"In His Image and Likeness"

# "In His Image and Likeness"

## POLITICAL ICONOGRAPHY
## AND RELIGIOUS CHANGE
## IN REGENSBURG, 1500–1600

Kristin Eldyss Sorensen Zapalac

Cornell University Press   *Ithaca and London*

PUBLICATION OF THIS BOOK WAS SUPPORTED BY A GRANT
FROM THE NATIONAL ENDOWMENT FOR THE HUMANITIES,
AN INDEPENDENT FEDERAL AGENCY.

First published 1990 by Cornell University Press.

International Standard Book Number 0-8014-2269-8
Library of Congress Catalog Card Number 89-71209

Printed in the United States of America
*Librarians: Library of Congress cataloging information
appears on the last page of the book.*

⊗ The paper used in the text of this publication meets the minimum requirements
of the American National Standard for Information Sciences—Permanence of Paper
for Printed Library Materials, ANSI Z39.48–1984.

# Contents

# Figures

# Preface

The chapters that follow explore the political languages used in a sixteenth-century German city and the impact of religious change on those languages. They examine written texts commissioned by the semiliterate and illiterate members of society as well as those authored by literate magistrates; they also examine visual images painted to hang on the walls of the chambers in which the magistrates met and inscribed in their law codes and legal handbooks. Although each chapter is in some sense an essay in the examination of a particular set of sources not generally utilized by historians of political discourse, these essays are designed to be read together and to reflect not only the diversity of the visual and verbal languages in which political relationships were discussed within one German city, but also the concepts and organizing principles that they shared and that were validated by contemporary epistemology.

Put another way, this book focuses on the power of the image in political discourses of the sixteenth century, as well as on two particular image clusters: one that disappeared and one that developed in Lutheran cities during this period. The term "image" is here broadly defined in an effort to avoid the religious iconoclasts' dichotomy between "word" and "image," a dichotomy the disciplinary boundaries of our own academic culture have tended to perpetuate. As used here, "image" refers not only to the object removed or threatened by the iconoclasts, to the painted, inscribed, or carved museum piece, or to that object as a means of conveying complex religious concepts to "the simple folk." In this sense, sixteenth-century images are being well explored by other scholars.[1] "Image" here refers instead to the peculiarly concrete languages, verbal as well as visual, in which abstract concepts were conceived and articulated in the medieval and early modern periods. The term "political discourse" also requires definition: it does not here refer to that canon of theoretical texts that have had the greatest or most obvious impact on our own political theories; those texts have been and are being explored by other scholars. Rather we explore the connection between theory and praxis, examining the expression and conceptualization of political relationships in the specific context of a city that underwent religious change in the sixteenth century.

It is my thesis that visual and verbal images, many of them having their origins in conceptions of the sacred, were a powerful—perhaps the most powerful—part of political thought in German cities in the sixteenth century, that political relationships were conceptualized and negotiated within the municipal walls more often in the languages of image, figure, and metaphor than in the rationalized language of legal categories. It is for this reason that the Reformation, which made certain images and certain methods of viewing images inappropriate and gave greater sanction and authority to others, had such an impact on political language. And it is to the Lutheran Reformation and the epistemological and cosmological transformations that it both wrought and presupposed that we must turn to understand the changes in political language which we discover. At least in Regensburg, the case study in the chapters that follow, the changes in the political languages spoken within the walls cannot be linked to the specific tensions of that city's troubled economic situation at the end of the medieval period, to the dramatic and even bloody political "upheaval" it witnessed in the second decade of the sixteenth century, to the pogrom with which it closed that decade, or to any change in political structure or access to political office. My own prosopographical research plays no rôle in the following account only because it reveals that the route to office in a political system much less patrician than that of nearby Nuremberg did not greatly change over the course of the century. In particular it should be noted that there was no change in the administration of justice in either its broad or its narrow sense to account for the radical change in the visual language in which justice was conceptualized within the council chamber. The transformation of the language of justice and magistracy was rooted not in a transformed political, social, or economic structure, but instead in a transformed view of the structure of the cosmos and of human thought. This suggests that the fit between the political relationships within the walls and the images in which the Wittenberg reformers explicated sacred relationships may help to account for the rapid spread of Lutheranism within German cities.

Why did visual and verbal imagery form the basis for the communication of political ideas and relationships at the end of the medieval period? How was the use and understanding of imagery changed by Lutheranism? These questions lie at the heart of our investigation. They are addressed theoretically in the prolegomena, an examination of the epistemological positions occupied by "word" and "image" as they were understood by Augustine of Hippo, whose discussion of psychological anthropology and epistemology dominated the medieval period, and by Martin Luther, who radically revised the Augustinian anthropology and epistemology. The chapters that follow the prolegomena address the same questions in a case study of the transformation of the political language of judgment and authority within the walls of Regensburg, a small (c. 10,000 population), free imperial city on the northernmost bend of the Danube roughly midway between Nuremberg and Munich.

For reasons both epistemological and cosmological, political relationships were conceptualized (I am tempted to write "made concrete") in imagistic rather than in rationalized language in both the late-medieval and the Lutheran city; chapters 1 and 2 explore the way images "meant" in late-medieval Regensburg and the impact of Lutheranism on that capacity for meaning. The Last Judgment panels that hung on the walls of Northern courtrooms in the late-medieval period were in the sixteenth century systematically replaced in Lutheran cities by allegorical depictions of Justitia. This replacement expressed a cosmological shift, one also evident in the transformed epistemology of the theological writings explored in our prolegomena: the late-medieval cosmology in which sacred history and eschatology were emphatically present in the temporal world had been replaced by a Lutheran cosmology in which the two realms were held apart by the concept of predestination. Painted images through which one had previously glimpsed the world beyond the temporal became opaque, examples rather than windows.

In the Lutheran epistemology the temporal and sacred realms were separated by a chasm unbridgeable by human efforts at communication; the mediating hierarchy of the medieval period was no longer a useful concept for understanding either sacred or political relationships. Luther's Reformation replaced the medieval hierarchical ordering of things with an ordering based on the dyadic relationship of paternity. In chapter 3 we see that reordering at work in the language of the Regensburg councillors' attempts to come to terms with the involvement of outsiders—whether emperor or neighboring prince—in the internal affairs of a city whose walls had been made porous by economic and political distress.

I have already suggested that the languages that have survived for Regensburg are not obviously marked by the sometimes violent "unrest" among the small tradespeople and craftsworkers just outside the circle of inner power in the last decades of the fifteenth and the first decades of the sixteenth century. Nevertheless, those people if not those events did play a rôle in the transformation of the language in which the political dialogue was carried out. Familiar sources—frescoes, painted panels, tracts on the responsibilities of magistrates, and ordinances—tend to reflect the perspective of the politically dominant. In a further effort to map political discourse as a dialogue between subjects and council rather than between more rarified political theorists, we turn in the fourth chapter to a reading of those more familiar sources together with less familiar documents directed to the city council by its subjects. The more nuanced picture of the use of political language which emerges reveals a paternal language of politics which developed not as the result of authoritarian imposition but in the course of a dialogue between governors and governed as each group sought to define and negotiate its relation to the other.

The breadth of my sources means, of course, that I have incurred a variety of debts in the process of my research. A grant from the Deutscher Akademischer Austauschdienst enabled me to spend the academic years 1982/1983 and 1983/1984 exploring the archives and libraries of Regensburg and Munich in the Federal Republic of Germany. My research in the Stadtarchiv, Regensburg, was aided by the courtesy and helpfulness of Guido Hable, former Archivdirektor, and Raimond Sterl. In the Staatliche Bibliothek, Regensburg, to which I retreated after the Stadtarchiv closed for the day, the generosity of Dr. Gisela Urbaneck and her staff made that retreat profitable for my research; much of the evidence and argument developed in chapter 3 appeared first in an exhibition Dr. Urbaneck kindly encouraged me to arrange on the second floor of the Staatliche Bibliothek. The director of the Museen der Stadt Regensburg, Dr. Wolfgang Pfeiffer, has allowed me access to the rare books held by the museum as well as to photographs of its collections. Professor Karl Möseneder and the students in the Institut für Kunstgeschichte at the Universität Regensburg provided an academic "home away from home" in seminars on the art historical and ritual aspects of *Feste* in Regensburg. An invitation from Dr. Hans Medick gave me a chance to discuss some of my research results with members of the Max-Planck-Institut für Geschichte in Göttingen; the fact that they would find in this book little trace of the project I described then in no way lessens my gratitude for their comments and hospitality. The extension of that Göttingen trip to Wölfenbüttel and a summer seminar run by Professor Peter Blickle at the Herzog August Bibliothek led me to meet Robert Scribner, for whose encouragement and scholarly advice I am immensely grateful.

My time in Munich was briefer than that in Regensburg, a fact that only increases my debt to Dr. H. Hauke and the staff of the Handschriftenabteilung of the Bayerische Staatsbibliothek, the scholar's haven amid the bustle of Munich, and to the reading room staff of the Bayerisches Haupstaatsarchiv. Escapes, even from scholarly havens, are essential, and for that I am grateful to the museums and musicians of Munich, but particularly to the Bayerische Staatsoper and the wide range of its operatic offerings in repertory. Also in Munich, I cherish the memories of stimulating conversations with Norbert and Inge Schindler, Winfried Freitag, and their friends, as of *Sekt-Frühstücke* with the members of the fifth-floor GAP in Studentenstadt.

Research provides its own stimulation; a surprise, a discovery, or the perfect piece of evidence lies always around the next corner. Writing, on the other hand, turns too easily into drudgery. That drudgery was greatly reduced by the unflagging efforts and courtesy of Vivienne Bourkoff, Jenny

Newman, and the staff of the Inter-Library Loan office in the Milton S. Eisenhower Library of the Johns Hopkins University. The inevitable isolation of writing was redeemed for me by the scholarly community that is the History Department at Johns Hopkins, and, although I have presented no part of the present book before the department, the memories of pointed comments made in seminars in which I have presented papers have, I hope, improved the argument here. For their comments on specific chapters, I am most grateful to Orest Ranum and Michael McCormick at Hopkins and to colleagues in Cambridge, particularly to Brian Daley, S.J., of the Weston School of Theology and Mark Edwards of the Harvard Divinity School.

If no scholarly project ever achieves true completion, this one has at least achieved a static form in publication thanks to the patience of John Ackerman and the production staff at Cornell University Press and to a subvention from the National Endowment for the Humanities. That this journey can be measured in terms of months rather than years is owing to the opportunity for uninterrupted work provided by the Junior Fellowship generously awarded me by the Harvard University Society of Fellows and by the facilities of the Houghton and Widener libraries of that university. My primary debt, however, is to Mack Walker, who from the beginning allowed me unusual freedom in pursuing historical questions into the realms of art history and—though I admit it hesitantly and with trepidation—the history of religion.

KRISTIN E. S. ZAPALAC

*Cambridge, Massachusetts*

# Note on Translations

Unless otherwise noted, the translations are my own. When translating biblical passages I have modified the text in the King James Version of the English Bible to agree with the Latin translation (Vulgate) in use during the late-medieval period or with Martin Luther's translations into either Latin or German. Wherever possible primary material has been quoted from editions published in the sixteenth century rather than from modern editions. I have, for example, preferred to quote Augustine from the edition edited by Erasmus in 1528/1529, although I have in each case compared the text with that of the Migne edition. The major exception is the work of Martin Luther, which I quote from the Weimar edition (unless noted otherwise) in order to avoid the confusion of the plethora of sixteenth-century editions of his individual and collected works. In order to shorten my still-lengthy notes, the original texts have been included in the notes only where the language itself is under investigation or where modern editions are not immediately accessible.

"In His Image and Likeness"

# "In His Image and Likeness": Luther's Revision of the Augustinian Epistemology

And God said, Let us make humankind in our image and likeness.

—Genesis 1:26

From the time of Augustine to that of Martin Luther there was little disagreement in the Christian West about the meaning of the biblical description of the creation of humankind. The medieval understanding of Genesis 1:26,[1] of what it might mean to have been created in God's image and of how words and images might function in a mind so fashioned, was based primarily on *De trinitate*, the amalgam of careful observation, Neoplatonism, and Christian mysticism completed c. 416 by Augustine (354–430), bishop of Hippo in North Africa. Augustine sought and found the sign of the creator inscribed in the whole creation;[2] nevertheless, in Genesis 1:26 he had the word of the creator himself that only one species had been created in the *imago dei* (image of God). Out of that assurance Augustine drew the epistemology that would empower so much of medieval theology and, indirectly, medieval art.

"Let us make humankind in our image and likeness": to the Christian philosopher, the use in the Genesis passage of the first person plural form in both verb (*faciamus* in the Old Latin translation used by Augustine and in Jerome's "Vulgate") and possessive (*nostram*) indicated that humankind had been created not to the image of the Father alone, or of the Son alone, but to the image and likeness of the triune god.[3] The passage therefore held out the possibility that some understanding of the doctrinally vexed relations among the three persons of the Trinity would be revealed by an investigation of the

This essay is "preliminary" both in the sense that its theoretical nature sets it apart from the other essays at the same time that it undergirds them and in the sense that it constitutes the preliminary sketch for a planned larger work on the sixteenth-century debate on the interpretation of Genesis 6:5 and 8:21 and the tension around the potential destabilization of the biblical text.

image of the Trinity in himself. In the latter books of *De trinitate*, Augustine investigated the human mind, in which, at least according to his late thought, the "divine image is inscribed . . . as an inalienable property."[4] In an effort to understand something of the relationship among the members of the Trinity in whose image the mind was created, he investigated not only the functioning of the mind's constituent parts, but also the mind's recognition of itself as the panel on which was inscribed the *imago dei*.[5] Because his project of knowing or apprehending the Trinity could be accomplished by nothing less than the fulfillment of the Delphic injunction to "know thyself," to which he himself alluded in the tenth book of *De trinitate*, Augustine's analysis would become a standard source not only for trinitarian theology, but also for medieval psychology.[6]

After considering other triads, Augustine had turned in the tenth book to the mental triad—memory, intellect, and will—which seemed by virtue of its consubstantiality and immortality to constitute "the image and likeness" of the godhead.[7] When he enjoined his readers to ascend with him "by whatever powers [or "faculties"] of intention we possess, to that peak and highest essence, of which the human mind is the imperfect image, but the image nonetheless,"[8] those "powers of intention" were themselves a part of the *imago dei* Augustine's project would discover. The unifying and motivating element in the mental trinity was its intention or will (Augustine used terms such as *voluntas*, *arbitrium*, and *intentio*, the last meaning literally the act of "stretching out toward" someone or something), the mind's motivation and striving, its activating desire to know things within and outside itself experientially, rationally, or intellectually.[9] Although the mind, according to Augustine, was imprinted with the image of the deity, just as soft wax bore the mark of the seal ring or the clay pot the imprint of the potter's thumb,[10] its postlapsarian recognition of this imprint, and therefore its knowledge or recognition of its true self, was impeded by the corporeal sense perceptions toward which this will, corrupted by the Fall, directed its attention.[11]

Much has been written on Augustine's insistence that human ability and capacity had been limited by the Fall; far less has been written of the context for that insistence—the Augustinian concept of grace. Because of Adam's sin, the bishop of Hippo argued, the will was not free to direct its attention to higher things unassisted but was inclined always toward the world. The intellect's vision of the mind's innate *imago dei* was therefore obscured by images of the temporal world to which the postlapsarian will directed its glance, filling its memory with earthly dust. Only the ineffable light of divine grace could pierce the temporal dust and make visible the mind's memory of itself and the eternal truths, could allow its recognition of itself as the *imago dei*.

Touched by grace, Augustine argued, the will turned toward its creator as naturally as a plant turned toward the sunlight: "It is reminded to turn to the Lord as if to a light by which it is touched in some way, even if it is turned

away from it."[12] "Those who, when reminded, turn away from the defor-
mities by which they were conformed to this world by secular lusts, and turn
toward the Lord, are reformed by him. . . . So that that image begins to be
reformed by him, by whom it was formed. For it is not capable of reforming
itself, as it was of deforming itself."[13] Conversion, "turning around" or
"turning toward," was therefore recognition of the divinity, even if only in
the darkened *imago dei* of the mind.[14] Recognizing himself as the flawed
image or mirror of God, Augustine read the Pauline promise for the future as
empowering his own temporal attempt to "see through the glass darkly" to
some limited apprehension of the Trinity itself.[15]

Inspired to see "through" an image, the will directed the mind's eye—the
intellect—to its memory. It was the relationship among these three that
Augustine explored as the image of the trinitarian relationship of the godhead. By "memory," Augustine understood the mind's repository both of the
images it had formed based on information gained about the material world
through its own bodily senses and from the sensually perceived communica-
tions of others, and of its visions of eternal forms and its vision of itself, since
these were not always held before the mind's eye but were always available,
just as the image of any objects once perceived were available in the memory.[16] Although not derived from the sensible world, such knowledge was
apprehended as an image nonetheless; like an image from the sensible world
it was called up from the memory to be viewed by the intellect.

The "intellect," the third element of the mental trinity, objectified, apprehended, or brought to the mind's attention. Intellection was, in Augustine's frequent phrase, the viewing in the mind's eye (*acies animi*) of
images stored in its memory.[17] When it dealt with images whose origins lay in
the material temporal world the intellect reviewed them discursively, combining and analyzing them in a rational process. When, however, the grace-
enlightened mind intended toward God, apprehending the imprint of its
innate *imago dei* and through that image apprehending the trinitarian relationship itself, intellection was not a discursive process. It was instead a
vision or intuition, the imperfect human image of divine intellection itself
which "does not hold thoughts singly, but apprehends everything completely in one eternal and ineffable vision."[18] At his most formal, Augustine
differentiated between these two functions of the intellect as "lower" and
"higher" reason (*ratio inferior* and *ratio superior*) or "reason" (*ratio*) and "intellect" (*intellectus*).[19] So distinguished, "reasoning" referred to discursive
thought where "intellection" was reserved as a technical term for nondiscur-
sive contemplation: "Intellect is the contemplative element of the spirit;
intellecting refers to a purely intuitive apprehension of which the spirit itself
is not necessarily conscious."[20]

In the eleventh book of *De trinitate* Augustine described the mental trinity
rather simply in terms of the result of its relatedness: the intellection or vision
of the mind's true self which arose out of its recognition of itself as having
been formed in the *imago dei* was objectified, as was all internal vision, in

conception or thought (*cogitatio*). "And so that trinity arises out of memory, internal vision, and that will which joins the two—which three when collected [*coguntur*] into one, are called thought or 'recollection' [*cogitatio*], that is, that which is collected [*coactu*]."[21] In the final book of *De trinitate* Augustine summarized the complex inner workings of the two trinitarian relationships:

> In this image of the trinity, the human memory, especially that memory which the beasts have not, that is, that in which intelligible things are contained which did not come to it from the senses, bears a relative, incomparable and indeed imperfect similitude, but nevertheless a similitude of a sort to the Father. In the same way, the human intellect, which is formed by the intention of thought when what is known is spoken [as] an internal word belonging to no language, has in its great disparity nonetheless the similitude of the Son. And human love proceeding from knowledge, and conjoining memory and intellect, as common to both parent and offspring yet somehow to be perceived as neither parent nor child, has in this image some similitude, albeit a very imperfect one, to the Holy Spirit.[22]

Augustine saw in the relation among intellection, thought, and expression, that is, in the objectification of memory-stored knowledge in conception and its external articulation, "an image of the Son's generation by the Father," an image of the "Word made flesh" of the first chapter of John: "This actual expression is obviously distinct from the latent memory of self it expresses, but it does not become detached from it; what becomes separate is only the exterior word whereby our inner knowledge is externalized in the form of words or other signs."[23] For the philosopher whose purpose was to understand trinitarian relations and the Father's generation of the Son through their imperfect reflection in the human mind, "word" (*verbum*) was less the spoken or written utterance than the mind's internal conception.[24]

With the issue of the mind's conceptualization of itself and the externalization of some portion of that conceptualization in signs, we come closer to the hermeneutic problem of how word and image meant and were to be interpreted. As we have seen, for Augustine "word" referred to both interior concept and its corporeal temporal expression: "For on the one hand, we call 'words' those things which occupy a space of time by syllables whether spoken or thought; on the other, anything that is noted, that is impressed in the mind, so long as it can be brought out and defined by the memory is called 'word,' however much the thing itself may be displeasing; finally, that thing which is conceived mentally and which pleases [is also called 'word']."[25] The interior "words" of Augustine's second and third definitions were also "images," and "therefore both image and word."[26] He wrote of the mind's action in representing itself to itself not only as "word" (*verbum*) but also as representation, as "image" (*imago*) and "vision" (*visio*). "Yet how can there be a word, which has not yet formed in the vision of thought? How could it be a likeness of the knowledge of which it was born, if it did not have that form, [since it was] because it was capable of having that form that it was called a word?"[27]

Augustine returned to the consideration of this interior word in the final chapter of *De trinitate*: "All this which the human mind knows—that which the mind itself has harvested, that harvested by the senses of its body, and that harvested by the testimony of others—all this it holds stored in the treasury of memory, out of which is born the true word, when we speak that which we know. But the word exists before all sound, before all thought of sound. For it is then that the word has its greatest likeness to the thing known, of which it is born and of which it is the image. The 'seeing' of conception arises from the 'seeing' of knowledge, which is a word of no language, but the true word of the true thing, having nothing of its own, but taking everything from that knowledge of which it is born."[28] The relation between intellection and interior word was described as generation, as the former giving birth to the latter, but the temporality that that might imply was only apparent.[29] The intellection of the human mind remained itself always an image of the generation of John 1. If the divine Word was "in the beginning," and "eternally begotten of the Father," the interior word of the human mind was the objectification of intellection, a reflection of the mind itself, an image simultaneous with the act of vision. This was the point made by Augustine at the end of a chapter on the generation of the "only begotten Son": "And this word of ours has neither sound nor thought of sound, but is of that thing which we speak within ourselves by seeing, and therefore belongs to no language; and thus in this enigma there is a likeness to that word of God which is very God, since this word was born of our knowledge in the same way that that Word was born of the Father's knowledge."[30] Just as the divine *logos* or *verbum* was incarnate in the Son's birth at Bethlehem, so the mind's internal word was temporally incarnate in external utterance. The *logos* of John 1 was not the sole source for Augustine's use of *verbum* for the mental conceptionalizations he otherwise referred to in terms of sight or vision;[31] nevertheless, the use of *verbum* for the mind's concepts as well as for their verbalized expression intentionally paralleled the use of the same Latin word in Scripture for divine conceptualization or generation.[32] The uncreated "Word" expressed and encompassed the limitlessness of "that which is"; in the Genesis account it was through this "Word," that is, through God's speaking, that the world and humankind had been created.[33] By insisting in *De trinitate* on the presence of an internal word, of which the external word (utterance) was merely an imperfect sign or image, Augustine established a parallel between divine and human "word," strengthening his argument for the human mind as the *imago dei*.[34]

The interior word was always held apart from its temporal expression in the realm of the senses ("word" in the sense of Augustine's first definition); because it was not subject to the dilutions and corruptions of the senses it remained the faithful representation,[35] not only word but truly image: "Yet when we call thoughts 'the heart's locutions' that is not to say that they are not also visions, which when they are true arise out of the visions of things known."[36] Because the internal human "word," unlike its externalized, uttered, or written form, was not confined within the linear temporality of discourse, Augustine conceptualized the nonanalytic apprehension, characteristic of the internal "word," as seeing: "For externally, where things are done by the body, locution is one thing and vision another; but inwardly, where we think, both are one. Hearing and vision keep their distance in the bodily senses, but in the mind to see and to hear are not separate."[37] Augustine's description of intellection's objectification in concept or thought drew on his experience of understanding both aural and visual material.[38]

We have already encountered in the human intellect the "eye of the mind," an eye unlike the bodily eyes in that grace could turn it from the temporal images that impeded the mind's recognition of itself as *imago dei* toward a vision of Wisdom itself.[39] Indeed, it was for Augustine not so much the case that the eye of the mind could be taught to turn *from* the things of this world to those of the world beyond as that it could be taught to see *through* the things of this world to those of the world beyond. In *De Genesi ad litteram*, Augustine gave as a simple example of this hierarchical progress the way in which the reader came to understand the command "Love thy neighbor as thyself."[40] Corporeal sight, rational and linear, perceived the letters of the command on the page.[41] Spiritual sight, internal and imaginative, turned inward to the memory to recall the neighbor to mind even were he or she not physically present.[42] Finally, through intellectual vision the meaning of the command was fully apprehended; it was intellectual vision that "intuited" (*intuit*) the meaning of the verb "love," which was neither a physically present object like a letter nor an object remembered like the body or face of a neighbor.[43]

The progress described in Augustine's deceptively simple example, from serial perception, through an analysis of images stored in the memory, to the apprehension that was "sensuous thought,"[44] the union of knowing and loving, was both progressive and hierarchical. It was for him characteristic of all apprehension or "infused" vision, whether of the eternal verities or of the godhead itself. Conversely, the union of knowing and loving was the goal toward which temporal perception and understanding, rightly used, intended and were the necessary first steps.[45] The process described in the example of "Love thy neighbor as thyself" is the process we have seen pursued in *De trinitate*. It is the process to which Augustine attributed his own conversion in the *Confessiones*.[46] More pertinently, it is the process by which Augustine and Monica, his mother, "extended ourselves and touched eternal Wisdom with consuming thought" in the same book.[47] The pair's brief encounter with Wisdom was passionate, but its context discursive.[48] Having had its origin in conversation, it ended when "we returned to the clatter of our mouths, where a word both begins and ends," in contrast to the infinite and eternal Word of God.[49] If the encounter itself was prototypically "felt thought," the ascent to divine Wisdom was the prototypical love-illuminated progress from sense perception, through the discursive analysis of (or analytic discourse on) images recalled from the memory, to intellectual apprehension: "we ascended, recollecting, and talking of you, and admiring your works."[50] Having briefly heard the Word that signified no other existence but was itself the thing signified, Augustine and his mother returned to their discussion, going on to imagine the joy of having progressed from hearing the Word as it was uttered (i.e., limited) in the *signum* (sign) of their own flesh, of the created world, even of their own souls, to hearing it in an eternal relationship of such absolute immediacy that there was no interval between speaking and hearing.[51]

The experience Augustine and Monica imagined—of perfect and eternal participation in the creator for whom the act of willing was also the act of creating and in whom there could be no interval between willing, speaking, hearing, and apprehending—was framed by their daily experience of mediacy, of uttered words that had beginnings and that ended, that had no existence other than as *signa* and yet were at best only imperfect signifiers of the speaker's interior words.[52] The relation between created humankind and its creator was mediated by *signa*, by things that were for the Christian philosopher significant not of themselves but of the creator who had willed them.[53] This was the starting point both for Augustine's examination of epistemology in *De trinitate* and for his examination of hermeneutics in *De doctrina christiana*. The former work became the medieval West's handbook to psychology and its triune god, the latter its guide to exegetics and rhetoric.

Unlike those things which signified and referred to the divine creator by virtue of having been created by him, the creations of humankind signified by convention rather than by nature. The created world tended toward transparency; a dark mirror, it was a mirror nonetheless. Human creations, however, were opaque, significant of the intentions of their human creators but revealing nothing of the world beyond. Of human words, only those of sacred Scripture, so divinely inspired that they might reveal to the believer more than their human agent had intended, were darkly transparent, appearing obscure on occasion only to entice the reader to search for multiple layers of meaning. Alone among the cases of human signing, in sacred Scripture meaning was not governed by the intention of the human signer. It was therefore possible for the reader guided by grace to discover in Scripture meaning not intended by the human scribe; alone the divine intelligence whose scribe the writer of Scripture was, had "without a doubt" already foreseen the meaning imputed by the reader.[54]

If in Scripture human *signa* that might seem opaque and obscure were in fact peculiarly transparent, the situation was reversed for the visual arts as *signa*. In contrast to the word, whose obvious arbitrariness and signification by convention stressed its character as *signum*, painting or sculpture was defined by Augustine as a human creation that signified by simulation (*simulatis operibus*), disguising its conventionality by disguising itself as the *res* (thing) signified.[55] Although the signification of the work of art was willed rather than natural,[56] it disguised the human intention behind its production by simulating rather than referring to the signified and even by pretending to an identity or to a natural transparency it could not attain.

In *De doctrina christiana* (c. 397), the handbook of rhetorical and exegetical practice to which Martin Luther would later frequently refer,[57] Augustine argued that "of the things that they have instituted themselves, there is nothing more peculiar to human beings than that which is false and deceitful." He counted the visual arts with fabulous stories and falsehoods among "those human institutions which were superfluous."[58] Viewed appropriately, a painting or sculpture was a *signum* like the spoken or written word, an intentional rather than a natural sign. According to Augustine it was therefore to be understood in relation to its author's intention rather than as a natural *signum* of the *res* it simulated; like "the fables and fictions by whose lies humankind is delighted," the work of art was to be investigated in terms of what had been intended by its commissioner: "for what reason, where, when, and by whose authority it was made."[59] The visual arts, however, were dangerous precisely because their simulative mode of signifying concealed their conventional (or intentional) character, and because the viewer was therefore tempted to treat them as natural rather than intentional *signa*. Faces appeared to be "reflected" by portraits as well as by mirrors,[60] a fact that obscured the primacy of human intention in the production and therefore in the meaning of the former.

Given the rarity of Augustine's references to the visual arts, their rôles in two tales of misunderstanding are striking. In an earlier section of *De doctrina christiana*, Augustine related Varro's story of the Muses, regarded as nine in number because a city had found itself unable to decide among the trio of three-figure groups sculpted by different artists in a competition to honor the three goddesses. Because of their equal beauty, all three groups, nine figures in all, were placed in the temple, with the result that they were later misunderstood by people who, neglecting the circumstances and intentions of their human production, misread the three simulations for the *res* itself or as a natural and hence transparent *signum* through which the *res* itself was to be seen.[61] A similar anecdote in *De consensu evangelistarum* (c. 400) proved the falsity of a treatise on magic attributed to Christ by demonstrating that the forgers themselves had been deceived by simulations of Christ.[62] According to Augustine, the forgers, confused by church frescoes, that is, by the appearance of the simulative *signa* of Christ on the walls of Roman churches together with the simulative *signa* of Peter and Paul (two saints who shared a common feastday), had sought to "legitimate" their treatise by including in it an inscription addressed by Christ to Peter and Paul, although those familiar with Paul's life from the New Testament canon knew he had never met Christ in the flesh. In the story of the Muses the sculptures themselves had been neutral; in the story of the heretical forgery, Augustine's identification of the visual simulations of Peter and Paul with the "very distinguished and solemn" celebration of those martyrs by the Roman church emphasized his point that it was the (mis)reading of a conventional human *signum* as a natural *signum* rather than the *signum* as *res* which was at fault.[63] It was appropriate that the heretics who had failed to recognize Christ, "the Word made flesh," as the *signum* that was itself also and inseparably the *res* (in this case, literally the incarnation of being, the inseparable expression of the *id quod est*),[64] but instead had seen in him only a man skilled in magical arts, should also have been deceived by the humanly created *signa* on the church wall: "Those who had sought Christ and his apostles on painted walls rather than in holy Scripture deserved to go completely wrong. It's not surprising that fabricators should have been deceived by painters."[65]

Paintings and sculptures were infrequently discussed by Augustine because they, as human creations, inevitably led away from God. The inherent deceitfulness of such representations was all the more critical for Augustine, for whom sight was the favored metaphor for the unmediated apprehension of the divinity toward which his strivings were directed. Augustine's writing was filled with light and mirrors; the image seen "through a glass darkly" of I Corinthians 13:12, alluded to throughout *De trinitate*, also provided its conclusion: "I know Wisdom to be an incorporeal substance and a light in which are seen those things which are not seen by the eyes of the body. And nevertheless [Paul] says: 'We see now through a mirror in an enigma, but then face to face.' If we ask how and what this 'mirror' might be, surely nothing other than an image of that which takes place is discerned in a mirror. This we have therefore undertaken: to see somehow through this image which is us ourselves to that which made us, as through a mirror."[66] In the end not only the writing creature himself but also the whole of the creation "spoken" by God during the first six days became mirrored windows through which the grace-filled viewer might glimpse the world beyond obscured only partly by his or her own reflection in the glass. That hermeneutic—the epistemological possibility of a rationally organized "seeing through" divinely created objects (*signum*) to a vision, albeit a darkened vision, of the uncreated, the creative "that which is" (*id quod est*) itself—was Augustine's gift to the medieval period.[67]

◆

And the Lord saw that the wickedness of humankind was great in the earth, and that the whole thought of the heart was always prone to evil. (Genesis 6:5 in Vulgate translation used by Luther in first decades of sixteenth century)[68]

And the Lord saw that the wickedness of humankind was great in the earth, and that the whole imaging of the thoughts of the human heart was wholly evil always. (Genesis 6:5 as translated from Hebrew by Luther in 1525)[69]

If Augustine's understanding of human intellect, memory, and will, and the interpretation of Genesis 1:26 on which it was based, dominated the medieval period, it was Martin Luther's understanding of the corruption or limitation of those faculties, based on his interpretation of two more passages from the same book, which fueled the theological controversies of the sixteenth century. Just as Augustine's venture into psychological anthropology had been rooted in his desire to understand his triune god, so Luther's psychological anthropology was inextricably bound up with his attempt to understand the mystery of salvation; any understanding of soteriology had to be rooted in an understanding of the corruption of human capacities which was result of the Fall.[70]

Although both Augustine and Luther insisted that salvation must be the result of divine rather than human action, Luther's insistence on the un-bridgeability of the gulf between creator and creature resulted in his direct attack not only on medieval hermeneutics but also on the Augustinian episte-mology in which they were grounded. In the eyes of the reformer, the relevance of Augustine's interpretation of Genesis 1:26 to the postlapsarian human condition was soon surpassed by Luther's own interpretation and retranslation of Genesis 6:5 and 8:21, the parallel passages that announced the cause and conclusion of the Flood. As they had framed the story of the Flood, the two texts came to frame his career. Martin Luther analyzed Gen-esis more often than any other book of the Old or New Testament. As he responded to criticism by both radical reformers and conservative Catholics, Luther's defense of his theological stance became increasingly a defense of his anthropological assumptions, and came more and more to rely on the scriptural interpretations on which they were based.

In 1533 and again in 1539, Luther acknowledged the extent to which his close reading of the scriptural text had been triggered by his critics, quoting from Augustine's handbook on exegetical practice *De doctrina christiana*: "The pope drove me to it; he woke me up. Augustine said the same thing of himself: 'It is the heretics who stimulate us to scrutinize the Scripture'— otherwise no one would pay attention to the words."[71] To support his thesis on the bondage of the will in the face of Catholic criticism, Luther turned first to Genesis 6:5 and 8:21 in their Vulgate translation; soon, beleaguered by radicals and conservatives alike, Luther and his collaborators looked to the "new" science of Hebrew philology for reinforcement. Retranslating and reinterpreting the two Genesis passages not only buttressed Luther's soteri-ology against his attackers, it also fueled the development of an increasingly revolutionary epistemology. Genesis 6:5 and 8:21, which Luther in the begin-ning had offered as proof of the bondage of the will, became for him proof of the postlapsarian limitations of the human intellect and memory as well. Virtually undiscussed by Augustine, the two passages lay at the heart of Luther's epistemological differences with both the sectarians and the Catholic church, at the heart of his positions on the sacramental nature of the Mass and on images.[72]

Even before the posting of his famous theses, as he was publishing his first edition of the *Theologia deutsch* (*German Theology*),[73] Luther, in contrast to Augustine,[74] was drawn to Genesis 6:5 and 8:21 to argue for the bondage of the will and to attack the limited definition of original sin he labeled "Scholas-tic." Although he would later credit his recognition that it was only God's gracious sacrifice of his son which could save (justify) the sinner to his reading of Paul's letter to the Romans,[75] his early lectures on Romans reveal the extent to which his Christocentric soteriology was grounded in an account of human inability to earn salvation based on the parallel passages from the first book of the Old Testament. In those 1515/1516 lectures, Luther quoted the Genesis passages five times in their Vulgate translation, primarily to argue for the corruption of the will. Nevertheless, the lectures, like the marginal annotations Luther made in the Erfurt monastery's copy of Augustine's *De vera religione* in 1509, show that Luther was already linking the Genesis passages with Augustine's trinitarian anthropology.[76] In his exegesis of Romans 5:12—"Therefore, as through one man sin came into the world, and through sin death, so death passed upon all men, in whom [or "in whose sin"] all have sinned"—Luther used Genesis to confirm what he saw as the Pauline account of original sin. "[Original sin] is not merely the loss of quality in the will; on the contrary, not merely the loss of light in the intellect, of virtue in the memory, but precisely the loss of all rectitude and of the power of all capacities whether in body or mind and of the whole human being within and without. Furthermore, it is the tendency itself to evil."[77] Luther's careful limitation of the capacities of each member of the Augustinian triad emphasized the debt he owed the African bishop and his trinitarian image of the human mind. Throughout his career Luther would criticize, limit, even rant against the results of Augustine's investigation of the mind, of the memory, intellect, and will as the "image and likeness of God." It was nevertheless to the tripartite mental scheme propounded in *De trinitate* that he would always return in his own analyses of Genesis.

Augustine's contemporary Jerome did not fare so well at Luther's hands. The development of a critical stance toward (or the destabilization of) the Bible translation attributed to Jerome was slow. Northern scholars' access to the Hebrew Old Testament was limited not only by the suspicion in which they held their Jewish contemporaries, but also by the difficulties of accurately printing a script in which crucial vowel sounds were represented if at all by small dots and lines. Moreover, the earliest published Hebrew/Latin vocabularies tended to reflect the canonical status of Jerome's translation, "defining" each Hebrew word simply by listing examples of its rendering in the Vulgate. Even the most critical of the early sixteenth-century lexicographers did not challenge Jerome's adoption of the special reading given by his rabbinic contemporaries to *yeser*, the Hebrew word that would become crucial in Luther's reinterpretation of the Genesis passages.[78]

In the *De rudimentis hebraicis* (1506), the work cited by Luther as an authority in his first lectures on the Psalms and a work explicitly critical of the Vulgate translation,[79] Johannes Reuchlin had included in an entry entitled *yasar* (the basic meaning of which was given as "he made, he formed, he created") several passages in which Jerome had translated *yeser* as *figmentum* ("creating/ creation" or "imaging/image/figment/fiction"), as well as passages in which Jerome's translation had taken the verbal form. In contrast, a separate entry headed *yeser* (the basic meaning of which was given as "thought or, better, desire and cupidity") included only one example, Jerome's translation of Genesis 6:5: "And all the thought of the heart was intent on evil."[80] The Aramaic vocabulary Sebastian Münster published a decade later added only *yeser hara*, the technical term used by the rabbinic commentaries on the Old Testament for the "evil desire innate" in humankind (the concept in which Jerome's special conative translation of *yeser* as "intent" or "inclination" in the two Genesis passages was rooted), to the vocabulary of the theologian struggling with the difficulties of Hebrew.[81] Nevertheless, whether lists of examples of the ways in which a given word had been rendered in Jerome's canonical translation or whether based on the research and vocabularies of medieval Jews like David Kimhi, these early vocabularies made apparent any variations in the rendering of a specific Hebrew word. The vocabularies therefore not only provided access to a previously closed text and encouraged the production of more accurate translations, they also indirectly challenged the authority of the received text itself, that is, of the traditional translations on which Catholic doctrine had been based and legitimated.[82]

Luther's notes for the lectures he delivered on the Psalms from 1513 to 1516 reveal his first steps in Hebrew. Reuchlin's *De rudimentis* had become his authority, but he made no reference in his notes to the noun *yeser* or to the variations in its rendering documented by Reuchlin.[83] Even in his attack on the papal bull *Exsurge, domine* in 1520, when Luther claimed the support of the Hebrew text in his critique of the Vulgate translation, it was not any discrepancies in Jerome's renderings of the noun *yeser* into Latin which troubled him, but rather a perceived softening of the passage.[84] Luther's second attack was launched against what he saw as Jerome's modification of the Hebrew text; it was, however, an attack that accepted the rabbinical, conative interpretation of *yeser*: "Additionally, we can turn back to the Hebrew text: 'Since whatever the human heart thinks and desires is only evil continually.' An exclusive particle was added to 'evil,' which [Jerome's] translation did not duplicate. Neither did it duplicate the verb 'to desire' nor did it fully duplicate the verb 'to think,' but instead transformed it into 'thought.'"[85] The complaint was that Jerome had misrepresented the Hebrew by translating what he saw as the two coordinate verbs "[the heart] desires and thinks" (*cupit et cogitat cor*) into the noun "thought" (*cogitatio*) and the weak participle "inclined, intended" (*intenta*). Not surprisingly, since it was his intention to defend his thesis on the bondage of the will against theologians he called "Pelagians," Luther here laid even greater stress on what he saw as the conative aspect of *yeser* than had Jerome himself: "For Moses meant not only the quick and spontaneous, but also the ingenious and that by which the human being industriously considers doing anything. And he says that even these are nothing but evil, in order that nothing made by those Pelagians who subscribe to free will should be evaluated as good, however studiously it labors."[86]

While in exile in 1521, Luther turned again to the Hebrew text of the

Genesis passages to explicate the Gospel for Christmas Day (printed in the *Weihnachtspostille* of 1522); this time the result was an attack not just against the "Pelagians" but also, albeit somewhat obliquely, against the psychological anthropology of Augustine himself. The context, an exegesis of the passage "In him was life, and the life was the light of humankind" (John 1:4), forced the Wittenberg theologian to confront his differences with the first of Augustine's Johannine treatises. Luther's primary task in dealing with the fourth verse of the Gospel was to demonstrate the limitations of Augustine's argument that the divine light was the source of the light of human reason (*vornunfft* = *ratio*).[87] Although Luther at first claimed agreement with his predecessor's interpretation ("No one, however, should throw it up to me that I differ here with Augustine, who understood [the verse] to refer to the natural light [of human reason]") and disclaimed any attempt to overturn it ("since I know well, that all the light of reason is kindled from the divine light"), he moved quickly to undercut human reason. Reason had, he argued, been so corrupted by the Fall that left to itself it could not even recognize the source of its light.

Luther brought that paragraph full circle by concluding—contrary to the agreeable pose in which he had opened the examination—that any discussion of natural light was "inappropriate at this point in the Gospel, since [John] was speaking only of divine light," and that after all "St. Augustine was human and one isn't required to accept his interpretation."[88] Any sense of closure this aroused was nevertheless illusory; after pausing only long enough to offer the weak excuse "since we have room," Luther returned in the next paragraph to the same topic. In this second paragraph Luther made little attempt to disguise his disagreement with Augustine's psychological anthropology despite his admiration for the man he considered his predecessor in the battle against the Pelagians.[89] Augustine's interpretation of John 1:4 as evidence that human reason was capable of recognizing the divine light because it was that light which was its origin and the source of its own enlightenment encapsulated the argument of the latter books of *De trinitate*.[90] Luther argued against that interpretation: far from being able to recognize the divine light and its connection to that light, human reason left to itself was a "false light," the cause of "all distress and misery." Although no one could doubt that humankind was created "in all its powers (faculties) through the eternal Word of God," there was, nevertheless, "no good in the human being, that is, as Moses says in Genesis 6: 'All its thinking and perception intend with all powers [or, "with all faculties'] only toward evil."[91]

The insertion "with all powers" (*mit allen krefften*) strikes the eye, interrupting an otherwise unexceptional German rendering of the (conflated) Vulgate texts at Genesis 6:5 and 8:21.[92] In one sense it is just an echo of the "in all its powers" of the previous sentence; nevertheless, the powers inserted into the Genesis text were not those of the whole human being but only those associated with its thinking and perception or with its intending. Another explanation is suggested by Luther's statement in a letter written from the Wartburg that he was using his plentiful free time while in exile to read the Bible in Greek and Hebrew, and would begin work on the *Postille* as soon as the necessary materials arrived.[93] If, as seems likely, the Greek text referred to by Luther was not simply a Greek New Testament but instead the recently printed Septuagint Bible, Luther's insertion may have been the result of the adverb *epimelôn* ("carefully, diligently"; translated as *diligenter* in the Old Latin versions)[94] that appeared in the Septuagint renderings of Genesis 6:5 and 8:21. Such an emphatic adverb would have had obvious appeal to the reformer who had employed the phrase *de industria* in his 1520 elucidation of the conative in Moses' description of the corruption of human thinking.[95] It should, however, be noted that this is the only case I have found in which Luther silently altered the translation of the Genesis passage. And that it echoed and subverted the exhortation that founded the epistemological project that was Augustine's *De trinitate*.

We have already seen the "powers of intention" in Augustine's injunction to the reader of *De trinitate* to ascend with him "by whatever powers [or, "by whatever faculties"] of intention we possess, to that peak and highest essence, of which the human mind is the imperfect image, but the image nonetheless."[96] Augustine's exhortation had founded his project with an acknowledgment of limitation which was paradoxically also an empowering affirmation of possibility. Luther's insertion of the Augustinian affirmation into the Genesis text subverted Augustine's epistemology. It constituted a literally scriptural grounding of Luther's critique of the Augustinian ascent to knowledge of the divinity.

It was, however, not the will alone which was bound in Luther's developed epistemology. Despite his faithfulness in 1522 to the canonical interpretation of *yeser* as motivational or directive, that is, as Augustinian *intentio* or will (here, as in Jerome's translation, rendered as a part of the verb), despite his use of precisely that canonical interpretation to limit if not to overturn the Augustinian theological anthropology, Luther's discussion of human reason presaged a more severe revision of that anthropology. The limitations of human reason, as described by Luther in 1521, were not only motivational, and thus the result of the governing will, but also directional: "like the one who should have gone to Rome, but went in the other direction instead—he knew perfectly well that whoever wanted to get to Rome had to follow the right route, but he didn't know which that right street was."[97] When the issue was the pathway to God, "intending" in the wrong direction might be more a matter of lack of information than of lack of motivation.[98]

*Ratio* rather than will was explicitly the issue in the broadside Luther fired at a Franciscan friar from Leipzig in 1522. Luther responded to Augustin Alveld's attempt to set papal authority on a scriptural foundation with a diatribe against what Luther characterized as the attempt to protect the divine Word with human reason (*vernunfft*). This time it was a straightforward German translation of the Vulgate text which constituted part of his evidence: "Scripture tells us not to obey reason: 'You shall not do what you think right' (Deuteronomy 12), because reason is always striving against God's law, as in Genesis 6: 'All the thoughts and perception of the human heart are in an evil way all the time.' " Reason, according to Luther, was not bad in its own limited sphere; in its postlapsarian state, however, it was incapable of understanding anything of the divine realm and therefore bad (i.e., incapable and inappropriately directed) when it was driven by the arrogant will to attempt such an understanding. There was no room in Luther's developed epistemology for a division of the eye of the mind into higher and lower reason or *intellectus* and *ratio*. His depiction of "presumptuous reason" bore a striking resemblance to the activity Augustine had described as the intellect's natural response to enlightenment by grace; Luther's usurpation of the Augustinian image of light demonstrated the presumption he thought it implied. Augustine's intellect had turned toward illuminating grace as naturally as a plant turned toward the sun; Luther saw any attempt to use human reason, "even human reason founded on or enlightened by faith," to interpret or defend divine order as "trying to illuminate the blazing sun with a dim lantern."[99]

The metaphor of sight proved useful against radical as well as Catholic. On a practical level, the radicals represented a threat to the acceptance of Luther's orderly reform by political authorities; in terms of Luther's epistemology, their "arrogance" was little different from that of the Catholic church. Where Catholics presumed to appease the deity and to earn salvation through their own works, radicals presumed direct contact with the deity, ignoring the sacraments and words he had instituted for their benefit. They were epistemological "iconoclasts," who went beyond the destruction of painted surfaces to the rejection of the scriptural *signum* through which God had chosen to communicate himself to humankind. Against them, therefore, Luther characterized the teacher who interpreted Scripture without acknowledging its nature as *signum* and without making use of the human learning of Greek, Latin, and Hebrew as "the blind man fumbling along the wall."[100] If Augustine's late-medieval successors were guilty of pretending to see through *signa* to the godhead, radicals were guilty of ignoring the divinely ordained *signa* and of pretending to direct converse with God. Even more than images of sight, Luther therefore turned the radicals' words against them. They were "prophets of no understanding" who "conjured up their living voice from heaven with . . . pompous words that they themselves don't understand."[101]

Luther's attacks on both the Catholic hermeneutic and on the radical rejection of *signum* were rooted in an epistemology that received a decided boost from philology in 1523 when Luther and his lieutenant Philipp Melanchthon rejected the particularist translation of *yeser* (at Genesis 6:5 and 8:21) which had been based on the rabbinic concept of *yeser hara* ("evil impulse"). "God saw that the evils of humankind were great in the earth, and that all the imaging of the thoughts of its heart was delusive and deformed all the time."[102] Philipp Melanchthon's translation of Genesis 6:5 in his commen-

tary on "some obscure chapters of Genesis" (1523) is the earliest I have found
in which *yeser* was rendered as *figmentum*, that is, as Jerome himself had
rendered *yeser* in Psalm 103 and in the other passages in which no reference to
the "evil impulse" had been seen by the rabbinic commentators.[103] In this
case, although it was human sinfulness rather than epistemology which
occupied Melanchthon in his commentary on the passage, the connection
between *yeser*, the word previously taken to refer to the human will, and the
processes of the *ratio* or *intellectus* was enhanced by the translator's rendering
of the Hebrew *ra* as "empty, vain, delusive" (*vanum*) and "perverse, bent,
deformed" (*pravum*). The former word, in particular, had been associated not
with evil motivation but with deluded mental processes by the classical
authors with whom Melanchthon was familiar.[104]

Reading *yeser* at Genesis 6:5 and 8:21 as it had been read in the other
passages in which it occurred put a stronger, philologically authorized
weapon into Luther's hands just in time for his response to Erasmus' famous
*Diatribe on the Freedom of the Will* (1524).[105] In his *Diatribe*, Erasmus had
dismissed the evidence of Genesis 6:5 and 8:21 on two counts: first, because it
pertained not to the whole of humankind (according to Erasmus, Noah
himself was exempted), but only to those "of that age most corrupted by
unspeakable vices," and second, because to accept it would be to leave no
space for human penitence: "And even if it is not possible to overcome it
without the help of divine grace, the proclivity to evil found in the majority of
humankind does not completely eliminate the freedom of the will."[106]

In the lengthy response he issued a year later under the equally Augustinian title *De servo arbitrio ad D. Erasmum Roterdamum*,[107] Luther followed a
reiteration of Erasmus' argument with new, and most Erasmian, evidence:
"Why did [Erasmus] not consult the Hebrew here, where Moses says nothing
of proclivity? Nor do you have cause for quibbling, for he has chapter six: *Chol
Ietzer Mahescheboth libbo rak ra chol ha iom*, that is, all the imaging of the
thoughts of his heart is entirely evil always. He doesn't say 'intent on' or
'prone to' evil, but rather 'directly evil' and that nothing except evil is made or
thought by the human being its life long. The nature of the evil of it is
described—that it can neither make nor be otherwise than evil; for, by the
testimony of Christ, an evil tree is not able to bear other than evil fruit."[108]
That Luther's translation was here less charged and more literal than
Melanchthon's had been only served to emphasize its rootedness in exacting
philological investigation, a powerful rhetorical weapon in the midst of a
rather bitter dialogue with the Dutch scholar. "Vitriolic" would perhaps be
the better description of Erasmus' brief response to Luther's philological
evidence (in the midst of a general response that was anything but brief): "To
this Hebrew [Luther] quotes, which agrees neither with the Septuagint, nor
with Jerome's interpretation, nor is annotated by any of the approved inter-
preters, I can reply that either Luther hasn't understood the force of the
Hebrew words, or that he has a corrupt codex."[109]

In light of the fact that recent Jewish, Catholic, and Protestant scholarship

has accepted Luther's translation if not necessarily the epistemological conclusions he drew from it, and that the Council of Trent itself was forced by
Luther's polemic to confront the evidence of Genesis 8:21,[110] we may be
excused for suggesting that the very brevity and vitriol with which Erasmus
dismissed Luther's translation were indicative of its power as evidence. At
any rate, in the next line Erasmus adopted the stance of the magnanimous
victor—"nevertheless, let's generously concede that everything which the
human being thinks on its own is bad"—in order eventually to reframe the
discussion in the more comfortable terms of the necessity of proper training
and the generality rather than the universality of Moses' statement: "I insist
that there's a minimum of this proclivity in those spirits which are well born
and well educated; the greater part of proclivity is not natural, but the result
of corrupt institutions, improper companions, and the cultivation of a sinful
and malicious will. At Genesis 6 Scripture is not actually speaking of human
nature, but of corrupt inclinations, and in general, for I don't judge it appropriate to Noah and his family."[111]

With Erasmus' position, redolent to our ears of the twentieth-century
incarnation of the same controversy, the worst of the shouting match over
Genesis 6:5 and 8:21 came to an end. After the discussion of the 1520s, most
Bibles published with scholia acknowledged the existence of two interpretations of *yeser*, although the translations of *yeser* in the passages themselves
continued to reflect the religious convictions of the editors.[112] Nevertheless,
neither this fact nor the bitterness of the debate with Erasmus deterred
Luther from presenting his own mature analysis of Genesis in what must be
one of the longest "courses" in the history of academic lecturing.

On 31 May 1535, in the manner universal to professors recruiting students
for their next courses, Martin Luther closed his lecture on Psalm 90 with the
announcement that he would follow his course on the Psalms with lectures
expounding the first book of the Bible, "thus laboring in the word and works
of God until I die."[113] Luther was very nearly right in his estimate; the lecture
"course" lasted a full decade, ending in November 1545, just one year before
Luther's death. As edited and published by his followers, the lectures fill
more than two thousand pages in the Weimar edition of his works. They
constitute sixteenth-century Lutheranism's longest and most complete statement of the epistemological implications of Genesis 1:26, 6:5, and 8:21, as
well as its definitive revision of the Augustinian epistemology.

As academic lectures, Luther's *In Primum Librum Mose Enarrationes* (*Exposi-
tions of the First Book of Moses*) often focused on the Hebrew text itself: more
attention than usual was paid to the Hebraists on whose published vocabularies and grammars the scholar depended, the Vulgate translation of *yeser* at
Genesis 6:5 and 8:21 was again rejected, and those who had relied on its
conative participles were accused of willful misreading.[114] The lectures displayed not the preacher or the polemicist but the scholar, who cited, commented on, and revised his scholarly predecessors as well as the text itself. As
a result, the discussion of Genesis 1:26 in the published version of the lectures

provides Luther's most sustained commentary on Augustine's *De trinitate*. Out of the "sea of questions" aroused by the Genesis passage, Luther chose to focus on the problem of the *imago dei*, reminding his listeners that Augustine had had much to say on the subject, "especially in his book *De trinitate*," and that "most of the other doctors had followed Augustine's lead, retaining the Aristotelian division in which the image of God was constituted by the mental faculties: memory, mind or intellect, and will."[115] Luther acknowledged that it was not only the tripartite division of the mind, but also the relationships among the members of the triad which had seemed to Augustine and his followers to constitute the *imago dei*; he therefore gave a brief but faithfully Augustinian account of the generation of the word in the heart as an image of divine generation.[116] The problem Luther saw in Augustine's meditation on what it might mean to have been created in the image and likeness of God was its potential for appearing to support the concept of free will with the flawed syllogism: "God is free. Therefore, since humankind was created in God's image, it must also have free memory, mind, and will." Luther's concern was not one of logic and the problem of whether an "image" could constitute a specification of the general case "God," but the soteriological conclusion the demonstration appeared to trigger: "If this is true, it follows that humankind is able to accomplish its own salvation using its natural faculties."[117] In the fear he expressed Luther was less than fair to Augustine, binding too tightly to those who claimed his support for the doctrine of free will the father for whom divine grace was the constant soteriological "middle premise" that could not vanish, however great the emphasis placed on the doctrine of "cooperation."[118] It was in the empowering epistemology of the father who had been his authority for the will's servitude that Luther now located the roots of the doctrine of free will itself.

At the level of soteriology the Augustinian understanding of the *imago dei* seemed to Luther dangerously close to sustaining the doctrine of freedom of the will; at the level of anthropology and epistemology it seemed to Luther to disguise the insuperable gulf between humankind and God, and even to falsify the functionings of the human mind. In Luther's final exposition of Genesis the discussion was shifted from the battle ground of soteriology (could salvation be earned by works performed by a free will?) to that of the epistemology on which it was based (could divine grace enlighten the intellect so that humankind might understand things beyond the material realm?). It was in Luther's discussion of the latter issue that grace was the middle term likely to disappear.[119] Although he did, on occasion, note that it was natural rather than enlightened reason that was incapable of recognizing God,[120] Luther was more likely altogether to dismiss the possibility that even an enlightened reason could apprehend the divine.[121] "Our nature is so deformed by sin, so corrupted and fallen, that we cannot recognize the naked God or comprehend what he is. It is for this reason that these coverings are necessary. . . . And it is therefore insane to do like the heretics and dispute about God and the nature of divinity without words or coverings."[122]

It was not only what seemed to him the rantings of the radical sectarians, or the academic disputations and allegorical "towers of Babel" constructed by the late-medieval Scholastics, that Luther's epistemology undermined. Luther's mature epistemology also undermined the possibility of a contemplative apprehension of the divine, whether achieved through the resignation and abnegation exemplified by the pseudo-Dionysian passages of the *Theologia deutsch* Luther himself had edited in 1516 and again in 1518,[123] or through the intellectual ascent exemplified by Augustine's *Confessiones*. The parable Luther told early in his lectures, of the failed attempt at ecstatic union, was not only a critique of the radicals he called "Neo-Arians"[124]: "Those, however, who want to reach out to God without this covering are straining to ascend to heaven without a ladder (i.e., without the word); they therefore fall back, overthrown by the majesty that they wanted to embrace naked, and perish. Thus Arius fell."[125] It was also a rewriting of the traditional mysticism approved by the Catholic church and exemplified in Augustine's *Confessiones*.[126] Not just the desired embrace, participation, or union with the divine,[127] but the verbs themselves (*attingere, ascendere ad coelum*) echoed Augustine's paradigmatic description of the experience of the divine he and his mother had shared shortly before her death.[128] In Augustine's description, however, the brief experience of union had been framed by the words of analytic discourse with which the ascent had begun and the "clatter" of temporal human expression to which the pair had returned; in Luther's revision the only appropriate ladder was the word of God, which the seekers failed to use. In Augustine's description, he and Monica had returned as victors (*remere*, a verb used of victorious returns in particular); in Luther's revision the seekers of such an experience were instead literally felled (*ruunt oppressi*) and destroyed (*pereunt*).

That Luther's revision was motivated by epistemological rather than purely doctrinal considerations—that it was in a sense Luther himself who had pulled the ladder out from under the seeker—is perhaps clearest in his rewriting of the definition of the human being itself. In both the final book of *De trinitate* (IV, vii) and in his earlier *De ordine* (II, xi), Augustine had defined humankind by quoting the "ancient sages": "The human being is an animal that is rational and mortal."[129] In Augustine's view that definition had to be understood as establishing a relationship between the human creature and God himself: the immense gulf between creator and creature was in some sense bridged by the very fact of creatureliness. Just as the pot unavoidably bore some fragmentary thumbprint of the potter, so too the creature was necessarily imprinted with some trace of the creator. The whole of creation was therefore the expression of God's will to create, but only the human mind possessed the *ratio* with which to recognize the *imago dei* impressed in it. It was in the context of a discussion of the implications of human rationality that Augustine quoted the ancient definition at *De ordine* II, xi: "*Ratio* is the mind's motion, that by which it analyzes, its power of separating and joining," that by which the mind was led, if only very rarely, to the recognition of

God. Augustine had acknowledged that such recognition was an infrequent occurrence, but the outlook was nonetheless empowering: to the *ratio* enlightened by grace the created world was transparent, revealing the hidden majesty of its creator. Channeled by Duns Scotus' translation and commentary on the writings of the pseudo-Dionysius, the Augustinian epistemology could turn even the visual arts Augustine had distrusted into windows on the spiritual realm.[130] "There is a formidable distance from the highest, purely intelligible sphere of existence to the lowest, almost purely material one (almost, because sheer matter without form could not even be said to exist); but there is no insurmountable chasm between the two. There is a hierarchy but no dichotomy. For even the lowest of created things partakes somehow of the essence of God—humanly speaking, of the qualities of truth, goodness and beauty. . . . therefore man, *anima immortalis corpore utens*, need not be ashamed to depend upon his sensory perception and sense-controlled imagination. Instead of turning his back on the physical world, he can hope to transcend it by absorbing it."[131]

Luther, speaking out of his own monastic experience, eventually rejected the Augustinian epistemology, not only as expanded to include visual images, but also in its narrower original version: Augustine had written that "the one who lives well, prays well, and studies well will also see."[132] Luther responded that that may once have been the case, that is, before the Fall, but it was the case no longer. Adam himself may have been able to walk in the garden with God and to see his glory in all things, "but, if a scintilla of recognition of the divine had remained intact in humankind, we would have long been different from what we are now."[133] Luther's authority for this was the wisest of the ancient sages, Moses himself.[134] "Therefore, if you want to define the human being truly, take your definition from this passage [Genesis 8:21]: that the human being is a rational animal, which has an imaging heart. What then does it image? Moses answers: 'evil; that is, against God or God's law and humankind.' "[135] The mind no longer saw clearly; instead, it imaged evilly, especially when it presumed to image the godhead.

The *Enarrationes* contains Luther's longest and most explicit discussion of what he understood the human "imaging" to be and of how it was "evil," a discussion in which it was epistemology rather than willful sin which was at stake. On this latter point Luther was quite clear. Moses had said that it was "imaging" that was evil, and "imaging denotes reason itself, together with will and intellect." Nor was the "evil" of "imaging" rooted in the body. In contrast to the Catholic churchmen, who usually interpreted the "from its youth" at Genesis 8:21 as a reference to the uncontrollable sexual urges of the adolescent male,[136] Luther insisted that the Hebrew word *neurim* denoted the age at which the human began to make use of reason.[137] The passage, he said, referred not to physical desire or concupiscence: "It is not lust, not tyranny, and not the other sins that Moses calls evil; it is the imaging of the human heart, that is, human industry, wisdom, and reason, together with all the powers that reason uses even in its highest actions."[138] "Imaging denotes reason, together with will and intellect, even when it is thinking about God, and when it is busy with the most honorable works, whether those of the political sphere or of the household."[139] With this last definition, Luther declared epistemologically invalid the Augustinian distinction between higher and lower reason or intellect and reason. The terms might designate two different goals toward which the efforts of reason were directed, but the operations ("imaging") involved were identical.[140] At the beginning of book seven of the *Confessiones*, Augustine had criticized his own inability to conceptualize God before his conversion: "I was unable to conceive of any kind of substance except what I was accustomed to see through these eyes." Nevertheless, he argued in the next section, the fact that the images in his mind had the same form as what he saw with his eyes had only disguised the fact that the process by which the mental images were formed was entirely different from physical seeing.[141] Because of this difference, the enlightened reason was capable of seeing through the created world, whose surfaces only were observed by the physical eyes, to a dark perception of the divinity itself.

The progress and difference Augustine had posited between the sight of the mind and the sight of the eyes was the crux of the epistemology Luther rejected. From 1525 he had argued that physical and rational seeing (imaging or mental conceptualizing) were essentially the same. Driven by the violent iconoclasm of Andreas Karlstadt and his followers to define his own attitude toward painted and carved representations of sacred figures and events, Luther argued that material images were acceptable because the mind itself created and looked upon images of the sacred events about which it heard and read. According to Luther, this internal imaging was as natural as the reflection of an object in a pool of water: "When I hear or think about something, it's impossible for me not to make a picture of it in my heart; whether I want to or not, when I hear [the word] 'Christ,' an image of a man who hangs on a cross appears in my heart, just as my face naturally appears in the water when I look into it."[142]

For Luther it was not, as it had been for Augustine, only the unconverted or graceless mind that in its ability to conceptualize was restricted to those forms the physical eyes had observed in the created world. The limitation extended to all humankind, whether justified or not; it was because of the restricted nature of human conceptualization that God had chosen to humble himself in the incarnation (literally, "enfleshment"), passion, and death of his son. Luther's insistence in 1538 that "humankind can't grasp spiritual things except in images"[143] reveals the impact of his reinterpretation of Genesis 6:5 and 8:21 on his earlier Augustinian understanding of the functioning of corporeal and spiritual vision. In 1520 he had defended the sacramentality of the Mass in terms of the Augustinian epistemology: "We poor human beings, because we live in our five senses, must at least have an external sign we can cling to, in addition to the word. This external sign is nevertheless sacramental, that is, it is not only external; it also is and means spiritually, in order that we should be pulled into the spiritual by the corporeal, and so that we can grasp the exterior with our bodily eye and the internal with our mind's eye."[144] Five years later, in a similar context, the direction was the same, but the mind's eye appeared to have dimmed. The word of God in the Gospel and the sacraments of baptism and communion still functioned on two levels;[145] only the understanding implied by the mind's eye was missing, replaced by a more general appeal to the "Holy Spirit and faith, together with other gifts."[146] Augustine had found his motto in the words of Isaiah: "Believe in order that you may understand."[147] For Luther, however, faith and understanding had—like the spiritual and temporal worlds, to which they were now applied, respectively and exclusively—been separated, and it was faith alone that pleased God.[148] *Solifidianism* (salvation by "faith alone") did not promise the enlightment of the cognitive faculties; it insisted that the believer's only option was faith, the faith in God's promise given in the New Testament and in his desire to be merciful as demonstrated by temporal event, that is, by his sacrifice of his son.[149] God had promised the believer justification, not understanding. Participation in divinity could not come even briefly while the human being lived in the material realm; it must await the "Father's kingdom, where the will will be truly free and good, the mind illuminated, and the memory constant."[150] Once he had reached the Father's kingdom in his description of the path to salvation, Luther's language became Augustinian: "What we say is taught by faith and word, which point to that glory of the divine image as if from a distance. Just as in the beginning before light had been added sky and earth were quasi-raw bodies, so the pious have that raw image within themselves which God will perfect on the last day in those who have believed his Word."[151]

In contrast, when he wrote of the temporal existence, Martin Luther described the mind not, as Augustine had, as darkened by the dust of material perceptions (which might appear to leave the door open for an Augustinian enlightenment by grace?), but as polluted and numb. Memory, will, and mind were "diseased and leprous," an analogy explained by Luther's description of lepers as those "whose leprous flesh was numb and almost dead except when they were driven to vehement desire." In *De trinitate* Augustine had also used the image of disease to describe the postlapsarian condition of the mind's *imago dei*; in his image, however, recovery was made possible by the gracious physician.[152] Luther's identification of the disease as leprosy, which no sixteenth-century physician could cure, subverted the Augustinian analogy.[153]

Images presented no threat to the Lutheran heart because it understood and accepted its limitations, and accepted the concept that the gap between the creator and his creation was unbridgeable except by the action of the creator himself. In one sense it was God's own decision to reveal himself through the incarnation and his other willful communication in history which legitimated the creation of visual images. Historical events like the advent of Christ had illuminated what had previously been dark; it was only through his expression in historical and material "reality" perceptible to the natural human faculties that God could make himself known to human-kind.[154] Strikingly, it is only in the context of revelations already made as the result of historical event that Luther used the contrasting images of darkness and illumination, enigmas and clarity, from I Corinthians 13:12, the passage Augustine had so made his own in the last books of *De trinitate*: "At that time it was appropriate that these things be said darkly by divine council, or at least for this reason, because all things were at a distance in that future Lord, to whose coming was reserved the restitution of everything, of all cognition and of all revelation. Therefore, those things which had formerly been pro-posed as if through enigmas, Christ unveiled and ordered to be preached clearly."[155] Christ's advent and passion had clarified the truth and the prom-ise that had until then been hidden in the Old Testament. It had redeemed humankind. But neither it nor grace could illuminate the mind's understand-ing of anything more than the historical reality of the event. Luther therefore defended visual images first as literal re-presentations of God's "will to sign;" images were appropriate memorials of God's self-revelations in historical time.[156]

This type of painted image was no more dangerous than the image, natural and inevitable as the reflection in a pool of water, that arose in the heart when it heard the word "Christ"; the viewer of the painted image "saw only histories . . . as in a mirror." In contrast to the Marian images at Regensburg and elsewhere, which, like the images of Peter, Paul, and Christ together on the wall of the fourth-century Roman church, were problematic because they did not represent historical events and exacerbated the human tendency to confuse the painted or sculpted *signum* for the *res* it simulated, the "mirror images" of God's temporal actions were not the material of superstition or subject to misinterpretation; they were therefore not to be discarded.[157] In a sense Luther had shared and resolved Augustine's concern about the mis-reading of images.[158] The problem Luther saw, however, was less the pos-sibility of their misreading in terms of the temporal realm; in a sense the images of the late-medieval period were protected from this type of misread-ing by their claim to reveal not temporal but spiritual truths. It was therefore this idolatrous misreading with which Luther had to deal. This he did by tearing the idolatrous understanding from the heart rather than by toppling their corporeal expressions with his fists.[159]

Once the visual *signum*, whether produced by the human hand or by the hand of God, had been transformed by Luther's epistemology from the glass through which the eternal Wisdom could be darkly glimpsed into the glass that reflected only God's intervention in the temporal sphere, it became less dangerous than the verbal *signum*. For Augustine the word had been herme-neutically unproblematic because it drew attention not only to the *res* it signified, but also to its own nature as *signum* and therefore to the intention of its speaker. This display of intentionality saved the word spoken by a human being from the misreading associated by Augustine with the visual *signa* created by human hands. The same display of intentionality made it possible to see through the Word that was the expression of God himself to his "essential will."[160] For Luther, in contrast, the "essential will" was unknowable; allegorical readings of Scripture, the attempts by theologians to pierce its veil, "do not illuminate, but are empty dreams."[161] Visual images, however, so long as they simply gave flesh to New Testament parable or a prophet's vision, did not pretend to illuminate sacred mysteries. But neither were they empty dreams. "Because we can't grasp it otherwise it's necessary to depict spiritual matters in such images. God doesn't have the human form in which Daniel paints him: a lovely old man with snow-white hair, a beard, wheels and fiery streams, etc. God has neither beard nor hair, but we nevertheless depict Him accurately in this image of an old man. We must paint such a picture of our Lord God for the children, and even for those of us who are learned."[162] "Even for those of us who are learned" the human power to image had been limited by Adam's Fall; "therefore God lowers himself to be grasped by our weakness and offers himself to us under similitudes or coverings with childlike simplicity, that he may in some way be known by us."[163] Viewed in these terms, images of God himself were acceptable so long as they concerned themselves with reminding the viewer of God's decision to involve himself mercifully with his human children. Less acceptable were images, such as those medieval depictions of the Trinity, that attempted to elucidate some aspect of the godhead rather than of its chosen relationship with humankind.

Luther's radical insistence on the limits of the human understanding, and his resulting rejection of medieval attempts to treat scripture as a glass through which one might glimpse spiritual truths, however darkly, had been rooted at least partially in the close examination of texts that those very attempts had necessitated. His insistence on the opacity of scriptural texts, on the human inability to see through divine words, resulted in an even greater insistence on recovering the exact and literal meaning of those words. And it resulted, ironically, in a text that itself became threateningly destabilized.[164] Luther's understanding of the relationship between word and painted image was not hierarchical, that is, no word except the word of Scripture was more valuable or revelatory than a picture. Even scriptural word had been made opaque by the limitations of human reason. Or, rather, it had been spoken by God in the knowledge that humankind could not go behind or through the word to a greater insight of the godhead, an acknowledgment of human limitedness which was most explicit in the parables spoken by the incarnate Word. The human psyche was capable only of understanding the flat surface of God's promised relationship with itself, not of penetration into the mysteries of the godhead. In 1528 Luther had dismissed the radical reformers' definition of the Mass as "a figure, symbol, or allegory" (*figur, symbolum odder gleichnis*) for Christ's sacrifice, saying that the Mass was "in no way to be compared with meaning and symbol."[165] If the Mass was something much richer, something beyond reason's comprehension, Luther's epistemology emptied figure, symbol, and allegory of their ability to do more than refer to the realm beyond the corporeal. No longer a window on the realm beyond, they only marked the existence of that incomprehensible realm without providing information or access to it. The existence of eternal verities such as Justice might still be signalled, but their conceptualizations were as opaque and unrevealing of the justice in the eye of God as the shallow "female forms" in which, according to an obviously disdainful Christian of the early fifth century, "pagans" depicted the virtues. For reasons that will soon become apparent, it seems appropriate to conclude this investigation into Luther's rewriting of the Augustinian epistemology with the passage, from a letter to Augustine, in which that fifth-century Christian defined his epistemological dilemma: "Just as we cannot give mental form to Justice or Piety, unless, perhaps, we image them with pagan shallowness in the form of women; so also God deserves to be conceptualized without any fantastic simulation as far as it is possible for us to do so."[166]

# Christ among the Councillors: The Iconography of Justice in the Late-Medieval *Rathaus*

 And [Jehosaphat] set judges in the land throughout all the fenced cities of Judah, city by city, and said to the judges, Take heed what ye do: for ye judge not for humankind, but for the LORD; for that judgment you judge shall redound on you. Wherefore now let the fear of the LORD be upon you; take heed and do it: for there is no iniquity with the LORD our GOD, nor respect of persons, nor taking of gifts.

—II Chronicles 19:6–7

Two miniatures, painted roughly a century apart and showing meetings of the *Ratsherren*, the city councillors, mark the transition from medieval to early modern visual language within the Regensburg *Rathaus*. The city council exercised both legislative and judicial authority in Regensburg, the small (c. 10,000 population) city at the northernmost bend in the Danube which held the status of a free imperial city; like Nuremberg, its larger and much more prosperous neighbor to the northwest, Regensburg owed no allegiance to any prince—not even to the Bavarian dukes whose territory surrounded the city—but only to the emperor himself.[1] The first miniature (fig. 1), painted by Hans Mielich in 1536 for the frontispiece of Regensburg's *Freiheitsbuch*,[2] showed the presentation of that book to the city council or *Rat*. The grave councillors and the *Stadtschreiber* (city secretary) looked on while the *Stadtcammerer* (the city's highest official) accepted the book on behalf of the city. On the wall above hung a large panel. The second miniature (fig. 2), painted in 1627 by an anonymous Regensburg artist,[3] commemorated the foundation of the Dreieinigkeitskirche, the Protestant church dedicated to the Trinity. As in the first miniature, the Stadtcammerer received the presentation while the Ratsherren looked on and the Stadtschreiber made his notes. On the wall above hung a different panel, half hidden by a drapery.

From Mielich's miniature we learn that the painting in the pre-Reformation

**1.** Hans Mielich, *Meeting of the Regensburg Rat*. Dedicatory miniature in Regensburg *Freiheitsbuch* of 1536. Museen der Stadt, Regensburg.

**2.** Anonymous, *Meeting of the Regensburg Rat*. Miniature commemorating foundation of the Drei-einigkeitskirche, 1627. Museen der Stadt, Regensburg.

council chamber was a square panel, four to five feet across to judge from its size in proportion to the door on same wall. It showed Christ, draped in a red cloak that left exposed the wounds in his right side, his hands, and his feet, sitting on a rainbow against a sand-colored sky, his feet resting on a globe. A lily extended behind his head at his right, a sword at his left; also to his right and left appeared angels blowing the trumpets that woke the dead. The dead themselves rose from their graves in a greenish-blue earth, to be interceded for by John the Baptist and Mary, who knelt to Christ's left and right. The panel on the wall of the *Ratsstube* in 1536 was, then, a typical late-medieval depiction of the Last Judgment, similar to the woodcut created by Albrecht Dürer c. 1510 for his *Small Passion* series.[4]

The actual panel shown in the miniature from 1536 disappeared in the course of the sixteenth century. An inventory made of the entire Rathaus at the century's end reveals that it not only had been removed from the wall of the council chamber, but had vanished from the building by that time.[5]

At the end of the sixteenth century a new image of judgment was hung in the place that had been occupied by the Last Judgment panel during the first decades of the century. This panel (fig. 3), half hidden in the miniature of 1627, still hangs in the same chamber in the Regensburg Rathaus.[6] Painted in 1592 by Isaac Schwendtner, governmental insider, member of the Äußerer Rat and assessor in Regensburg's municipal building office, it belonged to another tradition, that of the allegorical depiction of Good Government, of which the most famous example is the fresco painted in the fourteenth century by Ambrogio Lorenzetti for the Sienese Palazzo Pubblico.[7] In the medieval period such depictions were mainly to be found south of the Alps; the position held by the allegory of *buon governo* in the Sienese council chamber was generally occupied by a Last Judgment in the late-medieval council chambers of the North.[8] In Isaac Schwendtner's late sixteenth-century version of the allegory, the three Virtues of Good Government—Caritas, Justitia, and Prudentia—were accompanied by Pax and Ceres, the peace and prosperity that were the products of a virtuous government.

Whereas the weighing of evidence or souls was represented abstractly by the scales held aloft by Schwendtner's Justitia, it was the act of judgment itself that was the focus and subject of the medieval Last Judgment panel showing the division of the saved and the damned. The use of the earlier more active and explicit judgment scene on the walls of the Rathäuser, the halls in which the German town councillors met to write law and to judge the cases referred to their higher jurisdiction by the lower municipal courts, was common in the late-medieval period.[9] It was insisted on by Ulrich Tengler, the author of the most important German handbook for legal procedure of the early sixteenth century.[10] "As is the praiseworthy custom," he wrote, "it is common in the council chambers and in courtrooms where capital cases and other matters are judged, where oaths are sworn, and where other legal, corporal, and civil matters are decided, that a figure of the Last Judgment be depicted."[11]

**3.** Isaac Schwendtner, *Das gute Regiment*. Panel painted 1592 for Regensburg Rathaus. Museen der Stadt, Regensburg.

Art historians have not ignored this abundance of Last Judgment images. In 1885 Gustav Portig began the work of compiling descriptions of the Last Judgment in art, but his monograph is little more than a descriptive list that leaps around the continent and the centuries and makes no real attempt at analysis.[12] In her 1937 dissertation, Ursula Grieger Lederle restricted her geographical focus to include only those images in German and Netherlandish Rathäuser while expanding her iconographical focus to include a variety of judgment images.[13] She arranged her descriptions according to subject matter, frequently ignoring chronology and even neglecting to date the images she described. Religious and political context played no rôle in her discussion; although she considered works dating from the medieval period into the seventeenth century, neither Catholicism nor Protestantism is mentioned in the text.

Two years later, in 1939, Georg Troescher made a considerable contribution by refining Lederle's approach, cataloguing and analyzing only those Last Judgment images to be found in Rathäuser.[14] Both his catalogue and his analysis are more exact than those of his predecessors. However, Troescher's main purpose was to show that the appearance of the Last Judgment in Rathäuser had its roots in native German culture. The subsequent transformation or disappearance of the image lay outside the scope of his analysis and religious change played no rôle. In contrast, an attempt at discovering the impact of religious change on the image of the Last Judgment was made by Gisela Spiekerkötter in a dissertation published the same year as Troescher's article.[15] Spiekerkötter, however, like Portig, chose to consider the Last Judgment images in all their locations, which is to say, largely to ignore the contexts in which these images occurred, and to cover the entire period from 1500 to 1800. She concluded that "generally speaking, no dogmatic differences can be found in the depictions of the Last Judgment, because neither the length of punishment nor the ethical concept of grace can be easily represented visually."[16] For the particular case of images in council chambers, she referred the reader to the then forthcoming article by Troescher and commented only that "in a later period [after the eleventh century], the broad dissemination of the image made possible the occasional appearance of the Last Judgment in town halls. Even there it nevertheless remained in the sacral sphere, because of its eschatological meaning. . . . it even had the power to bridge the split between the Catholic and Protestant churches."[17]

Most recently, Craig Harbison has reopened the inquiry begun by Spiekerkötter into the impact of Protestantism on depictions of the Last Judgment in general.[18] Looking, in contrast to Spiekerkötter, for a sweeping transformation wrought by Protestantism, he nevertheless accepts her assertion that the Last Judgment in the council chamber belonged to the sacred world and posits a sharp division between the secular world of the town hall and the "intruding" sacred sphere of the Last Judgment image.[19] His approach emphasizes iconography, tending to ignore the way in which an image's location in relation to other images might affect its meaning.[20]

The disappearance of the Last Judgment image from the Regensburg council chamber and its eventual replacement by a completely different type of judgment depiction, one outside the range analyzed by Harbison, hint at a transformation that remained hidden to his approach.[21] The Regensburg material reveals a dramatic change in the image of judgment. That change is linked closely to the images incorporated in sixteenth-century Lutheran thought. Moreover, an examination of the lists of judgment depictions provided by Troescher and Harbison in the light of the Regensburg evidence suggests that the transformation of the visual language of judgment was general in Lutheran cities during the sixteenth century.

In Regensburg, as in other cities in Northern Europe in the late-medieval period, depictions of the Last Judgment gave visual substance to its verbal appearance in the oaths taken by the *Bürger* appointed or elected to serve in a municipal court: "I swear . . . to keep only God and the Law before my eyes, as I must answer for that before God at the Last Judgment."[22] As is the case with the Last Judgment image that hung in the Regensburg council chamber at the end of the medieval period, many of these panels no longer exist; their disappearance will be explained later in this chapter. The prominence of the Last Judgment in late-medieval courtrooms is, nevertheless, attested by those depictions that remain, and by miniatures and descriptions that record the existence of objects now lost.

One of the Last Judgment depictions now missing is the small panel that hung above the magistrates' bench in the lower court in Hamburg, illustrated in 1497 by a Hamburg miniaturist (fig. 4).[23] As depicted by the artist, that courtroom was a busy place: four judges listened to the appeals made by three parties before the bench, while two bailiffs escorted a prisoner away and other groups stood in conversation; at the windows eager citizens watched the proceedings and talked among themselves. If the urban character of the activities were not explicit enough, a scene of bustling city life could be seen through the window of the courtroom.

For the late-medieval viewer the two inscribed bands held by the hands of God above the scene underscored the meaning conveyed by the Last Judgment on the courtroom wall—the activities of the municipal court had implications beyond the municipal, secular realm. The first was inscribed in Latin with part of the judicial charge from II Chronicles with which we began this chapter: "You, who are about to judge others, consider what you do; for you judge not for humankind, but for the Lord."[24] The second combined the next, and quite ominous, line from that verse—"for that judgment you judge, shall redound on you"—with the equally awful and immediate reminder from the Sermon on the Mount: "with what measure you mete, it shall be measured back to you."[25]

**4.** Anonymous Hamburg artist, *Courtroom Scene*. Miniature, c. 1497, from *Van schickinge unde vorderinge des neddersten gherichtes*. Staatsarchiv, Hamburg.

It has been suggested that the Last Judgment panel was an appropriate decoration for the walls of the medieval council chamber because the Last Judgment was a symbol or allegory for earthly judgment, a legitimation for temporal judges. This is the rôle assigned the panels by Craig Harbison, who sees such depictions as "sacred intrusion" into an "acknowledged area of secular control."[26] "Every ounce of relevance that could be directly or obliquely applied to secular, earthly proceedings was methodically extracted from the Christian eschatological drama. . . . The original purpose of Town Hall Last Judgments was to infuse the profanity of the common law with the content of sacred dogma which seemed most appropriate."[27]

More recently, Samuel Edgerton has presented a more complex argument for the visual interconnectedness of temporal judgment and Last Judgment depictions and the legitimating function of the latter.[28] Analyzing material from the Italian Renaissance, he argues that although the medieval conception of the Last Judgment (and its visual depiction) was to an extent formed by the sights familiar to the medieval town-dweller, the influence ran both ways: "The rulers of the urban communes during the Middle Ages used the iconic arrangement of the Last Judgment, as described in scripture and depicted by artists, to lend legitimation and moral support to the secular dispensation of law and order. Here, even the seating of the local judges resembles that of Christ and his apostles, the criminal defendants appearing at the judges' left, just as Jesus consigns sinful souls to hell at his sinister side."[29] Edgerton's thesis depends on the presence of the Last Judgment "icon" in the mind of the citizen; the eschatological event was not generally depicted on the walls or furnishings of the Italian courtroom.[30]

Sources not examined by Edgerton or Harbison provide evidence of the availability of that icon or, rather, of the interconnectedness of the languages of eternal and temporal justice. Both north and south of the Alps dialogues by learned canon lawyers and the popular plays performed as part of the Easter liturgy explicated the theological issue of sin and salvation in the familiar language of the contemporary courtroom.[31] In the course of the fifteenth century a trial in which the devil challenged Christ's right to deprive him of his power over humankind had become a popular scene in the dramatic "Harrowing of Hell" associated with the liturgy of the church. Here, as in another drama popular at the time—the trial of the four daughters of God over the salvation of Adam—theological issues were treated in the more accessible language of the courtroom.[32] In twentieth-century terms, the secular was intruding on the sacred, but these juristic "intrusions" had their origins in the apocryphal Gospel of Nicodemus and in a sermon attributed to St. Bernard.[33] In the sermon, Psalm 85:10—"Mercy and truth are met together; righteousness and peace have kissed each other"—was interpreted as a statement of the peaceful outcome of a trial in which two of God's daughters, Pax and Misericordia, charged that their sisters, Veritas and Justitia, were punishing humankind too harshly after the Fall.[34] Christ substituted for his father as judge and in the end resolved the dispute by himself doing penance for the sins of humankind. In the enactment of the *"Teu-felsprozess"* ("Devil's lawsuit") associated with Christ's harrowing of hell, the devil complained before God or Christ that Christ had illegally stolen his human property. In its early printings, the second part of Ulrich Tengler's *Laienspiegel*, the first legal handbook published in German, concluded with a version of this latter trial in which Mary appeared as the attorney defending humankind against the devil before the judgment throne of Christ[35]—a legalistic interpretation of the rôle in which she usually appeared in depictions of the Last Judgment, and one justified by the great thirteenth-century Regensburg preacher Albertus Magnus' characterization of Mary as extremely knowledgeable in both Roman and canon law.[36] The woodcuts illustrating Tengler's text (figs. 5 and 6) combined elements (distinguishable for analytic purposes as) sacred and secular;[37] Maria Mediatrix appeared as the defense attorney, her cloak spread to protect the human spoils sought by the plaintiff Satan, her learned words recorded by the evangelists in their capacity as court scribes.

The subject of these sacred courtroom dramas remained the mystery of human salvation, their theme Christ's sacrifice for humankind. Nevertheless, the speakers in their manuscript and early printed versions argued with references to civil law, to the Institutes and Digest of Justinian, and to canon law. The illustrated German editions of Jacobus de Theramo's and Bartolus de Saxoferrato's versions of the "Teufelsprozess" published at Augsburg in 1472, Straßburg in 1477, Magdeburg in 1492, and Leipzig in the 1490s, represented Satan's appearance before the heavenly judge in the visual language of the temporal courtroom.[38]

This borrowing and adaptation of languages worked in both directions, evidence not just of the legitimation of secular actions by the insertion of sacred language, but of the perceived interconnectedness of the two realms as well. It is clear from the style of these sacred texts by canon lawyers, and from their prefaces, that the "Teufelsprozess" was often "a juristic game from the intellectual realm of the chancery, a piece of stylistic showmanship in which theological and legal knowledge are displayed, but which also serves as a pattern book for legal practice."[39] This was, in fact, one of the reasons given by Ulrich Tengler for his inclusion of a version of the "Teufelsprozess" in his widely distributed *Laienspiegel*. The drama, he explained, had been written in Latin "by a very learned man for the education of his students." Tengler himself had translated and added it to his handbook, but "not that anyone should think that this trial between the devil of hellish evil and the Virgin Mary over humankind actually took place before almighty God." Rather, he had included it as an illustration of some of the judicial processes described in his text, "so that a simple uneducated layman" should be better informed about how one should defend and represent someone before a judge.[40]

On the evidence of Tengler's *Laienspiegel*, the applicability of the Harbison/Edgerton legitimation argument for the Northern courtroom, where

**5.** Anonymous, *Mary Defends Humankind before Christ*. Woodcut for Ulrich Tengler, *Der neü Layen-spiegel* (Augsburg: Hans Otmar, 1511), fol. CLXIX'. Handschriftenabteilung, Res. 2° J. pract. 76. Bayerische Staatsbibliothek, Munich.

**6.** Anonymous, *Mary Defends Humankind before Christ*. Woodcut for Ulrich Tengler, *Der Layen spiegel* (Straßburg: M. Hupfuff, 1510), fol. LXIV'. Handschriftenabteilung, Res. 2° J. pract. 74. Bayerische Staatsbibliothek, Munich.

the depiction of the eternal judgment hung on the wall as a ready referent for the defendant who might otherwise fail to recognize his iconic position among the damned, seems clear. In fact, an apparently iconic ordering has been found in certain Northern courtrooms by Harbison.[41] For Regensburg no similar material exists; Hans Mielich's miniature (fig. 1) shows not a trial with magistrates and defendant, but a presentation made to the council, which was seated in an order not analogous to the Last Judgment. Whether the seating during a trial more closely resembled the iconic ordering of the Last Judgment must remain an open question, an interesting possibility.

Both Harbison's and Edgerton's arguments are convincing, as far as they go. The problem is that they do not go far enough. Despite the aura of showmanship and Tengler's innocent disclaimer, he did not view the trial explaining the mystery of human salvation with which he closed the second section of his *Laienspiegel* as a simple analogy to the trial held in a late-medieval municipal court, nor did it serve only as a subtle iconic legitimation of the power of the temporal judge. Instead, the Last Judgment itself was present in the courtroom, evidence for that final trial was there being collected and weighed. Before its introduction in his handbook, Tengler described the "Teufelsprozess" as a "figure and image of the Last Judgment in

German verse or dialogue." "Certain characteristics of the Last Judgment," he wrote, "may be seen as prefigured and indicated in the regulations already laid down [by me] for the handling of corporal cases." This was in order that "the simple layman may be excited that much sooner to justice," just as a rhymed "image of the Last Judgment" was added at the end of the third section, to show "truly how quickly and gruesomely and with what terrifying fear the damned receive their unavoidable and eternal punishment."[42]

If the Last Judgment was "sacred intrusion," into an area of "secular control," it was sacred intrusion at the very highest level, for the supposed secularity of the scene depicted by the Hamburg miniaturist was interrupted not only by the image of the eternal judgment, but, indeed, by the hands of God himself (fig. 4).

On the first of the bands held aloft by those hands, the charge of Jehosaphat to his judges could be read as simple confirmation of the rôle of the secular judge as God's temporal minister—therefore as a legitimation of the temporal judgment, and confirmation of the legitimating rôle of the visual icon. The second quotation, however, which combined the most ominous line from that judicial charge with an equally ominous passage from the Sermon on the Mount, delivered a more complicated message: "for that judgment you judge shall redound on you, and with what measure you mete, it shall be measured back to you." It was not just the defendant who found himself iconically threatened with damnation, but the literate judge, too, who was reminded of the importance of his temporal decisions for his own eternal sentence.[43] In fact, the complete text of Jehosaphat's charge to his judges was itself as much a warning to the judge as a legitimation of his right to judge: "Take heed what ye do: for ye judge not for humankind but for the Lord; for that judgment you judge shall redound on you. Wherefore now let the fear of the Lord be upon you; take heed and do it: for there is no iniquity with the Lord our God, nor respect of persons, nor taking of gifts."[44] In late-medieval Regensburg, an expansion of Jehosaphat's reminder to his judges served as warning in the oaths taken by the magistrate and his associates: "to judge correctly the poor as well as the wealthy, the visitor as well as the citizen, according to my conscience and best understanding, without consideration of affection, antipathy, patronage, fear, payment or gift, friendship, enmity or anything except God and the Law, as I must answer for this before the Almighty on Judgment Day, truly and without fraudulent intent."[45]

To speak of the intrusion of the sacred into the secular is to import a distinction alien to the late-medieval mind. "The Lord is with you in giving judgment." And the eternal sentences of both temporal judge and temporal judged were at stake, "prefigured" in Tengler's words, in the temporal courtroom. The relation between eternal and secular event was of a different order from that suggested by Harbison or Edgerton. This mode of associating events should be very clearly distinguished from the weaker mode Harbison terms "drawing an analogy."[46] The Last Judgment panel was hung on the wall of the Regensburg council chamber not in illustration of an analogy between eternal and temporal judgment, but as a sign of the immanence, of the "real presence" of the Last Judgment in the medieval courtroom.

Theologians use the term "real presence" to refer to the belief that the Mass is not simply a memorial to Christ's sacrifice, but that Christ is actually present, that the Mass is *in the strongest sense* a re-presentation of these events. This was the essentially medieval position adopted by Martin Luther in his attempt to protect the "real presence" of the Mass from the attacks of the more radical reformers in 1527/1528. "It is the greatest idiocy [to say] 'the bread means or is a symbol of the body he gave for us, and the chalice or wine is a symbol of the blood he shed for us,'" he wrote.[47] "The Communion is in no way to be compared with meaning and symbol. Since everything in the New Testament must be fuller than in the Old Testament, even its symbols, if our Communion were merely bread and wine, Christ would have better had us retain the customary Passover meal of Moses. Our Communion must greatly surpass that traditional meal; otherwise Christ would not have abolished the latter."[48] Luther denied that the Mass or Communion was a figure, symbol, or allegory (*figur, symbolum odder gleichnis*) for Christ's sacrifice; instead, he insisted that it stood in an entirely different relationship to that event—Christ himself was present in the bread and wine of the Mass, which was "God's sacrifice sacrificed to God."[49] It was the mystery of the Mass that in the bread and wine *signum* (sign) and *res* (thing), normally irreconcilably separate, were conjoined through God's mercy and love.[50] In Luther's explanation, Christ, sitting on the right hand of the Father, was, like the Father himself, omnipresent, but "there is a difference between his presence and your ability to grasp him. . . . Christ's humanity is on the right hand of God and now also in all and over all things in the manner of the divine right hand, but you won't chew or slurp him like the cabbage or soup on your table unless he wills it. He has now become incomprehensible; you can't touch him even if he is in your bread—unless, that is, he binds himself to you and summons you to a special table with his word and with his word points out to you the bread you should eat. This he does in the Last Supper."[51] Christ, like God himself, was immanent in his creation but graspable only in the elements of the Communion because it was only there that Christ himself had specified or localized his presence for humankind. With the words "This is my body. . . . This is my blood," the eternal divine permeated the temporal sign of the bread and wine and made of the Communion an event richer and fuller than any mere symbol could be. It was in order to emphasize Christ's promised presence in the bread and wine on the altar that Luther specified that only a panel depicting the Last Supper and inscribed with a verse from the Psalms should hang above it: "they should stand before the eyes, in order that the heart consider them."[52]

If the "real presence" of Christ in the Mass was an element in Luther's thought as a Protestant, it was a "real presence" of another sort, signaled by other panels in churches and council chambers, which had triggered his crisis of faith and which eventually led him to protest against the Catholic church: "When I was a papist I fled from Christ, and shuddered at his name, because I believed in my heart that Christ was a Judge, to whom I had to answer on Judgment Day for every word and deed."[53]

Luther's fear at the thought of the final judgment was given greater urgency by his perception of its imminence. The spread of diseases old and new, the threat of a Turkish conquest of Western Europe, the eruption of disturbances in city and countryside, and meteorological events appeared to many to be signs of divine wrath and the Second Coming. Like other Christians in the late-medieval period, Luther located himself "in the middle of eschatological history": "Looking around himself, he found a multitude of signs signaling the immediacy of the end of the world. The telescoping of present and future, history and the end of history was characteristic of his perspective. In his conception the wrathful judgment [of God] demonstrated in the present therefore approached the Day of Wrath as an event to come. The Last Judgment was already operative in the present since the effects of the Wrath of God were on the one hand occasioned by the Fall and on the other precursors of the Last Judgment."[54]

Whether or not medieval Christians perceived the event called the Last Judgment as chronologically immediate, it was both immanent and emanant in relation to their temporal world. It was at once a chronological event that was the natural outgrowth of their activities and the ending of all chronology in the eternal, and an eternal that permeated the world whose proper goal and perfection it was, but which—like the presence of Christ in the world— was graspable only in the summoning of the individual before the bench. That temporal existence was not viewed as a mere figure for the final disposition of the soul was the result of the medieval church's insistence on free will, on the individual's freedom to choose for good or evil in each act. The tension created by the view that each action represented a new opportunity to choose (and therefore a new datum to be inscribed in the book out of which the final judgment would eventually be read) made a reading of the earthly life as figure possible only at its conclusion when judgment and therefore closure had been achieved.[55]

Their perception of this causal connection between temporal deeds and the final disposition of their souls did not, however, necessarily lead medieval Christians to share Luther's terror. The unusual *psychostasis* or weighing of the soul (fig. 7) on the first sheet of a manuscript written at Prüfening, the Benedictine cloister just outside Regensburg, c. 1150, a manuscript that by the second half of the sixteenth century had found its way into the library of the Regensburg Rathaus, emphasized the same causal connection, but in a different mood.[56] Here the monk-author of the work embraced rather than feared the weighing of souls on the last day. In the lower right corner of the folio, the monastic scribe of the manuscript lay dead on his pallet; a large Christ sat in judgment on the left side of the panel; in the middle an angel held the scale of judgment while another placed the manuscript itself in one

**7.** Bruder Swicher (?), *Self-portrait with Psychostasis*. Lower half of dedicatory miniature, *Etymologiae*, ms. c. 1150. Handschriftenabteilung, Clm. 13031. Bayerische Staatsbibliothek, Munich.

pan, overbalancing the weight of the monk's sins and causing the devil to flee while the monk's soul was welcomed to heaven. Thus the monk depicted the happy result he anticipated from his prayer: "God, deign to pity the wretched scribe. Don't weigh the heaviness of my failures. Although the good deeds are few, may they yet be exalted above the evils; may night yield to light, death to life."[57]

Whether the result for the individual was the fear experienced by the monk Luther or the pious optimism implied by the Prüfeninger scribe's subjunctive plea, the concept of the Last Judgment as a day on which each soul would be called to answer for the deeds, good and evil, done in the temporal realm was a part of the teaching of the medieval church. Its biblical basis was the twenty-fifth chapter of Matthew, where the horrible end marked out for the sinner who had failed to give food and drink to the hungry and thirsty, to provide shelter and clothing to the homeless and naked, and to visit the sick and imprisoned was contrasted with the eternal life promised those whose deeds had merited it.[58]

The good deeds narrated by Matthew had been made canonical by the medieval church, for which they represented the Christian's chance to earn a place at the right hand of Christ;[59] at the end of the fifteenth century these "Seven Acts of Mercy" appeared in association with several Last Judgment depictions.[60] In the *Armseelenaltar*, a carved wooden triptych donated to the Alte Kapelle in Regensburg by Sigmund Graner and his wife, Elisabeth, c. 1488 (fig. 8), the central scene represented their patron saints' recommendation of the donors to the mediators Mary and John and to Christ himself at the Last Judgment. The two panels below the Last Judgment extended that scene, showing on Christ's right angels freeing the saved from a prison familiar from enactments of Christ's harrowing of hell, and on his left a devil guarding imprisoned souls. Scenes on the wings of the altarpiece depicted two acts of mercy—the clothing of the naked and the feeding of the hungry— together with acts associated with the devotion to the body of Christ— attendance at Mass and adoration of the crucifix.[61] The lower panel of each wing reinforced the relation of these deeds to the Last Judgment by depicting, on the one hand, an angel flying toward the closed prison and, on the other, an empty prison with door ajar.

Transferred from altar to courtroom, the demonstration of the importance of works for salvation stressed the inseparability of the just judgment of mortal deeds and the justification of the spirit; this was the case of the woodcut of Christ holding the scales before the kneeling figures of Adam and Eve, which introduced the preface to Ulrich Tengler's *Laienspiegel* (figs. 9 and 10).[62] Here, an image we might anachronistically label "sacred" appeared and was broadly disseminated in an explicitly "secular" context—again, an anachronistic term.

The real and immediate presence of the Last Judgment and the weighing of temporal deeds which decided its outcome were graphically demonstrated in the books and furnishings of the late-medieval courtroom north of the Alps. The causal inseparability of eternal and temporal event, taught by the medieval church and the source of Luther's anxiety, was there signaled both visually and verbally. These visual and verbal forms were not simply illustrations drawing analogies between temporal and eternal judgment, but rather signs and manifestations of the presence of the Last Judgment in the events of the temporal courtroom. The temporal courtroom was, of course, no altar—although an altar frequently stood nearby—nor was the trial a sacrament. Like the panels of the Last Supper which would hang above Lutheran altars, the panels on the walls of the late-medieval courtroom were signs created by human hands, not by God; they signaled the presence of the Last Judgment but did not themselves contain it.

In contrast to Christ's words at the Last Supper, the words that localized the Last Judgment, binding it specifically to the individual and making it graspable and manifest, were not divine promises but human oaths. Christians of the late-medieval period were nonetheless accustomed to discerning the dark outlines of the spiritual realm in the products of human hands. A mysticism rooted in the Augustinian epistemology, but channeled in a new direction by Duns Scotus' translation of the pseudo-Dionysian writings, had

8. Anonymous, *Armseelenaltar* for Regensburg Alte Kapelle. Carved and painted triptych, c. 1488. Museen der Stadt, Regensburg.

**9.** Anonymous, *Adam and Eve before Christ with Balance*. Woodcut for Ulrich Tengler, *Der neü Layen-spiegel* (Augsburg: Hans Otmar, 1511), fol. Ciii. Handschriftenabteilung, Res. 2° J. pract. 76. Bayerische Staatsbibliothek, Munich.

**10.** Anonymous, *Adam and Eve before Christ with Balance*. Woodcut for Ulrich Tengler, *Der Layen spiegel* (Straßburg: M. Hupfuff, 1510), fol. Av'. Handschriftenabteilung, Res. 2° J. pract. 74. Bayerische Staatsbibliothek, Munich.

in general triumphed over the distrust of the visual arts displayed by Augustine himself (and, with different roots, by Bernard of Clairveaux) to produce a plethora of images designed to model the piety of the beholder.[63] Ideally, the beholder would be led *through* the visual image itself to a spiritual vision of the saint depicted or of the godhead itself, that is, through the temporal object to the atemporal reality it signified. So successful were painted panels as windows on the world beyond that they can be shown to have modeled the ecstatic visions of medieval mystics. This "correct" use of images, the usage defended by Catholics against the attacks of the sixteenth-century iconoclasts, has been thoroughly explored by scholars;[64] it is in the context of this usage that the Last Judgment scenes that hung in Northern council chambers must be understood.

In a painting dated 1493/1494 (fig. 11), Derick Baegert depicted the Last Judgment to the left of the chief magistrate in a northern courtroom.[65] The artist teased the spectator—was the Last Judgment a panel hung on the wall of the court chamber or was it instead an event seen through an open window, as the architectural framing and the closed leaded window in a parallel location to the right of the magistrate seem to suggest? The gesture of the earthly judge was identical with that of Christ in the Last Judgment, and

**11.** Derick Baegert, *Oath-taking in Courtroom*. Painted panel, 1493/1494. Städtisches Museum, Galerie im Centrum, Wesel.

Mary and John interceded with Christ, just as the magistrate's associates interceded with him. Unlike the contemporary panel in the Regensburg Rathaus (fig. 1), the Last Judgment scene on this wall revealed no souls rising from their graves at the trumpet call; instead it was the soul of the living man, the oath-taking witness in the temporal trial, over which the angel and devil quarreled: for the sake of that living soul they had stepped from the Last Judgment directly into the scene of secular judgment.[66] To distinguish here between a distant sacred and a present secular judgment, to speak of sacred intrusions into secular space, is false. The boundaries between events were not distinct; rather, they had been intentionally obscured. Thus the city's late-medieval constitution commanded the Regensburg *Schultheiß*, the chief official of the city's principal court, to remind those who were to swear an oath in his courtroom of the danger and weight that attached to oath-taking—that the temporal discovery of their falseness would result in banishment, but also that their oaths must be answered for on Judgment Day.[67] The eternal battle and judgment were present in the temporal event.

The hands of God reached down into the temporal scene and angels and devils battled over the souls of the living in "profane" space, locally and

**12.** Anonymous, *Oath-taking with Devil and Angel*. Woodcut for Ulrich Tengler, *Der neü Layenspiegel* (Augsburg: Hans Otmar, 1511), fol. XCIX. Handschriftenabteilung, Res. 2° J. pract. 76. Bayerische Staatsbibliothek, Munich.

**13.** Anonymous, *Oath-taking with Devil and Angel*. Woodcut for Ulrich Tengler, *Der Layen spiegel* (Straßburg: M. Hupfuff, 1510), fol. LXXX'. Handschriftenabteilung, Res. 2° J. pract. 74. Bayerische Staatsbibliothek, Munich.

temporally present because it was in that locale and at that moment that the witness himself insisted in the oath he swore that the truth or falsity of his testimony be recorded for the final judgment. Nor did Baegert's panel represent an isolated case; a similar image in which an angel and a devil fought over the soul of a living man in a temporal courtroom introduced the discussion of legal oaths in Tengler's *Laienspiegel* (figs. 12 and 13).[68] And devils appeared as the whispering councillors of the man who handed a bribe to a notary and the notary who accepted the bribe in a woodcut from Rodericus' *Spiegel des menschlichen Lebens*, published in Augsburg in the 1470s.[69]

By the same token, the trial scene and portrait of the *Advocat* Niclas Strobel, c. 1478, a copy of which is now in Graz (fig. 14), cannot be read, as Harbison suggests, following Lederle, as simply a scene set in a courtroom where one wall was frescoed with a Last Judgment depiction in which the arrangement of heavenly intercessors was analogous to the ordering of the associate justices in the temporal courtroom.[70] Here the magistrate's gestures did not match those of the heavenly judge; devils carried off the souls of the dead and already judged who arose from their graves in the background, but Christ and his judgment of the souls of the living actors in the courtroom—judges, jurors, and attorneys, as well as witnesses and defendants—waited upon the

**14.** Anonymous seventeenth-century copyist, *Courtroom Scene with Last Judgment and Portrait of Niclas Strobel*. Seventeenth-century copy of painted panel executed c. 1478; oil on wooden panel. Inv. Nr. M39. Stadtmuseum, Graz.

earthly event. The presence of the two men behind the magistrate's bench who looked up toward Christ on his judgment seat in the mandorla, as well as the upward glance of one of the magistrate's associates, confused the viewer's perspectival understanding of the scene, made impossible a comfortably distinct reading of two scenes as discrete events, one temporal and one merely the painted depiction of a distant event. As in the formally similar woodcut from the *Laienspiegel* (figs. 15 and 16),[71] the gestures of the heavenly

**15.** Anonymous, *Courtroom Scene with Last Judgment*. Woodcut for Ulrich Tengler, *Der neü Layenspiegel* (Augsburg: Hans Otmar, 1511), fol. XXII'. Handschriftenabteilung, Res. 2° J. pract. 76. Bayerische Staatsbibliothek, Munich.

**16.** Anonymous, *Courtroom Scene with Last Judgment*. Woodcut for Ulrich Tengler, *Der Layen spiegel* (Straßburg: M. Hupfuff, 1510), fol. XIII. Handschriftenabteilung, Res. 2° J. pract. 74. Bayerische Staatsbibliothek, Munich.

and earthly intercessors were not analogous in the weak sense. It was rather the case that the perspectival confusions and the glances of three of the actors in the temporal drama indicated the inseparability of the two events: the continual weighing and inscribing of earthly event in the book of the Last Judgment, the eternal presence of the Last Judgment in the temporal court. The text accompanying the *Laienspiegel* woodcut explained the seating arrangement within the chamber and emphasized the weighty responsibility of the judge/magistrate. Although the text had insisted only that a painted depiction hang in the council chamber—"a serious illustration of the Last Judgment should stand before the eyes"[72]—the woodcut, with its chain of clouds (the familiar symbolic demarcation between two realms) separating the judging Christ from the temporal judges, translated the meaning of the required painted image by presenting the Last Judgment not as a painted icon but as an event occurring outside of temporal time and space and as a mental image in the mind's eye of judge and juror.

The late-medieval Last Judgment was not a panel hung on the wall of the courtroom as decoration but a figure in eternity, eternally at stake in the here and now. The battle for the human soul was waged both in and out of time, both in the here and now and in eternity; the judgment that was the outcome

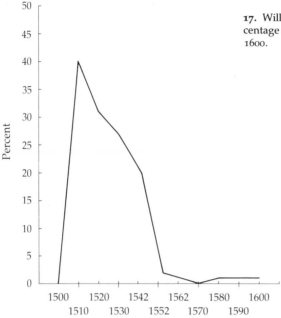

**17.** Wills referring to Last Judgment as percentage of extant wills, Regensburg, 1500–1600.

of that battle was at once immediate and eternal. This interconnectedness accounts for Ulrich Tengler's use of a "figure and image of the Last Judgment in German verse or dialogue" to conclude his legal handbook. "Certain characteristics of the Last Judgment," he reminded his reader, "may be seen as prefigured and indicated in the regulations already laid down for the handling of corporal cases."[73]

It is in this light that the oath taken by each Regensburg citizen elected to serve as a juror in one of the municipal courts—to judge each case according to his best understanding, to ignore friendship and enmity, and to be mindful only of God and Right, *because he will "answer for this to the Almighty on Judgment Day"*—is to be understood.[74] As in the case of the visual language of judgment, the lines of perspective blurred and the Last Judgment became strikingly immediate. The Regensburger whose will reminded each appointed executor that he had pledged to give an honest accounting in accordance with the testament's provisions, "as he will give an account of himself to God on Judgment Day," used a phrase common in the rather formulaic late-medieval testaments of the Regensburger (fig. 17), but it was scarcely an empty formula.[75]

Words, certainly legalistic words, may have been clumsier tools than pictures for depicting the real presence of the Last Judgment in the temporal courtroom;[76] they nevertheless made explicit the connection between "sacred" images and the legal handbooks and law codes in which they appeared. The *Brandenburgische halszgerichts ordnung*, printed in Nuremberg in 1516, was introduced by Erhard Schön's woodcut of the Last Judgment in

**18.** Anonymous, *Last Judgment*. Woodcut for Johann von Schwartzenberg, *Bambergische Halß-gerichts und Rechtlich ordnung* (Mainz: Ivo Schöffer, 1508), fol. I. Handschriftenabteilung, Res. 2° J. publ. g. 95. Bayerische Staatsbibliothek, Munich.

which was inscribed the admonition from the Sermon on the Mount, familiar
to us from the depiction of the trial in a Hamburg court, this time translated
from the Latin into German—an increased accessibility that strengthened its
urgency and immediacy.[77] "You will be sentenced in the sentence you issue":
the same inscription appeared at the top of the Last Judgment depiction that
had introduced the *Bambergische Halßgerichts und Rechtlich ordnung* (fig. 18)
and would introduce the *Constitutio criminalis Carolina*, the imperial law dealing with corporal punishment issued from Regensburg in 1532, both works
published in multiple editions by the Mainz printshop directed by Ivo Schöffer.[78] The Last Judgment and the issue of human salvation were made immediate and accessible to all late-medieval Bürger in drama, procession, and art
through the images and language of the temporal courtroom. As we have
seen, the literate Bürger, like the judge and councillor, found the same
conjunction of images at the altar where they worshiped, in the works of
literature with which they amused themselves, and in their legal handbooks.

# CHAPTER 2

# God among the Councillors: The Iconography of Justice after the Reformation

 How quickly you've made a wrathful judge into a generous father!

  —Johannes Geiler von Kaisersberg, c. 1510

The terrible immediacy of the Last Judgment in Catholic thought and paintings was a frequent theme in the writings of Martin Luther.[1] "The papists," he wrote, "make Christ nothing but a strict and wrathful judge, before whom one must be afraid—as if Christ wanted to shove us into hell; they paint him sitting in judgment on the rainbow, with his mother Mary and John the Baptist at either side, as intercessors against his terrible wrath."[2] While still a monk, he later recalled, he had "thought of Christ only as a wrathful judge sitting in heaven, as he is painted sitting on a rainbow. I couldn't call to him, couldn't even hear his name spoken, and had to seek refuge with our dear Lady, had to crawl under her cloak and call on my apostle St. Thomas. Afterward I thought 'Ach, I'll go to confession, and say Mass, and satisfy God himself with my good works.' Just so has the accursed Pope torn our dear savior Jesus Christ from our sight, thrown him away, and smeared his dear friendly tint with a horrible black color, so that we were more frightened of him than of the damned devil."[3] Luther's transformation of the image of Christ, or rather his insistence on the primacy of one of the multiplicity of images of Christ sanctioned by the medieval church, led to the eventual disappearance of the Last Judgment from the walls of Lutheran council chambers, the pages of lawbooks printed for Lutheran cities, and—as figure 17 shows—from the pages of wills executed in the Lutheran city Regensburg.[4] Christ the judge disappeared from the council chamber, to be replaced by an image that brought together an older vision of justice revived by the humanists and a vision of God the Father rather than the Son.

Luther, of course, was not the first to realize the necessity of dealing with the petrifying fear that might be provoked by the image of the Last Judgment and the constant recording of earthly deeds it signified; the medieval church itself had provided mechanisms for dealing with the "black ugliness" that was the Christian's fear of a wrathful god's righteous and eternal wrath. One of these mechanisms was the intercession of the saints—of the apostles like Luther's St. Thomas, of Burgkmair's Sts. Sebastian and Roche (fig. 32), but most frequently of Mary. It was Mary who pled efficaciously for the souls to Christ's right at the Last Judgment, Mary whose gesture toward or baring of her breast reminded her angry son that he too had been nourished on human milk,[5] Mary who spread her cloak to protect humankind from the arrows hurled by a wrathful god,[6] Mary who, in her superior knowledge of Roman and canon law, defended humankind before the Christ-Judge against the devil's charges in the "Teufelsprozess" that concluded Tengler's *Laienspiegel* (figs. 5 and 6). This was not simply folk custom but the teaching of the theologians who, in Luther's contentious phrase, "simply replaced Christ with Mary and made Christ into a judge":[7] "St. Bernard, who was otherwise a pious man, also said, 'See in the whole Gospel how horribly often Christ railed against, punished, and damned the Pharisees and quickly had done with them; in contrast the Virgin Mary is always friendly and mild and has never said a harsh word.' "[8]

Wolf Traut's woodcut for the Confraternity of the Rosary, c. 1510, combined visual and verbal languages to stress Mary's central rôle as intercessor (fig. 19).[9] Beneath the image of God the Father shooting arrows labeled *pestlencz*, *teurung*, and *krieg* appeared a hierarchy of intercessors for those who joined the confraternity: Anne folded her hands in prayer, Mary bared her breast to her son, and Christ gestured to the wound at his side. The banner and rosaries held by St. Dominic focused attention on Mary, for it was to her that the reader was to appeal (in the words used by Abraham to his wife as they were fleeing the famine): "Say, we pray thee, thou art our sister; that it may be well with us for thy sake; and our souls shall live because of thy grace."[10] Thus, in the carved wooden *Armseelenaltar* for the Alte Kapelle in Regensburg (fig. 20), the donors depended not only on their own good works to assure their salvation but more especially on the intercession of their patron saints and of the Virgin, who was depicted once as the mediator of the Last Judgment and again as the merciful guardian who spread her cloak to protect humankind.

The second *Heilmittel* ("means of healing") applied by the medieval church was the sacrament of confession and penance; as an aspect of "attrition," the fear of divine punishment could serve as the first step toward the sinner's absolution. Thus both penance and the intercession of the saints found their place in the *pater noster* for which Hans Burgkmair provided the title woodcut (fig. 32). And it was penance that ended the sinner's fear according to the gentle words of Johannes Geiler von Kaisersberg (1445–1510), the German preacher for whom the nave pulpit was erected in the Straßburg cathedral. Where Luther, while a monk afraid of eternal condemnation, "couldn't call to [Christ], couldn't even hear his name spoken," Geiler's book *Granatapfel* had

**19.** Wolf Traut, *The Rosary of the Virgin*. Woodcut, c. 1510 (G.1415). Staatliche Kunsthalle, Karlsrühe.

**20.** Anonymous, *Last Judgment with Maria Mediatrix*. Central panel of *Armseelenaltar* for Alte Kapelle. Regensburg, c. 1488. (Complete altar shown in figure 8.) Museen der Stadt, Regensburg.

begun with the invocation: "Jesus, you most worthy holy name, to hear you is sweet to all worshipful hearts, to name you is dear."[11] According to Geiler, who cited the church fathers as evidence, the transformation of a wrathful god into a loving one was the result of the sinner's act of confession and penance: "Now ye uplifted, you friend of God, when you have confessed your sin and have done what is required and want to do so from now on, as is appropriate to penance—now you are in God's grace. As St. Augustine says, there is no more healing medicine for sin than confession and penance. This medicine makes God's enemy into his friend, and makes the child of the devilish enemy into a child of God. . . . St. Bernard said, 'Oh, you saving penance; Oh, you good hope of the repentant sinner. . . . Oh, how quickly you've made the wrathful judge into a benevolent father!' "[12]

The gentle and emotive language in which Geiler characterized the relation between the penitent and God competed in the late-medieval church with the legalistic language of fine and indulgence. It was the translation of the penitential act into this latter temporal language which Martin Luther ultimately rejected, divorcing the languages of eternal and temporal judgment. He had pursued the medieval solutions to the dilemma of human impotence and sinfulness into the monastery at Erfurt; in his case their healing power had been short-lived.[13] In the end, Luther's response to the "real presence" of the Last Judgment in late-medieval thought and in his own tortured conscience, his response to a reckoning at once terrifyingly immediate and final, was the acceptance of his own utter incapacity to perform enough good to outweigh the inescapable evil he saw mounting on the other side of the balance, the mortal being's assured incapability of earning divine love and approbation. He abandoned any idea of his own capacity to justify his salvation and abandoned good works as a means of salvation. Although both attrition and confession would continue to play their rôle in his thought, it was not human works in the here and now which determined salvation, but the fatherly love of God, who had chosen to love his children and would not abandon them, however unworthy of his love. Thus Luther came round again to the language of Geiler and Augustine but with a shifted emphasis that eliminated the fearful presence of the Last Judgment: "The Trial has been set aside [for those who believe]; it is no more relevant to them than to the angels."[14]

Luther's solution was a radical rejection of the legalistic language of the church and a radical separation of the spiritual and temporal realms, placing salvation solely in the hands of God, and recognizing, even glorying in, the impotence of his children.[15] The stress laid by Luther on the difference between divine and human love was balanced by his need to conceptualize and declare divine love in terms intelligible to the human mind, that is, on the model of the parent's love for the child.[16] Luther's God, while still capable of displaying a justified wrath at his children's misdeeds, was a loving father who would not cast them aside eternally. For Luther, Christ was not the harsh judge but the one who transformed God from the lord and master to be feared to the Christian's *loving* father.

Luther's vision was broadcast to Regensburger by Paul Kohl's 1522 publication of his sermon on salvation: "See now that Christ does nothing other than make the Father sweet for us, and bring us to the Father through himself; that is Christ's goal in everything he does, that we should win a fine loving trust to the Father. If we fear the Father we've had it; we should instead bring him a fine childlike love. Now he says here, that the Father loved the world so much, that he gave his dear child for it, and gave us in Christ a means to come to the Father."[17] Christ had cried out "Abba, Father" at Gethsemane and extended the same filial relationship to his disciples by teaching them the prayer that would give the later Christians their "Father in heaven." Paul's letter to the Romans, often cited by Augustine, provided the basis for the emphasis on this image of expansive paternity and the contrast between fear and love: "For as many as are led by the Spirit of God, they are the sons of God. For ye have not received the spirit of bondage again to fear; but ye have received the Spirit of adoption, whereby we cry, Abba, Father."[18] A direct relationship between the Christian and his or her heavenly father (or a relationship mediated only by Christ himself) was not only the subject of Lutheran sermons published at Regensburg, it was also graphically demonstrated in the woodcut used by the Regensburg printer Heinrich Geißler to illustrate the 1561 tract by the Protestant theologian Matthias Flacius Illyricus, then resident in the city (fig. 21).[19] Just as, in the woodcut illustrating a 1525 tract on the difference between divine and papal indulgence, God had handed a letter of justification bearing Christ's head as its seal directly to the humble Christians who eschewed the papal arrogance,[20] in the Regensburg woodcut of 1561 God the Father handed the bread of life directly to the two men whose hands Christ held up to receive it—an image prefigured in the manna distributed by God the Father in the tabernacle design by Michael Ostendorfer (fig. 22).[21]

> Moreover, says St. Paul, [God] is not only *a* father, but rather the true father above everything which is called "father" on heaven and earth. . . . Everything which is called "father" here on earth, is merely an apparition or shadow and a painted imitation compared to this father. (Martin Luther, 1525)[22]
>
> God doesn't have the human form in which Daniel paints him: a lovely old man with snow-white hair, a beard, wheels and fiery streams, etc. God has neither beard nor hair, but we nevertheless depict Him accurately in this image of an old man. We must paint such a picture of our Lord God for the children, and even for those of us who are learned. (Martin Luther, 1538)[23]

Paradoxically, it was the heavenly Father's sacrifice of his only begotten Son, and the suffering such an act implied to the late-medieval Christian, which proved God's love for his adopted children. This was as emphatically the message of late-medieval art as it was the message of the Wittenberg

**21.** Anonymous, *God the Father Distributes Bread of Life*. Woodcut for Matthias Flacius Illyricus, "Eine Christliche Figur vnd Erklerung, wie vnd durch was Mittel, Gott die gerechtigkeitvnd seligkeit im Menschen wircke" (Regensburg: Heinrich Geißler, 1561). Single sheet, signed "M. Fl. Illir." by author. Inv. Nr. HB 24630. Germanisches Nationalmuseum, Nuremberg.

reformer. Whereas a hand extending from the clouds was all that the strictly enforced prohibition of graven images had allowed the Christians of the early medieval period to see of their god, the centuries before Luther's birth had prepared the way for the reformer's anthropomorphized vision. In the course of a gradual evolution, the masking clouds were rolled back to reveal God in a human form based on the description from the vision of Daniel. Soon the white-bearded Ancient of Days, who could be imaged because Daniel had seen him, appeared apart from the prophet's vision in depictions of the Creation, the receipt of the Ten Commandments, and the Baptism of Christ, where his presence in the biblical narrative justified his appearance.[24] By the century of Martin Luther's birth, moreover, God the Father appeared frequently in scenes from the life of Christ in which his presence was required by no biblical narrative but instead by a popular theological climate increasingly interested in his paternal relationship to Christ.[25] Earlier thought had discouraged attempts to explicate the relationship among the members

**22.** Michael Ostendorfer, *Distribution of Manna*. Detail of design for a tabernacle. Upper block of two-block woodcut, 1521. Museen der Stadt, Regensburg.

of the Trinity in human terms, creating an artistic climate in which the Trinity was represented as the *Gnadenstuhl*, a large male figure holding a small crucifix above which hovered a dove. Beginning in the thirteenth century, however, liturgical changes emphasized the body of Christ in the Mass; the elevation of the consecrated host became common and the Feast of the Corpus Christi was introduced to the whole church in Urban IV's bull *Transiturus de hoc mundo*.[26] This ritual emphasis on the broken body was given a static visual expression not only in the *imago pietatis* ("man of sorrows") that focused the viewer's attention on the solitary figure of the wounded Christ, but also in the *pietà* that modeled the viewer's response on the very maternal and human response of the Virgin who held her dead son in her lap.[27] The interest in the "pathetique" touched even the image of the Trinity, transforming the Gnadenstuhl depiction of God's display of his son's sacrifice for humankind into the depiction of a father mourning the dead son held in his arms, a scene of human grief called by Georg Troescher the *"Notgottes."*[28]

Just as Luther later would insist that it was only in the elements of the Mass that Christ made himself graspable to the human perceptive faculty, the Gnadenstuhl was an image that combined a representation of the triune nature of the godhead with the glorification of the eucharistic act, of God's gift of his son and of his receipt of the ongoing sacrifice offered up at the altar of the medieval church. By the end of the Middle Ages, the Gnadenstuhl had become the Notgottes, an emotional depiction not only of Christ's suffering but also of the divine response to his plea on the cross: "Father, I commend my spirit into your hands."[29] Thus Lucas Cranach the Elder depicted a crowned and radiant God the Father sheltering his naked son at the apex of *St. Bonaventure's Ladder* in a woodcut dated to the second decade of the sixteenth century (fig. 23). The dove of the Holy Spirit completed the Trinitarian image, but its focus remained clearly the father's protection of the thorn-crowned and shivering Christ.[30] Troescher discovered in the Notgottes a companion image to that of the Virgin and child; the latter showing the Man-God as a babe sheltered in the arms of his mother, the former showing the Man-God at his mortal death sheltered in the arms of his father.[31] The pairing is confirmed not only by the altar panels and tapestries he has found and in some cases reunited in print, but also by the woodcuts that illustrated early printed editions of St. Birgitta's *Book of the World* (fig. 24).[32] As depicted by these anonymous artists, Birgitta, accompanied by a praying monk and an angel, looked up to heaven, pen in hand, to see on one side God the Father holding the broken body of the dead Jesus, on the other Mary holding the infant Jesus, the dove of the Holy Spirit floating between the two parents.

In the medieval Gnadenstuhl version of the Trinity, God the Father had held the small crucifix before him as sign of the sacrifice he had carried out for the world and of the literal representation of that sacrifice on the altar of the church. The transformation of that image into a "Passion du Père," in which a father supported the broken and bleeding body of his son, an image that had its formal basis in the Marian pietà or the equally familiar Deposition scenes in which Joseph of Aremithea supported Christ between the Virgin and St. John (fig. 25), eliminated much of the presentational aspect of the older Gnadenstuhl depiction. In the Notgottes, the Father's glance was turned away from the viewer, his attention absorbed by the wounds and suffering of his Son.

Just as the Mater Dolorosa and pietà images had emphasized the mortal side of the Catholic church's Mary—her mortal grief at the death of her son—in contrast to the quasi–divine side represented by her appearance with the attributes of the Woman of the Apocalypse or the Immaculate Conception, so

**23.** Lucas Cranach the Elder, *Bonaventura's Ladder to Heaven*. Single-sheet woodcut, c. 1513. Germanisches Nationalmuseum, Nuremberg.

**24.** Anonymous, *Vision of St. Birgitta*. Woodcut for Birgitta, *Buch der Welt* (Nuremberg: Konrad Zeninger, 1481), fol. 91'. Handschriftenabteilung, 4° Inc. c. a. 183. Bayerische Staatsbibliothek, Munich.

**25.** Anonymous, *Deposition from the Cross*. Detail of Austrian processional cross, 1320–1330. The Walters Art Gallery, Baltimore.

too the late-medieval Notgottes might focus attention on the emotional relation between father and son. It might present God not only as one member of the triune godhead, not primarily as the planner of Christ's sacrifice, but as a man sorrowing over the dead body of his only son. God as father.

Like the pietà, this transformed Trinity image was capable of possessing an extreme, almost erotic quality, attributable in part to its origin in mystic religiosity and the writings credited to Bonaventure and the pseudo-

Anselm.[33] Despite the assertions by Otto Brunner and Jost Trier that the term "Vater" meant only "lord and master" until the mid-eighteenth century when it took on an emotional content,[34] the emotionalism of the paternal relation depicted in these images well into the sixteenth century argues for the preexistence of some emotional content in the human relationship which made it appear to the medieval theologians an appropriate model on which to image and explicate the triune godhead. Nevertheless, the idealization of that mortal relationship in an image appropriate to the divine, and the heightening of emotionalism appropriate to the loss of an "only begotten son," brought new emphasis to this aspect of paternity in the late-medieval period. It was in paternal terms that the late-medieval Christian had come to understand the relationship between the first two members of the Trinity; in paternal terms that Martin Luther, following Augustine and Paul, would explain the relationship between God and the Christian; in paternal terms that Martin Luther and his followers eventually would explain the relationship between governor and governed.

Transferred to the relationship between God and adopted child, the idealized paternity of the heavenly father was elevated above the paternity whose origins were "merely" biological. Thus Martin Luther consoled his friend the artist Lucas Cranach—who, in December 1537, still wept (*patrem lacrimantem*) for the son who had died two months before—with the greater sorrows of Adam, who had seen one son murder the other, and David, who had "howled" two years long over the murder of his firstborn son by Absolon. And, finally, reminded him that "God, the highest father, has more of your son than you, for you are only his corporeal father, you've only raised and fed him for a time; on the other hand, God, who has given him body and soul, defended and protected him up to now, and taken him from this life to the fatherland, is much much more father than you are; he can and will care, support, and nourish him better than can you and the whole world."[35]

It is especially important to establish the existence of this emotional side of the paternal relationship, not in order to prove that medieval or early modern parents were better or worse, more or less caring, than those today, but because of the frequency with which the Regensburger in the second half of the sixteenth century used the terms "Vater" and "*väterliche Liebe*," to describe the relationship between the Lutheran and his or her god, the magistrate and the subject, and the mortal father and his son or daughter.

Although the Notgottes itself was primarily an image of the late-medieval period, its most frequently imitated version was Albrecht Dürer's woodcut of 1511 (fig. 26).[36] A prayer published at Regensburg in 1555 by Paul Kohl could serve as a verbal illustration of any of the versions of Dürer's image or of Hans Schäufelein's later, more introspective woodcut (fig. 27): "O Lord God Father, see before the eyes of your majesty the work of your unutterable goodness, your sweet son, whose whole holy body is stretched out; look at all the parts of him, from his skull to the heels of his feet—no pain could be found to equal his pain! Look, dear Father, at his beautiful head—with what a wretched

**26.** Albrecht Dürer, *Notgottes*. Woodcut, 1511. Reproduced by courtesy of the Trustees of the British Museum, London.

**27.** Hans Schaüfelein, *Notgottes*. Woodcut for *Taschen büchlin Ausz ainem closter in dem Riess* (Augsburg: Hans Schönsperger der Jüngere, 1514), fol. B'. Inc. typ. Q.IX.27. Staatsbibliothek, Bamberg.

crown it is burdened, injured by those thorns! Heed the godly face—what living blood darkens it! Oh, the gentle corpse—how cruelly and painfully scourged; the holy breast, naked—how marked; the bleeding side—pierced through!"[37]

As Erwin Panofsky pointed out with regard to the imago pietatis, the emphasis on Christ's suffering contains a basic ambivalence: "There is for medieval thought no contradiction if the same wounds that cry out for vengeance at the Last Judgment also beg mercy for fallen mankind if shown to God the Father."[38] In later life, Luther claimed that as a monk, terrified of his inability to atone by his own actions for his sins, and terrified of the final judgment that awaited him, he had had such a horror at the sight of Christ wounded, hanging on the cross, that he could not look at depictions of the scene but "would rather have seen the devil."[39] The reformer resolved this problem for himself and his followers by the abolition of any causal connection between temporal action and final judgment and by a concurrent emphasis on divine fatherhood. The ambivalence was resolved; no longer a source of his or his father's wrath, Christ's wounds were now mouths speaking univocally, begging the father's mercy.[40] For Luther, the theme became the rôle of the Son of God as the means to salvation for the "unbelieving and hard children" of whom the mid-sixteenth-century Viennese preacher quoted above would write, "we have sinned against heaven and against you, Holy Father, and are not worthy to be called your children."[41] That author turned from his loving catalogue of Christ's wounds to pray to the Father-God who held his dead son: "Loyal Father, consider the humanity of your Son, and have mercy on our weakness, for which your Son labored and toiled so much. Think on the divine punishment of humanity and have mercy on those for whom he, innocent, suffered, look at the suffering of the Redeemer, and forgive the debt of the redeemed."[42]

The theme of the inexpressible depth of God's paternal love for his adoptive children became a familiar one to the sixteenth-century Bürger; the inexpressible was expressed not only in the visual arts and printed sources, but also in the sermons that were such an emphatic part of the Lutheran service: "The Holy Ghost can't articulate such love enough through the mouths of the prophets and apostles, nor can we in our depraved nature comprehend such love; we can't express it with our tongues."[43] The Viennese priest had stressed the depth of Christ's suffering in the course of reminding his god that the propitiatory sacrifice had already been completed; in contrast, the Regensburg preacher Wolfgang Waldner could only marvel in his will that his god had ordered such a sacrifice for one so undeserving as himself:

> First, I acknowledge and admit before God, that, because of original sin and also because of those additional sins which I myself have committed, I, like other mortals, have deserved to suffer not only mere mortal death and every unhappiness, but also eternal death and damnation a thousand times over; especially I acknowledge that He should and might, as a just God and judge, have allowed me—since I certainly wasn't lacking in godlessness—to have remained mired in my innate blindness, papist idolatry, unbelief, and the other sins I committed, to my eternal damnation. I acknowledge that, without any thought, action, deed, or desert on my part, my dear God and Lord, as a merciful father, nevertheless took pity on me, poor mortal and great sinner. . . . I acknowledge that the almighty heavenly father, out of heart's love, had his dearest Son Jesus Christ made mortal, suffer, and die for my sake, and that Christ through his own justification and redemption released me from my sins, from the devil, hell, and death, as well as from all the claims of the law, brought me back to his heavenly father and made me his child and an heir of eternal life.[44]

The transformation of the image of God in theological literature and in the woodcuts associated with it was in Regensburg eventually reflected in the language of the wills executed for its Bürger. In figure 17, we observed the decline in references to the Last Judgment in Regensburg wills as the Reformation took hold in the city. That decline was accompanied by a change in the way in which God himself was imaged in the wills (fig. 28): "First, when I have ended my days in this earthly vale of tears, and my suffering soul, which I want commended to God its Creator, to Mary Queen of Heaven, and to my holy angel to receive it into eternal salvation, has departed my body, I will and order that my body be carried out to the cemetery at St. Emmeram's,

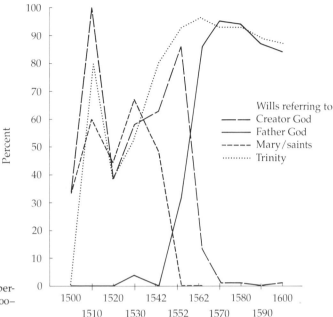

**28.** Invocations of God and saints as percentage of extant wills, Regensburg, 1500–1600.

to be committed to the earth under the same stone where my dear departed lies, with all appropriate ceremony for the salvation of my soul, according to the advice and good counsel of my executors."[45] In this will, executed in 1517 for a Regensburg citizen, God was invoked as creator, accompanied by Mary, Queen of Heaven, and the testator's guardian angel. Of the 229 wills extant for the years 1490–1552, 157, over 68 percent, invoked God as the creator of the soul.

The decade 1542–1552, between the official declaration of Regensburg's adherence to the Lutheran communion and the end of the imperially imposed Interim, marked the total disappearance of the invocation of Mary and the saints and the turning point in the language used to express the relation between God and testator in extant wills. Little more than 10 percent of the wills executed during the subsequent decade referred to a creator God. As was the case in a Nördlingen announcement for a sermon of public thanksgiving after the end of the Schmalkaldic War, God was instead pictured as the heavenly father of his earthly children.[46] As we have seen, it was not coincidental that the popularity of this paternal image in wills followed by a decade that of the Trinitarian image, in which God had appeared as the father of Christ (fig. 28).

The image of an immediate paternal relationship between God and the Christian did not eliminate the need for a secular authority or for temporal punishment. Martin Luther himself discussed the importance of his predestinarian doctrine for temporal government most explicitly in a sermon preached at Marburg in 1528. The sermon was first published at Wittenberg in 1530; in 1554 it was published in Regensburg itself with a preface by the Regensburg preacher Nicolaus Gallus.[47] In that sermon, Luther divided earthly justice or judgment sharply from heavenly justification, while still maintaining the medieval image of the wrathful god who hurled plagues on his people:

> We must know how to distinguish between the two regimes, between the two sorts of piety. The one here on earth, which was commanded by God and made subject to the second tablet of the Ten Commandments, is called worldly or human justice, and it exists in order that humankind may live together here on earth and use the goods that God has given us—since he wants even this life to be finely, peacefully, quietly, and appropriately governed and spent. . . . if one doesn't behave as he ought, God has ordered sword, gallows, the wheel, fire, water, etc., with which he commands that those who don't want to be pious should be hindered and taxed. Where that doesn't occur, where an entire land is evil and perverted and the hangman can't prevent it, he sends pestilence, dearth, war, or other horrible plagues in order that he may turn the land around and eradicate them, as happened to the Jews, Greeks, Romans, and others, in order that we should see that he wants us to maintain and protect piety, and to give us enough goods for this, or, if we're not pious, to take it all back and to exterminate.
>
> That is—in short form—the meaning and entire substance of earthly piety. . . .
>
> Above this exterior piety stands another, which doesn't belong to our temporal existence on earth, but has relevance only for and toward God, and leads us and preserves us in that life which comes hereafter. The first piety consists of works that life requires be practiced among people, toward those above and below, neighbor and brother; it has its reward here on earth, and comes to an end with this life; he who doesn't have this piety doesn't remain in this life. The second piety, however, carries and floats high above everything on earth, and has nothing to do with works. How could it deal with works, since everything that the body can do—what we call "work"—has already gone into the earthly judgment.
>
> This is what we call God's grace or the forgiveness of sin, and which Christ speaks of in this and other books of the Gospel, which isn't earthly judgment, but rather heavenly justification, not the result of our actions and capabilities, but God's work and gift. Mortal piety may well avoid punishment and the hangman, and enjoy temporal prosperity, but it can't demand God's grace and the forgiveness of sins. Therefore, even if we already have mortal piety, we must still have the higher piety as well, which exists before God and saves us from sins and bad conscience, and brings us from death to eternal life.[48]

It was the "higher piety" that, according to Luther, would bring the Christian "from death to eternal life" at the Last Judgment; the relevance of earthly deeds, "everything that the body can do," having already been exhausted in the earthly reckoning. Thus, when salvation was the issue, the law of the Old Covenant and the traditional image of the Last Judgment were together relegated to the side of the dead tree, and contrasted with the living tree and the Lutheran's freedom from the works-judgment of the Last Days, as in the case of Lucas Cranach's 1529 panel *The Allegory of the Law and Gospel*. Alternatively, the Last Judgment might be omitted altogether, as in the case of

Cranach's later (1553–1555) treatment of the same theme.[49] For the Lutheran convinced of God's grace, and of the efficacy of Christ's sacrifice, the Last Days were no longer to be feared as the time of the judging of temporal misdeeds but welcomed as the time of the resurrection to eternal life.[50]

The abandonment of the concept of a heavenly weighing of the sinner's deeds in favor of the belief in the sufficiency of Christ's merit and in God's paternal love for his children could itself be expressed in the language of the courtroom—this had, after all, been the intended message of the medieval "Teufelsprozess" dramas themselves. In 1556, the year after he arrived in Wittenberg from Transylvania, the printer Jacob Lucius designed and printed a single-sheet woodcut (fig. 29) showing a trial at which Christ pled for the pardoning of Adam and Eve. The defendants appeared, manacled by a serpent grasped firmly by a devil, before the open-air justice table at which the Trinity presided, the sword and lily of the Last Judgment laid before the Father and Son, the dove floating between them. In inscriptions, Justitia and Veritas defended the justice and truth of God's original damnation, while Misericordia and Pax supported Christ in his plea for mercy. Not only his words, but also the rose that lay next to the tablets bearing the Ten Commandments indicated God's acceptance of his son's argument. The most curious thing about this Lutheran woodcut, however, was its insistence that the whole came from the words of St. Bernard, the very man whom Luther had accused of turning Christ into a harsh judge who could only be appeased by his mother Mary.[51]

In 1571, when the Protestant Petrus Meckler wrote yet another version of the "Teufelsprozess," Christ himself replaced Mary as defense attorney and God replaced his son on the throne of judgment.[52] And, in another brief essay at explicating Christocentric justification, Andreas Musculus used the same language:

> Christ steps into the courtroom, invites the sinner to approach him, lifts him on his shoulders and carries him to his father who sits in the judge's seat. First he turns to the sinner. "Confide fili!" he speaks, "be of good cheer! I shall make a plea to our father as earnestly and dedicatedly as if your case were my own." Next he turns to God. "Father," he says, "here is a poor sinner who has come to me prayerfully seeking counsel and succor. He has reminded me of the love I have shown the world by dying and rising again in obedience to your command. I beg you now to continue to help him, as you have helped him in the past and, when the time comes, to perfect him with your righteousness." And to this plea God the Father replies: "My dearest son, I am well pleased with you. You have paid for this sinner with your own obedience to me, having fully satisfied all my demands. I can refuse you nothing. Go, take him with you."[53]

The Lutherans could continue to use the language of temporal law to explicate their understanding of justification, but the Last Judgment was no longer emanant or present in the temporal judgment; Meckler and Musculus might continue to retell the Lutheran's Last Judgment in the guise of a trial emphasizing Christ's prepayment of the penalty deserved by the sinner, but,

**29.** Jacob Lucius, *Pardoning of Adam and Eve according to St. Bernard.* Woodcut, 1556. Kupferstichkabinett, Staatliche Museen Preußischer Kulturbesitz, Berlin.

as we shall see, that retelling was no longer an appropriate conclusion to a handbook on temporal law.[54]

The shift in the meaning of the Last Judgment, the denial by the Lutherans of its "real presence" in the earthly reckoning of the temporal courtroom and their refusal to give temporal events any causal rôle in the sentence read on the Day of Judgment, is documented by the transformed inscription to be found on two panels in the council chamber of the Regensburg Rathaus. One, undated, said in Latin: "*Senator*, when you enter this council chamber in your capacity as public official put aside your private sentiments before the door, put aside anger, violence, hatred, alliance, and flattery and take up the persona and cares of the Republic, for as you have been impartial or inequitable, so shall you be judged by God."[55] The language was familiar, an expansion of Jehosaphat's charge to the judges he sent out into his cities and a restatement of the real presence of the Last Judgment in the late-medieval German council chamber.[56]

In 1554, however, twelve years after the official conversion of Regensburg to Lutheranism, another plaque was hung in the council chamber, a free translation of the one just quoted into more accessible German—and with one important additional line: "Den er ewig beschlossen hat." The addition significantly modified the final admonition to the councillors: "as you have been impartial or inequitable, so shall you be judged by God—*a judgment he has completed in eternity*."[57]

The new language of predestination was at odds with the medieval statement of the immediate connection between the Last Judgment and the temporal courtroom. In the Lutheran courtroom, the judge's decision, his work, no longer determined his own final sentence.[58] His sentence had already been determined—eternally, outside of time.[59] Similarly, the Bürger's execution of the testamentary provisions of a Regensburg will could no longer be seen as "guaranteed" by the threat of the coming Day of Judgment; his salvation or damnation was predestined. In the second half of the sixteenth century the Last Judgment appeared in the formulaic wills written in Regensburg only when the testator specified that the transformed image appear on a funerary monument (fig. 17).

Paradoxically, just as it was Luther's acceptance of his own unworthiness which convinced him of God's love and his own salvation, so too this extreme emphasis on the omnipotence and omnipresence of a divine plan severed the bond between temporal and divine judgment. The angels and devils of the Last Judgment no longer did battle for the soul of the oath-taker in the temporal courtroom; according to the Regensburg plaque, that battle had already been "completed in eternity." The judge was no longer to be judged by his temporal judgments; his eternal sentence had already been decided outside of time.

The abandonment of the concept of works-righteousness, of an omnipresent Last Judgment, which continually placed the actions of the here and now on the balance held by the archangel, must effect the language, visual and verbal, used by the Lutherans to describe temporal justice. In 1520 in a letter to Georg Spalatin, Albrecht Dürer called on God to grant him the opportunity to create an engraved portrait of Martin Luther as a "memorial of the Christian man who had delivered me from great anxiety."[60] We have no portrait of Luther by the Nuremberg master, but the reformer's impact on him is nevertheless clear. In 1521, the year after his letter to Spalatin, Dürer produced the *Sancta Justicia* for the reverse of the title page of the 1522 edition of the Nuremberg constitution (fig. 30). The allegorical figures depicted by Dürer for that 1522 edition of the *Reformacion der Stadt Nuremberg* stood in striking contrast to the image of judgment another Nuremberg artist, Erhard Schön, had depicted for the *Brandenburgische halszgerichts ordnung*, published in Nuremberg only five years earlier. In fact, Schön's illustration was a version of Dürer's Last Judgment from the *Small Passion* cycle of c. 1510, its artistic impact weakened somewhat by the spacing of the intercessory figures, its immediate relevance to the temporal book of laws for which it had been created made explicit in the two quotations borrowed from the *Bambergische Halßgerichts ordnung* of 1508: "In the sentence you issue will you be sentenced," and "The Lord gives mercy and judgment to all those who have suffered unjustly."[61]

Commissioned to produce a woodcut for the Nuremberg constitution, Dürer himself chose instead an allegorical image. According to his woodcut, it was not the Last Judgment that was present and at stake in the laws and sentences of the city. Rather it was a justice understood in allegorical terms, combining the Justitia of the sword (punishment) and the precise reckoning of the balance (weighing of evidence, but also careful assessment of each person's just deserts—justice broadly defined) with the generosity and love of a Caritas in whom theological and cardinal virtue came together, who emptied her coin-filled purse out of love of her neighbor and revealed a heart aflame with the love of God.[62]

This abstract personification of the justice of the temporal Christian government was, not surprisingly, an adaptation of earlier images rather than a Protestant invention. The woodcut *Zancken und zu gerich gen*, for the 1494 Basel edition of Sebastian Brant's *Narren schyff*, an edition in which Dürer had had a hand, had presented an image frequent in German books printed in the last decade of the fifteenth century—Justitia was depicted as a woman dressed in contemporary garb, crowned, her hair flowing loose, and holding scales and either sword or scepter, a figure probably based on an Italian model.[63] The winged figures of Dürer's Justitia and Caritas, in fact, recalled both the lily and the sword of Last Judgment images and the daughters of God in the late-medieval accounts of human salvation based on Bernard's sermon: Justitia, who punished humankind harshly as it deserved, and her sister Misericordia, who pled with her father that humankind be forgiven.[64] Nevertheless, the concept of the trial had vanished; the Last Judgment and the temporal courtroom had been relegated to separate spheres and real presence replaced by an allegory of justice that emphasized the councillor's

**30.** Albrecht Dürer, *Sancta Justicia*. Woodcut for *Reformacion der Stat Nüremberg* (Nuremberg, 1522), fol. 1'. 2° Bavar. 851. Staatliche Bibliothek, Regensburg.

obligations to justice not only in the narrower trial setting where written law might serve as a guide, but also in decisions involving the markets and other day-to-day activities where the unwritten law of custom and "God's law" of brotherly love and justice broadly defined were at issue.[65] The medieval concept of an unwritten divine law was a cornerstone of movements such as that which spawned the Peasants' War of 1524/1525, but also of less radical movements that repudiated the peasants' actions. Thus Martin Luther's violent rejection of the peasants who saw a political reformation where he had intended only a reformation of the church did not preclude his sharing with the rebels certain medieval notions of justice.[66] The faithful chroniclers of his "table talk" recorded an exchange between Luther and his friend Lucas Cranach, the artist and Wittenberg *consul*, about the hoarding of grain by Saxon *Junker*. Luther made it clear that he deemed guaranteeing the availability of grain at a fair price to be the responsibility of his prince, not in the courts as judge but in the normal execution of his authority on behalf of what accorded with God's law.[67]

It was some years before other Lutheran printmakers took up the challenge of producing a new image of justice with the enthusiasm displayed by Dürer in his 1521 woodcut for the Nuremberg constitution. The image produced by one of the first to do so, Dürer's successor as illustrator of Nuremberg's law code, will be discussed below. In the meantime, depictions of the Last Judgment were omitted in the versions of the *Carolina*, the imperial code dealing with corporal punishment, which were printed in Lutheran cities before mid-century. The formulaic oath given in that imperial code, like the wills written by Regensburg's municipal scribes after mid-century, contained no reference to the apocalyptic event.[68] Sebald Beham's woodcut border for the title page of Justinus Gobler's *Der Gerichtlich Proceß*, printed at Frankfurt in 1534, replaced the sign of an emanant Last Judgment with a series of biblical and secular analogies to the contemporary trial—the judgment of Solomon, Christ with the adulteress, the *Reichstag* at Worms, and other scenes of temporal judgment.[69] Despite the obvious economic pressures toward conservatism involved in reprinting popular texts, the editions of Ulrich Tengler's *Laienspiegel* published in cities turned Protestant also revealed deletions and replacements. The "Teufelsprozess" that had depicted the Last Judgment in the guise of a courtroom battle disappeared from the text, as did the versified Last Judgment that had closed the handbook.[70] The woodcut presenting the Last Judgment ringed in clouds above the temporal court was also frequently replaced.[71] The Straßburg editions of 1530, 1532, 1538, 1544, and 1550 used a woodcut showing God looking down and blessing a lord surrounded by musicians and advisers to replace the scene of Christ weighing the merits of Adam and Eve and to introduce the discussion of the responsibilities of the city councillor (fig. 31).[72]

Although the Last Judgment might continue to appear in the council chamber of the Lutheran city, what had been a statement of the causal relationship between temporal and eternal event was now only one of several

**31.** Anonymous, *Gottvater and Governor with Musicians*. Woodcut for Ulrich Tengler, *Layenspiegel* (Straßburg: W. Rihel and G. Messerschmidt, 1550), fol. H⁶. Special Collections DD3 .T4 1550 QC. Milton S. Eisenhower Library, The Johns Hopkins University, Baltimore.

possible analogies and exempla for the temporal judge.[73] At times, in fact, it appeared as a reminder of the difference between eternal and temporal judgment.

Such, for example, was the case with the Last Judgment painted by Anton Möller in 1588 for the Artushof in Lutheran Danzig. One of a series of five paintings, it was specifically contrasted with the canvas next to it, of a dignified judge in contemporary garb, labeled "Judex terrarum"—a phrase that in this context must be translated as "earthly judge."[74] In 1595, when, as the result of a second commission from the Danzig city council, Möller painted a single large canvas to hang above his first series, the Last Judgment by a wrathful god was not the central image. The depiction of Christ as judge, with Fides and Caritas (the gifts of divine grace, confirmation of the doctrine of *solifidianism*) as intercessors in addition to Mary and John, occupied only the top seventh of the work. Larger than Christ, more central and more active, was the figure of the archangel Michael, not with the balance but with the sword, driving into hell huge figures labeled as allegories of sin. These last occupied fully two-thirds of the canvas and show it to have been an allegory on the downfall of worldly sin and concupiscence related more closely to the image of the fall of the rebel angels than to the Last Judgment image of the late-medieval period.[75] Similarly, the Last Judgment painted by Vredeman de Vries in 1595 for the summer council chamber in Danzig, in which he replaced the traditional intercessors at Christ's sides with the four cardinal virtues, did not stand alone but was one of seven canvases commissioned from the artist. The other six were described by Troescher as allegorical, a grouping that demonstrates the transformation of the Last Judgment from a real presence with causal connection to the temporal courtroom to one of several allegories or exempla appropriate to the location.[76]

The elimination of the Last Judgment from the council chamber was, as we have already seen, a far cry from the elimination of God himself. Dürer's *Sancta Justicia* had referred not only to the justice of the sword but also to justice defined as giving each his or her due—justice extended to include brotherly love and the duty of the magistrate to provide for the common good. Lutheran allegorical depictions of the virtues and results of Good Government often included a depiction of God blessing that allegorical Good Government and the city that was its seat—an image wholly in accordance with the Lutheran understanding of the courtroom as the setting for secular judgments issued by the Ratsherren in their rôle as God's temporal "jailers, judges, and hangmen": those responsible for discipline and the maintenance of peace and harmony in earthly life.[77]

It was clear to Martin Luther that punishment was frequently necessary, that humankind had frequently to be forced to good behavior. The earthly authorities, therefore, must jail, judge, and hang because "where that doesn't occur, where an entire land is evil and perverted and the hangman can't prevent it, [God] sends pestilence, dearth, war, or other horrible plagues in order that he may turn the land around and eradicate them, as happened to the Jews, Greeks, Romans, and others."[78] The reference to the Jews was doubly appropriate, since in his involvement in the temporal sphere the god of Luther greatly resembled the Yahweh of the Old Testament.[79] Anxious to avoid anarchy, the Lutheran doctrine of two realms replaced the atemporal judgment and punishment of sin at the Last Judgment with an increased insistence on the judgment and punishment of sin by earthly authorities acting in God's stead lest God himself be forced to act in the temporal sphere.

More often than is generally acknowledged, Martin Luther drew his verbal imagery from the visual images around him.[80] He plagued himself and his listeners not only with the vivid image of the Last Judgment, and the continual minute recording of daily action in the great book to be read on the last day that that event implied for the Catholics, but also with the image of a god who in righteous wrath hurled angry arrows down on the world he had created. Luther lamented "the illness, pestilence, fever, war, dearth, and other troubles and suffering which are in the world and are God's punishments or plagues, where he shows his anger and judgment against the godless," reiterating the causal relation expressed in a book illustration at-

**32.** Hans Burgkmair, *Gotvatter and Plague Saints*. Woodcut for *Ain Patr noster zu beten / Und zü Betrachtenso vnns Der Allmechtig go zü sendet Die pestilencz Krieg / wider wertigkait / vnser gwissn zü rainigen / Got vnser sünd-beklagen / vnd in bitten sein zorne von vns wenden* (Augsburg: Grimm and Wirsung, 1521), fol. 1. Handschriftenabteilung, Asc. 775. Bayerische Staatsbibliothek, Munich.

tributed to Hans Burgkmair (fig. 32).[81] Printed in Augsburg in 1521, the woodcut showed a wrathful God the Father with sword raised to slash the huge world orb. To either side stood Sebastian, pierced through with the arrows that had made him the patron of plague victims as well as archers, and Roche, gesturing toward his festering plague sore; traditional medieval intercessors in time of pestilence, the two saints petitioned but did not actively intercede to stop God's righteous sword. In an earlier "Treatise against the Pestilence," no saints had appeared, but the God who in his wrath looked down on the men he had killed to eliminate sin held arrows linking him to the pagan Jupiter who had appeared a few pages earlier in the treatise.[82]

An increase in such divine wrath could be expected to accompany the increased godlessness that would mark the period before Christ's Second Coming, and city councillor and citizen alike perceived just such an increase in their own times. The inscription on the panels given by Albrecht Dürer to the Nuremberg city council in 1526 addressed "all worldly rulers in these dangerous times," using the words of Paul to warn that "in the last days perilous times shall come. For men shall be lovers of their own selves, covetous, boasters, proud, blasphemers, disobedient to parents, unthankful, unholy, without natural affection, truce-breakers, false accusers, incontinent, fierce, dispisers of those that are good, traitors, heady, high-minded, lovers of pleasures more than lovers of God."[83]

The fear of God's temporal punishment had kept the greater horror of the eternal punishment before the eyes of his people in the medieval period. If for Luther and his followers the severance of the bonds binding the two realms helped ease the horror of eternal punishment, the end of the notion of a cosmos organized in one continuous hierarchy also meant that the Virgin and saints could no longer be expected to intervene to prevent God's righteous punishment of sins in this world. The doctrine that comforted the individual with the knowledge that actions in this world would not determine fate in the next insisted that the sins of this world should be punished by temporal authority, else whole communities might be punished by God himself for the sins of individual members. Communities, then, must discipline themselves or face God's temporal discipline.

Gerald Strauss has argued that "the enormity of [human] degradation" was not only recognized by the Lutheran creed but was "the foundation of its preaching," and even that it was this pessimistic aspect of Lutheranism which accounted for the creed's spectacular success in the German cities since it "provided the city with a comprehensive ideology to explain, justify, and sanction what it was doing and to raise its dreary business of manipulating men and affairs to the exalted plane of divine purpose."[84] Whether or not Strauss is correct about the reasons behind magisterial Reformations, where the magistrate did accept the doctrine of two realms the result was an increased emphasis on the threat of God's temporal punishment of sin in the language of the decrees issued. Thus the lengthy prologue to a decree issued by the Regensburg Rat in 1543, the year after the council had embraced the Lutheran Communion, justified the conciliar interest in prohibiting blasphemy, adultery and fornication, drunkenness, usury, and the like in language drawn from Luther. According to the prologue, the council was issuing the decree "because many appropriate histories and examples, both in divine Scripture and in other trustworthy histories and chronicles, contain and demonstrate the gruesomeness and terrifying anger with which Almighty God has always punished those who despise his fatherly visitation, and especially those who worship idols and the Masses invented and created by men in disobedience to his Holy Word; that is, that he has often scourged great broad states and mighty cities with war, fire, and other similar plagues."[85] With the coming of the Reformation, in Regensburg as in Nördlingen, "the traditional recourse to the religious sanction of moral values [in municipal decrees] was expanded into a Rat's sermon" and "the council reached out into the realm of the church."[86]

As historians of fifteenth-century Germany have shown, the idea that earthly authorities held their offices from God was not a Protestant innovation.[87] Analyzing the Nördlingen Rat's rôle as the agent of godly order before the Reformation, Hans-Christoph Rublack concluded that "the explicitly religious legitimation of authority emphasized the authoritative character of the Rat that acted for the citizens, the subjects, even before and for God."[88] Nevertheless, Martin Luther, in his transformation of the vocabulary in which the relationship between God and humankind was discussed (or, better, in his insistence on the validity of only one of the competing vocabularies in which that relationship had been discussed in the late-medieval period), transformed the vocabulary in which the relationship between earthly authority and its subjects was discussed as well.

Although the judgments issued by the Rat were no longer intimately connected with the final reckoning, the authority of the Rat came from God, for whom it acted as earthly deputy or representative. The concept that earthly works were no longer subject to a final judgment and punishment at the end of time was ground for an increased insistence by the council on its rôle as overseer of earthly works; the end of Christ's atemporal rôle as the final judge of earthly actions was accompanied by an increased insistence on God's potential activity in the here-and-now of the temporal sphere. It should therefore come as no surprise to see God depicted as making a temporal choice between representatives of Catholic and Lutheran churches in Lutheran propaganda.

In part, the foundation for the visual rhetoric of the propaganda wars waged by the Protestants in the prints and broadsheets of the sixteenth century was laid in the late-medieval period by that era's increased willingness to depict an anthropomorphized God. Nevertheless, its sixteenth-century manifestation derived from the Augustinian/Lutheran extension of God's paternal involvement to his earthly children. God the Father, loving or wrathful, began appearing in the depictions of contemporary events. He had already appeared as the wrathful warrior hurling plagues down on humankind (figs. 19 and 32; notes 48, 80, and 81); now contemporaries saw him beaming approvingly on his Lutheran children, saw him glaring and raining stones on the offending Catholics in a woodcut by Lucas Cranach the Younger (fig. 33).[89]

This development was in some ways the natural outgrowth of the growing tendency in the late-medieval period to place donor portraits on the same panel with the Crucifixion or some other scene from the life of Christ or the saints or to locate the events of the life of Christ or the lives of the saints in the viewer's city in order to facilitate his or her internal *imitatio* of those events.[90] Thus, to take another of Cranach's woodcuts as an example, Friedrich the Wise and Martin Luther might appear at the baptism of Christ, kneeling, hands folded in prayer, on either side of Christ and John the Baptist while God the Father approvingly sent down the Holy Spirit (fig. 34).[91] Similar depictions located the baptism before a contemporary city. In a woodcut by Jacob Lucius, Wittenberg itself provided the background for a Baptism in which Friedrich's nephew, Johann Friedrich of Saxony, and members of his family appeared together with Martin Luther as witnesses (fig. 35).[92]

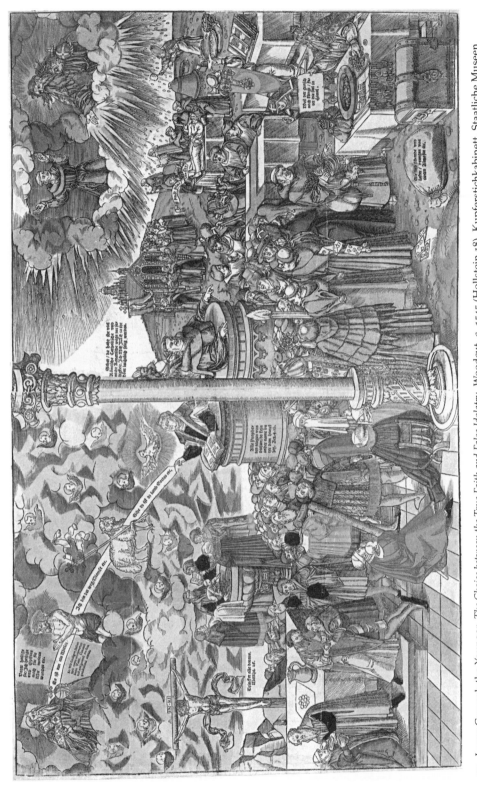

**33.** Lucas Cranach the Younger, *The Choice between the True Faith and False Idolatry.* Woodcut, c. 1545 (Hollstein 18). Kupferstichkabinett, Staatliche Museen Preußischer Kulturbesitz, Berlin.

**34.** Lucas Cranach the Younger, *Baptism of Christ with Luther and Friedrich the Wise*. Woodcut, c. 1548. Graphische Sammlung Albertina, Vienna.

It was but a short step from the appearance of a very human God the Father in the broadsheets of the Protestants in approbation or disapprobation of the combatants in contemporary religious disputes, and his appearance over contemporary cities in the cause of locating biblical truths within their walls, to the appearance of God the Father above a city in approbation of the good government of its city fathers. It seems to have been in the clouds over Lutheran cities depicted by Lutheran artists that God first appeared outside of sacred history or sectarian propaganda. He appeared, for example, above Regensburg in Michael Ostendorfer's small woodcut of 1553 (fig. 36). And above Nuremberg and the virtues of its government in the woodcut by the Nuremberg MS Master which provided the model for the Bocksbergers' fresco for the outer wall of the Regensburg council chamber (figs. 37 and 39).

In Regensburg, the frescoes painted in 1573 by Melchior Bocksberger distinguished the exterior of the chamber in which the Ratsherren met from the rest of the Rathaus (fig. 38). Two large scenes dominated that segment of the façade in the sketch Johann Bocksberger the Younger had made for this work (fig. 39).[93] The lower of the two scenes showed the wise Old Testament judge Solomon surrounded by his councillors;[94] above Solomon, higher than any

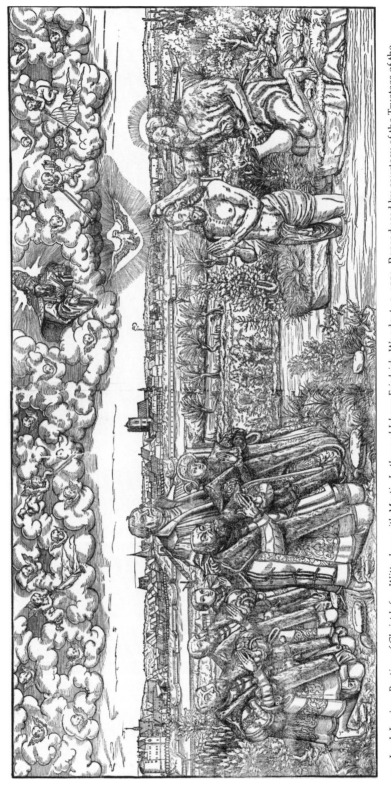

**35.** Jacob Lucius, *Baptism of Christ before Wittenberg with Martin Luther and Johann Friedrich.* Woodcut, c. 1550. Reproduced by courtesy of the Trustees of the British Museum, London.

**36.** Michael Ostendorfer, *View of Regensburg with God the Father*. Woodcut, 1553. Museen der Stadt, Regensburg.

other fresco on that wing of the building, was the Regensburg predecessor of Isaac Schwendtner's panel of 1592.[95] Bocksberger's *Allegory of Good Government* was based on the MS Master's woodcut for the *Stat Nurnberg verneute Reformation* printed at Nuremberg in 1564 (fig. 37), the year to which Goering dates Bocksberger's sketch for the Regensburg façade.[96] The MS Master's work was itself a sort of *explication de texte* of Dürer's woodcut for the 1522 edition of the *Reformation* (fig. 30). Justitia, identified by an inscription and by her familiar attributes, was seated, as Dürer's Justitia had been, on the viewer's left. At the viewer's right, in the position of Dürer's Caritas, sat Liberalitas, the limitation of Dürer's Caritas figure to an explicitly cardinal Virtue, an earthly generosity demonstrated by her duplication of Caritas' gesture of emptying the purse.

More cautious than Dürer's Caritas, Liberalitas caught the coins in a tray labeled PRO MERITO, a gesture eminently suited to the social consciousness of the fifteenth and sixteenth centuries, when Ratsherren began viewing beggars with suspicion, particularly in the economically straitened city of Regensburg.[97] Regensburg ordinances dating from the second half of the fifteenth century reveal the Rat's attempts to control begging within the city walls.[98] On the other hand, the *Regimentsordnung* or constitution written for the city in 1514 by a commission of imperially appointed outsiders no doubt reflected the broader perspective in its requirements that local and foreign beggars be licensed at their own cost and issued identifying insignia by a municipal beggar's overseer, whose job it was to see that foreign beggars remained within the walls only two or three days, that any illnesses claimed or indulgence letters shown prospective donors were authentic, and that all beggars received the Sacrament at Easter.[99] In 1523 public begging was halted in Regensburg and an *Almosen* office was established for visiting and providing for the worthy poor in their homes. The Christian obligation to "Brüderliche Lieb gegen den Nächsten" ("brotherly love to one's neighbor") was to be satisfied through contributions to the communal chest, whose funds were overseen and distributed by the Almosen officials.[100]

More significant in its message for the Bürger, the source of the wealth distributed pro merito by the MS Master's careful Liberalitas was clearly the

**37.** MS Master, *Allegory of Good Government*. Woodcut for *Der Stat Nurnberg verneute Reformation* (Nuremberg: Valentin Geißler, 1564), fol. 4. Handschriftenabteilung, Reserve 2° J. germ. 96. Bayerische Staatsbibliothek, Munich.

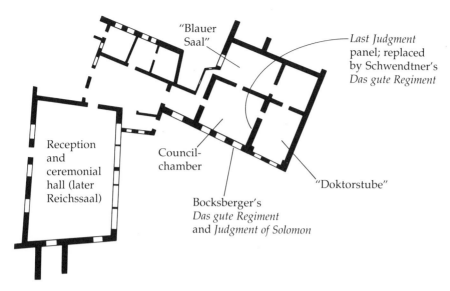

**38.** Regensburg Rathaus in the sixteenth century. Partial plan of second floor showing locations of panel paintings and frescoes discussed in text.

bees labeled CONCORDIA, who hovered around the inverted purse which was simultaneously a beehive.[101] In his effort to be explicit, the MS Master depicted his republic twice, once in the city view in the background made recognizable by the distinctive towers of Nuremberg's castle and churches, and once in the maternal Respublica, the community under law, who sat between Justitia and Liberalitas, dominating the woodcut.[102] At the feet of the allegorized republic slept Pax, her head in the lap of the Community. From the clouds above, God the Father showered his grace on the city where correct judgment and charity assured the peace and concord that made possible the council's generous charity.[103]

In Regensburg as in other Lutheran cities, the medieval image of the Last Judgment had by the end of the sixteenth century been replaced by an image related in its allegorical usage to Albrecht Dürer's *Sancta Justicia* of 1521 but combining the allegorical figures with an image of God which signaled his involvement in the temporal sphere. In the case of Bocksberger's *Allegory of Good Government*, the new image constituted an *explication* of Dürer's earlier *texte*. Schwendtner's panel of 1592 (fig. 3), based on another woodcut,[104] constituted a variation on the same theme, a variation that united God the Father and an allegorical Astraea (Justitia) who referred to the Iron Age from Ovid's *Metamorphoses* but also to Vergil's prophecy of the Golden Age to be expected under Augustus and Ariosto's echo of that prophecy on behalf of Charles V.[105] In Schwendtner's version, the three Virtues of the good governor—Caritas, Justitia, and Prudentia—appeared in the foreground, linked with a golden chain to the happy results of their regime, Pax and Ceres. The marble dais on which the allegorical figures were presented was separated by trees

**39.** Johann Bocksberger the Younger, *Allegory of Good Government* and *Judgment of Solomon*. Sketches for Regensburg Rathaus frescoes, 1564–1573. Detail of design for exterior wall of council chamber. Museen der Stadt, Regensburg.

from the profile of a city in the background, a profile whose rooftops, Rathaus tower, and cathedral identified it explicitly as Regensburg. In the clouds above, God the Father raised his right hand in benediction of the scene below; to his left and right two cherubs held the shields of empire and city. The whole was framed by the names and arms of the contemporary council members and by the inscription: "Come, see how pious is the connection [the golden chain linking the allegorical figures], how firm! And say: Life without this bond would be like a butchershop! Astraea, the goddess holding the sword and scales, commands each to yield for the sake of the agreement made. Storge [Caritas] joins spirits together; Prudentia governs deeds; Pax subjugates war; and Ceres is the foster-daughter of Pax. In this bond the Respublica stands solid. Tell me, Life, if this connection is absent from the city what sort of monster it becomes. Chaos."[106]

On Schwendtner's panel, Regensburg at the end of the sixteenth century found itself in an Age of Brass if not of Gold; Astraea was present with her virtuous attendants, but the encircling inscription warned of the chaos that would arise were she to flee heavenward. As citizen and public official of the city of Regensburg, Isaac Schwendtner was clearly an insider.[107] The distant city profile that named his city in the panel he painted was not therefore a view from outside the walls. Nor was it the citizen's view of buildings and market places. Hanging in the Rathaus council chamber, *Das gute Regiment* was, in fact, a turning inside out of the outsider's perspective; it was a view from the seat of government which saw all else as "outside." The city was defined by Schwendtner as a community under government, that government approved by God. The history of the adoption of these humanistically inspired allegorical personifications of good government is more than the history of the transmission of formal language. The humanistic figures were also shaped and filled by the problems of religious strife and by the position the city held in the empire.

# CHAPTER 3

# Widow, Wife, Daughter: The Iconography of Resistance to the Emperor

A peace must be forbidden and rejected if it is to be purchased at the Gospel's cost, if it hinders or damages the Gospel.

—Martin Luther, 1531

Membership in the Lutheran communion transformed the language in which political action and virtue were discussed in Regensburg. The elimination of the Last Judgment as a real presence in the courtroom represented a change in, rather than a severance of, the connection between religious and political thought, between religious and political action. The lexicon of that transformed language had soon to be adapted to meet new challenges.[1] Justitia assumed a dominant rôle in the council chamber as an allegorical alternative to a Last Judgment no longer perceived as effectively present, but also because the stresses of the fourth and fifth decades of the century brought her into association with Lucretia and made her particularly appropriate to the Lutheran councillor grown more militant under pressure from the Catholic emperor.[2] At issue was the relationship between city or Rat and emperor, crucial not just qua relationship but also because the emperor usually appeared second only to God himself as the source of the legitimation for the Rat's decrees. It was "to the almighty God himself first of all, also to the Roman imperial and royal majesties, their most merciful lords" that the Regensburg Ratsherren expected to answer for their subjects' actions and for their own.[3] Both aspects of the relationship, problematic since the last decades of the fifteenth century, had been strained in the decades surrounding the Reformation.

In 1542, one month after the announcement by the Rat of Regensburg's official conversion to the Lutheran communion, the Catholic dukes of Bavaria announced an economic blockade of the city: "We forbid each and every one of our subjects, . . . cleric and layman, poor and rich, of whatever dignity or status to ride, drive, or go into the city of Regensburg, or to live there"—a move of disastrous consequence to a city virtually surrounded by Bavarian territory.[4] The Rat's appeals to the emperor for relief from the blockade were without success; despite the gap in the blockade provided by the Protestant Upper Palatinate, Regensburg experienced a large loss in population in the fifth decade of the sixteenth century.[5] And, although the Reichstag of 1546 brought people and products and therefore some economic relief to the city, it also brought war. From the opening of the Reichstag through the end of the Schmalkaldic War, Regensburg was an occupied city; the Bürger watched the city's Protestant allies fall to the imperial forces while Spanish troops were quartered within Regensburg's walls.[6] Peace came in 1548 but brought with it the Interim, the temporary religious compromise signed by the imperial estates. The Interim closed Regensburg's Lutheran churches: no Lutheran Communion was celebrated in the city, no Lutheran sermon preached, no marriage or baptism according to Lutheran rite performed.

This much we know of the situation in Regensburg in the period of the Schmalkaldic War and the Interim, but little more. The nineteenth-century historian Carl Theodor Gemeiner carried his magnificent chronicle of the city only up to 1525; he devoted scarcely four thousand words (including documents) to the years 1546–1552, in his separate account of Regensburg's Reformation.[7] The history of the Reformation written in our own century by Leonhard Theobald relies heavily on Gemeiner's work, focusing almost exclusively on theological issues and diplomatic exchanges.[8] Only so much of the situation can be read in the official diplomatic documents and in the various accounts of troop movements, yet the sources familiar to the social historian are unavailable. Official municipal records necessary for a thorough investigation of the period disappeared at the turn of the nineteenth century.[9] Nor do Regensburg's two sixteenth-century chroniclers help: Leonhart Widmann, Catholic chaplain and diarist, kept no record of the years between 1543 and 1552; his Lutheran counterpart, the *Stadthauptmann* Heinrich Schmidt, participated in the Schmalkaldic War as a scribe for the imperial forces that captured Johann Friedrich of Saxony and did not settle in Regensburg until 1552.[10] Even the city's printer Hans Kohl fails us—we have only seven works printed by him from 1546, when Charles V issued the imperial ban against Johann Friedrich of Saxony and Philipp of Hesse, to the end of the Interim in 1552: the *Abschiedt* of the Reichstag (1546) and the ban itself (1546),[11] two comic school plays in Latin by Georgius Macropedius (1546),[12] accounts of Martin Luther's death (1546),[13] a litany (1547),[14] and a sermon collection (1546) and catechism (1547)[15] by Regensburg's Lutheran pastor, Nikolaus Gallus.

The publication of accounts of Martin Luther's death, of a litany, and of Lutheran sermons and a catechism confirms what we already know about the piety of the printer Hans Kohl and of much of the community. It reveals an ongoing concern with Lutheran issues despite the occupation of the city by imperial forces, but it does not reveal much about the attitude of the community or its leaders to their position. There is, fortunately, another source for understanding the impact of the pressure on Regensburg during the 1540s and 1550s, a source that at once expresses the inability of the Lutheran Bürger and Ratsherren to resist physically the limitation of their religious and political activities and celebrates their passive, internal resistance to those same limitations. The iconographical language of the stamped leather bindings in which the books owned by the city were bound provides a unique glimpse into the relationship among Lutheranism, resistance to the emperor, and the language of political virtue in a city allowed no overt display of resistance.

In 1546 the Regensburg Rathaus was the site not only of the Reichstag from which Charles V launched his attack on the Protestant princes but also of the *Ratsbibliothek*, the library that had been in existence at least since 1396, when the Rat purchased an illuminated codex of canon law from a deacon of the Alte Kapelle.[16] From the very beginning the library had contained works of history, medicine, and science in addition to the legal tomes that constituted the core of the collection.[17] According to Christine Ineichen-Eger, a special library was established by the city in the municipal Latin school by 1548, and the eldest Ratsherr given jurisdiction over it.[18] Since, however, the knowledgeable Grünewaldt praised the "Gemeiner Stadt-Bibliothec" located in the Gymnasium Poeticum in his discussion of the libraries in the city (1615), and mentioned no other municipal library, the "special library" probably represented a relocation of the Ratsbibliothek to the school for which the city would purchase a large building (the current site of the Staatliche Bibliothek at Gesandtenstraße 13) in 1558.[19] Two catalogues made of the Ratsbibliothek collection some fifty years apart display its rich resources in the realms of theology and literature as well as in law, history, and science. One of these catalogues is the *Index Generalis Secundum ordinem Pulpitorum confectus ostendens quae scripta singulis voluminibus contineantur; Ein gemein Register Uber alle bücher, so in eines erbarn Camerer und Rhats Liberei alhie zu Regenspurg an Ketten, gelegt sind, und dieselben nach einander auf den Pulpiten ligen, etc. Wievil auch Tractetlein in einem ieden buch zusamen gebunden sind*, compiled in the last quarter of the sixteenth century, perhaps in 1593, by Jonas Paulus Wolf.[20] As its title suggests, this catalogue constituted a shelf list and gave the contents of each volume. A second catalogue of the same collection, Elia Ehinger's *Catalogus Bibliothecae Amplissimae Reipub. Ratisbonensis* (1638), does not list the complete contents of each volume, but does give the date and place of publication for the principal work(s) in each binding.[21] These catalogues provide a fascinating view of the writings available in the sixteenth-century Ratsbibliothek; nevertheless, because books and pamphlets were acquired through donation as well as purchase, the lists by themselves are not reliable sources for the political or theological stance of the Rat during the period.[22] They do provide us with a rough guide to the lexicons or languages available to the Ratsherren and their advisers during the period under consideration— a guide by no means complete, since we have no lists of the books owned by the individual Ratsherren and by the same token have in most cases no indication which of the books in the Ratsbibliothek were actually consulted during the sixteenth century. Nevertheless, the lists are a guide and, more than that, provide the means for locating another source in which intent or willful choice and religio-political stance are more legible.

In the early days of printing, books and pamphlets were sold unbound; the purchaser him/herself then ordered the binding, generally of several shorter works together.[23] In combination, the *Index*, with its list of the works contained in each volume, and the *Catalogus*, with its dates and places of publication, contain the information necessary to identify exactly the particular volumes owned during the sixteenth century by the Regensburg Ratsbibliothek where those volumes have survived.

Led by my observation of a mid-century change in the bindings of lists of city officers to hypothesize that that transformation was the result of the acceptance of the vocabulary of militant Protestantism,[24] I have identified as many as possible of the actual volumes from the sixteenth-century Ratsbibliothek still extant in the collections of the Staatliche Bibliothek in Regensburg and the Bayerische Staatsbibliothek in Munich. My examination of the bindings of the surviving Ratsbibliothek volumes reveals the adoption during the 1540s of a consistent iconographical program, one highly interesting in the religio-political context of the middle decades of the sixteenth century. Although no similar examination has been made of the books bound for other cities in the sixteenth century, my discovery of an iconographical program for the books owned by the city of Regensburg leads me to suspect that such investigations in other Lutheran cities that felt themselves under siege might turn up similar results.[25]

## The Keys to the City

> May it please my dear lords and friends not only to accept this memorial of my eternal love for you and for this imperial city willingly and in friendly fashion, but also to consider for the salvation of your souls what a sign this is, that Regensburg's angel displays two keys in the shield.
>
> Since preachers are signified in the scripture by the dear angels, and the Gospel, which opens Heaven to all believers, by the keys, what better thing could I give this ancient and beautiful imperial city than to wish that mortal angels might unlock Heaven to all sinners and penitents with the preaching of the law and Gospels as keys? (Johannes Drach, address to Regensburg councillors, 1541)[26]

On 19 June 1546 the Augsburg Ratsherren declared the coming Schmalkaldic War a matter of religion rather than loyalty to the empire and reasserted their allegiance to the Protestant cause, thwarting Charles V's efforts to divide the Protestant princes and Protestant cities of his empire. On the next day, after having witnessed the unsatisfying conclusion of the *Religionsgespräch* and of the Reichstag within their walls, the Regensburg Ratsherren gave Charles V the key to their city.[27] In the absence of accounts of discussions within the council chamber, the gesture has been interpreted as an attempt to avert the damage that would have resulted from an effort to defend the city against the force of imperial arms.[28] The documents I have examined, the bindings of the books in the Ratsbibliothek, support this view, preventing us from seeing the gesture as either easy or acquiescent.

**40.** Anonymous Regensburger, *Regensburg Arms Held by Griffin*. Tempera sketch facing title page of Regensburger Ratsbibliothek copy of *Reformacion der Stat Nuremberg* (Nuremberg, 1522). 2° Bavar. 851. Staatliche Bibliothek, Regensburg.

As problematic as the keys handed an emperor already resident in the city were the keys that named the city on its own arms. In the woodcut he designed for the 1522 edition of the *Reformacion der Stat Nuremberg* (fig. 30), Albrecht Dürer had entrusted his city's arms and those of the empire to the hands of angels.[29] In contrast, the anonymous Regensburger who painted an ex libris for the Regensburg Ratsbibliothek's copy of the same work in 1548, after the defeat of the Protestant forces in the Schmalkaldic War had resulted in an Interim that closed the doors of Regensburg's Lutheran churches, depicted his city's arms clutched in a griffin's claws (fig. 40).[30]

The crossed keys had long named Regensburg on its walls, its coins and seals; they had named the city on the banner flown from the tower of the wooden pilgrimage chapel "zur Schönen Maria" under the protection of the city's political overseers rather than its bishop (fig. 41);[31] and they had linked city and salvation formally when affixed to the Gothic doorway at which St. Peter greeted the blessed in one of the city's painted late-medieval altarpieces (fig. 42).[32] Nevertheless, the keys borrowed from St. Peter, the patron of Regensburg's cathedral, are missing from the books, pamphlets, and broadsheets printed in Regensburg between the publication of the Schöne Maria broadsheets and miracle books (ended 1522) and the printed announcement

**41.** Michael Ostendorfer, *Kapelle zur Schönen Maria*. Woodcut, 1519. Museen der Stadt, Regensburg.

**42.** Anonymous, *Saved Enter Paradise.* Painted wooden wing from altar for Regensburg church, c. 1480. Inv. Nr. 13/284. Museen der Stadt, Regensburg.

by the Regensburg Rat of its decision to conform to the Lutheran communion (1542); St. Peter's keys are also missing from the stamped pigskin bindings in which the printshops' production was bound for the Ratsbibliothek.[33] In 1541, when the crossed keys appeared for the first time as the watermark for paper manufactured at the paper mill built by the city two years before, their appearance in print was still a rarity.[34] They did not appear on the bindings of the city's books until 1543.[35] Despite the execution in the city (c. 1530) of a large woodcut depicting a rather bored angel or putto resting its elbow on a shield bearing the familiar crossed keys (fig. 43), the eighteen ordinances printed as broadsheets for the city government before its official conversion to Lutheranism on 10 October 1542, by Paul Kohl and his successor (and presumed kinsman) Hans displayed no crossed keys; nor, for that matter, did

**43.** Workshop of Albrecht Altdorfer, *Angel with Regensburg Arms*. Woodcut printed in three colors, 75 x 39 cm, c. 1530. Museen der Stadt, Regensburg.

the ordinances printed for the see of Regensburg or the two editions of the papal bull *Indictionis concilii* printed in the city before that date.[36] The badge of ownership was also missing from the books bound for the Ratsbibliothek in wood boards with stamped pigskin quarter-bindings and the few municipal documents bound more elaborately.[37] The announcement and justification of the council's decision to institute the Lutheran form of Communion in the churches under its jurisdiction (fig. 47) was the first official document printed for the city to display the crossed keys.[38] Their appearance on the bindings of the city's books (fig. 48) had to await the following year.

The omission of the signifying keys before 1542 may be explained in part by the general lack of ornamentation which characterized works printed in the city and works bound for the city during the third and fourth decades of the sixteenth century. The forty-five pamphlets and broadsheets printed by Paul Kohl's shop between 1522 and 1530 were particularly plain, revealing an effort to attract readers through the use of visual image only in the news sheets that reported the battles of the period. In addition to the depictions of battles and troop formations, armorial bearings appeared in two of these "newspapers": the imperial eagle marked an account of "the imperial soldiers against the pope" (1527), and the Bavarian arms accompanied an account of Pfalzgraf Friedrich's attack on the Turks at Vienna (1530).[39] Regensburg's arms, however, appeared only once in Paul Kohl's publications, together with the imperial eagle, on the farmer's calendar for 1530.[40]

Hans Kohl, Paul's successor, displayed less interest in battles but considerably more in the use of the printed nonverbal image.[41] In contrast to those of his predecessor, his works were generally signed, occasionally with one of the two printer's marks designed for him in 1532, by Michael Ostendorfer.[42] Nevertheless, the only appearance of the city's arms in the pamphlets he printed before 10 October 1542 was in the pestilence regimen dedicated to and eventually distributed by the Regensburg Rat.[43] After the publication of the regimen in 1532, the city's arms disappeared from the products of Regensburg's presses for ten years, resurfacing for the first time in the conciliar announcement of the adoption of the Lutheran Communion in the churches under the Rat's jurisdiction and in the "Christian Instruction" written by the Nuremberger Johann Funck and printed shortly thereafter.[44]

The omission of St. Peter's keys from the works of Regensburg's printers in the third and fourth decades of the sixteenth century and their reappearance on the official announcement of 1542 were linked not only to an increasing interest in printed ornamentation but also to a gradual change in the propagandistic use of St. Peter's keys by Protestant artists and pamphleteers. In their attacks on the papacy, Protestant artists had made liberal use of the papal arms. Although it was the papal tiara that had identified the pope with the beast from the bottomless pit and the Babylonian whore in the famous illustrations of Martin Luther's "September Testament" of 1522,[45] other visual satires gave equal weight to the keys of St. Peter in the papal arms. For the pope, of course, these keys symbolized the papacy's direct descent from the "rock" on which Christ had built his church, and the papal ability to unlock heaven and hell. To the Bürger north of the Alps the keys of St. Peter on a wax seal confirmed the promise of an indulgence letter and symbolized papal authority on printed copies of bulls such as the *Bulla contra errores MARTINI LVTHERI ET SEQVACIVM* burned by Martin Luther on 10 December 1520.[46] They therefore figured large in Protestant attacks on the sale of indulgences and the authority claimed by the pope. The woodcut accompanying an anonymous Protestant's assertion in 1520, that "one can be saved without an indulgence from Rome," was a fairly straightforward representation of the sale of indulgences in a church with papal insignia prominently displayed on banners.[47] But the crossed keys, which to the Regensburger symbolized both the city and the papacy, were used to signal the failure of the claimed papal power over heaven and hell in the title page woodcut illustrating the "Tract on Divine and Roman Indulgence" published at Speyer in 1525.[48] Here a Protestant artist demonstrated his mastery of visual satire: the pope, accompanied by a cardinal, swung topsy-turvy in the pan of the balance scales familiar to the viewer from countless Last Judgment depictions; he clasped an indulgence letter impotently, its seal with the papal tiara and the falsely claimed keys of St. Peter mocking him. In contrast, God himself sat serenely in the other pan, far weightier in his majesty than the false claimants, handing three humble Christians a letter whose seal was Christ himself, the bread of life.

Another satirical pamphlet, adapted to the uses of Protestant propaganda by Hans Sachs and Erhard Schön from the pre-Protestant Bolognese *Vaticini Joachimi* (1515), included a particularly vivid image that united the keys with the language of the Last Judgment.[49] The pontiff stood holding the keys in one hand, the rods used in the scourging of Christ in the other, a snake-bodied devil at his side. From the pope's mouth extended the sword familiar from the Revelations and medieval depictions of Christ as the judge of the Last Days; it pierced the back of the haloed and banner-bearing lamb, symbol of the resurrected Christ.[50]

Also based on a pre-Reformation prototype was the immensely popular pamphlet depicting "the papal ass," adapted in 1523 from an equally satirical work of the end of the fifteenth century by Wenzel von Olmütz titled "ROMA CAPVT MVNDI," but now accompanied by a more explicit text written by Philipp Melanchthon at Martin Luther's instigation (fig. 44).[51] The "papal ass" was a scaled monster with an ass's head, the breasts and belly of a woman, two hooves, one hand, and one griffin's claw, with a dragon's head for a tail, depicted before the Castel Sant'Angelo at Rome, the keys of St. Peter flying mockingly on a banner above.[52] The tiara was gone, but the papal citadel and the crossed keys identical with those of the Regensburg arms sufficed as visual labels in the eighteen sixteenth-century editions of the woodcut accompanied by Melanchthon's text.[53]

In the context of a period filled with such images, and so long as the city remained officially uncommitted in the ongoing religious debates, an uninterpolated continuation of the use of Regensburg's traditional arms would have appeared to signal continued acceptance of the Catholic position by the city and its leaders. We know, of course, that such an acceptance was not the case. Although Schottenloher attributes three texts in praise of the miracle-working Schöne Maria of Regensburg to Paul Kohl's press in 1522, the remaining production of the press that year—eight sermons by Martin Luther—was already devoted to the Lutheran cause. A year later, in 1523, this tension was pointed up by Luther's own letter to the Regensburg Ratsherren condemning the pilgrimage chapel to the Virgin.[54]

That year the power of Luther's supporters in the council was strong enough to carry the appointment of the Johann Hiltner, a Lutheran, as *Stadtadvocat* or legal adviser, apparently at the recommendation of Jacob Fuchs, a former Bamberger monk who was brother to Thomas Fuchs, the emperor's *Hauptmann* in Regensburg.[55] In 1524 the Rat hired Johann Grüner, recently dismissed by the bishop from his post as cathedral preacher, for the city's pulpit in the pilgrimage chapel of the Schöne Maria.[56] By the next year the councillors had commissioned Johann Hiltner to seek Luther's advice concerning a preacher to be installed in the pulpit in the Minoritenkloster.[57] The city's official announcement of its adoption of the Lutheran Communion on 10 October 1542 did not, then, mark a sudden conversion but rather acknowledged, at a time made more propitious by the adoption of a Protestant position by the neighboring Pfalzgraf,[58] a decision already taken by many of the leading Bürger. During the Reichstag of 1541, Lutheran sermons had been preached in the homes of Schultheiß Ambrosy Amman and *Hanns-*

**44.** Anonymous, *Der Bapstesel zu Rom.*
Woodcut for Philipp Melanchthon and Martin Luther, "Deuttung der czwo grewlichen Figuren Bapstesels zu Rom und Munchkalbs zu freyberg" (Wittenberg: [Johann Rhau], 1523), fol. A[1] verso. Cage BX1763.M45 1523. Milton S. Eisenhower Library, The Johns Hopkins University, Baltimore.

*graf* Karl Gartner; at Easter some fifty leading Bürger and Ratsherren had attended the Lutheran Communion sponsored by Philipp of Hesse in his lodgings in the city.[59] Two visiting Protestant theologians, Rudolf Gualter and Anton Corvinus, trumpeted in separate reports from that Reichstag that the city belonged to their co-religionists.[60] Finally, on 30 May 1542, some four months before the Regensburg Rat announced its decision, a petition calling for that decision was delivered to the *Innerer Rat*, the small council. Among its signers were two physicians and nine members of the *Äußerer Rat*, the outer council; three of the latter group would later be elected to the inner council, another was Hans Kohl, Paul Kohl's successor in the Regensburg printshop.[61] In addition, the petition was signed by five members of the Schultheißen court (one of whom would later join the Innerer Rat) and one former or future member of the same court, one member of the Hannsgrafen court, one *procurator*, three city scribes, one future member of the municipal building office, and one future member of his quarter's tribunal.[62] For these literate men just outside the city's political center, and for the Lutherans on the council itself, the crossed keys of their city's arms were clearly an embarrassment so long as they were likely to be interpreted as a symbol of Catholic loyalty, as Erhard Schön had used them on the banners he hung from the tower at Worms in a woodcut illustrating the (partial) success of the papacy at

**45.** Erhard Schön, *Worms with Papal Banners*. Woodcut for Hans Sachs, *Eyn wunderliche Weyssagung von dem Babstum* (Nuremberg: Hans Guldenmund, 1527). Germanisches Nationalmuseum, Nuremberg.

the Worms Reichstag of 1521 (fig. 45).[63] Only if another meaning were attached to the keys, and if they could be presented in a context in which that new meaning would take precedence over the old, could the familiar sign signify a community under God for the Lutherans of Regensburg.

> Christ's keys serve and help toward heaven and eternal life, since he himself calls them the keys to heaven, that is, that they close heaven to the stubborn sinner, but open the gates to the sinner who is penitent. . . . In contrast, what do the pope's keys do? They forbid and create external laws—and what help are these things against sin, death, and hell? (Martin Luther, "Von den Schlüsseln," 1530)[64]

During the period that the keys, because of their reference to the pope and implied adherence to the Catholic cause, had awkward connotations for the unofficially Lutheran, but officially uncommitted, city of Regensburg, they were being reinterpreted by Protestant authors and artists who took them from the pope and claimed their power for the Lutheran sacrament of confession. When, c. 1538, Master BP depicted the keys shattered, their shafts turned to gallows to hang the pope as a companion to Judas Iscariot, he at once deprived the pope of their power over heaven and hell and damned him for his presumptuousness and, particularly, for the greed he had displayed in having claimed to possess them in the first place (fig. 46).[65] The print was followed by others less subtle, more scatological.[66]

In the Lutheran reinterpretation, the keys maintained their power to lock

**46.** Master BP, *Satire on the Papal Arms*. Woodcut, c. 1538. Kunstsammlungen, Veste Coburg.

or unlock the gate to heaven, but they had been given by Christ to no one living person. According to Luther himself in a sermon printed in Regensburg in 1522: "No one other than the churches has been appointed possessor of the keys. . . . The Christian church alone has the keys, . . . the priest performs the office of the keys, baptizes, preaches, and distributes the Sacrament, not on his own account, but on account of the community, since he is a servant of the entire community to which the keys have been given."[67] The altarpiece commissioned by the Wittenberg city council from Lucas Cranach the Elder for the city church therefore replaced St. Peter, the saint traditionally found on one wing of an altarpiece, with a depiction of confession within the city church itself; the keys claimed by the pope as his inheritance from the saint were held instead by Johann Bugenhagen, the pastor who heard confession.[68] Neither the theological concept nor its iconographical representation was new; Hans Schäufelein had depicted the crucified Christ

**47.** "Warhafftiger Bericht eines Erbern Camerers und Rats der Stat Regenspurg, Warumb und auswas ursachen sie des herrn Abentmal . . ." (Regensburg: Hans Kohl, 10 October 1542), title page. Handschriftenabteilung, 4° Liturg. 64. Bayerische Staatsbibliothek, Munich.

in the act of handing the key to a priest hearing confession in the upper left of his 1513 woodcut for the title page of the *Via felicitatis.*[69] Confession, praised by Geiler as the means by which the sinner was transformed into the child of God,[70] remained an important part of Luther's theology; he reiterated his position in the 1530 pamphlet "Von den Schlüsseln," and in two Latin disputations with representatives of Henry VIII in 1536: the keys claimed by the pope were "new," his absolutions "fictive." The Lutherans, in contrast, did not claim a personal jurisdiction over the keys; they were not a possession but an office: "We absolve sins in accordance with the Gospel. . . . Christ is the absolver."[71]

By metonymy, Christ's Gospel was the absolution; this, at least, was the claim made in the key interpretation of the Hessian theologian Johannes Drach: "The Gospel, which opens heaven to all believers, [is signified] by the keys."[72] In June 1541 the Regensburg printer Hans Kohl published Drach's sermon on Psalm 117 with a preface dedicating it to the Regensburg Rat and explicitly reinterpreting the meaning of Regensburg's crossed keys; they were no longer to be seen as a sign of the city's ties to Catholicism, but instead as an admonition to preach the Lutheran Gospel. However welcome such an interpretation may have been to the council's Lutherans, in 1541 the council had to admit itself officially embarrassed by the publication within the city and during the Reichstag of an explicitly Lutheran tract dedicated to them by a visitor.[73] The printer was formally chastised.

Before the next year was out, confessional changes in the Upper Palatine

**48.** Anonymous, Binding stamp with Regensburg arms. Used on *Concordantiae maiores sacrae bibliae* (Basel, 1531; bound 1543), recto of pigskin binding. 2° Script. 337. Staatliche Bibliothek, Regensburg.

made the time appear finally propitious for the same council to flaunt the city's reinterpreted keys on the title page of their commitment to the Lutheran Communion (fig. 47).[74] Every Saturday the Lutheran reclamation of the keys from the "papists" was reiterated in a lesson read from the pulpit of the city's Lutheran churches at vespers: "The power of the keys, that is, the power to free people of their sins, and to forgive their sins in his name, has been given and commanded to his community on earth by Christ our dear Lord."[75] Every Sunday the Sacrament was distributed from vessels bearing the keys that once again symbolized both city and salvation.[76]

Shortly thereafter, the keys made their appearance on the stamped pigskin bindings of the books in the city council library housed in the Rathaus. Up to that point even the elaborately stamped bindings of the large folio volumes of the *Ratswahlbücher* series had borne no city emblem.[77] The first datable use of the large stamp depicting the crossed keys on a shield (fig. 48) was on the *Concordantiae maiores sacrae bibliae* published at Basel in 1531, a volume whose binding can be precisely dated because its anonymous craftsman designed a cover incorporating not only the city shield and decorative roll-stamps, but also the title of the book "CONCORDANTIAE" and the date "MDXXXXIII".[78]

After their appearance on the concordance, the crossed keys of the Lutheran city appeared regularly as the central panel of the bindings of books in the Ratsbibliothek (fig. 49a); in the 1560s, after the rights of Protestants to the practice of their religion appeared secure from imperial interference, the symbol of the empire began appearing together with the city's arms—a separate stamp placed above the keys displayed the imperial eagle (fig. 49b).

**49a.** Anonymous, Binding stamp with city arms. Used on books bound for Regensburg Ratsbibliothek, 1540s–1560s. Here: 2° Hist. eccl. 10/4. Staatliche Bibliothek, Regensburg.

**49b.** Anonymous, Binding stamps with city and imperial arms. Used on books bound for Regensburg Ratsbibliothek, 1560s–1600. Here: 2° Theol. syst. 40/3. Staatliche Bibliothek, Regensburg.

## Luther and Lucretia

> If, however, I caught someone, who was not exactly a tyrant, with my wife or
> daughter, so would I want to kill him. Likewise if he took by force from this one
> his wife, from another his daughter, from a third his field and goods, and the
> citizens and subjects came together, and could no longer tolerate or endure his
> violence and tyranny; so could they kill him just as they would another mur-
> derer or robber on the street. (Martin Luther, 1530s)[79]

Manuscripts and incunabula had, of course, been bound in leather in the
late Middle Ages, but in binding, as in printing with movable type, interest in
ornamentation grew with the advance of technology. Where late-medieval
bindings had been decorated with repetitive designs made by the use of
simple metal stamping tools, the early decades of the sixteenth century
brought new tools influenced by the technology of woodcuts and engravings—stamping tools capable of producing elaborate panels as well as tools
that could be rolled across the leather to produce a repetitive pattern not
dependent on the craftsman's eye for its regularity.[80] These first roll-stamps
were used to create more complex versions of the vegetative and abstract
ornamentation of the Gothic period. The new technology, however, presented increased possibilities of expression, and craftsmen soon made use of
it to produce "frames" similar to those of the woodcut title pages becoming
popular at the same time. Like the woodcut title pages, these new binding
designs were capable of reflecting the subject matter of the text within or,
more frequently, the intellectual/spiritual concerns of the person who had
commissioned the binding.

Humanism and the growing interest in the art of ancient Greece and Rome
were early evident. The craftsman who bound the Basel concordance for
Regensburg in 1543 was following established practice when he made use of
a roll-stamp that produced a series of small medallions in imitation of antique
coins such as those mentioned in the inventory made of the property of the
Regensburg artist and Ratsherr, Albrecht Altdorfer, at his death in 1538.[81] At
the same time, however, craftsmen in other Lutheran cities, most notably
Wittenberg, had already replaced these imitations of ancient hero portraits
with portraits of their own heroes and the depictions of appropriate virtues.
Two of the tools created by these craftsmen were eventually adopted for use
on the volumes bound for the Regensburg Rat. Large detailed portrait busts
of four leaders of the Protestant Reformation filled the medallions in the strip
produced by one of the roll-stamps (fig. 50). The date of the roll's creation—
1539—was given on one of the medallions; the letters "I—H", the initials of
its creator or of the bookbinder who used it, appeared in the foliage that
linked the medallions; and the names of the men depicted were given on the
medallions' rims: "IOANNES HVS 1415—PHILIPPVS MELANTHO—IOANNES
FRIDE.D.SA—MARTINVS LVTHERVS."[82]

The second tool adopted for use on the Ratsbibliothek bindings was the
Virtues roll of 1546 by the same IH Master (fig. 51). Instead of portrait

**50.** IH Master, Reformer roll of 1539. 17.7 x 2.1 cm. Enlarged to show detail. Photograph by author, from 2° Theol. syst. 8. Staatliche Bibliothek, Regensburg.

**51.** IH Master, Virtue roll of 1546. 17.2 x 1.5 cm. Enlarged to show detail. Photograph by author, from 2° Theol. syst. 157. Staatliche Bibliothek, Regensburg.

medallions, its design was made up of rectangular "bay windows" in which the four figures of virtue were depicted in half length. The base of each window bore an identifying label: PRVDEN—IVSTICIA—LVCRETIA—VENVS.

These two stamped rolls first appeared in Regensburg in 1546, as the Protestants and Catholics of the empire were preparing for war, on the bindings of two Greek texts owned by Hieronymus Noppus, the preacher called to the city from Wittenberg on the recommendation of Martin Luther in 1543.[83] In neither of these two volumes do the endpapers bear the watermark of the Regensburg paper mill, nor were they bound in the pigskin typical of the city's books. They may, in fact, have been bound outside the city, perhaps in Wittenberg or Augsburg, the latter possibility suggested by the provenance assigned by Konrad Haebler and Ilse Schunke to one of the two roll-stamps used.[84] If this is the case, the two tools were subsequently purchased or copied for use in Regensburg itself, for they were soon in constant use on the books bound for the Ratsbibliothek, whose endpapers bore the watermark of the Regensburg paper mill.[85] The stamped designs they produced dominated the bindings of folio volumes bound for the city between 1546 and the end of the 1560s, when the position of the Protestants seemed no longer threatened by the emperor. At that point they were replaced by noncommittal New Testament scenes.

At the beginning of this chapter I claimed that we can read in these mid-century stamped leather bindings an account of the relationship among Lutheranism, resistance to the emperor in a city allowed no overt display of resistance, and the language of political virtue. This is to argue that we must treat the work of largely ignored craftsmen with the same seriousness that we normally dedicate to the print medium with whose artists we are more familiar—an argument supported by the generally high level of artistic ability and iconographical sophistication demonstrated by the IH Master.[86]

### The Reformers

In the context of the Schmalkaldic War and its aftermath, the message of the IH Master's Reformer roll on Regensburg bindings needed little interpretation. Even without the identifying inscriptions, the medallion portraits he produced with such care would have been easily recognizable; in three cases the sources of the portraits can be identified. The portrait of Philipp Melanchthon was a direct descendant of Albrecht Dürer's famous engraving of 1526 (fig. 52). The medallion portrait of Martin Luther was closely related to portraits by Lucas Cranach the Elder and Albrecht Altdorfer, the latter image itself taking the form of a medallion portrait (fig. 53). In contrast, Hus' profile on the medallion of the bookbinding stamp appears to have shared its origin with a silver medallion produced in honor of the martyred reformer (fig. 54).[87] The exact source for the profile portrait of Johann Friedrich of Saxony, recognizable and distinctive as were his features, has thus far eluded me.

1526
VIVENTIS·POTVIT·DVRERIVS·ORA·PHILIPPI
MENTEM·NON·POTVIT·PINGERE·DOCTA
MANVS

52. Albrecht Dürer, *Philipp Melanchthon*. Engraving, 1526. 17.5 x 12.8 cm. Graphische Sammlung, Staatsgalerie, Stuttgart.

Despite their apparent capitulation in 1546, the Lutheran Ratsherren rendered to Caesar only that which they held to belong to him: the city's keys were turned over to Charles V, but not the right to interfere in matters of faith and piety.[88] Nor was the council's claimed right and obligation to follow what they believed to be God's law stated timidly on the stamped bindings. Other rolls had included Desiderius Erasmus' portrait with those of Luther and Melanchthon;[89] on his 1539 roll, the IH Master substituted the portrait of Johann Hus, the fifteenth-century Bohemian claimed as a predecessor by the Lutherans and memorialized by them on medallions like the one below. Hus' medallion was distinguished from the others on the 1539 roll by its inclusion of a date—1415, a reference to the year of Hus' martyrdom for his faith. Seven years after its creation, in 1546—the year of the roll's appearance in Regensburg, the year of Martin Luther's own death at age sixty-three and of Charles V's declaration of war against the Protestants—the allusion to Hus' death at the stake must have seemed particularly apt. In the following years Johann Friedrich's imprisonment and his loss of the electoral office must have seemed another form of martyrdom, his portrait on the roll together with those of the other martyrs more poignant.[90] As a whole, the roll described the Protestants not as the pamphlet literature had frequently done, in terms of

**53.** Albrecht Altdorfer, *Martin Luther*. Engraved medallion portrait after Cranach the Elder. 6 x 4 cm. (Bartsch 61). Graphische Sammlung Albertina, Wien.

**54.** Anonymous German, Johann Hus centenary medallion (obverse). Sixteenth century. Silver, 43 mm. National Gallery of Art, Washington, D.C., Samuel H. Kress Collection.

their theological differences with Catholics, but as militants, prepared for martyrdom, a description particularly appropriate to Protestant sentiment in an occupied city during the Schmalkaldic War and, later, in a city forbidden Protestant services under the provisions of the Augsburger Interim.

### The Virtues

> God must finally defend and protect Truth and Justice, and punish evil and the evil poisonous doers of vice and tyrants; otherwise he would lose his divinity and in the end no one would consider him a god. (Martin Luther, 1541)[91]

If the depictions of the reformers celebrated the city's commitment to the Lutheran communion when it was most threatened, it was the rôle of the virtues depicted on the same bindings to clarify the link between piety and political resistance, defining good government within walls of Regensburg and in the empire as a whole. The history of such images in Regensburg went back at least as far as the tenth and early eleventh centuries, when miniaturists had surrounded depictions of Abbot Romualdus of St. Emmeramskloster and Abbess Uta of Niedermünster with medallions of the virtues necessary in the governors of cloisters.[92] With the illuminations in the *Gospel Book of Heinrich II* (1014–1024; fig. 55), the connection between governor and virtues was extended to the secular world.[93] An examination of the iconography of that work's dedicatory miniature helps elucidate the medieval understanding of the emperor's rôle—an understanding challenged by sixteenth-century Protestants—as well as the medieval concept of the virtues of good government, in particular those associated with the administration of justice.

Adolf Katzenellenbogen saw in this depiction the emperor's rôle as "mediator, not only formally but literally, between heavenly and earthly figures."[94] The divine grace received by the emperor at his coronation, and demonstrated in the miniature by the descending dove of the Holy Spirit, was the source of the Sapientia and Prudentia who were depicted to his left and right.[95] Justitia and Pietas, virtues mediate in the relationship between the emperor and the deity, occupied the upper corners of the miniature; their dependents, Lex and Ius, occupied its lower corners as carriers of the relationship between emperor and subject. Governed by Lex and Ius, and by divine Justitia and Pietas as mediated by the emperor, was the scene below the emperor's feet: a defendant with arms upraised in supplication to the emperor, and a sword-bearing executioner who also looked up to receive the imperial decision. In this vision, not papal but imperial judgment, the emperor as governor, was or should have been the mediation between the two spheres that Martin Luther would later radically divide. Whether the medieval emperor received at his anointment the benefit of the divine grace of the Holy Spirit or whether the act of anointment only confirmed its receipt, that grace set him apart from other mortals and fitted him for the administration of his realm.

55. Anonymous member of Regensburg school, *Heinrich II*. Miniature from *Gospel Book of Heinrich II* (ms., c. 1014–1024), fol. 193'. Cod. Vat. Ottob. lat. 74. Biblioteca Vaticana, Rome.

The artists of other medieval miniatures, such as those in a twelfth-century manuscript written at Prüfening, were not so sanguine; they used depictions of the virtues and vices together with scenes of the Old Testament not only to praise but also to warn of the downfall of rulers governed by vice rather than virtue (fig. 56).[96] The series began by contrasting the city of Babylon, where the daughter of Babylon paid homage to an enthroned Cupiditas, with the city of Jerusalem. The latter was characterized by four towers, one for each of the cardinal virtues—Prudentia, Justitia, Fortitudo, and Temperantia; here, in the virtuous city, the daughter of Sion paid her homage not to Cupiditas

**56.** Anonymous member of Regensburg school, *Vices and Virtues of Governors*. Pen drawings in *Glossary of Bishop Salomo of Konstanz* (Prüfening: ms., 1165), fols. 3'–4. Handschriftenabteilung, Clm. 13002. Bayerische Staatsbibliothek, Munich.

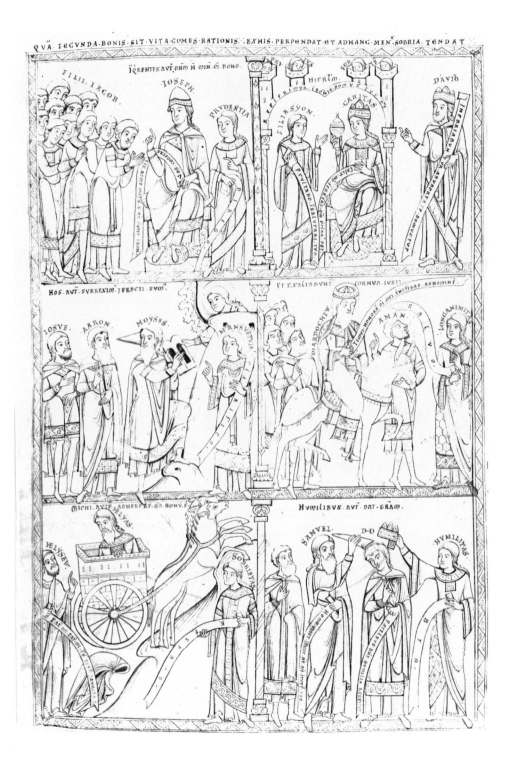

but to the queen of the theological virtues, Caritas. Following this contrasting pair, a depiction of Croesus, brought by Opulentia to stand prisoner before the throne of Cyrus, was balanced by a celebration of Prudentia as the power behind the throne on which Joseph sat and before which his brothers knelt. Below these images of the principal virtues and vices eight scenes depicted the vices originating from Opulentia and Cupiditas and the virtues growing out of Prudentia and Caritas. The final pair in the series presented the image of Gloria/Superbia, who watched Saul commit suicide after he had been overthrown, contrasted with that of Humilitas, who crowned David as he was being salved by Samuel, each image sealed with a biblical admonition to the temporal ruler: "God resisteth the proud" and "Though the Lord be high, yet hath he respect unto the lowly."[97]

In the sixteenth-century empire, similar messages of praise and admonition were conveyed in language that brought elements of Renaissance humanism to the traditional allegorical personifications of the virtues and their biblical analogues or exempla. The iconography adopted by the IH Master in the Virtues roll of 1546 is an example of such a visual communication, owning to both its medieval roots and its humanist heritage, but expressed more militantly in a visual language appropriate to its religio-political context, a language growing out of the bonds between northern humanism and militant Protestantism forged in the 1530s. The iconography of the Virtues roll of the IH Master had its origin both in accessible visual images and in the languages developed to discuss the acceptability of resistance against the emperor in the 1530s and 1540s; the two developments were intertwined, the one providing a form for the other, the other giving richer contextual meaning to the forms.

In 1531, at the time of the foundation of the Schmalkaldic League after the failure of the Protestants to carry their point at the Reichstag, Saul appeared again as an exemplary personification of *hochmut* or Superbia in *The Gate of Shame*, a joint effort in verse and woodcut by Hans Sachs and Erhard Schön describing the downfall of twelve Old Testament tyrants.[98] As in the twelfth-century miniature, these depictions of vice had their virtuous counterparts— the *Twelve Old Testament Heroes* of the same year. Unlike the medieval scribe, however, Hans Sachs contextualized the image of the twelve tyrants in an introduction stating the purpose of the piece: "to comfort all suffering Christians who bear the heavy burden of the yoke of the bloodthirsty Turk and other godless tyrants" with the knowledge that tyranny and evil government were God's fatherly way of punishing his people for their inattention to him and of drawing them near to him again. Sachs' verses were intended to demonstrate that "when God's people, oppressed by their own governors, or conquered by foreign heathen tyrants, raped, robbed, murdered, enslaved, imprisoned, captured, and forced to idolatry against God's law, recognize their trespasses and turn to him crying out for help, God takes pity on them mercifully and saves them from the tyrant's grasp. . . . With his mighty arm, God always shows wonderfully the arrogance of the tyrants and their supporters through their shameful dishonorable deaths, that their shameful lives are well balanced by their dishonorable deaths."[99] Erasmus had discussed tyrants in an even more specific context, devoting several pages of the "mirror of princes" that he dedicated in 1516 to the future Charles V to developing the distinction between the prince and the tyrant, a distinction made more accessible to the German audience with the publication in 1521 of two German editions of the text.[100] Sachs' text of 1531, however, like the medieval miniature, relied on exampla rather than abstract characteristics to define the tyrant: Saul was the murderer of "eighty-five innocent priests, their wives and babes, their asses and cattle," a description similar to Martin Luther's evocation in the early 1530s of the "not quite tyrant" whom it was justifiable to kill.[101] Attaching that language to the history of Saul made explicit the causal relationship between the tyrant's murder of those who resisted him because of the strength of their religious beliefs and his downfall.[102] It was a connection Luther himself would make explicit in his own reference to the Old Testament king in a 1539 letter to an advisor of Johann II of Brandenburg.[103]

LUCRETIA   During the same year, Sachs and Schön also collaborated on other works that exemplified and gave historical as well as visual form to the language of challenge and warning being developed by Martin Luther and his colleagues in the Schmalkaldic period. In two pieces they used the traditional pattern of the "nine heroes." The *Nine Most Loyal Romans* of 1531 took as its first exempla the heroes Lucius and Terentius. Lucius was praised for his willingness to desert wife, child, and property in order to help his friend Scipio Africanus escape prison and to abandon his fatherland, going with him into voluntary exile—a sacrifice recalling Martin Luther's frequently repeated advice that Lutherans whose princes would not allow the practice of their religion should not take up arms but should instead flee to Protestant princes.[104]

The second of the "most loyal Romans," as well as two of the heroines of Sachs' *Nine Most Loyal Pagan Women* of the same year, were associated with the name Brutus, the savior of Rome from Caesar's tyranny—a striking contrast to the traditional inclusion of Julius Caesar himself among the nine heroes.[105] While not himself a rebel, Terentius was praised for his willingness to sacrifice his own life to save his friend Decius Iunius Brutus after the latter had assassinated "Kayser Julium."[106] Portia, the wife of the more familiar leader of the conspiracy against Julius Caesar, Marcus Iunius Brutus, appeared in the *Nine Most Loyal Pagan Women* in a similar rôle; on learning that her husband had been killed by order of the Roman Senate, she committed suicide by swallowing live coals.[107] Eighth among the "most loyal pagan women" in Hans Sachs' verse of 1531 was Lucretia, the Roman matron later adopted by the IH Master as an exemplary personification of one of the four cardinal virtues. To understand the meaning of Sachs' choice requires a more thorough investigation into Lucretia's story as it was familiar to the German Bürger of the sixteenth century.

In Livy's account and in the closely related story told by Ovid,[108] the rape of

Lucretia, the most virtuous of Roman women, by Sextus Tarquinius, the son of the Roman king Tarquinius Superbus, had led her to commit suicide after having exposed his deed to her husband Tarquinius Colatinus, her father Lucretius, and a kinsman, Lucius Iunius Brutus. Thereupon Brutus roused his colleagues to overthrow the king, the father from whom Sextus Tarquinius had learned his arrogance.[109] Livy had dated the events to 510 B.C. and seen in them the origins of the Roman Republic. This interpretation of the story was not, however, stressed by Hans Sachs' verses of 1531—they told only of a beautiful woman who had committed suicide rather than sully her husband's bed with an imperfectly pure wife after her rape by the son of the Roman king.[110] Her rôle as catalyst in the overthrow of the king by Lucius Iunius Brutus was not mentioned. This was in keeping with the fact that it was not the three Brutuses, the tyrant-killers themselves, whom Sachs praised, but rather their friends and relatives, whose loyalty was twofold—personal and patriotic. We shall return shortly to this mediated support of just tyrannicide.

The story of Lucretia had served some medieval writers as a figure of the sacrifice of Christ,[111] but was rediscovered in its more classical form by the Italian humanists and popularized by Boccaccio's *De claris mulieribus*.[112] Like Sachs' later verses, Boccaccio's work, which appeared in illustrated versions from presses in Ulm and Augsburg as early as the 1470s, had stressed Lucretia's virtue and ignored her rôle in the overthrow of the king and foundation of the Roman Republic.[113]

Despite the availability of the Boccaccio editions illustrated with history scenes showing Lucretia in medieval garb, and Lucretia's inclusion among medieval accounts of the nine heroines of antiquity, the Old Testament, and Christian antiquity,[114] it was a nude and classicized Lucretia who began appearing in the North in the early decades of the sixteenth century. The Lucretia of the northern Renaissance was a figure based on Italian prints influenced by the discovery c. 1500 of a classical statue, declared a depiction of Lucretia by Cardinal Giovanni de' Medici.[115] Albrecht Dürer sketched an Italianate Lucretia as early as 1508,[116] and other Nuremberg artists soon gave the elegant classical nude iconographical justification by the addition of the column that was the traditional attribute of Fortitudo and an inscription stressing Lucretia's "Pudicitia" or "Sanctimonia" (fig. 57).[117] Nevertheless, the Roman woman gained her greatest popularity in the 1530s and 1540s in columnless versions by the Cranach school and its imitators outside Wittenberg.[118]

Some art historians have made tentative attempts to link Lucretia's popularity in the 1530s and 1540s with the religio-political position of the Protestants at that time, but without recourse to written sources;[119] a convincing explanation must take written as well as painted *Bildsprache* into account.

The story of Lucretia lent itself to personifications of both Sanctimonia and Fortitudo. The political context of Lucretia's suicide, however, made the story an equally appropriate parable for the downfall of the over-proud tyrant, in

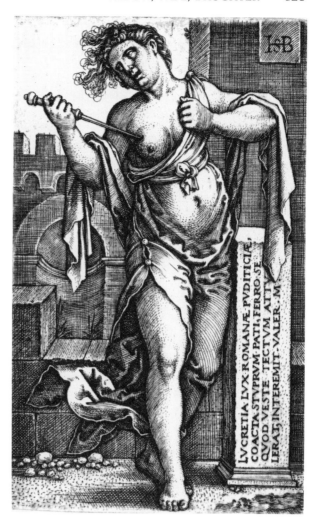

**57.** Hans Sebald Beham, *Lucretia with Column*. Engraving with inscription "LVCRETIA LVX ROMANAE PVDITICIAE COACTA STVPRVM PATI FERRO SE QVOD VESTE TECTVM ATTVLERAT, INTEREMIT.VALER.M." (Bartsch 79) Inv. Nr. 25–1882. Kupferstichkabinett, Staatliche Museen Preußischer Kulturbesitz, Berlin.

the vein of the story of Saul from the Hans Sachs / Erhard Schön woodcut of 1531 or even the miniature drawn by the twelfth-century Prüfening monk (fig. 56). This would not have escaped humanists such as Philipp Melanchthon—who lectured on both Livy and Ovid's *Fasti* and helped to spread the latter account with the publication of his own edition of the work (Halle, 1539)—or the Bürger who learned their Latin from the pages of Livy and Ovid and amused themselves with translated versions of the same stories.[120]

A pair of German plays written at the end of the 1520s exemplified two of the possible readings of the Lucretia story in the sixteenth century. The version by Heinrich Bullinger, a Swiss theologian who would become Zwingli's successor at Zurich, based on Latin editions of Livy and Dionysius of Halikarnassos, was titled *A Lovely Play concerning the History of the Noble Roman Lucretia, and How the Tyrannical King Tarquinius Superbus Was Driven from Rome, and especially concerning the Steadfastness of Iunius Brutus, the First Consul of Rome*; it was staged in Aarau, Basel, and Straßburg immediately after its publication at Basel in 1533.[121] In contrast, Hans Sachs' short one-act tragedy *Von der Lucretia*, based on the accounts of Livy and Valerius Maximus available in German translation, did not appear in print until 1561, long after it had been staged in Nuremberg.[122] As the two titles suggest, Bullinger's drama spoke more directly and more self-consciously to the contemporary political context in which it was composed. When Hans Sachs composed his *Lucretia* in 1527, the Peasants' War was still fresh in the memories of the Nuremberger; Sachs himself had just received an official warning from the Nuremberg Rat to avoid controversy—a response to his publication of anti-Catholic satires.[123] Perhaps for this reason, Sachs' story, like Boccaccio's account and Sachs' own later verses, was couched as a celebration of Lucretia's virtue, not as an invitation to revolt. Nevertheless, although the body of the play was concerned with the delineation of feminine virtue and the ethics of marriage, the epilogue reminded the audience of the political context of the action and of their own viewing of it, contrasting tyranny with honorable government, uproar with peace.[124] Bullinger's drama, in accordance with its title, took a different tack. Lucretia's rape and suicide were mere prologue to the chief action; even the revolt itself was taken for granted. The focus in the Swiss account was the period after the foundation of the republic and the story of Brutus' attempts to solidify the community and prevent the growth of a pro-Tarquin party in the city.[125] Since his steadfastness on behalf of the republic extended to the execution of his own sons when they joined the monarchial party, the drama had a particular message and poignancy in a period of religious dissension and of calls to unity among the Swiss cities following their de facto withdrawal from the empire.

Heinrich Bullinger's political reading of the story of Lucretia was known and staged in the Lutheran cities, yet in the face of imperial attempts to force their return to Catholicism, Protestants such as Hans Sachs praised the Roman heroine for her Sanctimonia rather than her catalytic rôle. In a dinner conversation concerning marriage, Luther himself included Lucretia as an exemplum of virtuous womanhood: "The Holy Spirit praises women. Judith, Esther, and Sara are exempla, and Lucretia and Artemisia are praised among the pagans."[126] More strikingly, in the lectures he gave on Genesis 39:13–18 in the early 1540s, Lucretia, the virtuous Roman matron, served Luther as a prominent counterexample to the seductive wife of Potiphar.[127]

It was Lucretia's piety and purity which the Regensburg artist Michael Ostendorfer emphasized in the inscription he added to his 1530 painting (fig. 58): "Pious, beautiful, and mild Lucretia was forced by Sextus, the son of the king of Rome, to be unchaste with him; she therefore committed suicide."[128] Not all German accounts, however, were so circumspect. In 1534 Heinrich Steiner printed the *Memorial der Tugent* written before his death in 1528 by Johann von Schwartzenberg, the jurist who had drafted the *Bambergische Halsgerichtsordnung* of 1507 and who had in later life become an outspoken

**58.** Michael Ostendorfer, *Lucretia*. Painted panel, 1530. Museen der Stadt, Regensburg.

Lutheran.[129] The pages dedicated by Schwartzenberg to Lucretia's story (fig. 59) focused on the political results of threatening "pious women and children," and are worth quoting in full:

> The son of the seventh Roman king, not ornamented with piety, envied and hated Lucretia for the praise given her. He therefore struggled against her out of vice and forced her into dishonor/adultery. With great pain she revealed what had happened and drove a knife through her heart. She preferred the pain of death to being an example of adultery, and was praised for this by pious pagans. The name of the criminal was Sextus. Because of the vicious sin here related of Sextus, all kings were driven from Rome—the same histories tell us this. For this reason the name of king was hated in Rome forever after, and still today no king rules Rome. One finds the same thing has occurred whenever pious women and children are forced. And the deed one forces often brings damage to one's own. Let all ranks be warned that this has destroyed many governments.[130]

Unlike Hans Sachs', Schwartzenberg's moral was clearly drawn: forcing dependents—"pious women and children"—to impieties and dishonor would likely harm the forcer; it had "destroyed many governments."

In Schwartzenberg's account, as in that of Hans Sachs, Lucretia was an exemplum of Sanctimonia or Humilitas.[131] The vagaries of sixteenth-century German orthography emphasized perhaps unintentionally the dual meaning of Lucretia's chastity: the word "eerbruch" in the edition of 1534 encompassed both dishonor (*Ehrbruch*) and adultery (*Ehebruch*); it was corrected in the edition of 1535 to the unambiguous "eebruch."[132] In his insistence on envied honor rather than lust as the primary motivation behind Sextus' deed, Schwartzenberg echoed a classical source. Cassius Dio, born in Bithynia around the middle of the second century A.D. and a clear partisan of Rome, had insisted that despite Lucretia's great beauty it was nevertheless her reputation rather than her body that Sextus Tarquinius wanted to ruin.[133] In Dio's version Lucretia made the connection between adultery and her own reputation and the honor of her house and men in the hortatory preface to her suicide: "Now I, because I am a woman, will treat my case as becomes me; but do you, if you are men and care for your wives and for your children, avenge me, free yourselves, and show the tyrants what manner of men you are and what manner of women of yours they have outraged."[134]

As a personification of Sanctimonia, Lucretia resembled the Old Testament heroine Judith, who was generally included among the three Old Testament heroines in the nine heroine cycle as an exemplum of the same virtue. Judith, however, had personally conquered the tyrant Holofernes, the personification of Luxuria or Superbia; Lucretia depended on the appropriate (male) defenders of her virtue to avenge her after her suicide. This distinction between the stories of Judith and Lucretia was emphasized by the Protestant authors themselves: although men and women loyal to Brutus were included in Hans Sachs' 1531 verses on the heroes and heroines of pagan antiquity, the tyrannicide himself was not. In this distinction lay a partial reason for Lu-

**59.** Hans Schäufelein, *Lucretia*. Woodcut for Johann von Schwartzenberg, *Memorial der Tugent* (Augsburg: Heinrich Steiner, 1534), fol. CXV'. Handschriftenabteilung, 2° A. lat. b. 273. Bayerische Staatsbibliothek, Munich.

cretia's greater popularity in the empire, and for her appearance on the Regensburg bookbindings.[135]

The passage reported from Martin Luther's conversation at table in the first half of the 1530s helps to clarify the connection between the pious Roman matron and the Lutheran Bürger of cities such as Wittenberg and Regensburg: "If, however, I caught someone, who was not exactly a tyrant, with my wife or daughter, so would I want to kill him. Likewise if he took by force from this one his wife, from another his daughter, from a third his field and goods, and the citizens and subjects came together, and could no longer tolerate or endure his violence and tyranny; so could they kill him just as they would another murderer or robber on the street."[136] The Lutheran whose family and property were threatened because of his religious practices stood in the position of the priests executed by Saul, and also was cast in the rôle of Lucretia's father or husband, his house's Sanctimonia destroyed by a member of the emperor's or pope's entourage.[137] The validity of the political hierarchy was attacked in terms of the rights and responsibilities of the *Hausvater* or *pater familias*. "Every father," wrote the Wittenberg theologians in a 1538 *Gutachten* to Elector Johann Friedrich of Saxony, "is obliged, according to his ability, to protect his wife and children against outright murder, and there is no difference between a private murderer and the emperor when he tries to exercise unjust force outside his office, and especially, open or notorious unjust force."[138] Four years later, when Luther lectured on Genesis 29:23–25, he acquitted Leah of compromising Jacob by comparing her situation with that of Lucretia (on which he dwelt at unusual length), and by stressing the force exerted by Leah's evil father—a force compared explicitly with the force exerted by the tyrannical Tarquins, and contrasted implicitly with the virtuous and correct action undertaken by Lucretia's father.[139] We are here dealing with the thorny and much discussed problem of the development of a Lutheran theory of resistance to the emperor from the point of view not of the political theorists and their historians, but in terms of the images in which resistance was ultimately couched by Martin Luther, by Phillip Melanchthon, and by the artists, advisers, and popularizers around them.[140] Resistance grounded in a theory of natural law was accessibly expressed in the language and image of paternity and that paternal rôle denied the emperor himself.[141]

In 1504 the First Herald of the Florentine Senate had said of Donatello's *Judith and Holofernes* that it was inappropriate to the Republic because it was a symbol of death and of the killing of a man by a woman.[142] The secret of Lucretia's appeal to the Wittenberger and their Lutheran cousins in Regensburg and elsewhere lay in the limitation of her rôle to resisting the corruption of her Sanctimonia and the promise her story offered that a tyrant whose entourage threatened his subjects' Sanctimonia would be removed by the "father(s)," the legitimate defender(s) of the subjects' virtue.[143] The "father" might be the Heavenly Father or his ministers the princes and, possibly, city councillors; what was important was the promise that the triumph of virtue would ultimately be accomplished.

The Peasants' War had taught the reformers wariness and a love of properly sanctioned authority; despite his attack on the papacy, the concept of authority—particularly of a paternal authority—was one of the foundations of Martin Luther's religious thought. In Lucretia's story, as the Lutherans told it, was to be found no license to mass revolt, but instead the statement that passive resistance was necessary to the maintenance of Sanctimonia, and that if that resistance were overcome by force of arms (the rape of Lucretia by Sextus Tarquinius), the tyrant who had sanctioned the violent actions of his entourage would himself be overthrown—by the appropriate authorities (in Luther's own view, God himself or, eventually, the princes).[144] The language that empowered the authorities and that might eventually require that they take up arms against their emperor insisted at the same time on the obedience of their childlike subjects.

PRUDENTIA    Of the three remaining virtues personified on the IH Master's roll, we have already met the allegorical Prudentia and Justitia, the

former in the Prüfening manuscript (fig. 56) and on the panel now hanging in
the Regensburg council chamber (figs. 2 and 3), the latter on the same panel
and in one of Albrecht Dürer's woodcuts (fig. 30). Whereas the Prüfening
Prudentia had been identified only by the appearance of her name on a scroll,
Isaac Schwendtner identified his Prudentia for the viewer twice: in the serpent that encircled her left arm and in the inscription that framed the image.
Confronted with the same problem in identification, the IH Master had taken
a different route, one that revealed considerable iconographical sophistication (on his own part or that of his intellectual adviser). He depicted his
Renaissance Prudentia gazing into a mirror, an attribute she shared in the late
Middle Ages and Renaissance with the goddess Venus and the vice Luxuria.[145] In Prudentia's case, however, the mirror had apparently replaced an
earlier attribute, a dove or a dove within a circle, a reference to the Holy
Spirit.[146] In the course of the Middle Ages the dove had vanished and the
circle had been reinterpreted as a mirror, a reinterpretation encouraged by a
line from the Wisdom of Solomon describing Sapientia as a "flash of eternal
light and unblemished mirror of God's majesty and image of his goodness."[147] The biblical passage emphasized the divine origin of the virtue, a
link made explicit when, at the end of the fifteenth century, Albrecht Dürer
returned the dove, clearly identified as the Holy Spirit by its halo, to Prudentia in a woodcut for the 1494 Basel edition of Sebastian Brant's *Narren schyff*.[148]
On its own, the mirror, emblem of reflection and introspection, could refer to
the Delphic injunction "Know thyself," quoted by Socrates in Plato's *Pro-
tagoras* and used so expansively by Augustine.[149] This was demonstrated
explicitly in the portrait of Hans Burgkmair and his wife painted in 1527 by
Lucas Furtenagel, in which the mirror whose reflection reminded the couple
of their mortality bore the Delphic command in German translation—"Erken
dich selbs"—on its rim.[150] Both traditions informed the Prudentia of the 1546
roll—the IH Master gave her a mirror to gaze into, but in it she must have
seen reflected not only her own image but also the dove that sat in the foliage
above her head.

   In the dove, emblem of the Holy Spirit in the eleventh-century miniature
from the *Gospel Book of Heinrich II*, we saw demonstrated the medieval understanding of the connection between the temporal and spiritual realms. The
Lutheran interpretation, of course, deprived both governor and pope of any
supernatural power and any ability to mediate between the two realms.
Governors were assigned by God for the peaceful administration of the
temporal realm. The good governor must consider the will of God in his
decisions; his knowledge of Lex and Ius must be tempered by his understanding of the divine will, an understanding given him as all other Christians by divine grace. The oath taken by the judge and jury in sixteenth-
century Regensburg to act "according to my conscience and highest understanding," to do "what is most right according to my best judgment," insisted on the connection among conscience, intellect, and judgment.[151] The
magistrate's office did not, however, make him a mediator between the
temporal and sacred realms.

JUSTITIA Justice narrowly defined, the obligation to see that individuals were rewarded or punished for their earthly deeds according to their individual merits, was in Regensburg the responsibility of the judges, the Schultheiß and the Hannsgraf, but also of the *Beisitzer*, the jurors elected on an annual basis to the two courts, and of the Ratsherren themselves.[152] Allegorized Justitia appeared on the bindings of the books in the Regensburg Ratsbibliothek, many of them legal tomes, in the garb she had assumed in the city after its adoption of the Lutheran Communion. More evident than the scales was the sword, which in that context seemed to promise the Protestants the help of the "mighty arm" of God in their battles, or at least that their heretical enemies would feel the sword of judgment in the Last Days. On the bookbindings executed in Wittenberg and in other Protestant cities in which the center of the binding face did not feature the city's arms, the armed figures of Justitia and Lucretia appeared in large stamped panels and were thus even more prominent than in Regensburg.[153] Queen and mother of the cardinal virtues,[154] Justitia owed her Northern ascendancy over the other cardinal virtues during the sixteenth century only partly to her suitability to the Lutheran courtroom; her traditional attribute the sword and her association with Lucretia in the iconography of militant Protestantism after the formation of the Schmalkaldic League in 1530/1531 accounted for her immense popularity outside of the narrow context of the courtroom. As the Lutherans used the story of Lucretia to display their virtue and to justify their resistance to the imperial authority, and even to hint at the danger in which a tyrannical emperor might ultimately find himself, they used the other weapon-bearing female, Justitia, to vouch for the justice of their cause and their confidence that God's justice would prevail.[155] On the books of the Ratsbibliothek, Justitia, depicted as she was next to Lucretia, and flourishing the sword familiar from depictions of the archangel Michael as he cast out the rebel angels or drove Adam and Eve from the garden, took on a militancy that had been modified in Albrecht Dürer's *Sancta Justicia* by the generosity and love of Caritas.[156]

VENUS Nor was Caritas omitted in 1546. On the IH Master's Virtues roll, the righteous judgment symbolized by Justitia's sword and scales was balanced by a humanistic Caritas, not an allegorized abstraction, but the goddess Venus, whose son Cupid flew overhead, his bow playfully drawn. Her antecedents were perhaps not so refined as those of Dürer's allegorical Caritas—familiarity with the winged female archer who was the medieval German *Minne* or *Liebe* had made acceptance of the classical Venus/Cupid image of earthly love all the easier in sixteenth-century Germany.[157] The IH Master nonetheless gave her an expressive gesture that referred as clearly as had the flaming heart of her predecessor to the love of God which was the source of all temporal charity. For Augustine and his successors the cardinal virtues remained without merit for salvation unless inspired by the three theological "virtues infused by God," of which Caritas was queen;[158] for Luther, of course, the separation was more radical. Nevertheless, although salvation was for him in no way related to possession of the cardinal virtues, love of God was a source of the exercise of temporal virtue. Formally repeating the militant diagonal of Lucretia's suicide in the arrow held pointed against her breast, the gesture of the IH Master's Venus referred also to the the divine love piercing the heart hidden beneath the flesh, and to formally similar images of the late-medieval period: to the lance-pierced heart of Christ, the sword-pierced heart of the sorrowing Virgin, and the arrow-pierced heart of Augustine. The interconnectedness of late-medieval symbology is nicely demonstrated in the woodcuts executed by the Nuremberg master Wolf Traut in the first two decades of the sixteenth century. We have already noted the serial gestures of Mary and Christ in Traut's *Rosary* woodcut of c. 1510 (fig. 19): Mary displayed her breast to Christ, who in turn drew his father's attention to the wound in his side. That work was accompanied by two more woodcuts, each with smaller rosaries in which the five large beads bore the images of Christ's wounds—in each hand, in each foot, and in the heart itself.[159] On the second of these woodcuts, the meaning and the primacy of the Mass among the seven sacraments of the church was demonstrated by lines connecting the side wound displayed by Christ in the Mass of St. Gregory with the other six sacraments. Analogically linked to the breast at which he had nursed, the wound in Christ's side was a sign both of the love of God and obedience to his will, and of God's love for the world and his sacrificial plan for its salvation.[160]

In collaboration with Sebastian Brant in 1512, Traut made the connection between the sacrificial suffering of mother and son even more explicit in a woodcut that promised the viewer the remission of 9,415 days in purgatory (fig. 60).[161] Brant's verses on the "plaintive consolation of Christ to the sad co-passion of the Virgin Mary" appeared under an image in which Christ, crowned with thorns and surrounded with the *arma christi*, gestured to his wound while Mary's folded arms emphasized the sword piercing her heart.[162] Traut divided his picture plane evenly between the two figures, and depicted them gazing deeply at one another, while Brant's verses constituted a dialogue between the two sufferers, beginning with Christ's query, "Oh, mother mild, what pierces your heart?" and ending with the indulgences promised to the viewer who contemplated it "with reverence, penitence, and sorrowful heart."[163] The "sword of compassion" which Simeon had warned Mary would pierce her heart, the love and co-passion that her son's death inspired in her, were to be taken as models for the viewer's own heartfelt response to the image.[164]

Popular culture also used the dialogue form, to connect the heart of the Christ child and that of the recipient of a New Year's card such as the tiny Bavarian engraving of c. 1520, which showed the Christ child climbing steps to a giant heart with open door:

> "I've sung the New Year in, and now I've been allowed in—that pleases my heart."

**60.** Wolf Traut, *Man of Sorrows and Mater Dolorosa*. Woodcut for Sebastian Brant, "Querulosa Christi consolatio: ad dolorosam virginis Marie compassionem" (Nuremberg: Hieronymus Hölgel, 1512). National Gallery of Art, Washington, D.C., Rosenwald Collection.

"Welcome, my dear lord; I open the door of my heart to you; come in with your mercy."[165]

A third woodcut by Wolf Traut, *St. Augustine and the Child* from 1518, brought together the images of arrow, heart, and love of God, and brings us nearer to the Caritas from the *Sancta Justicia* of 1521 by Dürer, in whose workshop Traut had worked in 1505 and from 1512 to 1515.[166] Traut's St. Augustine encountered a child who tried to empty the sea with a spoon; between the child and the saint hovered a heart pierced by an arrow. The former image had its origin in the tales told of the saint by "many medieval writers"; it was a reference to the impossibility of human attempts to comprehend the Trinity.[167] The latter, the arrow-pierced heart, was a favorite image in the writings of Augustine himself. In his exegeses of those Psalms most reminiscent of Job's laments, Augustine had turned God's wrathful arrows into a lover's *verba*; his interpretation of Psalm 38:2, "For thine arrows stick fast in me," combined allusions to the book of Job and to a line (spoken by the

Church, according to Augustine's—and, later, Luther's—interpretation) from the Song of Songs, "I am wounded with love": "And holy Job also commemorated these arrows [Job 6]—in the midst of those pains, he said the arrows of the Lord inflicted him. Although we are accustomed to accepting arrows as the words of God, how could he suffer when struck by these? Is it because love itself cannot exist without pain? Whatever we love and cannot have, we must feel pain for. For he who loves and is not pained, has what he loves. He who also loves, as I said, and does not possess what he loves, must cry out in pain. From this comes that said in the person of Ecclesia, the bride of Christ in the Song of Songs 2 and 5: 'I am wounded with love.' "[168] Despite his rejection of the magical powers attributed to Venus by popular and learned culture, Augustine had envisioned and written of the love of God in terms associated with the pagan goddess and her archer son: "You have shot the arrow of your Caritas into our heart and we bear your words inscribed in our viscera; the examples of your servants, whom you transformed from black to shining, from dead to alive, burn together in the bosom of our thoughts and consume our heavy torpor."[169] The image was recalled by medieval artists in the slit in his habit over his heart, the actual piercing of his chest by an arrow,[170] or the arrow-pierced heart held by the saint himself (fig. 61).[171] Later artists, in images painted for the Augustinian order, would formally associate the pierced heart of Augustine with Christ's pierced side and Mary's breast in images that placed the saint between Christ, who gestured to his wound, and Mary, whose breast flowed milk instead of blood.[172]

Associated by the IH Master with the allegories of two cardinal virtues and with the exemplum of a third, the Venus whose own heart was threatened by her son's arrow was, despite her pagan ancestry, more a representative of the love of God than of the dual love of God and neighbor demonstrated by the Caritas of Dürer's *Sancta Justicia* or the simple love of neighbor demonstrated by the later Liberalitas of Bocksberger's fresco for the Regensburg Rathaus.[173]

At mid-century, the emphasis lay on the governor's love of God, his resistance to attempts to compromise his religious beliefs, and his willingness to sacrifice himself for those beliefs in the knowledge that God's will would triumph. And so Lucretia, Justitia, Prudentia, and a Venus whose gesture spoke of divine love and potential self-sacrifice dominated in the visual vocabulary of books bound for the Regensburg Rat at mid-century. In contrast, the visual language of the 1570s, when the threat of imperial intervention in matters of religion was relaxed, spoke in terms less politically charged. The bindings of the books bound during that period for the Ratsbibliothek reflected less militant though equally religious concerns in a visual lexicon based on the New Testament but lacking in political overtones.

The temporary relaxation of attempts to enforce religious homogeneity in the last forty years of the sixteenth century had its influence on more public

**61.** Anonymous, *Augustine's Heart Pierced by Arrows of Caritas*. Woodcut for Augustine, *Sermones de Tempore* (Basel: Johann Amerbach, 1494), fol. 1ʳ. Handschriftenabteilung, 2° Inc. c. a. 3005. Bayerische Staatsbibliothek, Munich.

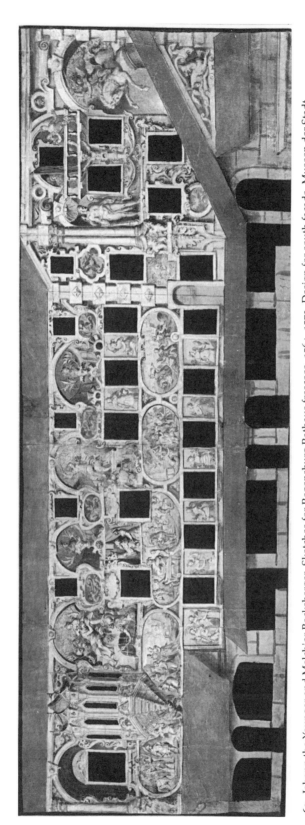

**62.** Johann the Younger and Melchior Bocksberger, Sketches for Regensburg Rathaus frescoes, 1564–1573. Design for south façade. Museen der Stadt, Regensburg.

political statements as well. It was exemplified by the frescoes painted by the Bocksbergers in the 1560s and 1570s on the walls of the Rathaus, a building used by both the Regensburg Rat and the imperial diet; these took no confessional stance, but—particularly in the fresco on the outside of the council chamber itself—stressed the governor's Liberalitas to the deserving and needy under the approving gaze of God. Allegories of virtue appeared on two of the outer walls of the Rathaus. On the outer wall of the council chamber itself, as we have seen (fig. 39), appeared a group of allegorical figures explicitly related to good government; to the right of that fresco, on the outer wall of the southeast wing of the complex, appeared the traditional seven virtues, individual figures classically draped, holding traditional attributes, and separated from one another by illusionistic architecture (fig. 62). Despite the illusionistic framing that turned the façade into a series of windows in which not only the virtues—conceptualized in the form disdained by Augustine's fifth-century correspondent as the work of "shallow pagan" minds[174]—but also heroines of the Old Testament and antiquity appeared, together with their not-to-be-emulated opposites, the scenes were flatter than the Last Judgment that had once hung in the council chamber. The façade, which seems to have owed as much to Boccaccio's *De claris mulieribus* as to Hans Sachs' expansion of the traditional nine heroes theme to include antiheroes, provided a series of illustrations, exempla, or memoranda, rather than a glass through which the practiced viewer could catch a dark glimpse of another realm. That the theme was no longer faith and resistance seems clear from the stories included; in addition to depictions of Judith with Holofernes' head, and Jael slaying Sisera, appropriate to the concerns of the Lutherans at mid-century if less popular than portrayals of Lucretia, the frescoed walls showed Phyllis riding Aristotle, Delila trimming Sampson's hair, Dido founding Carthage, and Cloelia swimming the Tiber, among other scenes. Are we are simply to label it a return to the medieval theme of "the power of women"?[175] Of that I am less certain; it remains a subject for future exploration. Lucretia herself, at any rate, had vanished from the political scene.[176]

# *Gottvater, Stadtväter, Hausväter*: Paternal Imagery in the Dialogue between Bürger and Rat

The Fourth Commandment follows the first three that concern God himself because it teaches how one should act toward all authority that stands in God's stead, to honor father and mother, master and mistress, etc.

—Martin Luther, "Sermon on Exodus," 1525(?)

Historians of the late-medieval period seem agreed that the second half of the fifteenth century was marked in the imperial cities by a growing "Oligarchisierung"[1] and that the greater distance between governors and governed was accompanied by the governors' increasing reliance on religious language to legitimate their authority.[2] In Regensburg, we have seen the impact on the temporal courtroom of Martin Luther's transformation of the angry judge of the Last Judgment into the loving son of a loving father who punished not so much out of wrath as out of the desire to teach; in addition, we have observed the growth of a language of resistance to the emperor's efforts to re-Catholicize Lutheran areas of the empire. We have been concerned with various ways in which religious change transformed the language in which the governors interpreted their relationship to a divine plan and to their emperor. In the opening chapters we saw the Last Judgment panel, which had reminded judge and judged of the presence within the temporal courtroom of the coming eternal judgment, vanish from the Regensburg courtroom to be replaced by a vision of justice at once more humanistic and more insistant on the immediate relationship between a Christian regime and God's threatened intervention in the temporal sphere, as the council's interpretation of its place in God's plan was transformed by its acceptance of Martin Luther's theological position. In the third chapter we observed the transformation of the Lutherans' relationship to imperial authority under the impact of religious dispute, and the development of a language of resistance to the Catholic emperor which stressed the paternal responsibilities of the prince or city ruler toward his subjects. Since it was the Rat's relationship to God and its relationship to the empire which in its own eyes gave it authority over the *Gemeinde*, the common citizenry of Regensburg, we should therefore expect a change in the way the relationships to God and emperor were viewed to affect the ways in which political relationships were defined within the walls. In this chapter we shall explore the impact of the Reformation and its transformation of the relations between town council and God, and between town council and emperor, on the relationship between town council and Bürger. We turn especially to the paternal image that was the basis of the Lutheran understanding of cosmological order—to the problem of the paternalization of the relationship between ruler and subject and its roots in Martin Luther's understanding of the relationship between God and Christian. We remain within the walls of the Rathaus, but this time the sources allow us to shift our focus and to examine one way in which the Bürger themselves used this new imagistic language to reinterpret a relationship, increasingly described by the Rat in impersonal and bureaucratic language, in more personal terms, terms borrowed from Luther's interpretation of the relationship between the Christian and his or her god.[3] If, as Max Weber argued, the defining element of *Herrschaft* is its "evocation of obedience," it was the terms in which that obedience was evoked and promised, in which the relationship itself was defined, which were at stake in this sixteenth-century dialogue.[4]

## The Dialogue: Voices

> This external and material regime has been established and ordered by God. And with the words: "Thou shallt honor thy father and mother," he has commanded that it, like everything he has divinely established, be observed and honored. (Justus Menius, 1529)[5]

As we have seen, the Rathaus in the sixteenth-century German city provides us with a variety of sources for an examination of the changing language of political legitimation: visual sources such as painted panels and leather bookbindings and written sources including the tracts of theologians such as Martin Luther on the responsibilities of princes and the rulers of cities, as well as the ordinances issued by the secular authorities themselves. These sources generally reflect the perspective of the politically dominant; their languages were chosen to legitimate commands addressed to subjects and to legitimate the right of those in power to issue commands. In the verb "legitimate" we here intend—in Weber's language—not only the authority's "appeal to material or affectual or ideal motives as a basis for its continuance," but also its "attempt to establish and cultivate the belief in its legitimacy."[6] Confronted with such sources and with analyses of the use of such languages of legitimacy by those in power, it is easy to forget that the subject, too, might use the same or a related language for his or her own ends, to legitimate his or her own petitions and to legitimate his or her right to make petitions. Legitimation, as an act of communication, a part of discourse, can proceed in either

**Table 1**

Comparison of extant decrees published in Regensburg, 1490–1600, as listed in Schlottenloher and Kayser

| Decade | Total number of decrees listed in Schottenloher | Number of decrees given in Kayser | Number of decrees given in Kayser which use language of legitimation |
|---|---|---|---|
| 1490–1500 | 0 | 0 | 0 |
| 1501–1510 | 0 | 0 | 0 |
| 1511–1520 | 0 | 0 | 0 |
| 1521–1530 | 3 | 1 | 1 |
| 1531–1542 | 15 | 11 | 5 |
| 1543–1552 | 4 | 3 | 3 |
| 1553–1562 | 3 | 3 | 3 |
| 1563–1570 | 6 | 6 | 6 |
| 1571–1580 | 4 | 4 | 4 |
| 1581–1590 | 5 | 4 | 3 |
| 1591–1600 | 7 | 6 | 6 |
| 1490–1600 | 47 | 38 | 30 |

direction; the act of legitimation itself acknowledges that the authority's dominance rests on some "minimum of voluntary compliance, that is, [on the subject's] *interest* (based on ulterior motives or genuine acceptance) in obedience."[7] Acknowledged is a potential power of the recipient to reject the action of the "authority" through some act or speech of his or her own. Add, then, to sources listed above the petitions directed by the Bürger to the Rat in semiprivate documents such as wills.

In this chapter we examine both conciliar decrees and the petitionary language of citizens' wills as a dialogue between governors and governed about their political relationship. The conciliar voice will be heard in the collection of Regensburg decrees published in 1754 by Johann Friedrich Kayser,[8] a collection that includes more than 80 percent of the forty-eight decrees listed by Karl Schottenloher in his catalogue of the products of Regensburg printshops in the sixteenth century (table 1).[9] The subjects' voices will be heard in their extant wills, in the admittedly formulaic language in which they petitioned the council's approval of their requests concerning the disposition of their property, their mortal remains, and their immortal souls.[10]

Ironically, the voices of the Ratsherren are more difficult to catch at this remove than the voices of their subjects. As we saw in chapter three, printing came slowly to Regensburg; Regensburg's Rat began issuing printed decrees late, in 1523, and only a few survive for each of the succeeding decades. Their distribution is given in table 1.

On the other hand, Regensburg is rich in extant wills. Deposited in the Bayerisches Hauptstaatsarchiv in Munich are several thousand testaments from the period 1400–1750, previously in the Regensburg city archives.[11] Of

**Table 2**

Number of extant Regensburg wills, 1490–1600, by gender of testator

| Decade | Total number of testators | Males | Females |
|---|---|---|---|
| 1490–1500 | 3 | 2 | 1 |
| 1501–1510 | 5 | 2 | 3 |
| 1511–1520 | 16 | 7 | 9 |
| 1521–1530 | 45 | 27 | 18 |
| 1531–1542 | 75 | 36 | 39 |
| 1543–1552 | 85 | 38 | 47 |
| 1553–1562 | 127 | 62 | 65 |
| 1563–1570 | 150 | 73 | 77 |
| 1571–1580 | 235 | 108 | 127 |
| 1581–1590 | 238 | 121 | 117 |
| 1591–1600 | 268 | 129 | 139 |
| 1490–1600 | 1247 | 605 | 642 |

*Note:* With regard to table 2 and the following figures that relate
to the chronology of testamentary language, the actual numbers
involved in the first two or three decades are quite small (3, 5, and
16 wills respectively), and the results given are therefore to be
read only as possible indications of a trend.

these, the wills executed in the years 1490–1600 on behalf of some 1,200
testators are of interest to us (table 2).[12] The question of their representativeness is difficult to answer since population estimates for Regensburg c. 1500
vary between 6,000 and 15,000 people.[13] One of the most careful estimates is
that provided by Matthias Simon from calculations based primarily on the
baptisms and weddings recorded annually in the series of registers kept by
the city's Lutheran clergy beginning in 1542; unfortunately, comparable
sources do not exist for the Catholic population.[14] Simon's figures give an
average—Catholic and Protestant—population of 11,300 when the Catholic
clergy (whose wills were outside the purview of the city council) are omitted.
Using his estimate, we arrive at the figure of about 5,000 for the total number
of adult deaths in the period 1521–1600, assuming a death rate of between 5
and 6 adults per 1,000.[15] (I am here disregarding the first three decades
shown in table 2 because the number of wills extant for that period is clearly
too small to be statistically significant.) The 1223 testators whose wills survive
represent, then, roughly one-quarter of the total number of adults who are
calculated to have died during the period.[16] Of course, not all those who died
made wills; the very nature of a will implies an economic bias. Nevertheless,
the wills surviving from Regensburg reflect a surprising variety of economic
and social conditions among the testators and appear therefore to provide an
early-modern source remarkable for its representativeness. Wills dictated by
Ratsherren and merchants, but also by masons, leather workers, and bath-
house attendants survive, as do wills dictated by widows, servants, apprentices, and elderly pensioners spending their final years in the city's
hospitals.[17]

In the medieval period the Regensburger had written out his or her will or dictated it to a notary; only the wax seals of one or more of the city's citizens were required to establish the will's authenticity. After a brief late-medieval effort to make the city's wills conform to the practices of Roman law, the sixteenth century marked the return to a less rigid form that emphasized local authority over Roman law: wills were established as legitimate when written by the Stadtschreiber or his appointed substitute and witnessed by two members of the Innerer Rat.[18] The increasing institutionalization of the Regensburg Rat in the late-medieval period was reflected in the language of the wills written by city scribes for the citizens and residents of the city. Not only because of the city's jurisdiction in the case of disputes between heirs, but also and especially because of the taxes brought in on the goods inventoried after a resident's death, last wills and testaments were the affairs of the Stadtschreiber, the *Steuerschreiber*, and the Innerer Rat. The *Regimentsordnung* of 1514 said of wills: "The testament and business of the last will must always be drawn up as is orderly and in accordance with Law, and with all due solemnity; it must be written out with special care. From now on all testaments of the last will must first be opened and read before the honorable Rat, and the parties are to receive copies of the same at their request. And in order that the division of the same testament and transaction be adjudicated, the Hauptmann, Cammerer, and Rat should try earnestly to get the parties to agree among themselves regarding the property. Where they cannot agree concerning the property, the adjudication should be turned over to the Schultheißengericht as the appropriate court."[19]

Then as today, wills were written or dictated out of the wish to demonstrate love and favor or hatred and anger, out of the desire to keep the patrimony within the lineage or to reward a spouse to the near exclusion of the lineage, out of the testator's need to secure him- or herself an acceptable retirement or to make secure the rearing and education of his or her children. They were made also to ensure the proper burial and—for Catholics—eternal well-being of the testator and his or her ancestors and descendants. In Regensburg these intentions and motives were expressed in phrases fixed by the conventions and laws of the period; they were framed by formulaic invocations. Initially, I approached the Regensburg wills as a potential source for the confessional allegiances of the individuals involved. Unfortunately, however, it soon became clear that the formulaic nature of the invocations used in most Regensburg wills does not allow us to determine confessional allegiance on the basis of invocation alone; only in the comparatively infrequent pious bequests do confessional loyalties become apparent.[20]

Even provisions for burial, like the one quoted in chapter two from the will drawn up in 1517 for Niklas Schweller,[21] were apt to provide only that the burial arrangements be made according to the advice and good counsel of the will's executors; intentionally or unintentionally, they avoided committing to paper the deposition desired. Although Schweller's will gave the prospective burial location, even that detail was omitted in most later wills.[22]

The formulaic character of the invocations and the fact that the vast majority of Regensburg wills surviving from the sixteenth century were drawn up by the Stadtschreiber or his designated *Substitut*, though they make difficult the analysis of confessional loyalty on an individual basis, nevertheless allow us to chart changes on a broader scale in what must be characterized as at least the semiofficial language in which the city's inhabitants petitioned the Ratsherren before whom the wills would eventually be opened at their deaths.

How much, then, was the language of the will the choice of the testator? In the period between 1490 and the official conversion of the city to Lutheranism in 1542, the most popular image used to invoke the support of the Regensburg Rat for the provisions of a will depicted that authority in the rôle of *Beschirmer* (literally, "shielder" or "shelterer") (fig. 63). I have closely analyzed the frequency of the invocation of the Rat as protector in an effort to discover what indicators, if any, might account for its appearance or nonappearance in testaments drawn up between 1521 and 1542, during the two decades of its greatest popularity.

The Stadtschreiber Hans Reysolt drew up 30 percent of the 120 wills extant for the decades 1521–1542. Of those he wrote, 64 percent included the invocation of the Rat as Beschirmer. Neither Reysolt's presence as notary nor the making of pious bequests by the testator appears to be a reliable predictor of the invocation. In the wills written by the Stadtschreiber, gender is the strongest predictor of the choice of this invocation. The Ratsherren were apostrophized as protectors by 86 percent of the male testators, regardless of their confession, but by only 36 percent of the female testators. Those testators who made bequests to the Catholic church were slightly more likely to invoke the Ratsherren as protectors: 88 percent of the males did so, but, again, only 42 percent of the females. The situation, however, changes when the testaments drawn up by Reysolt, his son Hans Reysolt the Younger, and the *Hanns- und Kanzleischreiber* Wolfgang Pickl during the same period are considered as a group. Together these three men accounted for 61 percent of the wills extant for the two decades and for 69 percent of all the wills invoking the Rat as Beschirmer. Of the wills they drew up, 67 percent invoked the Rat as protector. In this case, both pious bequests and gender are fairly strong predictors of the invocation: 75 percent of all those making bequests to the Catholic church and all those making Protestant bequests (there were only two, one man and one woman) did so in wills that invoked the Ratsherren as protectors; in addition, the invocation appeared in the testaments drawn up for 73 percent of the males but only 59 percent of the women. Only in the wills drawn up for those who did not include pious bequests did such invocations appear less than half the time (40 percent in the case of men, 37 percent in the case of women). Unfortunately, the paucity of the confessional data does not allow us to reach more substantial conclusions in that direction. It does appear clear, however, that the testator as well as the scribe or notary influenced the decision to invoke the Ratsherren and the choice of invocation.

Close analysis of the occurrence of one particular formula in Regensburg

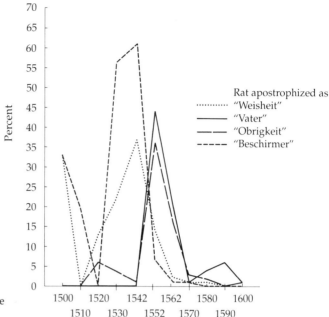

**63.** Wills apostrophizing Rat as percentage of all wills, Regensburg, 1490–1600.

wills confirms that not only the scribe or notary but also the testator had some say in the particular formulas chosen, which is to say that the testator must have accepted to some degree the normative understanding of the relationship between Rat and Bürger expressed by the invocative formula used in the will drawn up for him or her. Just as the Ratsherren addressing the Regensburg inhabitants in an ordinance used language calculated to impress the recipients with the legitimacy of their authority and that of their decree, so, too, the inhabitants who sought the Rat's approval of the provisions of their wills used language calculated to achieve that approval.

In a different context Hans-Christoph Rublack has concluded that "it was the Rat which expressed the norms and in its own self-conception formulated the elements of a political theory."[23] Although the political troubles of the late-medieval period make it clear that the self-conception of the city council was not always and everywhere identical with the citizenry's understanding of the relationship between council and community, Rublack's statement that "since the council was able to enforce what it legally defined as communal values, the council's conceptions remain central to an understanding of city politics" has application outside Nördlingen as well.[24] Certainly the council and citizens shared a discourse—that idea is implicit in our description of their "dialogue."[25] Nevertheless, the evidence for Regensburg reveals a citizenry capable, as was the council itself, of making lexical choices within their common vocabulary. Those shared values and that communal language shaped the discourse, but did not impose an absolute limit on the interpretations of the political relationship they expressed.

As figure 63 reveals, the language of one-half of the dialogue, the language used to petition the Rat's support for the provisions of the wills written for Regensburg's Bürger—the terms, in other words, in which the Bürger understood and chose to express this basic political relationship between governors and governed—underwent several changes in the course of the sixteenth century. The two most popular invocations of the Rat during the sixteenth century were "Beschirmer" and "Father"; neither was used exclusively— most often more than one image was used in an individual will—but each image held sway for two decades, and the transition from one to the other was demonstrably linked to the changes in the way divine as well as political relationships were perceived. In order to understand these transformations we must return to the dialogue itself. We begin with the Ratsherren.

### Before the Reformation: Rat as *Obrigkeit* or *Beschirmer*?

The wills and ordinances composed in the decades before the official acceptance of the Reformation in Regensburg reflected the multivocality of the medieval period. They reflected, as well, the different rhetorical strategies taken by Rat and Bürger in their efforts to legitimate their different goals.

In the first decree reprinted in Kayser's collection, the Rat justified its actions based on a perceived obligation to fulfill expectations, particularly those of their "most merciful lord, His Roman Imperial Majesty, and all of the estates of the holy empire."[26] Although it had, in times of stress, summoned the entire community together in an effort to achieve a consensus within the walls,[27] in 1523, as later, the Rat expressed its authorization as coming in the first place from above rather than from the community. By 1531, if not before, the council had adopted the language of "aboveness"; it referred to itself as the "hohern Obrigkeit," literally that or those set above the community. An ordinance issued in that year to clarify the jurisdictions of the various municipal courts ended with the possibility of final appeal to "an honorable Cammerer and Rat, as the higher *öbrigkeyt*, as is proper. Where anyone appears disobedient and contravenes this, the honorable Cammerer and Rat's necessary resolution, he should expect serious punishment."[28]

In this case, "Obrigkeit" referred specifically to the Cammerer and Innerer Rat sitting as the highest municipal court, but the judicial authority they exercised was only a part, if a very important part, of the councillors' duties. In the decrees which followed, "Obrigkeit" was used in other contexts, contexts that revealed a clear intention on the part of Cammerer and Rat to describe themselves as not only exercising authority, but also *as* authority. The Regensburg council claimed for itself recognition as a duly constituted and self-conscious institution, the "upper hand" cited by Rublack.[29] Recent research into the concept of Obrigkeit in other late-medieval German cities reveals a similar duality of meaning; examples from Speyer, Hamburg, and now Regensburg confirm Heinrich Bornkamm's conclusion that the initial meaning of government as function was soon institutionalized.[30] In the case of Regensburg, exercising authority in the judicial system within the town was transformed into *being* the authority. Nor is this "institutional" awareness surprising in Regensburg, a city for which lengthy constitutions were written by imperial commissioners in 1500 and 1514. In 1514 the election to the Rat was overseen, and the Ratsherren themselves inducted, by the imperial commissioners. Although in a complicated and carefully circumscribed fashion the Cammerer and Rat were elected annually with the participation of representatives of the "community," they did not refer to this communal sanction in any of the extant decrees; instead, they sought legitimation in the approval of the emperor and of God himself.[31]

In this attitude the Ratsherren were supported by the annual oaths sworn in the city. The oath taken by the Ratsherren on their election reflected the council's separation from and responsibility for the community; they swore "to advance the good of his imperial majesty, the holy empire, and, thereafter, the municipal community."[32]

As both Erich Maschke and Rainer Postel have pointed out, the acceptance of a usage such as "Obrigkeit" with its implied separation of Rat and community could take place only at the right "sociological moment"—when such a separation had in fact occurred.[33] In Regensburg, particularly after the unrest of the second decade of the sixteenth century which had required imperial intervention, the participation of the Bürger in political decisions was carefully circumscribed; the outsiders who wrote the city's new *Regimentsordnung* in 1514 to mark the end of the disorder were faced with the difficult task of eliminating the possibility that such disorder would recur while ensuring against the recurrence of the abuses of fiscal authority which were alleged to have been its partial cause—charges of fiscal malfeasance had resulted in the execution of one elderly former member of the Innerer Rat in addition to the several members of the outer council and community who were executed as leaders of the unrest.[34] In the constitution they wrote, the imperial commissioners tried both to ensure a closer oversight of economic matters by representatives of the community and to ensure a closer oversight of potentially disruptive elements such as craft guilds by the council. The emphasis was on the latter goal: if the Regensburg Rat was not so closed a patrician circle as the Nuremberg council in its membership criteria,[35] its day-to-day practices, as sanctioned and even required by the constitutions of 1500 and 1514 out of the fear of factions building around individual councillors, consciously set the council apart from the community. The Ratsherren had to vow to keep all council business secret until their deaths; after 1514 this last vow was extended to include a prohibition against the keeping of either public or private memoranda of the council's business by the Ratsherren—a prohibition unfortunate in the extreme for the historian![36]

The discussions within the walls of the small council chamber were to be held secret not only from the community at large but also from the outer council; the relation between the two councils was carefully circumscribed. The larger of the two councils, which had by definition to include at least twelve guildsmen after 1500, was called into deliberation with the Innerer Rat only on clearly defined occasions: "When one wants to discuss tax matters / When one wants to sell rents or interests / When the city conquers a sworn enemy / When accounts are examined / When a payment or some large undertaking is requested by his imperial Majesty and the Holy Empire, or any time when unusual business occurs such that the Innerer Rat holds it necessary to summon the Larger Council. The Hauptmann, Cammerer, and Innerer Rat may also summon the Äußerer Rat in all other matters as often as they want and consider useful."[37] The occasions for summoning the community at large were fewer: when an imperial missive or order was addressed to the "Cammerer, Innerer and Äußerer Rat, and community"; when sales or purchases of city property were contemplated; and when an order was to be issued which was binding on "the community, its children and descendents."[38] After the unrest of 1512–1514, communal participation in politics was even less frequent: on the occasions specified above only forty representatives of the community, elected by quarter, were consulted; this *Ausschuß* was to be fully empowered by the community to act and reach decisions on its behalf in the matters in which the imperial Hauptmann, Cammerer, inner and outer councils consulted it.[39] The community at large was to be summoned to the Rathaus only once a year on St. Stephen's day for the annual reading of the *Regimentsordnung* itself.[40]

The Regensburg Rat, then, acted "von Oberkeyt wegen," because of its high position, in the early decades of the century.[41] The legitimation of its power was a hierarchical one; its authority was based on its position above the citizens and inhabitants of the city, but was by no means absolute—it stood under and owed allegiance to the emperor who stood above it in the hierarchy ordained by God.[42] The emperor might be the "natural" lord of the empire,[43] the Regensburg city council, however, issued decrees by virtue of its "office," a term that, at least as used by Martin Luther in his translation of the Bible, referred to the position rather than the individual; the office continued to exist although the individual might be removed from it, and not only by his mortality.[44] Nevertheless, although the position of city councillor was in Regensburg an elective office de jure, none of the decrees extant from the sixteenth century appealed to the council's election by representatives of the citizenry or to any presumed rôle as "voice of the community" to legitimate its power;[45] instead, it was to "Almighty God" and "their Roman Imperial and Royal Majesties" that the Cammerer and Rat, "by virtue of their office," were first of all responsible; "the councillors themselves, their common obedient citizenry, and other peaceful people" came in the second place.[46] The council's primary activity might be in governing the community. Its authority, however, came not from the community itself, but rather from authorities outside and above it, from the emperor and from God himself— hence the appearance of the Last Judgment on the council chamber wall in

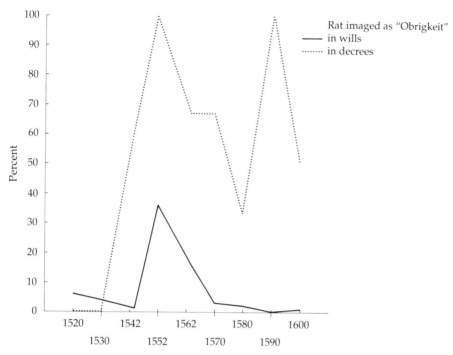

**64.** Wills and decrees imaging Rat as "Obrigkeit" as percentage of all wills and decrees, Regensburg, 1510–1600.

the late-medieval period, as reminder of the final judgment of judge as well as defendant, emanant in the temporal trial.[47]

If the language used by the Rat in the first decades of the century described an authority responsible for but distanced from the ordinary citizenry, the petitionary language used to legitimate the Bürger's last requests before the Rat revealed another perspective. Although the council most often described itself as Obrigkeit in its decrees, the Bürger, though they acknowledged the council's authority, tried to establish a more personal relation between governed and governor (compare figs. 63 and 64). As the Lutherans, including finally Martin Luther himself, would come to argue that an emperor whose treatment of his subjects was unjust was not an emperor but a tyrant, so the Bürger's language contained the implicit argument that the town councillors' office was dependent on their faithful care of the citizenry rather than solely on their recognition by the emperor or God. The image most commonly used to invoke the Rat's support of the testator's will in the decades before that body's official acceptance of the Lutheran Communion, an image often linked with the less personal invocation of the Rat as "Wisdom," was not that of the Rat as "Obrigkeit," but, as we have seen, that of the Rat as guardian or protector.[48]

The motif of protection was here literally that of a lord holding a sheltering hand or cloak over the head of an individual petitioner. As such, it had had its origin in the realm of customary law. In the Old Testament, as in Middle Eastern practice, the cloak's shelter implied the offer of the protection of marriage to or the social redemption and rehabilitation of the person sheltered.[49] During the medieval period a child in Northern Europe was declared legitimate or adopted by a father's sheltering gesture with his cloak; the same gesture, particularly when made by a high-born lady, could signify the assumption of lordship over and protection of the weak.[50] In the twelfth and thirteenth centuries legends began granting the lowly virgin who had become Queen of Heaven the privilege already accorded earthly women.[51] By the late-medieval period, therefore, it was most often Mary—present so often as a fourth member of the Trinity that art historians have coined the term "Quaternity"—who was depicted giving shelter and nurture.[52] Nevertheless, the gesture had not come to stand for maternal protection alone. Jesus or God himself might occasionally appear as just this sort of protector.[53] In the woodcuts (figs. 65 and 66) that illustrated at least two editions of the book by the theologian Heinrich Amandus, called Suso (Sweet), God sheltered the author under his swirling cloak; an inscription confirmed the gestural promise in language that would later appear in invocations of the Regensburg Rat in wills executed during the two decades between 1521 and 1542 (fig. 63): "Under my divine shelter, I will hold you who bear my name IHS in your hungry hearts.—The eternal Wisdom."[54]

The language in which the Rat's approval was sought, while it did not make a direct appeal to religious sanction, was borrowed from a religious context, for which it had earlier been adapted from legal and customary practice. The image of shelter appeared in Lutheran as well as Catholic discussions of both political and religious relationships.[55] It appeared, for example, as an analogy drawn from the animal kingdom, in two *Meisterlieder* written by Hans Sachs in 1527 in praise of Nuremberg and its city council.[56] In Sachs' "Sweet Dream," Nuremberg was imaged as an eaglelike bird that flapped its wings protectively about its offspring and fed them through the cold winter.[57] In his "Explication," Sachs interpreted the image for his listeners: "The bird symbolizes the imperial city Nuremberg who bears the eagle (its left side red and white) given her by the Roman empire in her coat of arms. [The young birds] symbolize the citizens everywhere in the city, wealthy and poor, merchants and craftsmen; that the eagle beats its wings means that the honorable Rat is truly attentive to its subjects, truly shielding and protecting them."[58] His image had its origin not only in the arms of the city he praised (fig. 30), but also in the language of the psalmist David, who had cried out to his god to "protect me under the shadow of thy wings," and—still more—that of the prophet Isaiah, who had promised that "the Lord will protect Jerusalem, as do the flying birds."[59] Here, then, the language had come full circle: applied to Yahweh by the writers of the Old Testament, the gesture that was a part of the legal custom of the Old Testament and medieval worlds was by the end of the medieval period a part of the gestural language of visual images depicting the relationship between God or

**65.** Anonymous, *God as Protector and Eternal Wisdom*. Woodcut for Heinrich Suso, *buch genant der Seusse* (Augsburg: Anton Sorg, 1482), fol. LXXXVIIII. Handschriftenabteilung, 2° Inc. c. a. 1260. Bayerische Staatsbibliothek, Munich.

In meinē götlichem schirm will ich sy haben.
die meinē namē ihs ī īrer begird wellē trayē
Die ewiḡ weyſheit.

**66.** Hans Schäufelein, *God as Protector and Eternal Wisdom*. Woodcut for Heinrich Suso, *Diss buch das da gedicht* (Augsburg: Hanns Othmar für Joh. Rynmann, 1512), fol. 61. Handschriftenabteilung, Reserve 2° P. lat. 1430. Bayerische Staatsbibliothek, Munich.

Mary and humankind. The two Old Testament passages are particularly apropos, for we find in them not only the image used by Sachs but also, in the German translations by the translator of c. 1466 and by Martin Luther, the verb "beschirmen," the term used in the Regensburg wills.[60] Nor have we moved so far from the cloak that emblemized the protection offered by a lord or a divinity; in Hebrew the word for the sheltering cloak and the sheltering wing were the same: *kanaph*. Thus Ruth, in appealing to Boas for protection and redemption, sought the shelter of his wing / the hem of his cloak using the same image he had used in blessing her with Yahweh's protection. Martin Luther stressed the repetition, as Jerome and the German translator of c. 1466 had not, by repeating the word *Flügel* metaphorically in Ruth's plea to Boas.[61]

If the Old Testament Yahweh was like a phoenix or "an eagle who flies over his young, and spreads his wings" as a shelter for his chosen people,[62] Jesus was reported by Matthew and Luke as having transformed the lordly language into the comfortable metaphor of the barnyard in the midst of a lament: "O Jerusalem, Jerusalem, thou that killest the prophets, and stonest them which are sent unto thee, how often would I have gathered thy children together, even as a hen gathereth her chickens under her wings, and ye would not!"[63] The eagle had become a mother hen, an image echoed by Martin Luther outside his translation of the Bible. Christians, he wrote, "shouldn't flee from Christ and God the Heavenly Father. He wants us to cling to him like the chicks who gather under the wing of the mother hen; like children who cling to their parents. This is the childlike protection we should seek from Christ and the Heavenly Father."[64]

It was to this last, extremely personal, explication of both spiritual and political relationships that the Regensburger would eventually come round, and we shall do so in their footsteps. Nevertheless, it is clear that even in the pre-Reformation period the language used by the Bürger to invoke the protection of the Rat in Regensburg wills defined the relationship between governed and governor in more personal terms than the language used by the Rat in contemporary decrees directed to the Bürger. In the wills the Rat, which in its own decrees was depicted in relationship with God and emperor, was brought face to face with the individual citizen.

## The Reformation and the Rat as "Father" in Wills

> We, the undersigned, most humbly beg Your Honorable Wisdom, as our Fathers and Magistrates, ordered and set over us by God, graciously to consider this, our Christian request and heartfelt plea, because the Father of all Mercy, Almighty God, in these last perilous times, acting out of great love and mercy, has given us his Holy Gospel and allowed it to be preached. (petition signed by thirty-one Regensburg Bürger, 1542)[65]

> As Plutarch skillfully said, a wholesome prince is to a certain extent the living image of God. (Erasmus of Rotterdam, 1516; German translation, 1521)[66]

> The authorities are made in God's image, as power proceeds from God. (Hans Trumer, town clerk in Augsburg, 1601)[67]

Although the Reformation brought no immediate change to the official language of the decrees issued by the Regensburg Rat—the language of "Obrigkeit" remained dominant into the 1560s[68]—it did transform the formulaic language in which the Regensburg testator petitioned the council. Martin Luther's very personal image of the relation between the Christian and his or her God, extended by Luther himself to certain political relationships, was adopted by the Regensburger in their wills to express the political as well as the religious relationship and was eventually appropriated by the council itself.

When, in 1562, Johann von Mathesius, son of a Rochlitzer Ratsherr and himself table companion and biographer to Martin Luther, wrote that "long ago the *Landesherren* used to be called 'fathers' and their subjects, 'people' or 'children,'" he was probably referring to the *pater patriae* of the Roman empire.[69] Certainly, in Regensburg, an imperial city with no temporal *Herr* save the emperor, the expression of political relations in paternal language was not the residue of a tradition with origins in the city's foundation as a Roman army camp, but rather the result of the Reformation and the new emphasis on the paternal love of the Father God for his earthly children.

Most medieval theologians had extended the protection of the Fourth Commandment to priests, but not to their lay counterparts.[70] In a sermon on the Ten Commandments delivered in German, the powerful thirteenth-century Franciscan preacher Berthold von Regensburg had urged his listeners to honor and obey their "spiritual fathers—that is, the priests—since God himself has dignified and honored them above all mankind," but had not extended the justificatory language of paternity to worldly magistrates.[71] In fact, though the Christian "shall also honor your spiritual mother, that is, Holy Christianity," God himself did not appear as a father in Berthold's sermon except insofar as the fellow Christian should be honored "because we Christians are all brothers in God, as we say every day in the pater noster."[72] Similarly, even in his sermon on God's love, God was referred to not as *unser Vater*, but as *Herre*.[73] God's love was compared to parental love, but to that of the mother rather than that of the father for the child.[74] Berthold's language, however, was no match for the emotive imagery of the mystics in his own century and later. Men such as Thomas Aquinas might deny that the triune relationship of the godhead was accessible to human understanding, but the human need to comprehend, and to comprehend in human terms, resulted in visual and verbal explications of even that most impenetrable of sacred relationships in an emotional vocabulary suggested by Christ's own language as reported in the New Testament. According to Luther, "God has neither beard nor hair, but we nevertheless depict him accurately in this image of an old man. We must paint such a picture of our Lord God for the children, and even for those of us who are learned."[75] As we saw in chapter two, by the century of Luther's birth God the Father was appearing more and more frequently in scenes from the life of Christ in which his presence was required by no biblical narrative but was justified by a popular theological climate increasingly interested in his paternal relationship to Christ and in the pathos of his response to the sacrifice of his son on the cross, the sacrifice he himself had commanded.

Thomas Aquinas had denied the applicability of human terms to the triune godhead and acknowledged only reluctantly that a "certain similarity" might exist between rulers and fathers.[76] Nevertheless, paternal language had won wide acceptance by the end of the medieval period; following Gerson, Johannes Geiler von Kaisersberg, for example, had extended the protection of the fourth commandment, if not exactly the language of paternity, to both spiritual and secular authorities.[77] Writing in Latin, late-medieval humanists had echoed earlier authors in their application of the term *pater* to secular authorities.[78] In the "mirror of princes" he addressed to the future Charles V, Erasmus had used the analogy of the *pater familias*: "A pious prince should have the same disposition and heart toward his people as a good *Hausvater* has toward the members of his household."[79] Erasmus' work was translated into German and published at Augsburg and Zurich in 1521,[80] but Martin Luther seems to have been the first writing in German to combine consideration of the Fourth Commandment with the classical notion of the pater familias. In a work addressed not to a governor but to the governed, he suggested that "just as the Romans and other languages traditionally called the men and women in the house 'pater familias' and 'mater familias,' so they called the princes and authorities 'pater patriae,' that is, 'father of the entire country.' It is a great scandal that we who want to be Christians don't call them the same, or at least hold them in the same regard and honor.[81]

Even before this *Great Catechism* of 1529, the Wittenberg theologian had included in his discussion of the Ten Commandments an analysis of the honor owed worldly authority.[82] There appears, in fact, to have been an evolution in thought from his brief discussion in 1518, through the more extended treatment he gave the subject in a sermon delivered at the time of the Peasants' War, to the discussion in the *Great Catechism* itself. In 1518 the fulfilment of the Fourth Commandment consisted only in "willing obedience and submission to all forms of authority for the sake of God's pleasure, as the apostle Peter says, without any dissatisfaction, complaint, or muttering."[83] In contrast, Luther's sermons on Exodus, delivered most probably in October 1525, revealed the impact of the Peasants' War and his fear of anarchy—as well as a newly careful distinction between the relationship based on responsibility and authority and that based on emotional bonds. He opened his discussion of the Fourth Commandment by explaining to his listeners that the injunction to honor father and mother followed the first three Commandments, which related to God himself because it taught "how one should act toward all Authority that acts in God's place."[84] Not surprisingly, considering the violence with which Luther had insisted that the nobility should take up arms against the rebellious peasants, he went on to draw an explicit contrast between political and paternal authority. "The Authority of Princes and Lords isn't a loving authority, but rather a frightening one, since they are the Lord God's jailers, judges, and hangmen, whom he uses to punish bad boys; fathers and mothers, however, aren't frightening but instead wholly friendly."[85] Parents, Luther continued, had only love to give, without harshness or anger.

The Peasants' War did, however, come to an end, and with it Luther's need to portray the civil authority in terms familiar from his harshest attacks on the Catholic church's depiction of Christ himself as an unforgiving judge. If the Catholic emperor did not behave exactly as a loving father toward his subjects, in their more sanguine moods Lutherans might nevertheless model his exercise of authority on that of the good pater familias. In 1530 Luther would offer the servant's obedience to the *Hausherr* as analogue for the obedience the electors owed Charles V in questions of attendance at sermons and liturgical ceremonies; in 1532, the reformer's optimism at the pacifistic letter the emperor had addressed to the imperial estates made Charles V at least momentarily "Caesar vere pater Germaniae."[86] As we have seen, the reformer had already recommended the use of the honorific title in his exegesis of the Fourth Commandment in the *Great Catechism* of 1529.[87]

Martin Luther's use of such paternal language of Charles V may well have expressed the same sort of gentle coercion attempted centuries earlier with no more noticeable success by Seneca.[88] In an essay "On Clemency," addressed to his recalcitrant pupil Nero, Seneca had reminded the emperor: "No one resorts to the exaction of punishment until he has exhausted all the means of correction. This is the duty of a father, and it is also the duty of a prince, whom not in empty flattery we have been led to call 'the Father of his Country.' . . . to 'the Father of his Country' we have given the name in order that he may know that he has been entrusted with a father's power, which is most forbearing in its care for the interests of his children and subordinates his own [interests] to theirs."[89]

Was it coincidence that Luther applied the honorific to his emperor for the second time in the year in which Jean Calvin published his commentary on Seneca's essay?[90] Possibly. By citing Julius Pollux' injunction to Commodus, Erasmus had made the same point in the instruction he addressed in Latin to Charles V in 1516, an instruction published in German at Augsburg and Zurich in 1521: "A king should be praised with the names 'father,' 'virtuous,' 'gentle,' 'mild,' 'gracious,' 'prudent,' 'just,' 'friendly,' 'magnanimous,'. . ."[91] A comparison of various editions of Ulrich Tengler's *Laienspiegel* reveals the popularity of similar language in the 1530s. The editions of that legal handbook published at Straßburg in 1527, 1530, 1532, 1538, 1544 included a phrase to be found in the Augsburg edition of 1512 but missing from the Straßburg editions of 1514 and 1518. In the Straßburg editions of 1527 and later, the sentence "Where the subjects honor and are obedient to authority peace and unity are that much more enduring and each remains in his appointed place," was altered to read: "Where the subjects are held dear by the authorities and the authorities in their turn are honored and obeyed by their subjects peace and unity are that much more enduring and each remains in his appointed place."[92] The same lesson was taught by the Lutheran preacher Johann Agricola in his explication of one of *The Three Hundred Common Proverbs* he dedicated to Herzog Johann Friedrich of Saxony in 1530. After explaining that the Württemberger had even compared Herzog Eberhard I to God because of the "fatherly friendly charity" he had shown them, Agricola went on to contrast Eberhard's government and the honor paid it with the situation under the Roman emperors: "The Romans may have called Augustus, Cicero, and others 'pater patriae'—a father who treated them as a father behaves to his children—but they raised no one so high voluntarily, for Augustus and Domitian insisted on such treatment, that their subjects must sacrifice to them as to gods, under penalty. It was a matter of force."[93]

The possibility of modeling the behavior of princes was not the only reason for the use of paternal language. The adoption of the paternal rather than the hierarchical model might also be used to deny the authority of those who did not behave as "fathers." When—shortly after he had referred to Charles as pater patriae—Martin Luther was pushed finally to allow resistance against the emperor's increasingly militant Catholicism, he attacked the absolute validity of the political hierarchy of the Holy Roman Empire in terms of the rights and responsibilities of the Hausvater or pater familias; this time, of course, it was the prince rather than the emperor who was viewed as enacting the paternal rôle.[94] Luther responded to the imperial threat by questioning the concept of an absolute natural hierarchy in secular affairs and positing instead a structure based on paternal responsibility. In the previous chapter we saw, in a passage from Luther's *Tischreden* of the first half of the 1530s and in the theologians' *Gutachten* to Johann Friedrich of Saxony, how the Lutheran—or rather the Lutheran magistrate whose charges had been forcibly deprived of their religious piety—was cast in the rôle of the protector, in the rôle of Lucretia's father or husband.[95]

Although it may have been nourished by Greek concepts of the family and the political realm, accessible in the writings of medieval and Renaissance authors,[96] Luther's own eventual understanding of the secular order of things had its birth in his anthropomorphized understanding of sacred relationships.[97] The accessibility of Luther's own imagery contributed to the broad appeal of his theological message and at the same time helped to transform the language of political discussion in the empire.

In 1542, six years after the release of the recommendations of the Wittenberg theologians, a group of Regensburg Bürger used the same symbolic language when they petitioned their "city fathers" to allow the use of the Lutheran rite of Communion in those churches under the jurisdiction of the Ratsherren. Given the social and cultural status of the signers, just outside the circle of the inner council,[98] the language of the appeal, quoted above, is particularly interesting; their use of the language of paternity to refer to both earthly and divine magistracies echoed Luther's and seems to have marked the first appearance of this imagery in the city. It would soon find its place in other petitions and in the other strategies by which the Bürger sought to influence the actions of the Rat by emphasizing and reestablishing the immediacy and priority—and even the intimacy—of the relationship between council and citizen.

In Chapter 2 (fig. 17), we observed the decline in references to the Last Judgment in Regensburg wills as the Reformation took hold in the city. As we saw, that decline was accompanied by a change in the way in which God himself was invoked in the wills (fig. 28). God the Creator became God the Father, not only of his only begotten Son but also of Christ's adoptive siblings, the Regensburg testators. In turn, it was this divinely generous father who became the paradigm on which the Regensburger would try to model the behavior of the Ratsherren whose approval they sought in their wills.

The decade 1542–1552 thus saw a transformation in the language used to beg the acquiesence of the Regensburg Ratsherren in the provisions dictated by the testator (fig. 63), as well as in the language used to invoke the divinity himself. The will written by Stadtschreiber Nicolaus Dinzl for Margaretha, widow of the woodcarver Philip Hemerl, in 1545, is the earliest extant testament to have reminded the Ratsherren of their "fatherly love" for their subject as it sought their acquiesence to the testator's bequests.[99] During the next two years both Dinzl and Hans Trost, his Substitut, included the paternal image in wills they wrote. Nevertheless, by no means all of the wills either wrote were phrased in paternal terms: 66.7 percent of the ten wills that survive from Dinzl's hand in the years 1545–1549, and 21 percent of the nineteen wills written by Trost during the same period include the reference to the Rat's "paternal love." By 1548 Hans Pilgerl, another Substitut, was following suit; of the thirteen extant testaments he wrote between that date and 1551, 76.9 percent included the paternal language.

The figures indicate, once again, that while the scribe might have influenced the choice of language, he did not control it. No scribe used the phrase in all of the extant wills he wrote, and none who wrote many wills did not include it at least occasionally. Even Steffan Pöder, who wrote 26 percent of the total wills for the two-decade period when the phrase was dominant in testaments included it in three wills. The twelve scribes whose wills made no references to "fatherly love" accounted for 17.3 percent of the extant wills, but here the numbers are so small that, in light of the evidence from more active scribes, we cannot attribute the lack of such language entirely to the scribe: only two of the twelve wrote more than five wills, none wrote more than ten.

Let us consider more closely the period of "fatherly love"'s greatest popularity in Regensburg's wills—more than 75 percent of the forty-five extant wills written 1548 to 1552 included the image in invocations of the council's support. The dominance of the paternal language becomes even more striking when we realize that 17.7 percent of the extant wills from that half-decade omit any apostrophy of the Rat. In other words, almost 92 percent of the extant wills that apostrophized the Rat between 1548 and 1552 included the paternal image. Nevertheless, we cannot conclude that that language was the only one available during the period: many wills must be characterized in this sense as having been multilingual and both "Beschirmer" (twice) and "Obrigkeit" (once) appeared during the period in wills that omitted the paternal language. Nor can we conclude that the scribes insisted on its use: even Hans Müllner, whose fourteen wills (13 paternal references) written during the two-year period, 1551/1552, accounted for almost 29 percent of the paternal references of the five-year period, did write one will with no such reference. In fact, each of the active scribes wrote wills with and wills without the paternal reference during the period.[100] Nor does gender appear to have greatly influenced the language chosen: women represented 46.7 percent of the testators during the half-decade and 44 percent of those using paternal language.

Although in most cases the language of paternity appears formulaic, part of a standard although by no means requisite phrase whose purpose was to ensure the Rat's approval of the will's provisions, in some cases the paternal image seems to have arisen out of the specific circumstances of the execution of an individual will, a situation that allows us a glimpse of the meaning that might lie behind the formula. Thus a woman concerned on her deathbed about the welfare of her children might, like Elisabeth, Lutheran widow of the patrician Ratsherr and Hannsgraf Karl Gartner, commend her soul and her children to her god in the same language: "I commend my poor sinful soul, through Christ my savior and salvation, to my true dear God and Father, full of grace and mercy, into his powerful hands. Amen. To him I commend also the children I leave behind, as to a wealthy father who can preserve them from all harm."[101]

Elisabeth herself had no special need to beg the care of the Rat for her children; for that she could rely on relatives such as the Stadtadvocat Johann Hiltner, the Lutheran minister Nikolaus Gallus, and her son-in-law and member of the Innerer Rat Caspar Portner.[102] Others, less fortunate, felt greater need for shaping a paternal and protective relationship between their heirs and the Rat. This was particularly the case for Katherina, Catholic widow of the prince bishop's wine steward Hans Haider. On her deathbed she commended to the paternal care of the Rat her niece Elisabeth Erhard, a single woman who had served her fifteen years. Through a gift to the city's tax office of fifty Rheinish Gulden as well as through language paternal and complimentary, she tried to ensure both her heir's protection and her right to continue to pursue her Catholic religion unmolested: "And I comfort myself modestly that their Noble, Honored, Farsighted, Honorable Wisdoms will therefore allow my universal heir to be commended to their paternal protection, but nevertheless without interference in Religion."[103] Similar language appeared natural to the testator who, like the young bath-house attendant Michael Schuester, who had cared for his younger sister in Regensburg although their father was still alive in another town, wanted to leave a sum of money for the benefit of his siblings (all referred to using diminutives) in the municipal *Vormundamt*, the bureau that had been established in 1537 to oversee orphans with legacies as well as for those without: "And I obediently beg the honorable Cammerer and Rat here, as my generous dear overlords and fathers, that their Wisdoms will lay down my abovementioned dear siblings' *Legata* in their praiseworthy Vormundamt, to [my siblings'] advantage and better support."[104]

Where orphans and widows were concerned, the connection between divine and secular protection was a natural one, one justified by the Old Testament itself. Several of the extant wills referred specifically to Psalm 68:5, in which God himself appeared as the "father of the fatherless and a judge of the widows." Lorenz Ludwig, minister in Regensburg's St. Lazarus chapel, used the passage to commend his "dear wife Margareth to my dear faithful God and the honorable Cammerer and Rat of this praiseworthy and ancient imperial city Regensburg." The temporal authorities should "show her all goodly and paternal will because she is without relatives. The true and merciful God, as father of orphans and judge of widows, will not let such action go unrewarded—of this I am certain in my heart."[105] In other wills an interesting elision occurred: God, the father of the Christ who would no longer judge the temporal works of Christians on the last day, was himself no longer judge of widows, but father only. Thus, in a will dictated to an imperial notary in Schwandorf, the Lutheran Margaret Meier (née Kradl), mother of Regensburg's Catholic chronicler Jeremiah Grünewaldt, commended both her second husband and her sons by her first marriage to the "Noble, Honored, Farsighted, Honorable, and Wise Lords Cammerer and Rat" of Regensburg with the reminder that "the Almighty, who is a father to all widows and orphans, would reward them richly" for their care.[106]

The contrast between judge and father was made explicit by another Lutheran clergyman, Wolfgang Waldner, preacher in Regensburg's Neupfarrkirche. God, who "might and should" have acted "as a just God and Judge," leaving the testator mired in the blindness of his sins and papist idolatry, had instead acted as a "merciful father," redeeming him from his deserved damnation.[107] Having acknowledged God's paternal goodness, Waldner turned to the paternal goodness shown him by the Regensburg Rat, "my dear lords and fathers, [who] have cared for me with generous support for more than twenty years, first in the preacher's office in this true church under their gracious protection, and now in my weak old age," and finally to the "paternal loyalty and goodness" he himself had shown his own children.[108]

Other testators used similar language, like Waldner not attempting to model the Rat's future behavior, but rather acknowledging and giving thanks for a special relationship already perceived as existing between the testator and the council. Barbara, widow of Wolfgang Klopfinger, scribe in the municipal salt office, was commanded by her husband's will personally to give each Ratsherr a Rheinish Gulden because the councillors had "not only admitted me to citizenship but also and above all accepted me for one of their offices in order that I could that much more easily keep and feed myself; in fatherly fashion they kept me and advanced my well-being in other ways."[109]

In 1525, Martin Luther had preached the difference between governors and parents. "The Obrigkeit of the princes and lords," he said, "is not a loving Obrigkeit, but a terrifying one, since they are our Lord God's jailers, judges, and hangmen, with whom he punishes the bad boys, but father and mother aren't terrifying but wholly friendly. In Romans 13 it says of the Obrigkeit, that they should turn away the bad wild people and protect the pious, for this reason they take money, customs duty, and taxes; but father and mother is a gentle, fine, happy Obrigkeit, they don't take anything from their children; instead they risk body and life, put all their property and possessions in the balance, wager neck and stomach and everything they have for their children. Worldly Obrigkeit wants only to have; parents can't do anything but give, for their children are their own flesh and blood."[110] Nevertheless, by 1529 Martin Luther was using paternal language in a way that suggested an effort to model the emperor's behavior toward the Lutherans as well as an effort to model the behavior of subjects toward the authority.[111] Our examination of the wills executed at Regensburg in the decades after the Rat announced the city's official conversion to Lutheranism reveals that the Bürger too could use paternal language in an attempt to create or acknowledge a new type of governmental Obrigkeit.

### The Reformation and the Rat as "Father" in Decrees

That the Lord Christ loves us so much beyond our comprehension is proven by the fact that he rendered obedience to his father and willingly let himself in for suffering for our sake. (Bartholomeus Rosinus, Regensburg preacher, 1577)[112]

Although they have preferred up to now to carry out their office of Obrigkeit toward their beloved Bürger and Gemeinde with paternal gentleness and leniency rather than with sharp, harsh, and serious punishment, their Wisdoms nevertheless have learned with heavy hearts and pain that paternal love and partiality alone doesn't lead to or bear the fruit of appropriate obedience. . . . (Regensburg Rat, 1591)[113]

If paternity required special care on the part of the parent, it expected filial piety of the child in return. Thus, in choosing to use paternal language to model their relationship to the Rat, the Bürger had to acknowledge their childlike dependency on the greater power and wisdom of their governors in order to claim the personal benefits of a more intimate relationship with them. Similarly, when, after 1565, the Rat itself began using paternal language in its decrees (fig. 67), it not only laid claim to greater power and

**67.** Decrees imaging Rat as "Obrigkeit" vs. "Vater" as percentage of all decrees, Regensburg, 1520–1600.

wisdom in such language; it also acknowledged a special responsibility for its subjects, a special concern to treat them, in fact, not as subjects but as beloved children.[114]

Analyses of *Hausväterliteratur* have often ignored the fact that, at least in the sixteenth-century examples of the genre, a distinction was preserved between the Hausvater's relationship to his children and his relationship to his servants. If, as Justus Menius and his modern successors have argued, "*Politia* or the government of a land must have its origin in *Oeconomia* or housekeeping, out of which it springs like a fountain,"[115] we must remember that for Menius government was to be understood in terms of household, not household in terms of government. More important, Menius carefully preserved the distinction between child and employee, recommending: "It is not enough that pious children should merely fear their God, creator, lord, and father; they should rather also recognize that he wants to be gracious and merciful, and in everything show himself to them and treat them as a true, friendly, dear father would treat his beloved children,"[116] but *not* using similar language of the relationship between master and servants.[117] Luther himself, in his translations of Christ's parables, was careful to preserve the distinction between Vater and Hausvater, using the term "Hausvater" only where the masterful rather than the parental relationship was intended.[118]

With this in mind, then, we turn to the use of the paternal analogy by the Regensburg Ratsherren.

In 1537, in the decree that established the same Vormundamt to whose care Bürger like Michael Schuester would leave legacies for their children and siblings, the Regensburg Rat wrote of its responsibilities as Obrigkeit to act "to the praise of Almighty God and for the advantage of the common good."[119] Supervision of orphans was necessary because "there is and can be no more upright and God-pleasing regime than one where such upright and well-reared people govern and are governed,"[120] but also out of concern for easing the anguish of parent on their deathbeds: "In order that the parents may feel and see that their children won't be abandoned at their deaths, but that they may be considered, supervised, and raised through the care of the Obrigkeit, no less than as if the parents themselves still lived and were there."[121] Nevertheless, despite the fact that the Rat offered itself in the parent's stead with the erection of the new municipal bureau, it acted in 1537 "von Oberkeyt wegen," rather than out of paternal love for its Bürger. A half-dozen years later, after the city's official conversion, the Rat, in what could be described as a council's "sermon" on moral issues, referred repeatedly to God's "paternal visitations," his warnings and temporal punishments of his adopted children's sins.[122] As in the earlier decrees, the councillors held their office from God, at least implicitly: they acted "in order that the honorable Rat here, as the established Obrigkeit, not be despised, as if such shameful sins and vices occurred with their knowledge and approval, but instead that their just disapproval be felt herein, that they may be acquitted of this before God and the world."[123]

The language of authority changed slowly; what worked was abandoned with reluctance. In fact, in Regensburg's decrees the distancing language of Obrigkeit was not abandoned but rather supplemented by the paternal imagery already common in the wills written for the Bürger. After almost two decades of usage in the Regensburg wills opened and read before the Rat, and in references to God in the decrees written for the Rat itself, in the second half of the 1560s we encounter the first reference to paternity applied to the Rat itself in Regensburg's extant decrees (fig. 68). In a decree dealing with religious issues, God was praised for his paternal concern, for his caring salvation of humankind from the deep darkness of the papacy, and particularly for his having first of all delivered the message of salvation to "Germany, our dear fatherland."[124] Neither the Rat nor the Bürger were, however, to be allowed to forget God's just wrath and the punishment he was forced daily to administer to his ungrateful children. The councillors must play their rôle in the divine plan; acting "wholly true and paternal," they therefore required all subjects, Bürger, and relatives to attend Communion and sermons willingly and often.[125] Whoever did not—and here both "fathers" are joined explicitly—would be punished as a despiser of God and Obrigkeit, as well as of the religious peace published by the Reich.[126] The

**68.** Wills and decrees imaging Rat as "Father" as percentage of all wills and decrees, Regensburg, 1542–1600.

Obrigkeit never disappeared, but it coexisted throughout the remainder of the century with the more intimate view of municipal government implied in paternal language.

The more intimate and concrete conceptualization of political relationships implied by the use of paternal language did not vanish from Regensburg's decrees although the invocation of the Rat as father virtually disappeared from the testamentary petitions of the Bürger after 1570 (fig. 68). While the transformed language of the wills was apparently connected with a change in the will-making process itself, the reason for the continued popularity of paternal language in decrees after it had for the most part disappeared from the wills in which it had first appeared was probably connected to contemporary perceptions of paternity.[127] Gerald Strauss has reminded us of the pessimistic affinity between the *Weltanschauung* of the Ratsherr forced to deal daily with recalcitrant Bürger and the Lutheran acceptance of the impossibility of the mortal's ever achieving true goodness and earning salvation.[128] If we look at the wills and decrees issued in the Lutheran city Regensburg, we discover another, more emotionally compelling, affinity. Bartholomeus Rosinus, the Lutheran preacher at Regensburg who, in the Good Friday sermon quoted above, had emphasized Christ's obedience to his father's command, even unto passion and death, felt himself forced to restrict his own son Peter's inheritance a half-dozen years later; he complained in his autograph will: "He left his occupation and studies, ran away from me, conducted himself badly in Zwickau and then ran away from that city, making his mother sick to death. His unfilial disobedience has brought me into extreme and deathly bitterness. Neither has he shown contrition for this nor begged forgiveness."[129]

Such ingratitude and disobedience seemed to sixteenth-century parents all too common. In the words of one "familiar German proverb" quoted by Johann Agricola in his collection of 1530: "A father is more capable of supporting ten children than ten children are of supporting one father."[130] The 1566 decree, quoted at the end of the last chapter, in which the Regensburg Rat reminded its Bürger of the daily punishment visited by God on his ungrateful children, had opened with another reminder—that the last days of the world were at hand. Disobedience to parents was, in fact, one indication that the world was in its final days according to the passage from Paul's second letter to Timothy inscribed at the bottom of the panel of the *Four Apostles* painted by Albrecht Dürer and given by him to the Nuremberg Rat.[131] That being the case, it was natural that many of Regensburg's Bürger should have been convinced the end was near.

In any decade in the sixteenth century, between 10 and 25 percent of the extant Regensburg wills mentioning children indicated tension between parent and child strong enough for the parent to attempt to cut off or to limit the child's inheritance (fig. 69).[132] The conditions under which such a step could be legally taken were carefully circumscribed: (1) when the child had raised his or her hand against the parent or conspired to poison the parent; (2) when the child had brought criminal charges involving capital or corporal punishment against his or her parent, except in cases of heresy and treason; (3) when the child had attempted adultery with a stepparent; (4) when a son had refused to put up bond for his unjustly imprisoned father; (5) when the child had prevented the parent from making a proper will; (6) when the child had taken up the baiting of wild animals or some other frivolous or dishonorable occupation (procurer or prostitute), unless the parent had also done the same; (7) when a daughter under twenty-five years of age had refused to marry according to her father's advice and, in addition, had led an unchaste life; (8) when the parent was simple or poor and the child had refused relatives' pleas that he or she provide care and medication; and (9) when the parent was a Christian and the child a heretic.[133]

The relative difficulty of disinheriting a child meant, at least in the case of the extant wills for Regensburg, that even where tension existed complete disinheritance was rare. Attempts at partial disinheritance were generally accompanied by some specification of the child's misdeeds, as well as by a phrase indicating that the child should be completely disinherited if he or she were to contest the will's provisions—apparently a powerful threat since no

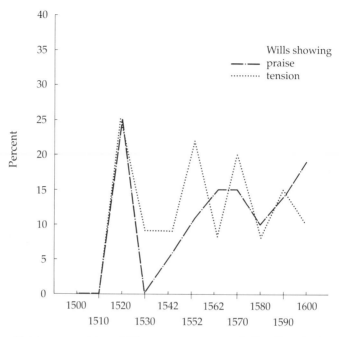

**69.** Wills criticizing or praising children as percentage of all wills referring to offspring, Regensburg, 1500–1600.

challenges are recorded in the surviving documents. In most cases, the parent protested that the limited legacy provided for was given not because the child deserved it but only out of parental partiality and unwillingness to cut off flesh and blood. Among other bequests, the Lutheran Margaretha, widow of Leonhart Aichenseer, set aside three Gulden for the Almosenamt, the municipal charitable bureau, two Taler for her *Beichtvater* or confessor, four for her stepdaughter, three for her stepsister, and three Gulden for her niece, but provided ten Gulden for her daughter Margaretha "in order that this, my last will and testament, be that much less subject to challenge," claiming that her daughter "throughout her life has shown herself and acted toward me and my dear husband, her deceased father, not as an obedient pious child, but instead conducted an unchaste and irregular life while single, had a child out of wedlock, and then married without my or her father's (my dear dead husband's) knowledge and permission."[134] As was frequently the case, the will concluded with a provision that the residue of the property go to another child "from whom I have received much filial love and loyalty."[135] The language of the last will of the Stadthauptmann Heinrich Schmidt and his wife Margaretha, who had taken their grandchildren into their own home, was fairly typical, but it allows us to see the same speaker using paternal language in personal and political contexts and in private as well as in semipublic documents. Schmidt and his wife left a limited inheritance to their son Hans Heinrich, whose troubled adolescence, marriage, and debts Heinrich Schmidt had described in his personal chronicle together with the actions he himself had performed "out of fatherly love," not because they owed it to him, since "as everyone knows, he has acted in such a manner that we would have true and just cause to legally disinherit him," but because of "fatherly and motherly partiality."[136] If Hans Heinrich should dispute the provisions of the will, he was to be entirely disinherited in favor of his children. In the chronicle Schmidt kept for his heirs we find strikingly similar paternal language used of the Ratsherren, despite the fact that Schmidt proved himself capable of criticizing their actions in the same private document. An entry bemoaning the fact that the Rat would not grant him temporary release from his municipal contract in 1575 in order that he might take up a profitable position in the imperial army was followed by an entry for the same year about a dispute among Rat, school rector, and popular preacher in which Schmidt's approval of the concilliar position was manifest in the paternal language he used to describe their actions. The Rat had several times cautioned the pastor and rector "very paternally;" they had then written of the dispute to other cities "out of fatherly concern"; finally, "since the fraud they didn't understand was daily becoming more rooted among the ununderstanding Bürger," the Rat was forced to drastic measures—and here the metaphor changed—"they had to discover a medicine by which the rotten flesh would be cut away from the body while the remaining limbs stayed fresh and sound."[137]

Theologians such as Johann Agricola sometimes argued that even the carefully reared offspring of the best and wisest parents might turn out badly as a display of divine power,[138] but an analysis of the family situations in which the tension between parent and child was severe enough to influence the testamentary provisions made by the parent suggests that temporal factors, particularly remarriage and the existence of a stepparent, could play key rôles in intrafamilial stress. Whether because of actual tension between the child and the stepparent, or because the testator found it necessary to argue that such tension existed in order to make more generous provision for the recently acquired spouse, 57.9 percent of the disobedience reported in the wills took place in families where remarriage had occurred, although only 45.8 percent of all testators with children reported more than one marriage in their wills (figs. 70 and 71). Looked at differently, 15 percent of all remarried testators with children complained that one or more had been seriously disobedient. The figure was highest for men who had remarried—19 percent of those with children complained of them and their children accounted for over 42 percent of all cases of filial impiety reported in wills despite the fact that only 25 percent of the children mentioned in wills were mentioned by fathers who had remarried (figs. 70, 71, and 72). The impact of such figures on the society looks more serious when we consider that remarriage was a common phenomenon in early modern society, particularly among men—

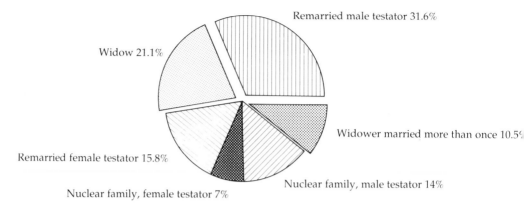

**70.** Family situation and gender of testator of Regensburg wills with complaints of disobedient children, 1500–1600.

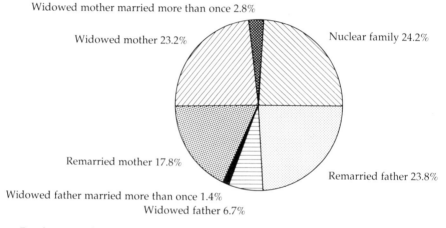

**71.** Family status of testator with offspring reported in Regensburg wills, 1500–1600.

fewer than 15 percent of all male testators in Regensburg were alone because of the loss of a spouse or failure to marry by the time they dictated their wills; the figure for women was over 40 percent (fig. 73).[139]

In light of the very apparent impact of remarriage on family relations it would be unjust to suggest that tensions between parents and children were a result of the spread of Lutheranism.[140] Nevertheless, the emphasis on the filial piety demonstrated by the willingness of Christ's sacrifice confronted the Christian with an unattainable ideal, and the splintering of the Christian church provided, at the least, an arena for the display of such tensions. In his autograph will, Friderich Sebaldt, Lutheran deacon in Regensburg, cut his son Niclas off with only ten Gulden "because, although I arranged for him to learn an honorable trade, he nevertheless abandoned that trade and—against my will—committed himself to the Jesuit cult, falling away from the pure teaching of the divine Scripture."[141] Other parents included provisions

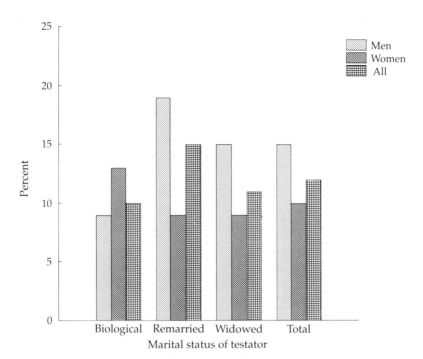

**72.** Marital status of testators of wills restricting children's inheritance as percentage of all Regensburg wills, 1500–1600.

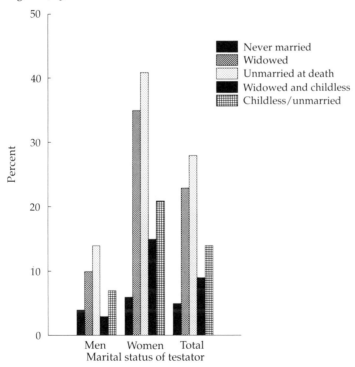

**73.** Testators unmarried at time will written as percentage of all Regensburg testators, 1500–1600.

that their children inherit only if they abided by the true Christian faith—naturally that was understood to be the faith of the parent. Herr Georg Weynsbrünner, Ritter von Salzburg and lord of Eggmuhl, owner of two houses in Regensburg, announced in his will his adoption of a cousin's son to replace the son he had never had. The emperor himself had approved the former Hans Praunsehe's adoption of the Weynsbrünner name and privileges. Nevertheless, should the "adopted son and heir fall away from the right and true Christian church and Religion, the Augsburg Confession," the Obrigkeit of the city of Regensburg was to take two thousand Gulden from Hans' legacy and dedicate it to the good of the churches of the Augsburg Confession.[142] The elimination of heresy as a just cause for the disinheritance of a child by the *Nürnberger Reformation* of 1564 is probably the result of a marked increase in such charges.[143]

If biological parenthood provided mixed blessings in the form of grateful and ungrateful children, the parental rôle of the Regensburg Rat, as expressed in the language it addressed to its subject "children" in its decrees as opposed to the language in which it was addressed by those "children" in their wills, appears to have had more in common with the parental rôle of God the Father, whose adoptive children, in contrast to Christ himself, were constitutionally incapable of acting with the love, respect, and obedience his paternal love and generosity deserved. Certainly the decrees issued after the Rat itself had adopted paternal language for the description of its relationship to the Bürger spoke of the loving parent's need to punish for the good of the child and of the child's disobedience and lack of filial respect, rather than of the parent's pleasure at the child's obedience. This may explain why, in the end, the paternal language seemed more appropriate to the expression of the governor's perspective than to that of the governed, why the Rat itself continued to find paternal language an appropriate expression of its relationship to the Bürger in the decrees it issued into the seventeenth century.

# Frequently Used
# Abbreviations

| | |
|---|---|
| AHVR | Archiv des Historischen Vereins für Oberpfalz und Regensburg, Regensburg |
| HStAM | Hauptstaatsarchiv, Munich |
| StAR | Stadtarchiv, Regensburg |
| StBM | Staatsbibliothek, Munich |
| StBR | Staatliche Bibliothek, Regensburg |
| Bartsch | Adam von Bartsch, *Le Peintre-Graveur* (Vienna, 1808). |
| *Catalogus* | Elia Ehinger, *Catalogus Bibliothecae Amplissimae Reipub. Ratisbonensis* (Johann Rhelino, amanuensis, 1638). StBR, Rat. civ. 430. |
| Grünewaldt | Franciscus Hieremia Grünewaldt, *Ratisbonae oder Summarische Beschreibung der Uralten Nahmhafften Stadt Regenspurg Auf- und Abnehmung, und wie man sie heut nach siehet; deren führnehmsten Geist- und weltlichen Zierden, darum sie sowol heut als ein Kayl. Gefreyte ReichsStadt, als vor Alters ein Bayl. Königl. und Fürstl. Residenz und Haupt-Stadt, ansehnl. u. beruhmt ist* (1615). StAR, MS Ratisb. IAe2 Nr. 9. |
| *Illustrated Bartsch* | Adam von Bartsch, *The Illustrated Bartsch*, ed. Walter L. Strauss. Multiple volumes (New York, 1978–   ). |
| *Index* | *Index Generalis Secundum ordinem Pulpitorum confectus ostendens, quae scripta singulis voluminibus contineantur; Ein gemein Register Uber alle bucher, so in eines erbarn Camerer und Rhats Liberei alhie zu Regenspurg an Ketten, gelegt sind, und dieselben nach einander auf den Pulpiten ligen, etc. Wievil auch Tractetlein in einem ieden buch zusamen gebunden sind* (compiled after 1574, possibly in 1593 by Jonas Paulus Wolf). AHVR, AA R 44. |
| Kayser, *Dekretensammlung* | Johann Friedrich Kayser, ed., *Sammlung derer von einem Wohledlen Hoch- und Wohlweisen Herrn Stadt Cammerer und Rath der des Heil. Röm. Reichs Freyen Stadt Regenspurg an Ihre untergebene Burgerschafft von Zeit zu Zeit im Druck erlassenen Decreten* (Regensburg 1754). |
| Meder | Joseph Meder, *Dürer-Katalog* (Vienna, 1932). |

| | |
|---|---|
| Panofsky | Erwin Panofsky, *Albrecht Dürer* (Princeton, 1943). |
| *Patrologia* | *Patrologiae cursus completus omnius ss. patrum, doctorum scriptorumque ecclesiasticorum sive latinorum, sive graecorum. Series latina*, ed. J.-P. Migne, 221 volumes (Paris, 1844–1864). |
| Passavant | J. D. Passavant, *Le Peintre-Graveur*. 6 volumes. (Leipzig, 1860–1864). |
| Schmidt, *Chronik* | Heinrich Schmidt, *Item In dissem Buech ist beschriben Allerlay Handlungen so mich Hainrichen Schmidt der Zeyt Stadthauptman zu Regenspurg sambt den Mainigen von Jharn zu Jharn betroffen unnd durch unns ist gehandellt worden wellchs von dem 1523 Jar Anfacht unnd ferner bis Ins 1583 Jars beschribn worden unnd gendt ist gott der Almechtig gebe sein genad ferner Ammen.?* (begun 1583). AHVR, Ms. Ratisb. 357. |
| Schottenloher | Karl Schottenloher, *Das Regensburger Buchgewerbe im 15. und 16. Jahrhundert mit Akten und Druckverzeichnis* (Mainz, 1920). Items from the catalogue that makes up the bulk of Schottenlohr's work are cited by number following his name. |
| Schramm | Albert Schramm, *Bilderschmuck der Frühdrucke*, 23 volumes (Leipzig, 1920–1943). |
| *WA* | Martin Luther, *D. Martin Luthers Werke. Kritische Gesammtausgabe*, Section 1: *Werke*, 63 volumes (Weimar, 1883–1987). |
| *WA Bibel* | *D. Martin Luthers Werke*. Section 3: *Deutsche Bibel*, 13 volumes (Weimar, 1906–1961). |
| *WA Briefe* | Martin Luther, *D. Martin Luthers Werke*. Section 4: *Briefwechsel*, 18 volumes (Weimar, 1930–1985). |
| *WA Tischreden* | Martin Luther, *D. Martin Luthers Werke*. Section 5: *Tischreden*, 6 volumes (Weimar, 1912–1921). |
| Weller | Emil Weller, *Annalen der politischen National-Literatur der Deutschen im XVI. und XVII. Jahrhundert*, 2 volumes (Freiberg i. Br., 1862–1864). |
| Widmann, *Chronik* | Leonhard Widmann, *Chronik von Regensburg*, ed. E. V. Oefele [Die Chroniken der deutschen Städte 15 (Leipzig, 1878)]. |

# Notes

1. Most recently and usefully by Robert W. Scribner, *For the Sake of Simple Folk: Popular Propaganda for the German Reformation* (Cambridge, 1981).

*Prolegomena* "In His Image and Likeness": Luther's Revision of the
                    Augustinian Epistemology

1. Vulgate translation: "& ait. Faciamus hominem ad imaginem & similitudinem nostram." Quoted from the "Complutensian Polyglott": *Vetus testamentum multiplici lingua nunc primo impressum. Et imprimis Pentateuchus Hebraico Greco atque Chaldaico idiomate. Ad iuncta unicuique sua latina interpretatione*, vol. 1 (Academia Complutensi, Alcalá de Henares: Arnaldus Guillelmus de Brocario, 1517), fol. aii.

In my translation, I have replaced "man" with "humankind" to reflect the Vulgate text's *hominem* and the insistence of both Augustine and Luther (based on the following verse, Genesis 1:27) that the passage referred to both male and female: "huic quod scriptum est in Genesi, Fecit deus hominem, ad imaginem dei fecit eum, masculum & foeminam fecit eos, & bene dixit eos. Ad imaginem quippe dei naturam ipsam humanam factam dicit, quae sexu utroque completur, nec ab intelligenda imagine dei separat foeminam. Dicto enim quod fecit deus hominem ad imaginem dei, fecit eum inquit masculum & foeminam: vel certe alia distinctione, masculum & foeminam fecit eos." Augustine, *De trinitate* XII, vii; quoted from Augustine, *Opera omnia*, ed. Desiderius Erasmus (Basel: Johann Froben, 1528 [vols. 1–7 dated 1528; vols. 8–10, and table of contents and index bound at front of first volume dated 1529]; hereafter cited as Erasmus ed. [1528]), vol. 3, p. 281 = *Patrologia*, vol. 42, col. 1003. This was the first complete edition of Augustine's works. In the copy I used (Houghton Library, Harvard University, *fNC5 .Er153 .528a2, vol. 2/3), the above passage was annotated in the margin by a sixteenth-century reader: "& foemina non excluditur"—a point I stress because a misreading of this passage has been included in the plethora of charges of sexism recently leveled against Augustine. In fact, Augustine concluded the chapter quoted above, in which he assigned himself the difficult task of reconciling Genesis 1:26–27 with I Corinthians 11:7 by interpreting Paul's description of man as the "image and glory of God" and woman as the "glory of man" "figuratively and mystically." As his sixteenth-century reader correctly noted, Augustine closed the chapter insisting that the *imago dei* of Genesis 1:26 referred to that portion of the mind capable of turning toward the eternal verities, that portion "which it is obvious that not only males but also females possess" ("quam non solum masculos sed etiam feminas habere manifestum est"). Luther made the same point by referring to Adam and Eve: "Heva fuerit praestantissima creatura, similis Adae, quod ad imaginem Dei attinet. . . . ut significet Hevam quoque a Deo factam fuisse, consortem imaginis et similitudinis divinae, item imperii super omnia." Martin Luther, *In Primum Librum Mose Enarrationes* (delivered 1535–1545; published 1544–1550), *WA* 42–44; here, 42:51–52.

2. "[According to Augustine] there is nothing in nature that does not bear some resemblance to the Trinity and that may not, as a result, help us to get some idea of it. In its proper sense, however, the distinction of being an image belongs only to man, and in man it belongs by right only to his soul, and in his soul it belongs by right only to the mind (*mens*), for this is the highest part and the one nearest to God." Etienne Gilson, *The Christian Philosophy of Saint Augustine*, trans. L. E. M. Lynch (New York, 1960), p. 219.

3. On the trinitarian interpretation of the first-person plural "let us create" (Vulgate: *faciamus*): "At vero illa imago, de qua dictum est: Faciamus hominem ad imaginem & similitudinem nostram, quia non dictum est, ad meam vel ad tuam, ad imaginem trinitas factum hominem credimus, & quanta potuimus investigatione comprehendimus." Augustine, *De trinitate* XIV, xix; quoted from Erasmus ed. (1528), vol. 3, p. 313 = *Patrologia*, vol. 42, col. 1055. See also *De civitate dei* XVI, vi, and *De trinitate* I, vii; XII, vi, and Ambrose's similar analysis of the passage: *Hexaemeron* VI, vii = Ambrose, *Opera omnia*, ed. Desiderius Erasmus (Basel: Johann Froben, 1527), vol. 4, p. 82 = *Patrologia*, vol. 14, col. 272–273. On the relation between the *Hexaemeron* and Augustine's thought, particularly the question of whether the *Hexaemeron* contains the substance of the sermons Augustine heard Ambrose preach in Milan, see Gerald A. McCool, "The Ambrosian Origin of Augustine's Theology of the Image of God in Man," *Theological Studies* 20 (1959), pp. 62–81, esp. pp. 65–68, 71, citing P. Courcelle, *Recherches sur les "Confessions" de saint Augustin* (Paris, 1950), pp. 101–102.

Martin Luther insisted at somewhat greater length on the same interpretation of *faciamus* in the lectures he delivered on Genesis, 1535–1545: *In Primum Librum Mose Enarrationes*, *WA* 42:43–44.

The use of *faciamus* was crucial to Augustine in another context as well. While the definition of *similitudo* was limited to "likeness" in our sense of "simulation," *imago* might be used in a limited and stronger sense. For an object to be an "image" of another required not only that it displayed a likeness to the other, but also that it had been generated in some way from the other. Thus humankind was not only in some weak way "like" the godhead, but also in its image, because created by it. A perfect image required the further identity of substance; a son might stand in this relationship to his father. In this sense, only Christ was the perfect image of the Father. Michael Schmaus, *Die psychologische Trinitätslehre des Hl. Augustinus* [Münsterische Beiträge zur Theologie 11 (Münster, 1927)], pp. 361–364.

4. Gilson, *Christian Philosophy*, p. 219. For Gilson's very useful interpretation of this aspect of Augustine's thought, see pp. 221–223.

5. *De trinitate* XIV, viii. Gilson's cautionary words are here appropriate: "It is tempting, but it would be dangerous to separate the problem of the *mens* from that of the Trinity and apply it to the study of the human soul, for while this kind of transposition would gratify our taste for order and distinctions, it would cut Augustinian psychology off from its theological roots and Augustinian theology from its psychological roots. What the philosopher has joined together let us not sunder artificially." Gilson, *Christian Philosophy*, p. 220. To separate Augustinian psychology from Augustinian theology appears to me not so much dangerous as impossible.

6. *De trinitate* X, ix; cf. X, v, viii. On the problem of self-knowledge in Augustine's work in general, see Pierre Courcelle, *Connais-toi toi même de Socrate à saint Bernard* (Paris, 1974), pp. 125–163. In addition to *De trinitate*, Augustine's letters to Nebridius and his *De Genesi ad litteram* constitute the starting point for discussions of the medieval understanding of the human intellect and psyche as well as of the medieval church's understanding of its triune god. The year 1927 saw the publication of two important works on Augustine's triads in general and *De trinitate* in particular: they were analyzed briefly by Murray Wright Bundy, *The Theory of Imagination in Classical and Mediaeval Thought* [University of Illinois Studies in Language and Literature 12 (Urbana, 1927)]; and in much greater detail by Schmaus, *Psychologische Trinitätslehre*. Cf. also, Alfred Schindler, *Wort und Analogie in Augustines Trinitätslehre* [Hermeneutische Untersuchungen zur Theologie 4 (Tübingen, 1956)], and Erich Dinkler, *Die Anthropologie Augustines* (Stuttgart, 1934). More generally, see Gilson, *Christian Philosophy*, esp. pp. 217–224, and the chart given in Eugène Portalié, *A Guide to the Thought of Saint Augustine*, trans. R. J. Bastian (London, 1960), pp. 134–135.

7. *De trinitate* XIV, iii. On the consubstantiality of the mental trinity, see XIV, vi–vii; XV, iii. Cf. Schmaus, *Psychologische Trinitätslehre*, pp. 220–225.

Augustine further explained that these three aspects of the mind constituted the true "image and likeness" of God not only because of the ways in which they related to one another, but also because, working together, memory, intellect, and will "can remember, understand, and love that by which they were made." *De trinitate* XIV, xii; cf. Schmaus, *Psychologische Trinitätslehre*, pp. 264–281.

8. "Iamne igitur ascendendum est qualibuscunque intentionis viribus ad illam summam & altissimam essentiam, cuius impar imago est humana mens, sed tamen imago." *De trinitate* X, xii; quoted from Erasmus ed. (1528), vol. 3, p. 269 = *Patrologia*, vol. 42, col. 984. On the meaning of *intentio* in Augustine's writings, see below, note 9.

9. The phrase "qualibuscunque intentionis viribus," translated by McKenna as "exert ourselves to the utmost of our mental powers," and by Burnaby as "with such power of concentration as is at our disposal," seems to me to refer not generally to the capacities of the human mind, but specifically to the powers of the human will, limited (*qualibuscunque*) by the Fall. Cf. the conjunction of *intentio* and *voluntas* as "the will's intention" in the following passage, Augustine's summary of book XI of *De trinitate*: "Deinde in ipso animo, ab his quae extrinsecus sensa sunt velut introducta inventa est altera trinitas, ubi apparerent eadem tria unius esse substantiae, imaginatio corporis quae in memoria est, & inde informatio cum ad eam convertitur acies cogitantis, & utrunque coniungens intentio voluntatis." *De trinitate* XV, iii; quoted from Erasmus ed. (1528), vol. 3, p. 316 = *Patrologia*, vol. 42, col. 1060. *The Trinity*, trans. Stephen McKenna [The Fathers of the Church 45 (Washington, D.C., 1963)], p. 312; Augustine, *Later Works*, trans. John Burnaby [The Library of the Christian Classics 8 (Philadelphia, 1955)], p. 89. It is worth noting that Burnaby omitted *intentio* from the "Note on terminology" with which he prefaced his translation of the second half of *De trinitate*; nevertheless, under the rubric "*Amor* and *Charitas*" he noted that the primary connotation of the *amor* in Augustine's work was "desire": "It is the motive of all human action, the source of energy which compels a man to seek the satisfaction of his needs; and Augustine compares it to the force of gravity. . . . it is important to observe that both *amor* and *charitas* include feeling as well as striving or conation. . . . So Augustine can define love as 'nothing else but the will, seeking after *or holding in possession* an object of enjoyment' (*De Trin.*, XIV, 8 (vi))—a definition which makes clear the difference in connotation between 'will' and 'love.' The two words denote one and the same activity, but *voluntas* fixes attention upon the conative element in this activity, while *amor* always connotes feeling." Ibid., pp. 35–36 (emphasis in the original).

Of "love" and "striving," which "cannot yet be called 'love,' but nevertheless is found in the same region and belongs to the same type of activity," Schmaus writes: "All of these activities belong to the realm of the will." *Psychologische Trinitätslehre*, p. 381. Cf. *De trinitate* IX, iii. I agree. The connection of "striving," "attention," "intention," and "will" makes much more sense of the following passage from *De trinitate* XI, i: "tamen, ut dixi, tanta facta est in corporibus consuetudo, & ita in haec miro modo relabens foras se nostra proiecit intentio, ut cum ab incerto corporum ablata fuerit, ut in spiritum multo certiore ac stabiliore cognitione figatur, refugiat ad ista, & ibi appetat requiem unde traxit infirmitatem." Quoted from Erasmus ed. (1528), vol. 3, p. 269 = *Patrologia*, vol. 42, cols. 984–985. And, in fact, the capacity to which Augustine has referred five times as *animi intentio* in the first half of the second chapter of the same book, has by the end of the same chapter become the *voluntas animi*. Cf. Erasmus ed. (1528), vol. 3, pp. 276–277 = *Patrologia*, vol. 42, cols. 985–987. Cf. the other uses of *intentio* in *De Genesi ad litteram* XII, xii: "cogitationis intentione," "in sensibus corporis intentione," and "animi intento a sensibus corporis." Quoted from Erasmus ed. (1528), vol. 3, p. 487 = *Patrologia*, vol. 34, col. 463; and XII, xxi–xxii: "quorum dormiendo avertitur intentio a sensu vigilandi," "Ita quamvis diversa sit causa intentionis alienatae," and "Vigilantibus etiam neque ullo morbo afflictis nec furore exagitatis, occulto quodam instinctu ingestas esse cogitationes quas promendo divinarent, non solum aliud agentes, sicut [printed marginalia: Ioan. 11] Caiphas pontifex prophetavit, cum eius intentio non haberet voluntatem prophetandi, verumetiam id suscipientes ut divinandi modo aliquid dicerent, novimus." Quoted from Erasmus ed. (1528), vol. 3, p. 492 = *Patrologia*, vol. 34, col. 472. On the translation of the passages from *De Genesi* XII, xii, see the comments of Taylor, who prefers "attention" or "impulse"; Augustine, *The Literal Meaning of Genesis*, trans. J. H. Taylor [Ancient Christian Writers 42 (New York, 1982)], p. 303 n. 19. We will return to the meaning of *intentio* with our discussion of Martin Luther's interpretations of Genesis 6:5 and 8:21.

10. *De trinitate* XV, xxii; Portalié, *Guide to Thought*, pp. 111–112. Portalié's "solution" (pp. 112–

114) ignores Augustine's insistence that the image of God, however marred, is *always* inscribed in the human mind—the divine grace in the sunlight metaphor does not inscribe the image but rather touches the human mind, turning the mind that responds willingly to the *recognition* of its creation *ad imaginem dei*.

11. Earlier in his career, Augustine had thought that the *imago dei* impressed in the mind of Adam had been lost by Adam's sin. To the inquiry: "How can we be said to be renewed if we have not received that which the first person lost," he replied in *De Genesi ad litteram*: "We are renewed in the spirit of our mind according to the image of him who created us, the image that Adam lost"; *De Genesi ad litteram* VI, xxiv. Discussing Paul's injunction to the Ephesians (4:22–24) to "put off the old Adam," Augustine had been more specific concerning the restoration of what was lost: "The image impressed in the spirit of the mind which we receive by the grace of justification is that which Adam lost by sin." Ibid. VI, xxvii. Cf. the similar problem in Ambrose, *Hexaemeron* VI, vii–viii; esp. at the end of chapter vii. For this position in other treatises by Augustine, see Schindler, *Wort und Analogie*, pp. 66–72.

In the *Retractiones* he wrote c. 427, Augustine explicitly modified the statements he had made in that early work. "In the sixth book," he wrote, "where I said that by sin Adam had lost the image of God according to which he had been created, it should not be taken to mean that nothing of the image remained, but rather that it was so deformed that work in re-formation had to be undertaken." *Retractiones* II, xxiv. Augustine's new position was reflected in *De spiritu et littera*, but especially in book fourteen of *De trinitate*, in which he gave his most complete formulation of the reformation of the *imago dei*, again with reference to Ephesians 4:22–24. In Augustine's revised position, the image was no longer something lost as it had been in *De Genesi ad litteram*, but rather something "deformed and discolored," to be "reformed and renewed" by the one "by whom it had been formed." Cf. Schmaus, *Psychologische Trinitätslehre*, pp. 291–297.

12. *De trinitate* XIV, xv. Cf. *De trinitate* XII, xv.

13. *De trinitate* XIV, xvi.

14. The divine light toward which the will naturally turned was blinding, but in necessarily shielding itself from that glare the eye of the mind recognized in its remembered self-knowledge the *imago dei* gleaming with reflected light like a mirror obscured by darker images of corporeal origin. *De Genesi ad litteram* XII, xxxi. Cf. *De trinitate* XV, vi: "Sed quia lux illa ineffabilis nostrum reverberabat obtutum, & ei nondum posse contemperari [*sic*; Migne: "obtemperari"] nostrae mentis quodammodo convincebatur infirmitas"; quoted from Erasmus ed. (1529), vol. 3, p. 318 = *Patrologia*, vol. 42, col. 1064.

15. The allusion was to I Corinthians 13:12, probably the most frequently quoted verse in *De trinitate*. See, particularly, *De trinitate* XV, viii–ix, and xxiii, but also III, iv; V, i; VI, x; VIII, iii; IX, i; XII, xiv; XIII, xx; XIV, ii, xvii, xix; XV, xi.

It should be noted that, even aided by grace, the renewal or cleansing of that imprinted image of the accumulated dust from the material world was not to be instantaneous, as was the forgiveness of Original Sin which was the result of baptism, but—like recovery from some life-threatening illness—involved an arduous process of healing which lasted from the moment of conversion to the moment of physical death and beyond. *De trinitate* XIV, xvii. Cf. Dinkler, *Anthropologie Augustins*, pp. 170–171. At first glance Augustine appears here to have taken a narrower view of the illuminating rôle played by divine grace than he would in arguing that Plotinus and the Gospel were in agreement concerning the source of wisdom in *De civitate dei* X, iii. On the basis of this latter text, and particularly of Gilson's discussion of wisdom and mathematics (*Augustine*, pp. 128–129), Dinkler argues that "no cognition (*Erkenntnis*) is possible without God's help, without divine illumination." His next sentence, however, offers an important limitation of *Erkenntnis* without acknowledging it as such: "The conceptualizing of the Good, of divine illumination, of the eternal forms (*rationes aeternae*) or even of numbers are given to humankind as *a priori* wisdom made visible in the present through divine illumination." Dinkler, *Anthropologie Augustines*, p. 169. If we leave aside for the moment the complex problem of the position assigned mathematics by Augustine and return to the text of *De civitate dei* X, ii, in which Augustine sought to demonstrate the agreement between his theory of divine illumination and that of Plotinus' exposition of Plato's views, we see that there Augustine repeatedly corrected "rational" with "intellectual," suggesting that it was the *acies animi* functioning as *intellectus* or *ratio superior* rather than as *ratio inferior* which was illuminated by divine light. For a similar distinction between *scientia* and *sapientia*, the products of *ratio* and *intellectus*, see *De trinitate* XII, xiv–xv. On *ratio* and *intellectus*, see below, notes 19, 20. Ronald H. Nash, *The Light of the Mind: St. Augustine's Theory of Knowledge* (Lexington, Ky., 1969), pp. 94–124, offers a simplified summary of the competing interpretations of Augustine's theory of divine illumination.

16. *De trinitate* X, viii–ix. On *memoria* in general, see Schmaus, *Psychologische Trinitätslehre*, pp. 313–331.

Augustine's use of the term "memory" did not, however, imply that the mind's knowledge of eternal principles or of itself was the result of sense perception or imaginary modelings (*imaginaria figmenta*); in fact, he insisted to a correspondent that memories were not "necessarily of previous physical states." Rather, the mind's image of eternal forms and of itself, the vision in which the mind illuminated by grace could recognize the image of God in the mind itself, was inscribed in the memory. Bundy, *Theory of Imagination*, pp. 156–157; citing Augustine's letter to Nebridius = epistola vii in *Patrologia*, vol. 33, cols. 68–69 (epistola LXXII, pp. 217–219, in Erasmus ed. [1528]).

17. *De trinitate* XI, ix. On the *acies animi*, see Schmaus, *Psychologische Trinitätslehre*, pp. 266–267.

18. *De trinitate*, XV, vii. Cf. Schmaus, *Psychologische Trinitätslehre*, p. 411; Gilson, *Christian Philosophy*, p. 218.

19. Dinkler, *Anthropologie Augustins*, pp. 258–261. The line of demarcation between the two functions was, however, far from distinct, and it is not entirely clear whether the judgment of temporal matters on the basis of eternal verities (*rationes aeternae*), as in the case of temporal justice, was regarded by Augustine as the province of *ratio* or of *intellectus*. Cf. *De trinitate* XIV, xv, with the following passage. Augustine's division of the functions of the intellect or reason has been the source of much scholarly controversy, generally over the exact location of the dividing line between *ratio inferior* and *superior* and the rôle played by divine illumination (see above, note 15). Even those less concerned about the location of the line take very different views of its rôle in Augustine's thought. For O.J.-B. du Roy, it represents Augustine's salvation by "the Neoplatonic experience of interiority and transcendence" from "materialism of a sense-dominated imagination." "St. Augustine," *New Catholic Encyclopedia* (Washington, D.C., 1967), vol. 1, p. 1043. For Bundy, on the other hand, Augustine's mystical impulse "might at any moment cause him to deny the reality of the phenomena which his scientific impulse had led him to describe. . . . In the description of intellectual vision as a capacity of reason transcending imagination the mystical impulse led to the assertion of the old dualism with its insistence upon the materiality of imagination." *Theory of Imagination*, p. 167.

Since Augustine held that all moral action had its origin in the images of the eternal verities innate to the memory (even to the memories of pagans), it seems most logical that temporal moral action was the function of *ratio*, and that the grace-enlightened *intellectus* was given the task of "seeing through" the human moral action or category to apprehend or compare it to the divine verity of which it was the image. Cf. *Confessiones* VII, xvii; quoted below, note 48.

On the analogy of the creation of woman as Adam's appropriate helper (Genesis 2:18), lower reason was formed from higher reason to deal with matters essential to human existence in the material world (Augustine, *De trinitate* XII, iii). "Lower reason" was concerned with the analysis, combination, and arrangement of images based on sense perception; it was this "lower reason"—the ability consciously to commit to memory, to analyze, and to create imaginative visions (*fictas visiones*) by combining bits of images from the material world—which set humankind apart from the beasts. In contrast, it was "the property of higher reason to judge those corporeal perceptions according to incorporeal and eternal forms." *De trinitate* XII, ii; cf., however, *Confessiones* VII, xvii.

20. Schmaus, *Psychologische Trinitätslehre*, p. 267. Cf. Nash, *Light of the Mind*, pp. 5, 7–9, 64–66. Leaving aside the problem of contemplation in Augustine's thought, it is clear that the bishop of Hippo discriminated between the activities of the second member of the mental trinity in dealing with images originating in the material world (*ratio*) and its activities in recognizing the image of the godhead in itself (*intellectus* or *intelligentia*). Cf. Burnaby, "The Trinity: Introduction," in *Later Works*, p. 35: "To 'understand,' therefore, is simply to 'see with the mind,' to 'apprehend' rather than to 'comprehend,' and the act of understanding is intuitive, not discursive." See also the comments on generation and process below, notes 29, 32, 34.

*Scientia* and *sapientia*, the results of *ratio* and *intellectus*, were also held apart by Augustine; cf. *De trinitate* XII, xiv–xv.

21. "Atque ita fit illa trinitas ex memoria & interna visione, & quae utrunque copulat voluntate, quae tria cum in unum coguntur, ab ipso coactu cogitatio dicitur." Augustine, *De trinitate* XI,

iii; quoted from Erasmus ed. (1528), vol. 3, p. 272 = *Patrologia*, vol. 42, col. 988. It is difficult to capture in English the triad *coguntur, coactu, cogitatio*, which Augustine thought had the same etymological origin. My use of "collect"/"recollect" is borrowed from Rex Warner's translation of the same serious word play in Augustine's *Confessiones* X, xi: *The Confessions of St. Augustine* (New York, 1963), p. 222.

Although *cogitatio* is translated conventionally as "thought," we will soon see that "conception" would more accurately reflect the understanding of *cogitatio* expressed in *De trinitate*; cf. B. Darrell Jackson, "The Theory of Signs in Augustine's *De Doctrina Christiana*," in *Augustine: A Collection of Critical Essays*, ed. R. A. Markus (New York, 1972), pp. 92–147, esp. pp. 104–107 (reprinted from *Revue des études augustiniennes* 15 [1969], pp. 9–49). The translation of *cogitatio* as "knowledge" in the English edition of Gilson's *Christian Philosophy*, pp. 221 and 356–357 n. 22, seems misguided.

22. *De trinitate* XV, xxiii.

23. Gilson, *Christian Philosophy*, p. 222. Cf. *De trinitate* IX, vii.

24. On *verbum* in general, see Schmaus, *Psychologische Trinitätslehre*, pp. 331–369.

25. "Aliter enim dicuntur verba quae spatia temporum syllabis tenent, sive pronuntientur, sive cogitentur: aliter omne quod notum est verbum dicitur, animo impressum quamdiu de memoria proferri et definiri potest, quamvis res ipsa displiceat: aliter cum placet quod mente concipitur." *De trinitate* IX, x; quoted from Erasmus ed. (1528), vol. 3, p. 259 = *Patrologia*, vol. 42, col. 969.

26. "Ideoque & imago & verbum est. . . ." *De trinitate* IX, xi; quoted from Erasmus ed. (1528), vol. 3, p. 260 = *Patrologia*, vol. 42, col. 970. Cf. Schmaus, *Psychologische Trinitätslehre*, pp. 367–369; Schindler, *Wort und Analogie*, pp. 217–219.

27. "Sed quomodo est verbum, quod nondum in cogitationis visione formatum est? Quomodo erit simile scientiae de qua nascitur, si eius non habet formam, & ideo iam vocatur verbum quia potest habere?" *De trinitate* XV, xv; quoted from Erasmus ed. (1528), vol. 3, p. 327 = *Patrologia*, 42, col. 1078.

28. "Haec igitur omnia & quae per seipsum, & quae per sensus sui corporis, & quae testimoniis aliorum percepta scit animus humanus, thesauro memoriae condita tenet: ex quibus gignitur verbum verum, quando quod scimus loquimur, sed verbum ante omnem sonum, ante omnem cogitationem soni. Tunc enim est verbum simillimum rei notae de qua gignitur & imago eius, quoniam de visione scientiae visio cogitationis exoritur, quod est verbum linguae nullius, verbum verum de re vera, nihil de suo habens, sed totum de illa scientia de qua nascitur." *De trinitate* XV, xii; quoted from Erasmus ed. (1528), vol. 3, p. 325 = *Patrologia*, vol. 42, col. 1075.

29. Cf. Augustine's carefully drawn distinction between "generation" and "procession" in *De trinitate* XV, xxvii.

30. "Verbum autem nostrum illud quod non habet sonum neque cogitationem soni, sed eius rei quam videndo intus dicimus, & ideo nullius linguae est atque inde utcunque simile est in hoc aenigmate illi verbo dei quod etiam deus est, quoniam sic & hoc de nostra nascitur, quemadmodum & illud de scientia patris natum est. . . ." *De trinitate* XV, xiv; quoted from Erasmus ed. (1528), vol. 3, p. 327 = *Patrologia*, vol. 42, col. 1077. Cf. *De trinitate* XV, xi.

31. Although his comments in Tractatus 108 of *In Ioannis Evangelium* (416–417) show that Augustine was aware of manuscripts in which the Greek *logos* of John 1 had been translated as *sermo*, he himself adhered to the more accepted translation *verbum*; Schindler, *Wort und Analogie*, pp. 75–76, 115–118. On the question of the source of Augustine's internal *verbum*, see ibid., pp. 97–104. Cf. Augustine, *De diversis quaestionibus octoginta tribus liber unus* LXIII.

32. On the similarities and differences between human and divine *verbum*, see *De trinitate* XV, xi, xv–xvi.

33. For God as the *id quod est*, see Augustine, *Confessiones* VII, x, xvii; quoted below, note 46.

34. In his earlier *De fide et symbolo*, Augustine had moved in the course of three sentences between calling the human utterance *verbum* and calling it the *signum* by which "whatever secret we produce in our heart is proffered to the cognition of another." In either case it was contrasted to the *logos* or "Word" of the Incarnation. Schmaus, *Psychologische Trinitätslehre*, pp. 331–342; quotation from *De fide et symbolo* iii, given by Schmaus, p. 332 n. 1.

Although the human utterance of necessity limited the very conception it strove to express in order to express it, it was, like the second person of the Trinity, "word made flesh," albeit imperfectly as befit that which was only an imperfect image of divine generation: "For as our word in some way becomes a corporeal sound, assuming that in which it may be manifested by human senses, so the Word of God was made flesh, assuming that in which it itself might be manifested to human senses" ("Ita enim verbum nostrum vox quodammodo corporis fit, assumendo eam in qua manifestetur sensibus hominum: sicut verbum dei caro factum est, assumendo eam in qua & ipsum manifestaretur sensibus hominum"). *De trinitate* XV, xi; quoted from Erasmus ed. (1528), vol. 3, p. 323 = *Patrologia*, vol. 42, cols. 1071–1072.

35. *De trinitate* XV, xi.

36. "Nec tamen quia dicimus locutiones cordis esse cogitationes, ideo non sunt etiam visiones exortae de notitiae visionibus, quando verae sunt." *De trinitate* XV, x; quoted from Erasmus ed. (1528), vol. 3, p. 322 = *Patrologia*, vol. 42, cols. 1070–1071.

37. "Foris enim cum per corpus haec fiunt, aliud est locutio, aliud visio. Intus autem cum cogitamus, utrunque unum est. Sicut auditio & visio duo quaedam sunt inter se distantia in sensibus corporis, in animo autem non est aliud atque aliud videre & audire." *De trinitate* XV, x; quoted from Erasmus ed. (1528), vol. 3, p. 322 = *Patrologia*, vol. 42, cols. 1070–1071.

38. *De trinitate* XV, xi.

Similarly, the mind in which the *imago dei* was inscribed was called the image of God "just as a panel is also called an image because a picture is painted on it": "Aliud est itaque trinitas res ipsa, aliud imago trinitatis in re alia, propter quam imaginem simul & illud in quo sunt haec tria imago dicitur: sicut imago dicitur simul & tabula & quod in ea pictum est, sed propter picturam quae in ea est, simul & tabula nomine imaginis appellatur." *De trinitate* XV, xxii; quoted from Erasmus ed. (1528), vol. 3, p. 335 = *Patrologia*, vol. 42, col. 1090. The inscription of the *imago dei* in the human mind was like the imprint of a seal ring in wax, the engraved portrait on a coin, the transcription of a law from a book. Portalié, *Guide to Thought*, pp. 111–112.

39. Augustine, *De trinitate* XI, ix.

40. *De Genesi ad litteram* XII, vi.

41. For clarity's sake, I here follow Bundy, *Theory of Imagination*, pp. 157–158, in including both the action of the will and the internal impression that resulted from the will's desire to see and the bodily eyes' seeing in "corporeal vision." In *De Genesi ad litteram* XII, xi, Augustine ranked the three types of vision, insisting that the internal impression of the object seen by the bodily eyes was not perceived as an impression unless the bodily eyes were turned away from the physical object and the internal impression was sought out in an act of spiritual vision: "Nam cum aliquid oculis cernitur continuo fit imago eius in spiritu, sed non dignoscitur facta, nisi cum ablatis oculis ab eo quod per oculis videbamus, imaginem eius in animo invenerimus." Quoted from the Erasmus ed. (1528), vol. 3, p. 486 = *Patrologia*, vol. 34, col. 462. Although Augustine's corporeal vision involved the spirit as well as the corporeal eyes, it was a vision in its own right: "corporaliter litterae videnter, spiritaliter proximus cogitatur, intellectualiter dilectio conspicitur" (ibid.). This is, it seems to me, rather different from arguing, as Schmaus does (*Psychologische Trinitätslehre*, p. 366), that "corporeal seeing cannot exist without spiritual seeing," since "if a spiritual vision does not occur together with a corporeal vision the corporeal vision cannot be perceived." Schmaus' argument is the result of his having insisted on the preceding page that corporeal sight is carried out "with the bodily senses," while spiritual sight is "neither purely spiritual nor purely corporeal." In contrast, Augustine, after describing the seeing of the letters on the page as corporeal vision, assigned no rôle in their internalization to spiritual vision, but instead attributed to spiritual vision the task of recalling the absent neighbor to mind. *De Genesi ad litteram* XII, vi. Cf. Taylor's brief note to his own translation of *De Genesi*: "The three types of vision here described are distinguished by the objects seen and the power of the soul that sees: bodies seen by the soul through the instrumentality of the body, likenesses seen by the spirit, and immaterial realities seen by the intellect." *Literal Meaning of Genesis*, p. 303 n. 20.

42. Cf. Bundy, *Theory of Imagination*, pp. 158–167.

43. Ibid., pp. 167–168. On "intellect" and "apprehension," see above, notes 15, 19, 20.

44. The quoted phrase—whose application to Augustine I owe to Brian Daley, S.J.—is taken from T. S. Eliot, "Imperfect Critics," *The Sacred Wood* (2nd ed. London, 1960), p. 23. The corollary, Augustine's restless straining to "rest in God," is suggested by a comment from Eliot's essay "The Perfect Critic": "you never rest at the pure feeling. . . . The moment you try to put the impressions into words, you either begin to analyse and construct, or to 'ériger en lois,' or you begin to create something else." Ibid., p. 3. Cf. Allan Mowbray, *T. S. Eliot's Impersonal Theory of Poetry* (Lewisburg, 1974), pp. 76–93.

45. On this, see the prologue to *De doctrina christiana* and the comments on that work by Cornelius Mayer, "Res per signa," *Revue des études augustienne* 20 (1974), pp. 100–112, esp. pp. 111–112.

46. In *Confessiones* VII, x, Augustine described an ascent that began with the reading of philosophy that admonished him to turn inward: "Et inde admonitus [by the reading of philoso-

phy] redire ad memetipsum, intravi in intima mea duce te, & potui, quoniam factus es adiutor meus. Intravi & vidi qualicunque oculo animae meae, supra eundem oculum animae meae, supra mentem meam lucem domini incommutabilem. . . . Et cum te primum cognovi, tu assumsisti me ut viderem esse quod viderem, & nondum me esse qui viderem. . . . Et clamasti de longinquo, immo vero ego sum qui sum [printed marginalia: Exo. 3]. Et audivi sicut auditur in corde." Quoted from Erasmus ed. (1528), vol. 1, p. 94 = *Patrologia*, vol. 32, col. 742. It should be noted that here—before his recognition of the soteriological centrality of the God-Man Jesus (*Confessiones* VII, xviii)—Augustine described his experience as perceiving light but not being strong enough to look on it; he heard only a voice from afar. In *Confessiones* VII, xvii, he described the progress from corporeal perception through interior investigation to "that which is": "atque ita gradatim a corporibus ad sentientem per corpus animam; atque inde ad eius interiorem vim, cui sensus corporis exteriora annunciaret, & quousque possunt bestiae, atque inde rursus ad ratiocinantem potentiam, ad quam refertur iudicandum quod sumitur a sensibus corporis. Quae se quoque in me comperiens mutabilem erexit se ad intelligentiam suam, & abduxit cogitationem a consuetudine, subtrahens se a contradicentibus turbis phantasmatum, ut inveniret quo lumine aspergeretur, cum sine ulla dubitatione clamaret, incommutabile praeferendum esse mutabili, unde nosset ipsum incommutabile, quod nisi aliquo modo nosset, nullo modo illud mutabili certa praeponeret, & perveniret ad id quod est in ictu trepidantis aspectus. Tunc vero invisibilia tua per ea quae facta sunt intellecta conspexi. . . ." Augustine, *Confessiones* VII, xvii; quoted from Erasmus ed. (1528), vol. 1, pp. 95–96 = *Patrologia*, vol. 32, col. 745.

In some sense my argument that the progress to conversion described in the *Confessiones* (and particularly the progress to a vision of God in VII, xvii, and IX, x) is the same process as that described paradigmatically in the individual's comprehension of the meaning of "Love thy neighbor as thyself" can be related to J. J. O'Meara's characterization of Augustine's *Confessiones* as a paradigmatic account, "the story of a typical conversion: it is the story of Everyman." *The Young Augustine* (London, 1954), p. 13. I will argue below (notes 125–127) that Luther, at least, viewed the conversion/mystical experiences detailed in the *Confessiones* as having established a paradigm in need of revision.

47. *Confessiones* IX, x; see following note for complete quotation.

48.

Colloquebamur ergo soli valde dulciter, & praeterita obliviscentes, in ea quae ante sunt extenti, quaerebamus inter nos apud praesentem veritatem quod tu es, qualis futura esset vita aeterna sanctorum, quam nec oculus vidit, nec auris audivit, nec in cor hominis ascendit. Sed inhiabamus ore cordis in superna fluenta fontis tui, fontis vitae qui est apud te, ut inde pro captu nostro aspersi, quoquo modo rem tantam cogitaremus. Cumque ad eum finem sermo perduceretur, ut carnalium sensuum delectatio quantalibet in quantalibet luce corporea prae illius vitae iocunditate, non comparatione, sed ne commemoratione quidem digna videretur, erigentes nos ardentiore affectu in idipsum, perambulavimus gradatim cuncta corporalia,* & ipsum coelum, unde sol & luna & stellae lucent super terram. Et adhuc ascendabamus interius cogitando & loquendo te, & mirando opera tua, & venimus in mentes nostras, & transcendimus eas, ut attingeremus regionem ubertatis indeficientis, ubi pascis Israël in aeternum veritatis pabulo, & ubi vita sapientia est,** per quam fiunt omnia ista, & quae fuerunt, & quae futura sunt: & ipsa non fit, sed sic est ut fuit, & sic erit semper, quin potius fuisse & futurum esse non est in ea, sed esse solum, quoniam aeterna est. Nam fuisse & futurum esse non est aeternum. Et dum loquimur & inhiamus illi, attigimus eam modice toto ictu cordis, & suspiravimus & reliquimus ibi religatas primitias spiritus, & remeavimus ad strepitum oris nostri, ubi verbum & incipitur & finitur. Et quid simile verbo tuo domino nostro in se permanenti sine vetustate, atque innovanti omnia? Dicebamus ergo: Si cui sileat tumultus carnis, sileant phantasiae terrae & aquarum & aeris, sileant & poli, & ipsa sibi anima sileat, & transeat se non cogitando, sileant somnia & imaginariae revelationes, omnis lingua & omne signum & quicquid transeundo fit, si cui sileat omnino: quoniam si quis audiat, dicunt haec omnia, Non ipsa nos fecimus, sed fecit nos qui manet in aeternum, His dictis si iam taceant, quoniam erexerunt aurem in eum qui fecit ea, & loquatur ipse solus, non per ea, sed per seipsum, ut audiamus verbum eius, non per linguam carnis, neque per vocem angeli, neque per sonitum nubis, neque per aenigma similitudinis, sed ipsum quem in his amamus, ipsum sine his audiamus: sicut nunc extendimus nos, & rapida cogitatione attingimus aeternam sapientiam super omnia manentem, si continuentur hoc, & subtrahantur aliae visiones longe imparis generis, & haec una rapiat & absorbeat & recondat in interiora gaudia spectatorem suum, ut talis sit sempiterna vita, quale fuit hoc momentum intelligentiae, cui suspiravimus, Nonne hoc est, Intra in gaudiam domini tui [printed marginalia: Matth. 25]? Et istud quando? An cum omnes resurgemus, sed non omnes immutabimur. Dicebamus talia, & si non isto modo & his verbis, tamen domine tu scis quod illo die cum talia loqueremur, & mundus iste nobis inter verba vilesceret cum omnibus delectationibus suis, Tunc ait illa: Fili quantum ad me attinet, nulla re iam delector in hac vita. Quid hic faciam adhuc, & cur hic simnescio, iam consumpta spe huius seculi.

Augustine, *Confessiones* IX, x; quoted from Erasmus ed. (1528), vol. 1, p. 113 = *Patrologia*, vol. 32, cols. 774–775. *Erasmus noted here that other manuscripts had *temporalia*. **In the copy of the Erasmus edition I used, "vita sapientia est" was emphasized by a sixteenth-century reader who recopied it in the margin. Houghton Library, Harvard University, *fNC5 .Er153 .528a2, vol. 1, p. 113.

It is impossible fully to capture the images of the Latin text. The reflexive *extendimus nos* referred back to the more obviously conative *extenti* in the Pauline quotation ("intent on those things which lie before," Philippians 3:13) in the chapter's opening paragraph; *attingeremus*, *attigimus* and *attingimus* ("to touch" or "reach out to") had sensual as well as covetous connotations, including not only the idea of "eat," but also of "grab" and "embrace" (even the "embrace" of sexual intercourse); and *rapida* referred not only to the fleeting character of the encounter with eternal Wisdom, but was also an adjective that frequently modified (or, rather, conveyed the violence and destructiveness of) the two turbulent elements, fire and water. This last aspect was particularly to the fore in a scene that opened with a discussion of the "delights of the carnal senses" (*carnalium sensuum delectatio*) and "burning emotion" (*ardentiore affectu*), of "the tumult of the flesh" (*tumultus carnis*) and of "fantasies of earth, water, and air" (*phantasiae terrae & aquarum & aeris*).

49. Ibid.

50. Ibid.

51. See Augustine's influential distinction between *signum* and *res* in *De doctrina christiana* I, ii, and II, i.

52. Cf. Augustine's description of his vision's conclusion, quoted above, note 48, with: "Quomodo venit, nisi quia verbum caro factum est & habitavit in nobis? Sicuti cum loquimur, ut id quod in animo gerimur, in audientis animum per aures carneas illabatur, fit sonus, verbum quod corde gestamus, & locutio vocatur: nec tamen in eundem sonum cogitatio nostra convertitur, sed apud se manens integra, formam vocis qua se insinuet auribus sine aliqua labe sine mutatione assumit: ita verbum dei non commutatum, caro tamen factum est ut habitaret in nobis. . . ." Augustine, *De doctrina christiana* (c. 396), I, xiii; quoted from Erasmus ed. (1528), vol. 3, p. 7 = *Patrologia*, vol. 34, col. 24.

53. *De trinitate* VI, x. On the general issue of *verbum* and *signum* in Augustine's writings, see R. A. Markus, "St. Augustine on Signs," in *Augustine: A Collection of Critical Essays*, ed. R. A. Markus (New York, 1972), pp. 61–91 (reprinted from *Phronesis* 2 [1957], pp. 60–83); Jackson, "Theory of Signs," esp. pp. 99–108.

54. *De doctrina christiana* III, xxvii.

55. Cf. Augustine's descriptions of "word" and "picture": "Si enim hoc verbum quod nos proferimus temporale & transitorum, & seipsum ostendit, & illud de quo loquimur. . . ." *De trinitate* VII, iii; quoted from Erasmus ed. (1528), vol. 3, p. 240 = *Patrologia*, vol. 42, col. 937. And: "In picturis vero & statuis, caeterisque huiusmodi simulatis operibus, maxime peritorum artificum, nemo errat cum similia viderit, ut agnoscat quibus sint rebus similia." *De doctrina christiana* II, xxv; quoted from Erasmus ed. (1528), vol. 3, p. 25 = *Patrologia*, vol. 34, col. 54. Cf. the discussion of audible *signa* in *De trinitate* X, i. On the difference between *imago* and *similitudo* in Augustine's thought, see above, note 3.

56. The categories are Augustine's: *De doctrina christiana* II, i.

57. "Randbemekungen Luthers zu *Augustini Opuscula*" (1509), *WA* 9:11–12; and the various quotations/citations indexed in *WA* 63:59.

58. "Et hoc totum genus inter superflua hominum instituta numerandum est. . . . Et nulla magis hominum propria, quae a seipsis habent, existimanda, quam quaeque falsa atque mendacia." Augustine, *De doctrina christiana* II, xxv; quoted from Erasmus ed. (1528), vol. 3, p. 25 = *Patrologia*, vol. 34, col. 54. The human creations to which we refer as "the visual arts" are strikingly absent from Augustine's writings. Presumably it is for this reason that they are not mentioned—and this section of *De doctrina christiana* is not discussed—in Robert J. O'Connell's *Art and the Christian Intelligence in St. Augustine* (Cambridge, 1978). Cf. *Confessiones* X, xxxiv.

59. "Et hoc totum genus inter superflua hominum instituta numerandum est, nisi cum interesset quid eorum, qua de causa, & ubi, & quando, & cuius autoritate fiat. Milia denique fictarum fabularum & falsitatum, quarum mendaciis homines delectantur, humana instituta sunt." Augustine, *De doctrina christiana* II, xxv.

60. ". . . sicut in speculo vel pictura, quia imagines sunt, etiam similes sunt." Augustine, *De*

*Genesi ad litteram imperfectus* xvi; quoted from Erasmus ed. (1528), vol. 3, p. 353 = *Patrologia*, vol. 34, col. 242. Johann Mader, *Die logische Struktur des personalen Denkens aus der Methode der Gotteserkenntnis bei Aurelius Augustinus* (Vienna, 1965), p. 136 and n. 3.

61. Augustine, *De doctrina christiana* II, xvii.

62. *De consensu evangelistarum* I, x.

63. "Credo quod pluribus locis simul eos cum illo pictos viderunt, quia merita Petri & Pauli etiam propter eundem passionis diem celebrius & solenniter Roma commendat." *De consensu evangelistarum* I, x; Erasmus ed. (1528), vol. 4, p. 267 = *Patrologia*, vol. 34, col. 1049.

64. See above, note 46.

65. "Sic omnino errare meruerunt, qui Christum & apostolos eius non in sanctis codicibus, sed in pictis parietibus quaesierunt. Nec mirum si a pingentibus fingentes decepti sunt." *De consensu evangelistarum* I, x; Erasmus ed. (1528), vol. 4, p. 267 = *Patrologia*, vol. 34, col. 1049.

66. "Incorporalem substantiam scio esse sapientiam, & lumen esse in quo videntur quae oculis carnalibus non videntur: & tamen vir tantus tamque spiritalis, Videmus nunc, inquit, per speculum in aenigmate, tunc autem facie ad faciem. Quale sit & quod sit hoc speculum si quaeramus, profecto illud occurrit quod in speculo nisi imago non cernitur. Hoc ergo facere conati sumus, ut per imaginem hanc quod nos sumus, videremus utcunque a quo facti sumus, tanquam per speculum." *De trinitate* XV, viii; quoted from Erasmus ed. (1528), vol. 3, p. 320 = *Patrologia*, vol. 42, col. 1067. The discussion of I Corinthians 13:12 continued through the next chapter.

67. For the phrase *id quod est* in Augustine's *Confessiones* VII, xvii, see above, note 46.

68. The problems and issues involved in the translation of the Hebrew text at Genesis 6:5 and at the parallel passage at 8:21 will be addressed in the rest of this prolegomena. I therefore include here the Latin translations in use when Martin Luther began his own consideration of the passages.

Jerome's (Vulgate) translation of Hebrew texts:

6:5 "Videns autem dominus quod multa malitia hominum esset in terra: et cuncta cogitatio cordis intenta esset ad malum omni tempore."

8:21 ". . . sensus enim et cogitatio humani cordis in malum prona sunt ab adolescentia sua."

Translation of the Greek Septuagint text (the basis of the Old Latin text used by Augustine) in use at the beginning of the sixteenth century:

6:5 "Videns autem dominus deus, quod multiplicate sunt malitie hominum super terram: & omnis cogitat in corde suo diligenter ad mala omnibus diebus."

8:21 ". . . incumbit cogitatio hominis diligenter ad mala: ex adolescentia sua."

"Interpretation" of the Chaldean (= Aramaic) text in use at the beginning of the sixteenth century:

6:5 "Et palam fuit coram domino, quod multa esset malicia hominis in terra: & omnis sensus cogitationis cordis sui esset malus omni tempore."

8:21 ". . . sensus cordis humani malus est ab infantia sua." Complutensian Polyglott: *Vetus testamentum multiplici lingua nunc primo impressum*, vol. 1, fol. b, b', biiii.

For Augustine's use of the passage, see below, note 72.

69. The translation I give here is of Martin Luther's translation of the Hebrew text into Latin in his response to Desiderius Erasmus' *De libero arbitrio diatribe* (Basel: Johann Froben, 1524): "Aut cur non et hic Ebraicum consulvit, ubi nihil de pronitate Moses dicit? ne cavillandi caussam habeas. Sic enim habet cap. 6: Chol Ietzer Mahescheboth libbo rak ra chol ha iom, hoc est: omne figmentum cogitationum cordis eius tantum malum cunctis diebus. Non dicit intentum vel pronum ad malum, sed prorsus malum ac nihil nisi malum fingi et cogitari ab homine tota vita." Martin Luther, *De servo arbitrio ad D. Erasmum Roterdamum* (Wittenberg: Johann Lufft, 1525), *WA* 18:736. Cf. the same translation in the lectures he gave in Latin on Genesis a decade later: "Sed ipsa verba Mosi quoque diligentius sunt consideranda. Usus enim his est singulari Phrasi certo consilio, quod non simpliciter dicit Cogitationes hominis esse malas, sed ipsum figmentum cogitationum. Sic vocat hoc, quod homo potest in suis cogitationibus, seu cum ratione et libero arbitrio, etiam in summo gradu. Ideo enim figmentum vocat, quod homo summo studio excogitat, deligit, facit, sicut figulus, et putat pulcherrimum esse." Luther, *In Primum Librum Mose*, *WA* 42:291. Luther usually conflated the parallel passages from Genesis, especially before his retranslation and reinterpretation of them c. 1525.

70. An attempt in which Luther was constantly confronted by, and frequently acknowledged, the soteriological writings of Augustine himself against the Pelagians.

71. Martin Luther, in conversation (Autumn 1533), recorded by Veit Dietrich, *WA, Tischreden*

1:297 Nr. 626; conversation (18 March 1539), recorded by Anton Lauterbach, *WA, Tischreden* 4:302 Nr. 4412. Cf. Augustine, *De doctrina christiana* III, xxxiii. The source of Luther's quotation is not given in *WA*.

72. I have been unable to discover any substantive use of the two Genesis passages in Augustine's writings apart from the references cited by McIntosh: *De civitate dei* XV, xxiv; *Questionum super Genesim* I, questio xv. John S. McIntosh, "A Study of Augustine's Versions of Genesis" (Ph.D. dissertation: Chicago, 1912), pp. 24, 126.

Augustine offered the first quotation as good reason to think that everyone in the world at that time deserved to die a horrible death, but undercut its universality by adding, before the quotation itself, a reference to the descendants of Seth: none of those known from Scripture was drowned in the Flood; *De civitate dei* XV, xxiv. Even more striking is Augustine's complete omission of the passage at 8:21 from the subsequent discussion. Chapter xxv was devoted to the argument that God's "anger" (*iratus sum*) did not indicate that his spirit was changeable but was intended as a metaphorical warning to the most ignorant reader. The next two chapters closed book XV with a discussion of the Ark as a symbol of the "city of God." And book XVI opened after the Flood had ended, ignoring Noah's sacrifice, our passage at 8:21, and even the rainbow that was a sign of God's promise.

Augustine ignored the Genesis passages even in his attacks on the Pelagian Julian; no reference to them was contained in *Contra Julianum*, in *Opus imperfectum contra Julianum*, or in the treatise he had earlier written for Marcellinus, *De spiritu et littera*. Nor did Augustine feel the need to cite them in order to preclude or respond to their use by his earlier Manichaean opponents; there were again no references in *De libero arbitrio* or *De gratia et libero arbitrio*.

If Augustine himself omitted Genesis 8:21 from his account of the Flood in book XV of *De civitate dei*, his contemporary (and teacher) Ambrose had done rather more in his own treatise on Noah and the Ark. His brief discussion there focused (as would Augustine's own proof of original sin in his *Confessiones*) on the sins of the flesh. Ambrose, *De Noe et arca liber unus*, chapter XXII; *Patrologia*, vol. 14, cols. 419–420.

Later Gregory the Great would also interpret Genesis 8:21 in primarily sexual terms (*Moralia in Iob* XXVIII, xix), but it was Jerome, Augustine's contemporary and the Bible translator to whom Luther would be compared and whose translation of the passage Luther would challenge, who made the most frequent use of Genesis 8:21. Given what we have seen in Ambrose and Gregory, Jerome's perspective comes as no surprise. I cannot avoid quoting one of his usages of the text: "Et quia appositum est cor hominis diligenter ad malitiam ab adolescentia, et paene omnes offenderunt Deum; in hac ruina generis humani, facilior ad casum est mulier. De qua et poeta gentilis: . . . varium et mutabili semper / Femina." Jerome, *Commentarium in Ecclesiasten* VII, 28/30; quoted from *Corpus Christianorum* (Turnholti), vol. 72, p. 312. The poetic fragment is from Vergil's *Aeneid* 4, 569–570. Other references to Genesis 8:21 in Jerome's works: *Commentarioli in Psalmos* XVII (*Corpus Christianorum*, vol. 72, p. 195); *Commentariorum in Hiezechielem libri XIV*, VIII, xxv; XIII, xliv; XIV, xlvii (*Corpus Christianorum*, vol. 75, pp. 343, 661, 711); *In Ionam prophetam*, i (*Corpus Christianorum*, vol. 76, p. 380); *Commentariorum in Matheum libri IV*, I (*Corpus Christianorum*, vol. 77, pp. 42–43).

Cf. the reference to Genesis 8:21 in Bernard of Clairvaux, *Tractatus de gratia & libero arbitrio*, *Opera* (Louvain: Jacobus de giuncti, 1530), fol. 267 = *Patrologia*, vol. 182, col. 1024. On Bernard's anthopology in general, see Wilhelm Hiss, *Die Anthropologie Bernards von Clairvaux* [Quellen und Studien zur Geschichte der Philosophie 7 (Berlin, 1964)]; on his teaching on original sin, see Julius Gross, *Entwicklungsgeschichte des Erbsündendogmas im Zeitalter der Scholastik (12.–15. Jahrhundert)* [*Geschichte des Erbsündendogmas. Ein Beitrag zur Geschichte des Problems vom Ursprung des Ubels*, vol. 3 (Munich, 1971)], pp. 79–83, which does not mention the Genesis quotation.

73. Concerning the debt owed by Luther to his more immediate predecessors the German mystics, and particularly to the anonymous author of the *Theologia deutsch*, which Luther himself edited in 1516 and again in 1518, Steven Ozment has concluded: "of the three areas of mystical theology—(1) ontology and anthropology, (2) the steps to salvation, and (3) the union with God—Luther is interested primarily in what the *German Theology* has to say about the second and he shies away from the conclusions drawn in the first and third areas. This is consistent not only with his prefatorial comments, but also with the evolution of his thought in the formative years 1513–1517." Steven E. Ozment, *Mysticism and Dissent: Religious Ideology and Social Protest in the Sixteenth Century* (New Haven, 1973), pp. 20–24, esp. p. 24. In an earlier work, Ozment compared the anthropologies of Johannes Tauler and Jean Gerson with that of Luther in the years imme-

diately preceding his publication of the *Theologia deutsch*, concluding (as he would later in the passage just quoted) that Luther had by 1516 already recognized and defined the areas of his anthropological disagreement with the mystics. Challenging Artur Rühl's conclusion "that it is not until 1522 that Luther finally *discovers* his basic differences with mysticism," Ozment argues "that there are decisive, irreconcilable differences between Luther and Tauler and Gerson in the period 1513–1516. There is, to be sure, no outspoken attack by Luther on either in this period. There are, however, quite significant and *conscious* modifications directed against both [emphases mine]." *Homo spiritualis: A Comparative Study of the Anthropology of Johannes Tauler, Jean Gerson, and Martin Luther (1509–1516) in the Context of Their Theological Thought* [Studies in Medieval and Reformation Thought 6 (Leiden, 1969)], p. 5 n. 4; citing Artur Rühl, *Der Einfluss der Mystik auf Denken und Entwicklung des jungen Luthers* (Oberhessen, 1960), p. 110.

If, as Ozment has argued, Luther had already recognized his differences with the anthropologies of the mystics by 1516, it is difficult to see why he would have issued so thoroughly mystical a pamphlet as the abbreviated *Theologia deutsch* in 1516, let alone the full version of 1518. I will suggest that Luther's definition of anthropology (i.e., of human limitations) was evolved and clarified as he turned again and again to Genesis 6:5 and 8:21 in his arguments against the church of Rome and against the sectarians. Clearly his soteriology influenced his understanding and translation of the texts, but just as clearly the activity of translating and the controversies surrounding the translation of *yeser* in the two passages influenced his understanding of anthropology.

74. On Augustine's use of Romans 5:12 as evidence for original sin and the resulting bondage of the human will, his sources, and his influence, see J. Freundorfer, *Erbsünde und Erbtod beim Apostel Paulus* [Neutestamentische Abhandlungen 13 (Münster i. Westfalen, 1927)], pp. 132–146; B. Leeming, "Augustine, Ambrosiaster and the *massa perditionis*," *Gregorianum* 11 (1930), pp. 58–91; Philipp Platz, *Der Römerbrief in der Gnadenlehre Augustins* [*Cassisiacum* 5 (Würzburg, 1938)], pp. 54–56, 100–106.

The most recent (and hostile) treatment of Augustine's interpretation of Romans 5:12 is Elaine Pagels, *Adam, Eve, and the Serpent* (New York, 1988), pp. 109, 143. Following the careful philological study by Stanislaus Lyonnet, "Le péché originel et l'exégèse de Rom. 5:12–14," *Recherches de science religieuse* 44 (1956), pp. 63–84, Pagels concludes that the phrase *in quo omnes peccaverunt* (as it was rendered by Jerome as well as by the pre-Jeromian Old Latin translations used by many of the Latin church fathers including Augustine) was an appropriate translation of *eph' hôi pantes hemarton* only when *in quo* was understood as the causal conjunctive "because." Pagels, however, goes beyond Lyonnet, in implying that it was Augustine who invented the reading of *quo* as a relative referring to Adam: "But Augustine misreads and mistranslates this phrase (which others translate 'in that [i.e., because] all sinned')" (p. 143). Augustine himself, as many scholars have pointed out, discussed the ambiguity of *quo*—which he understood always as a relative, referring either to Adam or to *peccatum*—as early as 412. Augustine, *De peccatorum meritis et remissione* I, x = *Patrologia*, vol. 44, col. 115. Eight years later, Augustine cited Hilarius as the authority for his interpretation of Adam as the referent of *quo*, the reading Augustine accepted for the rest of his career: "Nam et sic sanctus Hilarius intellexit quod scriptum est, in quo omnes peccaverunt: ait enim, In quo, id est in Adam, omnes peccaverunt. Deinde addidit: Manifestum in Adam omnes peccasse quasi in massa. Ipse enim per peccatum corruptus, omnes quos genuit, nati sunt sub peccato. Haec scribens Hilarius sine ambiguitate commonuit, quomodo intelligendum esset, in quo omnes peccaverunt." Augustine, *Contra duas epistolas Pelagianorum*, IV, iv = Migne, *Patrologia*, vol. 44, col. 614. Augustine's "Hilarius" was apparently the "Ambrosiaster" (= "pseudo-Ambrose"), whose commentary on the letters of Paul, dating from the late fourth century and attributed by later medieval authors to Augustine's own mentor Ambrose, is our earliest source for the interpretation (*Commentaria in epistolam ad Romanorum*, printed in *Patrologia*, vol. XVII, cols. 45–508, esp. 92–93). See, in addition to the first three works cited above, Julius Gross, *Entstehungsgeschichte des Erbsündendogmas. Von der Bibel bis Augustinus* [*Geschichte des Erbsündendogmas. Ein Beitrag zur Geschichte des Problems vom Ursprung des Übels*, vol. 1 (Munich, 1960)], pp. 54–55, 230–231, 304–305.

A good brief summary of the development of the Catholic position on original sin from the Greek fathers through the Council of Trent is G. Vandervelde, *Original Sin: Two Major Trends in Contemporary Roman Catholic Reinterpretation* (Amsterdam, 1975), pp. 2–41; also Henri Rondet, *Original Sin: The Patristic and Theological Background*, trans. of *Le péchè originel dans la tradition patristique et thèologique* (Paris 1967) by Cajetan Finegan (Shannon, 1972). For a summary of the doctrine on original sin in the offical proclamations of the Lutherans (Augsburg Confession,

Apologia, Schmalkald Articles) as well as on Augustine's doctrine, Luther's Catholic critics, and the decrees issued at Trent, see, in addition to works cited above, Urs Baumann, *Erbsünde? Ihr traditionelles Verständnis in der Krise heutiger Theologie* [Ökumenische Forschungen, ed. Hans Kung and Joseph Ratzinger, II. Soteriologische Abteilung 2 (Freiburg, 1970)], pp. 24–81; Julius Gross, *Entwicklungsgeschichte des Erbsündendogmas seit der Reformation* [*Geschichte des Erbsündendogmas*, vol. 4 (Munich, 1972)], pp. 11–52, 73–79, 84–118.

75. *WA, Tischreden* 4:72 Nr. 4007. On the crucial rôle of Romans 1:17, see esp. *WA* 54:179–187. Although Vogelsang's essay remains controversial in its particulars, scholars now generally accept that, however dramatic Luther's (later and undatable) *Türmerlebnis* may have been for him, his "discovery" of justification by grace alone was rooted in the reading and thinking he did in preparation for the lectures he delivered on the Psalms in 1513/1514, and that the roots extend back into late-medieval theology. Erich Vogelsang, *Die Anfänge von Luthers Christologie nach der ersten Vorlesung* (Berlin, 1929). Cf. Ozment, *Homo spiritualis*, pp. 6, 46 n.

76. In the margin of Augustine's *De vera religione*, chapter lii, next to the question "Quid enim appetit curiositas nisi cognitionem quae certa esse non potest nisi rerum eternarum & eodem modo se semper habentium?" Luther wrote: "Sic ergo nulla perfecta voluntatis in hac vita potest haberi perfectio, ita nec intellectus. Unde omnis philosophia de rebus tali ac tanta pascit intellectum veritate, quali ac quanta bonitate pascit voluntatem eadem creatura. Sed quid hoc? punctum et momentum utrimque." Luther made his annotation in a copy of the *Opuscula plurima* (Straßburg: Martin Flach, 1493), fol. CCXI', owned by the Augustinian monastery at Erfurt. Martin Luther, autograph annotations in Augustine's *Opuscula plurima*, *WA* 9:14. I have quoted Augustine from the edition with the same pagination published two years earlier at Straßburg by the same printer, fol. CCXI' = Erasmus ed. (1528), vol. 1, p. 515 = *Patrologia*, vol. 34, col. 167. Cf. Martin Luther, autograph manuscript of lectures on Paul's letter to the Romans (delivered 1515/1516), *WA* 56:234, 253.

77. Martin Luther, autograph manuscript of lectures on Paul's letter to the Romans (delivered 1515/1516), *WA* 56:312.

78. Although Gross mentions Genesis 6:5 and 8:21 (in order to dismiss their relevance) in his discussion of the concept of original sin in Jewish thought, and Baumann lists Genesis 8:21 together with the other scriptural sources considered at the Council of Trent, none of the works listed above discusses the importance of the interpretation of the Genesis passages for the controversy in the sixteenth century, or, indeed, their use by any of the medieval theologians into whose discussions of original sin they crept despite Augustine's nonreliance on them for his foundational argument. Gross, *Entstehungsgeschichte*, p. 34, and *Entwicklungsgeschichte*, loc. cit.; Baumann, *Erbsünde?*, p. 62. G. M. Lukken, *Original Sin in the Roman Liturgy: Research into the Theology of Original Sin in the Roman Sacramentaria and the Early Baptismal Liturgy* (Leiden, 1973), extends the consideration of the doctrine of original sin to its expression in the liturgies developed in the fourth through the seventh centuries. Although his index of Latin terms (pp. 419–424) includes *concupescentia*, there are no entries for *arbitrium, intentio, voluntas*, or, in the index of Greek terms (pp. 425–426), for *dianoia* (the Septuagint translation of *yeser* at 8:21; it is replaced by the verb *dianoeitai* in 6:5). Neither Genesis passage appears in the index to scriptural citations (pp. 403–406). Nor do they appear in the scriptural index to A.-M. Dubarle, *Le péché originel: Perspectives theologiques* (Paris 1983), pp. 175–178, although that work also includes a short chapter on "Le péché originel dans la confession d' Augsbourg et au concile de Trente."

The neglect was, nevertheless, relative. In addition to its use by Ambrose, Jerome, and Gregory (see above, note 72), Genesis 8:21 was cited in a commentary on Peter Lombard's *Sententiae* on original sin by the Parisian Dominican, Durandus de Saint-Pourçain, *Lectura prima super Sentencias* (but not by Peter Lombard himself: *Sententiae*, II, xxxi, 3). Durandus' commentary on the sentence is printed in *La controverse sur le péché originel au début du XIV<sup>e</sup> siècle. Textes inédits*, ed. Raymond Martin, O.P. [Spicilegium sacrum lovaniense. Etudes et documents 10 (Louvain, 1930)], pp. 169–170.

I have been unable to find any discussion of Luther's retranslation and reinterpretation of the two passages, presumably because Luther scholarship has focused almost exclusively on the problem of locating the moment of Luther's soteriological and hermeneutic "breakthrough" and thus on the so-called "young Luther."

79. Johannes Reuchlin, *De rudimentis hebraicis libri III* (Pforzheim: Tho. Anselm, 1506; photographic reprint: Hildesheim 1974). On Luther's extensive use of Reuchlin's vocabulary in his lectures on the Psalms (1513–1516) and in his *Operationes in Psalmos* (1519–1521): *WA* 3:30,10; 4:331,38 n. 5; *WA* 5:343,29; *WA* 63:524. No direct reference to Reuchlin's entries on *yeser* appears

in Luther's writings. On Reuchlin's *De rudimentis*, especially on his criticism of the Vulgate, see Ludwig Geiger, *Johann Reuchlin, sein Leben und seine Werke* (Leipzig, 1871), pp. 110–135, esp. pp. 122–123 n. 3.

The classic study of Reuchlin, Melanchthon's great uncle and the father of the German-speaking Christian Hebraists, is Ludwig Geiger, *Johann Reuchlin, sein Leben und seine Werke* (Leipzig, 1871; reprinted Nieuwkoop, 1964). Two brief essays on the German Hebraists of the sixteenth century, especially Sebastian Münster: Erwin I. J. Rosenthal, "Sebastian Muenster's Knowledge and Use of Hebrew Exegesis," in *Essays in Honour of the Very Rev. Dr. J. H. Hertz, Chief Rabbi of the United Hebrew Congregations of the British Empire on the Occasion of His Seventieth Birthday*, ed. I. Epstein, E. Levine, and C. Roth (London, 1942), pp. 351–369; Frank Rosenthal, "The Rise of Christian Hebraism in the Sixteenth Century," *Historia Judaica* 7 (1945), pp. 167–191.

80. "*yasar* Finxit. formavit. creavit. orsus est. Gen. ii. In quo posuit hominem quem formaverat. & psal. xxxiii. Qui finxit singillatim corda eorum. & Isaiae. xliii. Creans te Iacob et formans te Israel. Inde figulus. psal. ii. tanquam vas figuli. et figmentum. psal. cii. Ipse cognovit figmentum nostrum.

"*yeser* Cogitatio vel potius desyderium atque cupiditas. Gen. vi. Et cuncta cogitatio cordis intenta esset ad malum. et dicitur de bono et de malo." A double entry followed, for *yesar* and a second *yeser*, both rendered as verbs: *artavit, trepidavit*. Reuchlin, *De rudimentis*, p. 222.

In Reuchlin's *De rudimentis*, the creation of two separate entries tended to disguise the variations in Jerome's translation of the same Hebrew word. Other word lists, however, such as the vocabulary of Old Testament Hebrew and Aramaic commissioned by Franciscus Ximenez de Cisneros, archbishop of Toledo, primate of Spain, and chancellor to the Spanish monarchs, and published in 1515, defined *yeser* as *figmentum, plasmatio, formatio*, but followed two examples in which Jerome had rendered the word as *figmentum* with Jerome's translations of both Genesis 6:5 and 8:21. In this case there was no break in the entry, only the prefatory remark that "it is also rendered as 'sense' or 'thought.'" A series of comments completed the entry after two more examples: "For which the Hebrews read 'thought' whether it is well formed or obstinate. Also according to the Hebrews, in the text cited above *yeser* means human appetite or desire, whether for good or for evil. Whence in the place cited it could thus be *sensus* ('senses') in our letters." "Iasar. formare. fingere. plasmare. creare. coangustare. arctare. Gen. 2. Formavit igitur dominus deus hominem. & in eodem. Formatis igitur dominus deus de homo cunctis animantibus terre. pro quo hebrei legunt. Et formavit dominus deus de homo omnia animalia terre. . . ." *Vocabularium hebraicum atque chaldaicum totius veteris testamenti cum aliis tractatibus prout infra in prefatione continetur in academia complutensi noviter impressum* (Academia Complutensi: Arnaldus Guillelmus de Brocario, 1515), fol. 67'. "[printed in margin: Figmentum] Iéser. i. figmentum. Plasmatio. formatio. Ps. 102. Quia ipse cognovit figmentum nostrum. Esa. 29. Et figmentum dicat fictori suo. [printed in margin, but no break occurs in text column: Sensus et cogitatio] Ponitur etiam pro sensu vel cogitatione. ut Gen. 6. Et cuncta cogitatio cordis intenta esset ad malum. & in eodem. 8. Sensus enim & cogitatio humani cordis in malum prona sunt. 1. Paralip. 28. Et universas mentium cogitationes intelligit. [printed in margin: Vetus error] Esa. 26. Vetus error abiit. Pro quo hebrei le. Cogitatio. s. bona firmata est sive confirmata est. & secundum hebreos predicta dictio Iéser. significat appetitum vel desiderium hominis ad bonum vel ad malum. [printed in margin, again without interruption of text column: Appetitus] unde in predicto loco poterit esse sensus sicut in littera nostra." Ibid., fol. 68.

Although it did make the variation in definition/translation clear, the Complutensian entry for *yeser* is also confusing. The examples of *yeser* = *figmentum* are the same as Reuchlin's. However, both Genesis 6:5 and 8:21 are given as examples of *yeser* = *cogitatio* (or "sensus et cogitatio," "sense and thought") while no examples are given of *yeser* = *appetitus* ("desire"). In fact, the word *cogitatio* in Jerome's translation of Genesis 6:5 translates another word in the Hebrew text, while *yeser* is subsumed in the participle *intenta* ("striving," "tending toward"); in Jerome's translation of Genesis 8:21, in contrast, *yeser* is translated by *sensus* and *cogitatio* as well as by the participle *prona* ("inclining toward"). The reference to unspecified rabbinic commentaries ("secundum Hebreos," possibly David Kimhi) announced by the marginal note *Appetitus* seems intended to clarify—if only obliquely! ("predicta dictio" and "in predictio loco")—the participles *intenta* and *prona* in Jerome's translation of the two Genesis passages. Not surprisingly, the Complutensian Old Testament, the first to provide side by side the Hebrew text with Latin translation, the Septuagint with a Latin translation, and an Aramaic text with Latin "interpretation," reprinted Jerome's Vulgate as the translation of the Hebrew rather than offering a revised translation.

81. *"yeser* Sollicitus & anxius fuit: Inde *yesera* sollicitudo, cura: Jos. 22. Et *nepesh yesera* Anima anxia: Iere. 31. Item *yesera* idem quod *machshevel* offendiculum: 1. Regum 25. *yeser* Formavit, plasmavit. Item appetivit, concupivit: Inde *yisera bysa* Concupiscentia mala: Psalmo 91. Et *yeser hara* Mala innata concupiscentia: frequens in commentariis." Sebastian Münster, *Dictionarium Chaldaicum, non tam ad Chaldaicos interpretes quam Rabbinorum intelligenda commentaria necessarium ex baal Aruch & Chal. bibliis atque Hebraeorum peruschim congestum* (Basel: Johann Froben, 1527), p. 180.

Cf. the *Dictionarium Hebraicum* published by Münster with the same press in 1523 (p. 179):

*"yasar* Creavit, formavit, finxit, plasmavit. . . .

*"yeser* Creatura, figmentum . . . Ipse cognovit figmentum nostrum.

*"Yeser* Chald. *yesera* cogitatio, concupiscentia, fomes, cupiditas, appetitus."

Although I was eventually able to read this passage in British Library copy of the *Dictionarium hebraicum*, I am most grateful to Christa Sammons and Rick Hart for their courtesy in reading this passage to me telephonically from the copy in the Beinecke Library, Yale University.

82. In the end, this was as true of the vocabulary commissioned by the primate of Spain as of the vocabulary compiled by the soon-to-become-infamous Reuchlin. Nevertheless, the destabilizing potential of philological investigation was not immediately apparent, and the first modern translation of the Bible from Hebrew, Aramaic, and Greek was sanctioned by three popes, including Luther's archenemy Leo X. Sanctes Pagninus of Lucca had begun his translation in the last decade of the fifteenth century, before the advent of printed Hebrew/Latin lexica, and must have completed it before 1520, the year in which he showed it to Leo X. Although the pope agreed to fund its publication, only a small amount had been printed before he died; despite the papal privileges Pagninus had received for his work from both Adrian VI and Clement VII, problems in fund-raising caused the publication of Pagninus' translation to be delayed until 1528. Remarkable for its separation of the Apocrypha from the rest of the Old Testament and for its division of each chapter into numbered verses, Pagninus' translation is of interest here for its author's recognition of the problems with Jerome's translation of Genesis 6:5 and 8:21 (apparently even before they had become proof texts for Luther and his followers) and for his attempt to reconcile accurate translation with Catholic orthodoxy. Although Pagninus' independence from Jerome's translation was clear in his rendering of *yeser* as "imagination" in 6:5 and as "thought" in 8:21 and in his replacement of the conative verb "intends" with the simple "is" in the same passages, Pagninus offered an implicit explanation of the discrepancies in the *Hebrew Thesaurus* he published a year later, in 1529. In the entry on *yeser* he brought "desire," "thought," and "creation" together in a single definition: "desire, thought of the human heart, which forms and causes many things which the heart desires: creation." "Et videt dominus, quod multa esset malitia hominum in terra, et quod omnis imaginatio cogitationum cordis eorum, tantummodo esset malum omni die." *Biblia. Habes in hoc libro prudens lector utriusque instrumenti novam translationem aeditam*, trans. Sanctes Pagninus (Lyon: Antonius du Ry, 1528 [1527]), fol. 2'. ". . . cogitatio cordis hominis mala est à pueritia sua. . . ." Ibid., fol. 3. *"yeser* Desiderium, cogitatio cordis humani, *qui multa format & efficit, quae cor concupiscit:* Figmentum." Sanctes Pagninus, *Thesaurus linguae sanctae: lexicon Hebraicum* (Lyons: S. Gryphius, 1529) [*Short-Title Catalogue of Books Printed in France and of French Books Printed in Other Countries from 1470 to 1600 Now in the British Museum* (London, 1924), p. 334]; quoted from Pagninus, *Thesauri Hebraicae linguae* (Antwerp: Christophor Plantin, 1572), p. 41. The definition and commentary were considerably augmented in a later edition: Pagninus, *Thesaurus linguae sanctae, sive lexicon Hebraicum*, augmented by Johann Mercer, Antonius Cevallerius, B. Cornelius Bertram (Lyons: Bartholomaeus Vincentius, 1575), cols. 1030–1031.

On Pagninus of Lucca and his translation, see T. H. Darlow and H. F. Moule, *Historical Catalogue of the Printed Editions of Holy Scripture in the Library of the British and Foreign Bible Society* (London, 1911), vol. 2, part 2, pp. 924–925.

83. Nor is there evidence that Luther had investigated the Hebrew texts at Genesis 6:5 and 8:21 in preparation for the Heidelberg *Disputatio* of 1518. Martin Luther, "Disputatio Heidelbergae habita" (1518), *WA* 1:371.

84. Following the path suggested by his own explication of the passage in his *Disputatio* of 1518, Luther in 1520 argued that Jerome's use of the noun "thought" rather than the verb "thinks" misrepresented what he saw as the sense of active striving in the Hebrew original. In fact, the *yeser* of the Hebrew texts was not a verb but a noun. The confusing entries for the word in Reuchlin's *De rudimentis hebraicis* (1506) may well have been the source of Luther's mistake. For the entries themselves, see above, note 80. Luther's criticism seems to indicate that the noun

*cogitatio* had by the sixteenth century lost its more active, gerundive aspect. Both the more active "thinking," i.e., "the power or act of thinking," and its result, "thought," would be acceptable renderings of *cogitatio* in a classical author. *A Latin Dictionary Founded on Andrew's Edition of Freund's Latin Dictionary*, ed. Charlton Lewis and Charles Short (Oxford, 1879), p. 360.

85. Martin Luther, "Assertio omnium articulorum" (1520), *WA* 7:143. In the German defense of his theses, published in 1521, Luther did not refer to the Hebrew text, but used the verbal forms *gedenckt* and *begerd* in his translation of the two passages, reserving the noun forms *gedancken* and *begird* for his elaboration of the passages' force: "Item Moses Gen. vi. und viii. 'Alles was des menschen hertz gedenckt und begerd, ist nit mehr denn bosz zu allen stunden'. Horet hie lieben Papisten. Moses thut hie seinen mund wol auff widder euch, was wolt yhr datzu sagenn? ist ein guter gedanck oder will ym menschen zu einer stund, szo mussen wir Mosen lugen straffen, der alle stund, alle gedancken, alle begird des menschlichen hertzen bosze schilt. Was ist denn das für ein freyheit, die nit mehr denn zum boszen geneigt ist?" Martin Luther, "Grund und Ursach aller Artikel D. Martin Luthers szo durch Romische Bulle unrechtlich vordampt seyn" (1521), *WA* 7:447.

86. Martin Luther, "Assertio omnium articulorum M. Lutheri per bullam Leonis, X. novissima damnatorum" (1520), *WA* 7:143. Despite his lack of reference to it, Luther may have been influenced here by the adverb *epimelôn*, which occurs in the Septuagint text at both Genesis 6:5 and 8:21 (or by its rendering as *diligenter* in the Old Latin and Complutensian translations of the Greek text). On this possibility, see below note 94.

I do not mean to suggest that Luther was at this time aware of the rabbinic commentaries on *yeser hara*; he himself was not a Hebraist, nor had the term appeared in the sort of vocabularies he was likely to have encountered.

87. Augustine, *In evangelium Ioannis expositio*, Tractatus I = *Patrologia*, vol. 35, col. 1388. Luther may also have had in mind the passage at *Confessiones* VII, ix, in which John 1:8—"He was not that light, but was sent to bear witness of that light"—was applied not to John the Baptist but to the human soul: "Et quia hominis anima quamvis testimonium perhibeat de lumine, non est tamen ipsa lumen, sed verbum dei deus est lumen verum quod illuminat omnem hominem venientem in hunc mundum." Quoted from Erasmus ed. (1528), vol. 1, p. 93 = *Patrologia*, vol. 32, col. 740. "Et quia hominis anima quamvis testimonium," the first phrase of the sentence (i.e., up to the first line break) was underlined by the sixteenth-century reader of the copy I used: Houghton Library, Harvard University: *fNC5 .Er153 .528a2 v.1, p. 93.

88. Martin Luther, "Das Evangelium ynn der hohe Christmeß auß S. Johanne am ersten Capitel," *Weihnachtspostille* (1522), *WA* 10,1:203, 204.

89. In fact, the Christmas sermons written at Wartburg in 1521 and published in 1522 display an attitude very different from that of the young Augustinian monk writing in the margins of Augustine's treatises and annotating Peter Lombard's already Augustinian *Sentences* with yet more references to the African father, or that of the crusader who in 1525 chose a quotation from Augustine's attack on the Pelagian Julian as the title for his response to Erasmus. As will become clear, it was precisely Augustine's Neoplatonic psychological anthropology that aroused Luther's criticism in the *Weihnachtspostille*. Cf. the evidence of "Randbemerkungen Luthers," ed. Georg Buchwald, *WA* 9:2–94, and Luther, *De servo arbitrio ad D. Erasmum Roterdamum* (Wittenberg: Hans Lufft, 1525), *WA* 18:600–787, with *Weihnachtspostille* (1522), *WA* 10,1:210. Additionally, on the fallibility of Augustine, see *WA* 10,1:195–196, 278, 580, 589.

90. Precise dates for the works are not available, but Augustine seems to have begun work on *De trinitate* c. 400, on the second half (with which we have been most concerned) c. 410. The work was published in unfinished version (i.e., without the last three books) against Augustine's wishes c. 414 and finally completed c. 417. The *Tractatus*, begun perhaps a half dozen years later, was completed at about the same time as *De trinitate*. Cf. Augustine, *Retractiones* II, xv = *Patrologia*, vol. 32, cols. 635–636; Burnaby, introduction to *Later Works*, p. 13; Schmaus, *Psychologische Trinitätslehre*, p. 4; Schindler, *Wort und Analogie*, p. 7; Peter Brown, *Augustine of Hippo* (2nd ed.: New York, 1986), pp. 184, 282.

91. "Unnd dieweyl es der rawm gibt, wollen wyr dasselb falsch naturlich liecht, das alle iamer und ungluck anricht, baß antzeygen. Es ist mit dem naturlichen liecht wie mit allen andernn gelieden und krefften des menschen; wer tzweyffellt daran, das der mensch sey durch das ewige wort gottis geschaffen ynn alle seynen krefften wie alle andere ding? und ist gottis creatur. Aber dennoch ist keyn guttis ynn yhm, das ist (wie Moses sagt Gen. 6.): alle seyn gedancken unnd synn mit allen krefften sind nur zu dem bößen geneugt." Luther, *WA* 10,1:204.

92. As usual, Luther has here combined the two texts or, rather, quoted Genesis 8:21

omitting "from its youth." I offer the following translation of 8:21 in the Bible published in 1483 by the Nuremburg printer Anton Koberger (fol. VIII') as an unprejudiced German rendering of the Vulgate text: "Wann der syn unnd der gedanck menschlichs hertzen die seyn genaiget zu dem ubel von der kintheit."

No such insertion occurred in any other quotation of the Genesis verses by Luther, although they did vary among themselves. The following are quotations from the same period. "Sensus et cuncta cogitatio cordis humani prona est ad malum omni tempore." "Disputatio Heidelbergae habita" (1518), *WA* 1:366. "Item Moses Gen. vi. und viii. 'Alles was des menschen hertz gedenckt und begerd, ist nit mehr denn bosz zu allen stundenn'." "Grund und Ursach aller Artikel D. Martin Luthers szo durch Romische Bulle unrechtlich vordampt seyn" (1521), *WA* 7:447. ". . . alle gedancken unnd syn des menschlichen hertzen stehn zu dem ergisten alletzeyt. . . ." Martin Luther, *Von dem Bapstum zu Rome: widder den hochbreumpten Romanisten zu Leiptzck* (Wittenberg, 1522), *WA* 6:291.

93. Luther, letter to Georg Spalatin (14 May 1521), *WA, Briefe* 2:337. For the chronology of Luther's work on his *Advents-* and *Weihnachtspostillen*: *WA* 10,1,2:xlvii; Gottfried G. Krodel, "Excursus," *Luther's Works*, vol. 48: *Letters I* (Philadelphia, 1963), pp. 237–243.

94. The Septuagint, familiar to late-medieval theologians in the West primarily in the biblical quotations from the Old Latin Bibles (translations of the Septuagint) scattered throughout patristic writings (including those of Augustine himself), was made available with an interlinear Latin translation by the publication in 1517 of the polyglottal Old Testament by the Spanish Academia Complutensi under the patronage of Cardinal Francisco Ximenes de Cisneros, archbishop of Toledo and regent of Castile (Erasmus would address the dedicatory letter in his 1528/1529 edition of Augustine's *Opera omnia* to Cisneros' successor as archbishop and Spanish primate, Alfonso Fonseca; vol. 1, p. 3). Both the Complutensian interlinear translation and the Old Latin versions faithfully rendered the Septuagint's verb *dianoeitai* in Genesis 6:5 as *cogitat* and its noun *dianoia* in 8:21 as *cogitatio*. Compare the Complutensian: "& omnis cogitat in corde suo diligenter ad mala omnibus diebus" and "incumbit cogitatio hominis diligenter ad mala: ex adolescentia sua" with the very infrequent quotations of the passages in Old Latin translations by Augustine and other church fathers (see above, note 72). *Vetus testamentum multiplici lingua*, vol. 1, fol. +iii, b–b', biiii.

The "Greek" in Luther's letter to Spalatin could, of course, be simply a reference to the Greek New Testament, which had been made available by Johann Froben's press at Basel in editions edited by Erasmus in 1516 and 1519, as well as by a Venetian edition (1518) and an edition printed at Hagenau (1521), or even to Septuagint psalters, of which at least three editions had been published by 1500. *Historical Catalogue*, vol. 2, part 1, pp. 2–6 no. 1412; vol. 2, part 2, pp. 574–578.

95. Luther, "Assertio omnium articulorum" (1520), *WA* 7:143; cf. above, note 86. It should, however, be noted that Luther used *de industria* in 1520 only in a greatly expanded paraphrase intended to display the conative implication of Moses' supposed use of active verbs. Here as in the other examples quoted above (note 92), Luther's own version of what the Hebrew text "actually" said made no reference to the effort and industry he stressed in his paraphrase: "Insuper textum haebreum sic referre licet: 'Quoniam quicquid cupit et cogitat cor humanis, solummodo malum est omni die'." Ibid.

As was the case with Luther's quotations of the Genesis passages in works written before the *Weihnachtspostille*, the German translation of the Pentateuch prepared by Luther immediately after his return to Wittenberg from the Wartburg in 1522 showed no insertions from the Septuagint or elsewhere:

6.5: "Da aber der HERRE sahe, das der menschen bosheyt gros war auff erden, und alles tichten und trachten yhrs hertzen nur boss war ymerdar"; 8.21: "denn das tichten des menschlichen hertzen ist bose von der iugent auff." Martin Luther, trans., *Das Allte Testament deutsch* (Wittenberg: [Melchior Lotther], 1523), fol. 4, 5'. Only Luther's translation of the Pentateuch was published in 1523; his translation of the Histories appeared in the next year; his translation of the Prophets was printed in 1532; the Apocrypha, translated primarily by others but with introductory matter by Luther, was finally published together with the other section in 1534 as *Biblia. Das ist: Die gantze heilige Schrifft: Deudsch* (Wittenberg: Hans Lufft, 1534).

96. "Iamne igitur ascendendum est qualibuscunque intentionis viribus ad illam summam & altissimam essentiam, cuius impar imago est humana mens, sed tamen imago. . . ." *De trinitate X*, xii; quoted from Erasmus ed. (1528), vol. 3, p. 269 = *Patrologia*, vol. 42, col. 984. On the meaning of *intentio* in Augustine's writings, see above, note 9.

97. "Aber dahyn mag das naturlich liecht nit reychen, das es mocht sagen, wilchs gutt und

böße ding sey, und geschicht yhm eben alß dem, der da sollte gen Rom gehen und gienge hynder sich; denn derselb wißte wol, das man sollte die rechte straß gehen, wer gen Rom wolte, er wißte aber nit, wilche dieselb rechte straß were." Luther, "Evangelium ynn der hohe Christmesß," *WA* 10,1:203.

98. Luther acknowledged in the same paragraph that human reason was quite capable of attending to things that did not involve either moral or spiritual matters—his example of an activity within the capacity of human reason was taken from mathematics, a sphere that Augustine, in contrast, had identified as spiritual.

99. Martin Luther, *Von dem Bapstum zu Rome: widder den hochberumpten Romanisten zu Leiptzck* (1522), *WA* 6:291–292.

For just one example of the connection between Luther's earlier pursuit of the fourfold seeing through Scripture to some dim vision of divine truth and his Augustinian reliance on the promise of I Corinthians 13:12, see his comment on Psalm 80: ". . . thou that dwellest between the cherubim shine forth. . . . Turn us again, O God, and cause thy face to shine," in the "Dictata super Psalterium" (ms., 1513–1516), *WA* 3:606–607.

100. Particularly striking here is Luther's appeal to the *De doctrina christiana* written by the bishop whose "monoglossic" interpretations he had once praised above those of the linguist Jerome, as an authority for the necessity of linguistic knowledge in the interpretation of Scripture. "An die Radherrn aller stedte deutsches lands: das sie Christliche schulen auffrichten und hallten sollen" (1524), *WA* 15:40.

101. Martin Luther, "Eyn brieff an die Christen Zu Straspurg widder den schwermer geyst" (1524), *WA* 15:396.

102. "Videns Deus quod multa esset hominis malitia in terra, & omne figmentum cogitationum cordis eorum vanum & pravum omni tempore." Philipp Melanchthon, *In obscuriora aliquot capita Geneseos annotationes* (Hagenoa: Johann Secerius, 1523), fol. Kiii' = *Commentarius in Genesis*, in *Opera omnia*, ed. Caspar Peucer (Wittenberg: Johannes Crato, 1562), vol. 2, pp. 396–397.

The German translation of work appeared the next year under the title *Erklärung oder anzaygung in etliche schwersten Capittel des ersten Buchs Moysi* (s.l., 1524); in it the Genesis passage was rendered as it had been by Luther in his German translation of the Pentateuch: "Da der herr sach das der menschen boßhayt groß was auff erden, und alles tychten unnd trachten ires hertzen nur ymmerdar böß was" (fol. Fiii); cf. *Das Allte Testament deutsch*, trans. Martin Luther, vol. 1: Pentateuch (Wittenberg: [M. Lotther], 1523/24), fol. 4. An English equivalent for the sixteenth-century German "tychten unnd trachten" (= *dichten und trachten*) is supplied by William Tyndale's rendering of the same passage in the English Bible condemned by Thomas More as having been translated "after Luther's counsel": "And whan the LORDe sawe ye wekednesse of man was encreased apon the erth, and that all the ymaginacion and toughtes of his hert was only evell continually, he repented that he had made man apon the erth and sorowed in his hert." *The fyrst boke of Moses called Genesis*, trans. William Tyndale (Malborow in Hesse: Hans Luft, 1530), fol. viii. Cf. Tyndale's translation of Genesis 8:21: ". . . for the imagynacion of mannes hert is evell, even from the very youth of hym." Ibid., fols. x'–xi. I have chosen in my translation to substitute the more active "imaging" for "imagination" because of Luther's emphasis on the active verbal quality he perceived in the Hebrew and because of the somewhat restricted meaning "imagination" has acquired in our own culture.

103. For Jerome's translation at Psalm 103 (102), and in other contexts, see the lists in Reuchlin's *De rudimentis hebraicis* and the Complutensian *Vocabularium hebraicum*; quoted above, note 80.

104. *Vana imago* referred to ghosts in Horace's odes, but the adjective was more often applied to deceitful speech by other authors. Cf. Cicero, *De amicitia* 26, 98; *Oratio pro Quinto Roscio Amerino* 40, 117; Ovid, *Metamorphoses* 13, 263; Quintillian, 1, 8, 20; 7, 2, 34; Suetonius, *Caligula* 38. For these and other examples, see *A Latin Dictionary*, p. 1957.

105. *De libero arbitrio voluntatis* was the title of the treatise Augustine had written against the Manichaeans c. 387–395.

The translation given by Melanchthon in 1523 also appeared in the published Latin version of the lectures Luther himself delivered on Genesis in 1523/1524: "Cuncta cogitatio cordis humani. Pugnantia in hoc textu esse videntur, cum dicit generaliter: Videns Deus, quod multa esset malicia hominis in terra et omne figmentum cogitationum cordis eorum vanum et pravum omni tempore." Martin Luther, *In Genesin, Mosi librum sanctissimum . . . declamationes* (presumably read as lecture 1523/1524; published 1527), *WA* 24:1–710; here, 169. There was no discussion of the passage in the German version of the lectures published by a different editor in the same year (i.e., 1527). The two theologians rendered the word they had translated into Latin as *figmentum* as *tichten* in their German translation. Cf. note 103 above and Luther's Bible translation, *Das Allte Testament deutsch* vol. 1 (Wittenberg: [M. Lotther], 1523/1524), fol. 4, 5'.

106. "Et tamen hoc dictum non pertinet ad universum genus hominum, sed tantum ad illius aetatis homines nefandis vitiis corruptissimos. . . . Nec tamen simpliciter ad universos illius aetatis homines pertinebat., [sic] quandoquidem laudatur Noë ut vir iustus & deo gratus. . . . Proclivitas autem ad malum, quae est in plerisque hominibus, non adimit in totum libertatem arbitrii, etiamsi vinci in totum non potest, sine auxilio gratiae divinae. Quod si nulla pars resipiscentiae pendet ab arbitrio, sed omnia necessitate quadam geruntur à deo, quur inibi datum est hominibus spatium paenitendi?" Desiderius Erasmus, *De libero arbitrio diatribe, sive Collatio* (Basel: Johann Froben, 1524), fol. d6'–d7.

107. Luther's title, in contrast to Erasmus', was not taken from the title to any of Augustine's treatises; the idea of the lack of freedom of the will in its natural state was, however, articulated by Augustine in his *De spiritu et littera* III = Erasmus ed. (1528), vol. 3, p. 572 = *Patrologia*, vol. 44, col. 203. The actual phrase *servum arbitrium* was to be found in Augustine's *Contra Iulianum Pelagianum* II; vol. 7, p. 665 of the edition edited by Erasmus in 1528 = *Patrologia*, vol. 44, col. 689; it was the latter passage that Luther cited in *De servo arbitrio*; WA 18:665.

108. "Aut cur non et hic Ebraicum consuluit, ubi nihil de pronitate Moses dicit? ne cavillandi caussam habeas. Sic enim habet cap. 6: Chol Ietzer Mahescheboth libbo rak ra chol ha iom, hoc est: omne figmentum cogitationum cordis eius tantum malum cunctis diebus. Non dicit intentum vel pronum ad malum, sed prorsus malum ac nihil nisi malum fingi et cogitari ab homine tota vita. Natura maliciae eius descripta est, quod nec faciat nec possit aliter, cum sit mala; neque enim arbor mala fructus alios quam malos ferre potest teste Christo." Martin Luther, *De servo arbitrio ad D. Erasmum Roterdamum* (Wittenberg: Johann Lufft, 1525), WA 18:600–787; here, p. 736.

109. "Quod autem hebraismum nobis citat, qui nec cum Graecis, nec cum interpretatione Hieronymi consentit, nec ab ullo probatorum interpretum annotatur, respondere possum, aut Lutherum non intelligere vim Hebraei sermonis, aut codicem habere corruptum." Desiderius Erasmus, *Hyperaspistae liber secundus adversus librum Martini Lutheri, cui titulum fecit Seruum arbitrium* (Basel: Johann Froben, 1527), para. 181, pp. 340–343 = *Opera omnia*, vol. 9, part 2 (Basel: Hieronymus Froben and Nicolaus Episcopius, 1540), pp. 1195–1196.

110. Responding to a question posed in advance concerning the biblical and patristic sources appropriate to its discussion, the theologians appointed to the select committee on original sin at the Council of Trent gave precedence to Genesis 8:21: "Esse peccatum originale probarunt pluribus scripturae locis, sed praecipue: Genesi 8: Sensus enim et cogitatio humani cordis in malum prona est ab adolescentia sua; et ibi Ambrosius." "Summa responsionis theologorum ad suprascriptos articulos" (25 May 1546, 10 A.M.), *Concilium tridentinum, diariorum, actarum, epistolorum, tractatum nova collectio*, ed. Societas Goerresiana (Freiburg 1901–   ), vol. 5 = Actorum pars altera (1911), pp. 164–165. Joannes Morellus, one of the members of the select committee (*congregatio theologorum minorum de peccato originali*), composed a treatise on original sin during the session (i.e., after 24 May 1546). The treatise opened by offering the two Genesis passages as proof of the "morbidity of nature itself": "An sit peccatum originale? Constat esse ex scripturae testimoniis, ex diversorum conciliorum sententiis, ex universali ecclesiae consuetudine, ex consense patrum et omnium theologorum et ex philosophorum quaerimoniis de conditione naturae nostrae, quamquam unde sit ignorarent. Gen. 6: Cuncta cogitatio cordis intenta est ad malum omni tempore. Gen. 8: Sensus et cogitatio humani cordis in malum prona sunt ab adolescentia.—Haec satis indicant ipsius naturae morbum." Joannes Morellus, *De peccato originale* (after 24 May 1546), I; *Concilium tridentinum*, vol. 12, p. 553. Similarly, the third paragraph of the prefatory remarks in the notes on the proposed decree on original sin itself closed with another reference to Genesis 8:21: "infirmi denique et inepti ad omne opus bonum et e contrario ad omne malum idonei et proni ab adolescentia." "Decreti de peccato originali minuta" (June 1546), ibid., vol. 12, p. 567.

111. "Fateor in quibusdam ingeniis bene natis ac bene educatis minimum esse pronitatis. Maxima proclivitatis pars est non ex natura, sed ex corrupta institutione, ex improbo convictu, ex assuetudine peccandi maliciaque voluntatis. Et scriptura Genes. 6. non proprie loquitur de natura hominis, sed de corruptis affectibus, & in genere loquitur. Necque enim arbitror haec in Noe & in huius familiam congruere." Erasmus, *Hyperaspistae liber secundus*, loc. cit.

Several theologians at the Council of Trent used Genesis 8:21 in this same limited way to argue for the reform of the cathedral schools attended by adolescents. "Decreta super reformatione [of the clerics and orders] publicata in eadem sessione septima Tridentina sub Pio Quarto Pontifice Maximo" (15 July 1563), canon 18; *Concilium tridentinum*, vol. 9, p. 628. Cf. the report made to Ferdinand himself on the discussion of the difficult question of clerical marriage at Trent: "Primum Ferdinandi Imperatoris circa concilium indicendum responsum" (Vienna, 20 and 26 June 1560); ibid., vol. 8, p. 47.

112. We have already noted Pagninus' new Latin translation of the Bible (completed by 1520 but not published until 1528), which quietly revised the rendering of the Hebrew *yeser* at Genesis 6:5 and 8:21: "Et videt dominus, quod multa esset malitia hominum in terra, et quod omnis imaginatio cogitationum cordis eorum, tantummodo esset malum omni die." *Biblia*, trans. Pagninus (1528 [1527]), fol. 2'. And "cogitatio cordis hominis mala est à pueritia sua." Ibid., fol. 3.

Among the most distinguished of Pagninus' successors was the Hebraist Sebastian Münster, whose influential Latin translation of the Old Testament (1534) agreed with Melanchthon and Luther in its translation of *yeser* as *figmentum*: "& omne figmentum cogitationum cordis eius tantummodo esset malum per singulos dies" and "nam figmentum cordis humani malum est ab adolescentia sua." *Hebraica Biblia Latina planeque nova*, ed. and trans. Sebastian Münster (Basel: Michael Isingrinius and Henricus Petrus, 1534), fol. 6, 7'. Münster's *scholium* on 8:21 acknowledged and accounted for the existence of alternate readings, a practice continued by most of his Protestant successors: "Figmentum,] Formatur hoc nomen à verbo *yeser* id est, formavit. Exponunt tamen Hebraei pro *ta'avah* id est, concupiscentia & inclinatione, sive ea sit bona sit mala." Ibid., fol. 8. Münster's translation was particularly influential among Swiss and English Protestants; Darlow and Moule, *Historical Catalogue*, vol. 2, part 2, no. 5087. Cf. The *scholium* added at Genesis 8:21 in 1542 by Isodorus Clarius, a later participant in the discussions of the Vulgate text at the Council of Trent. *Vulgata aeditio veteris ac novi testamenti, quorum alterum ad Hebraicam, alterum ad Graecam emendatum est diligentissimè*, ed. Isodorus Clarius Brizianus (Venice: Peter Schoeffer of Germany, 1542), vol. 1, pp. 5, 7.

113. G. Koffmane, "Einleitung und handschriftliche Entwurf zur Genesisvorlesung," *WA* 42:VII–XXV.

114. *In Primum Librum Mose Enarrationes* (delivered as lectures 1535–1545; edited and published 1544–1550), *WA* 42–44. It is only the first volume of the lectures, published with Luther's knowledge two years before his death, with which we will be concerned.

In the *Enarrationes* we finally encounter explicit references to the philological researches of Sanctes Pagninus, the first modern translator of the entire Bible into Latin. On Pagninus's work as a Bible translator and author of vocabularies, see above, note 82. For Luther's use in the *Enarrationes* of the philological researches by Pagninus and the more familiar Nicolaus de Lyra, see Peter Meinhold, *Die Genesisvorlesung Luthers und ihre Herausgeber* [Forschungen zur Kirchen- und Geistesgeschichte 8 (Stuttgart, 1936)], pp. 201, 343–359, 364–370. Meinhold's useful work is primarily concerned with the problem of separating Luther's own thought from that of the students who made notes and that of Veit Dietrich, the editor of the published *Enarrationes*. Although it is unimportant to my argument whether this most complete version of Luther's epistemological revision should be attributed to Luther himself or to his followers, it should be noted that all of the positions taken by the speaker of the *Enarrationes* in the discussion that follows can be found in other of Luther's mature works and none was taken from sections attributed by Meinhold to other minds. For a comparison of Luther's own preparatory notes on Genesis 1:26 with the printed version, see Meinhold, *Genesisvorlesung Luthers*, pp. 186–189.

On the intentionality of the misreadings by the advocates of free will, see esp. *Enarrationes*, *WA* 42:347–348.

115. *Enarrationes*, *WA* 42:45.

116. Ibid.

117. Ibid. Although he did not use the technical terms of logic at this point in his discussion, Luther approved of the use of logic (dialectic), "which teaches what is true and certain," in biblical exegesis: "Historia enim est, quae, ceu Dialectica, vera et indubitata docet." *Enarrationes*, *WA* 42:173. Not surprisingly, he was particularly fond of using the tools of dialectic against his Scholastic opponents. See, for example, his discussion of "efficient," "formal," and "final" cause in interpretations of Genesis 8:21; ibid., *WA* 42:350–351.

118. A doctrine Luther correctly associated with the Augustinian maxim, "God, who created you without you, will not save you without you," but unfairly accused of positing the natural human will as the preceding and efficient cause of salvation. "Simile est, quod citatur: Deus, qui creavit te sine te, non salvabit te sine te. Hinc conclusum est: liberum arbitrium concurrere tanquam causam praecedentem et efficientem salutis." Ibid.

119. Luther himself argued that the "Sophists" wanted to achieve the impossible by combining the doctrine of free will with the doctrine of the indispensibility of grace—a fairly accurate summary of Augustine's efforts against the Manichaeans and Pelagians. *Enarrationes*, WA 42:348.

120. "Nam ratio sine Spiritu sancto est simpliciter sine cognitione Dei. . . ." *Enarrationes*, WA 42:291.

121. A few pages later, Luther argued that any more direct vision of God should be avoided "unless you are a perfect man like Moses or David" (one of the few instances in which Luther—or his editor—used gender-specific language). Even David and Moses, according to Luther, had apprehended God without ever turning away from the visible *signa* in which he had revealed himself. *Enarrationes*, WA 42:295.

122. *Enarrationes*, WA 42:9–10, 11. It was for the same reason that Luther dismissed the Augustinian distinction between lower and higher reason or intellect as irrelevant. Ibid., 42:138.

123.

> Man fragt. Ob es müglich sey, das die seel die weil sie in dem leib ist, müge dar zü kommen, das sie thü ein anblick in die ewigkait, und da empfach ein vorschmack ewigs lebens und ewiger säligkeit? Man spricht gemeinlich nein, unnd das ist war in dem synn. Alle die weil die seel ein sehenn hat auff den leib, und die ding die dem leib zügehören, und auff die zeit und sunst auff die creaturen, und sich darmit verpildet und vermischet, so mag es nit gesein. Wann sol die seel dahyn lügen oder sehen, so müß sie lauter unnd bloß sein von allen bilden, und abgeschaiden von allen creaturen, und zü forderst von ir selber. Und diß meint man es sey nicht geschehen in der zyt Aber sant Dionysius der wil es müglichen, das maint man auß seinen worten die er schreibt zü Timotheo. Zü der schauwunge göttlicher heimlichait soltu lassen synn und synnlichhait, unnd alles was synn begreiffen mügen, und vernunfft vernünfftigkliche wirckung, und alles das vernunfft begreiffen und erkennen mag, geschaffen, und ungeschaffen, unnd stand auff einem außgang dein selbs, unnd in einem unwissen alles diß vorgesprochnen, unnd kumme in ein einigunge des das da ist über alles wesen unnd erkantnüß.

*Theologia. deutsch.*, ed. Martin Luther (Straßburg: Johann Knobloch, 1519), fol. Aiiii.
The passage continued, with the argument that it was possible with practice to achieve such a state of mystical union at will and that that union was more dear and valuable to God than any corporeal action:

> Hielte er dises nicht für müglich in der zeyt, warumb lernet er es, oder redet einem menschen in der zeyt. Auch wiß das ein meister spricht über die wort Dionysii, das es müglich sey, und das es auch einem menschen also dick geschähe, das er darinn würt verwenet das er das lüget oder sehe als offt er will, und der blick ist keiner er sey edeler und got lieber und wirdiger, dan alles das das alle creatur geleisten mügen als creatur.

Ibid., fols. Aiiii–Aiiii'.
Luther edited an abbreviated version of the work in 1516 under the title *Eyn geystlich edles Buchleynn. von rechter underscheyd und vorstand. was der alt und new mensche sey. Was Adams und was gottis kind sey. und wie Adam ynn uns sterben unnd Christus erseten soll.* (Wittenberg: Johann Grünenberg, 1516); a longer one in 1518 with the following preface: "ist mir nächst der Bibel, und sant Augustin, nit fürkommen ain büch, darauß ich mer erlernet hab und will, was Gott, Christus, Mensch und alle ding seyen." Martin Luther, "Vorred" to his edition of *Theologia. deutsch. Das ist ain edels und kostlichs büchlin, von rechtem verstand, was Adam und Christus sey, und wie Adam in uns sterben, und Christus ersteen soll* (Wittenberg: Johann Grünenberg, 1518), fol. i' = WA 1:378. For discussion of the *Theologia deutsch* as it relates to the development of Luther's soteriology, see above, note 73. By the last decade of his life Luther himself rejected the claims made by the pseudo-Dionysius to Pauline discipleship; WA 42:175.

124. The term *novi Ariani* occurs two pages later than this passage. *Enarrationes*, WA 42:11, 13. The translation "Neo-Arians" is used by George Schick in *Lectures on Genesis, Chapters 1–5* [*Luther's Works* 1 (St. Louis, 1958)], p. 16.

125. "Qui autem extra ista involucra Deum attingere volunt, isti sine scalis (hoc est verbo) nituntur ad coelum ascendere, ruunt igitur oppressi maiestate, quam nudam conantur amplecti, et pereunt. Sicut Ario accidit." *Enarrationes*, WA 42:11.

126. On the *Confessiones* as designedly paradigmatic, see above, note 46. In his reported table conversation for 1532, Luther explicitly refused to grant the *Confessiones* exemplary or didactic authority, a refusal that seems rather to confirm the extent to which they had become for him, at least, paradigmatic of access to God as it was understood by the Catholic church. Veit Dietrich's account was considerably more negative than the conversation reported by Johannes Aurifaber. In both accounts Luther claimed to have given up his study of the father after having been led by

Paul to the discovery of justification by faith; there were, he said, only two worthwhile sentences in all of Augustine's writings. In Aurifaber's report, however, the whole was prefaced by Luther's praise for Augustine's service as a defender of the faith against heretics, especially the Pelagians. Both accounts are given in *WA, Tischreden* 1:140 Nr. 347.

For Luther's use of Augustine's *Confessiones* elsewhere, see the classic work by Pierre Courcelle, *Les Confessions de saint Augustin dans la tradition littéraire. Antécédents et postérité* (Paris 1963), pp. 353–370.

127. The differences between the two vocabularies were only accented by their resonance. In Augustine's account, written from within, to be overwhelmed was to surrender to the indescribable pleasure of the divine embrace. In contrast, Luther's vocabulary was stripped of sensual connotations; arrogance and appetite remained only in the attempted embrace—it was for lèse majesté that the arrogant libertine (understood not in a sexual but in the epistemological sense of *liberum arbitrium*) was sentenced to death.

128. Augustine described their experience in *Confessiones* IX, x; for the quotation, see above, note 48.

129. The chapter from *De trinitate* was cited by Luther in his annotations (1509/1510) on Peter Lombard's *Sententiae*. Cf. *WA* 9:33.

130. Erwin Panofsky, "Introduction," *Abbot Suger on the Abbey Church of St.-Denis and Its Art Treasures* (Princeton, 1946), pp. 17–25. On the relation between late-medieval art and religious piety, see especially the work of the following scholars: Emile Mâle, "L'art religieux traduit des sentiments nouveaux le pathetique," *L'art religieux de la fin du moyen âge en France. Etude sur l'iconographie du moyen âge et sur ses sources d'inspiration* (2nd ed., Paris, 1922), pp. 85–144; Erwin Panofsky, " 'Imago Pietatis'. Ein Beitrag zur Typengeschichte des 'Schmerzensmanns' und der 'Maria Mediatrix,' " in *Festschrift für Max J. Friedländer zum 60. Geburtstage* (Leipzig, 1927), pp. 261–308; Gert von der Osten, *Der Schmerzensmann. Typengeschichte eines deutschen Andachtsbildwerkes von 1300 bis 1600* [Forschungen zur deutschen Kunstgeschichte 7 (Berlin, 1935)]; Sixten Ringbom, "Devotional Images and Imaginative Devotions. Notes on the Place of Art in Late Medieval Private Piety," *Gazette des beaux-arts*, ser. 6, 73 (1969), pp. 159–170; Craig Harbison, "Visions and Meditations in Early Flemish Painting," *Simiolus. Netherlands Quarterly for the History of Art* 15 (1985), pp. 87–118; James H. Marrow, "Symbol and Meaning in Northern European Art of the Late Middle Ages and the Early Renaissance," *Simiolus. Netherlands Quarterly for the History of Art* 16 (1986), pp. 150–169; Robert W. Scribner, "Popular Piety and Modes of Visual Perception in Late-Medieval and Reformation Germany," *Journal of Religious History* 16 (forthcoming, 1990).

131. Panofsky, "Introduction," p. 19.

132. Augustine, *De ordine* II, xix. For a thorough investigation of Luther's earlier position with regard to the Aristotelian and Augustinian definitions of humankind and of the rôle of *ratio*, see Gerhard Ebeling, *Lutherstudien*, vol. 2: *Disputatio de homine*, part 2: *Die philosophische Definition des Menschen: Kommentar zu These 1–19* (Tübingen, 1982), pp. 1–22, 184–202, 211–332.

133. *Enarrationes*, *WA* 42:348.

134. According to Luther's own reckoning, Plato himself had perhaps garnered his learning in Egypt from the writings of the "fathers and prophets." *Enarrationes*, *WA* 42:4. Cf. Erich Seeberg, *Studien zu Luthers Genesisvorlesung; Zugleich ein Beitrag zur Frage nach dem alten Luther* [Beiträge zur Förderung christlicher Theologie 36, 1 (Gütersloh, 1932)], p. 73; Seeberg, *Christus, Wirklichkeit und Urbild* [Luthers Theologie 2 (Stuttgart, 1937)], p. 447. The *Schedelsche Weltchronik* (*Nuremberg Chronicle*) described him both as the "true and highest prophet" and as "a prince among historians": "Moyses der warhafftig und höhst prophet ein fürst der geschichtschreiber." *Das büch der Croniken und gedechtnus wirdigern geschichten von anbegynn der werlt bis auf dise unßere zeit*, trans. Georg Alt (Nuremberg: Anton Koberger for Sebald Schreyer and Sebastian Kamermaister, 1493), fol. XXIX'.

135. "Si igitur Hominem voles vere definire, ex hoc loco definitionem sume, quod sit animal rationale, habens cor fingens. Quid autem fingit? respondet Moses: malum, contra Deum scilicet seu legem dei et homines." *Enarrationes*, *WA* 42:348. It is here worth noting that Seeberg's German summary of this passage—"Der Mensch ist 'ein vernünftiges Tier, mit einem Herzen, das auf Böses sinnt' "—comes close to maintaining the very translation Luther had challenged so strenuously in the previous paragraphs as subject to the weaker interpretation of "tending toward," "inclining toward." Cf. Seeberg, *Christus*, p. 449; Seeberg, *Studien zu Genesisvorlesung*, p. 76; *Enarrationes*, *WA* 42:347–348.

136. See above, note 110.

137. *Enarrationes*, *WA* 42:352. This is not to suggest that Luther did not follow Augustine and

many other theologians in seeing the sexual urges of the adolescent as confirmation of the existence of original sin; cf. ibid., 42:351.

It was in a digression associated with this passage that Luther made his most direct response to Erasmus' good nature, good nurture argument (quoted above, note 111).

138. ". . . non libidinem, non tyrannidem, non alia peccata vocat mala, Sed figmentum cordis humani, hoc est, industriam, sapientiam, rationem humanam, cum omnibus viribus, quibus etiam in optimis actionibus ratio utitur." Ibid., *WA* 42:346.

139. "Vocat autem figmentum, sicut aliquoties supra dixi, ipsam rationem cum voluntate et intellectu, etiam tum, cum de Deo cogitat, cum honestissimis operibus exercetur sive politicis sive oeconomicis." Ibid., *WA* 42:348.

140. Luther had already criticized the distinction on other grounds; *Enarrationes*, *WA* 42:138. Cf. ibid., *WA* 42:347–348.

141. *Confessiones* VII, i.

142. Martin Luther, "Wider die himmlischen Propheten, von den Bildern und Sakrament" (1525), *WA* 18:83. Cf. the complaint against images by Luther's colleague at the University of Wittenberg, the professor and iconoclast Andreas Bodenstein von Karlstadt, which placed even greater emphasis on the naturalness of images: "Alßo magk ich sagen, wan man eynen bey den horen tzeugt. ßo merckt man wie vest seine hare stehnd. Hette ich den geist gottis nit wyder die olgotzen horen schreyhen, und sein wort geleßen. Szo hett ich alßo gedacht. Ich hab kein bild lieb. Ich forcht kein bilde. Aber itzt weiß ich, wie ich yn dyßem vall, kegen got und den bildern stehn, und wie vest und tieff bilder yn meinem hertzen sitzen." Andreas Bodenstein von Karlstadt, *Von abtuhung der Bylder, Und das keyn Betdler unther den Christen seyn soll* (Wittenberg: Nikell Schytlentz, 1522), fol. civ'.

Although I have profited greatly from Margarete Stirm's analysis of *Die Bilderfrage in der Reformation* [Quellen und Forschungen zur Reformationsgeschichte 45 (Gütersloh, 1977)]—as from that of her predecessor Hans Preuß, *Martin Luther der Künstler* (Gütersloh, 1931)—I disagree with Stirm's argument that the "Bilderfrage" was "marginal" (*nur eine Randfrage*) in Luther's thought. As I have tried to demonstrate here, the post-lapsarian limitation of the human intellectual faculty to image-based understanding was crucial to Luther's entire epistemology and to his attack on both Catholic and sectarian soteriologies.

143. "Man kan die geistlichen Sachen nicht begreiffen, nisi in bilder fasse." Martin Luther, "Predigt am Sonnabend vor Ostern" (20 April 1538), *WA* 46:308.

144. Martin Luther, "Eyn Sermon von dem newen Tewtament. das ist von der heyligen Messe" (Wittenberg: Johann Grunenberg, 1520; also printed in Leipzig, Nuremberg, Augsburg, and Basel in 1520), *WA* 6:353–378; here, 359.

145. The difficulties of Luther's position between Catholicism and radicalism are clearest in the problem of the Sacrament, the *signum* that was peculiarly effective but whose efficacy and operations were not to be probed by the human mind. The issue was of particular importance in the discussions that prefaced the Marburg Colloquy between Martin Luther and Huldreich Zwingli; on 1 October 1529, Luther's lieutenant Philipp Melanchthon and Zwingli agreed that "the Word is taken as an expression of the mind of God. This mind is the will of God garbed in human words. The human mind grasps this expression of the divine will, when it is drawn by the Father." Hermann Sasse, *This Is My Body: Luther's Contention for the Real Presence in the Sacrament of the Altar* (revised ed., Adelaide, 1977), p. 184. Cf. J. K. S. Reid, *The Authority of Scripture: A Study of the Reformation and Post-Reformation Understanding of the Bible* (London, 1957), pp. 66–72.

In a late work, the anti-Semitic tract "Von den Letzten Worten Davids" (1543), Luther used the Augustinian distinction between *res* and *signum* in an attempt to show that Christ's incarnation was more than mere *signum*. *WA* 54:62–63.

146. Martin Luther, "Wider die himmlischen Propheten, von den Bildern und Sakrament" (1525), *WA* 18:136.

147. Quoted in Henry Chadwick, *Augustine* (Oxford, 1986), p. 42.

148. Martin Luther, "Wider die himmlischen Propheten," *WA* 18:68.

149. Luther, *Enarrationes*, *WA* 42:48.

150. Ibid., *WA* 42:48.

151. Ibid., *WA* 42:48. Cf. Augustine's description of the divinity as the voice at a distance: "Et clamasti de longinquo, immo vero ego sum qui sum [Exo. 3]. Et audivi sicut auditur in corde. . . ." Augustine, *Confessiones* VII, x; quoted from Erasmus ed. (1528), vol. 1, p. 94 = *Patrologia*, vol. 32, col. 742.

152. *De trinitate* XIV, xvii. The metaphor was a frequent one in Augustine's writings.

153. Luther, *Enarrationes*, WA 42:46. Striking here is the contrast between the clear hopelessness of Luther's account and Christ's healing of lepers as recounted by the authors of the synoptic Gospels: cf. Matthew 8:2–3; 10:8; 11:5; Mark 1:40–42; 14:3; Luke 4:27; 5:12–13; 7:22; 17:12.

154. On the historical nature of God's self-revelation, see Seeberg, *Studien zu Genesisvorlesung*, pp. 86–97.

155. Luther, *Enarrationes*, WA 42:44.

156. I have here rendered as "will to sign" *voluntas signi*, the phrase Luther borrowed from the Scholastics to distinguish what humankind could know of God from God's essential will (*voluntas substantialis*), which the Scholastics regarded as hidden from minds without grace or scholarship and which Luther regarded as entirely hidden.

On the appropriateness of painting on walls images of God's actions in the world, see Luther, "Wider die himmlischen Propheten," WA 18:82–83, and Luther's introduction to his illustrated *Passional* (added in 1529 to the *Bett buchlin*, which had been in print since 1522), WA 10, 2:458–459.

157. Luther, Sermon on Deuteronomy 7:6 (31 October 1529; first printed from notes by Georg Rörer, Anton Lauterbach, Philipp Fabricius in 1564, ed. Johann Aurifaber), WA 28:677.

158. See above, notes 58–65.

159. Martin Luther, "Wider die himmlischen Propheten," WA 18:67–68.

160. On the term *voluntas substantialis*, which was Scholastic rather than Augustinian, see *Enarrationes*, WA 42:294–295.

161. Ibid., 173.

162. Martin Luther, "Sabbato paschae. 20. Aprilis. A prandio" (1538), sermon notes taken by Georg Rörer, WA 46:308.

163. Luther, *Enarrationes*, WA 42:294.

164. This destabilization became in its turn the basis on which at least one rather ordinary Catholic clergyman, Bishop Berthold of Chiemsee, a bishopric southeast of Munich, defended his church against the Protestants. In the fascinating albeit unoriginal *summa* he published at the end of the 1520s (admittedly a decade of singular disorder and disagreement among the Protestants), Bishop Berthold charged that the Protestants ("Luterisch und mer ander aberglawb") could not agree among themselves on their texts, but relied on disordered and false exegeses: "Dieselben all haben kain gewisse veraynigung noch gegründte schrift noch glaublich kundschafft irer ketzerey anders dann sovil sy heylige schrift an ettlichen ortten, sonderlich das Ewangeli und Epistel Pauli, felschen oder sonst äbich auslegen und auff iren mütwilligen syn betrüglich ziehen." Berthold Pürstinger, Bishop of Chiemsee, *Tewtsche Theology* (Munich: Hans Schobfer, 1528), chapter 1, para. 8 = fol. Bii'.

Long before the Council of Trent's discussions on the validity of Jerome's Vulgate translation, Bishop Berthold criticized the new translations precisely because of their reliance on Hebrew and Greek texts, which the bishop argued had likely suffered intentional pollution over the centuries at the hands of the Jews and Greeks (the latter, of course, were now all Turks):

> Man pfligt yetz auf ain newes heilige schrifft zedulmatschen aus allten hebreischen und kriechischen Texten der Bibel, die durch juden und kriechen, als veind römischer kirch, dickmals gefelscht und auf ungerechten syn, wider new gesetz, an ettlichen orten gezogen und zü betrug der cristen, unrecht außgelegt ist. . . . [of Jews:] Sy erwegen auch heilige schrift nur fleischlich nach dem püchstab, nit geistlich nach rechtem verstand. Wie sy vom herren bezigen seinn. do er zü in sprach, ir irret unnd versteet nit die schrifft noch die krafft gottes. . . . [after discussing the schism between East and West and insisting that the Greeks were now all heathens and Turks] Daraus zevermüeten daz sy den Text alltes und newes gesetz, gefelscht unnd auf iren vortail gezogen haben. Aus denen und anndern ursachen, ist mer zeglawben Jheronimo unnd andern heiligen lerern, die vor langen zeiten heilige schrift, aus hebreisch und kriechisch, in latein verdulmatsch und awßgelegt haben, dann ihenen die diser zeit heilige schrifft, auß der juden und hayden püechen nemmen. nachdem dieselben püech zwischen solher zeit vil gefelscht mögen sein. Darumb ist unzymlich in denselben frembden püechen grund oder auslegung zesüechen heiliger schrift.

Ibid., chapter 15, para. 4 = fol. Giiii'. Not surprisingly, it was Luther's presuming to pronounce on the accuracy of the traditional translation and exegeses which was most troubling to the Catholic churchman:

> Aber verkhert Lerer schamen sich nit vor gelerten, wo sy gleych mit listen die schrifft verkeren oder gefärlich auslegen und die warhait verplüemen. dieweil sy zü vodrist süchen iren aygen

lob und rüeme bey gemainen unschrifftgelerten lewten und bey denselben mit hässigen worten die gerechten lerer zegeswaigen und nyderzedruckhen. Dann wo sich die verkerten mit der schrift, wider die warhait nymmer können behelffen, alßdenn kömen sy mit dewfels stymm und waffen, nemlich dz sie die warhafftigen lerer verschmähen, verspotten schennden lesstern, verflüchen, verurtailen und verdammen. Und sy hat doch nyemandt (wie im Luca steet) darüber zü Richter erkiest, weder zu auslegung der schrifft noch zü urtailen annder lewt. Wer hat ye wider allt unnd new gerecht lerer gehört oder gelesenn grösser gespött, unzüchtigere wordt, windiger kallen, unfridsamere weis, ungeduldiger erzaigen und grössern trutz, dann ausm Luther und seinen gesellen.

Ibid., chapter 15, para. 5 = fol. Giiii'.

165. Martin Luther, "Vom Abendmahl Christi. Bekenntnis" (1528), WA 26:391, 395–396.

166. ". . . sed sicut justitiam vel pietatem corpoream cogitare non possumus, nisi aliqua forte nobis feminea corpora gentili vanitate fingamus; ita et Deum sine aliqua phantasiae simulatione in quantum possumus cogitandum." Consentius, letter to Augustine (410); quoted from *Patrologia*, vol. 33, col. 451 (letters to Augustine were not given in Erasmus' edition). Augustine's response, in a portion of his reply missing in Erasmus's edition, was to argue that although intellectual apprehension of God was possible and should be striven for, corporeal images of the Trinity should at all cost be avoided: "Et quidquid tibi, cum ista cogitas, corporeae similitudinis occurrerit, abige, abnue, nega, respue, abiice, fuge." Augustine, letter to Consentius (410); ibid., cols. 458–459.

## Chapter 1   Christ among the Councillors: The Iconography of Justice in the Late-Medieval *Rathaus*

1. In 1315 the Regensburg Rat had received the privilege "de non appellando"—that cases tried in lower courts within the city could not be appealed beyond the Rat itself—from King Ludwig the Bavarian. Berta Ritscher, *Die Entwicklung der Regensburger Ratsverfassung in der gesellschaftlichen und wirtschaftlichen Struktur der Zeit von 1245–1429* [*Verhandlungen des historischen Vereins für Oberpfalz und Regensburg* 114 (1974)], p. 99. There is evidence in the late-medieval period of imperial and princely efforts to limit the jurisdiction of councillors untrained in Roman law in favor of courts and judges more narrowly defined and academically trained. In Regensburg, for example, the prescriptive notes made c. 1488 for the Bavarian duke regarding the city's judicial system listed the Schultheißengericht as the highest court, the Rat itself only as the court responsible for adjudicating cases of inheritance involving the wealthy. HStAM, Kurbayern Äußers Archiv 1567, fol. 250. The duke's intent, however, had no lasting effect after the city regained its free imperial status. In 1531 the Regensburg Rat made an effort to reduce the number of cases that were being brought before it by ordering that all charges first be heard by the *Cammerer*, who would assign the case to the appropriate lower court; if the results were not satisfactory the case could then be appealed to the Rat itself. "Die Verweisung an nachgeordnete gerichtliche Behörden betreffend" (Decretum in Consilio; Regensburg, Hans Kohl, 18 October 1531). Schottenloher 51. Reprinted in *Sammlung derer von einem Wohledlen Hoch- und Wohlweisen Herrn Stadt Cammerer und Rath der des Heil. Röm. Reichs Freyen Stadt Regenspurg an Ihre untergebene Burgerschafft von Zeit zu Zeit im Druck erlassenen Decreten*, ed. Johann Friedrich Kayser (Regensburg, 1754), pp. 3–4.

The chronicler Franciscus Hieremia Grünewaldt insisted even in the seventeenth century on the judicial responsibility of the Regensburg Innerer Rat and described the limitation of the rôle of the university-trained lawyer to that of an adviser: "[Die Cammerer], so sonst anderwo *Consules* genennt seyn, verwalten, bey deren jedlichen, so lang dz Amt an ihm ist, der Oberste Sitz und Vorzug im Rath bestehet, und tägl. und stündl. nach vorfallender Gelegenheit daheim die Verhör und Fried-Gericht hat, die leicheste Fäll nach Gebühr entscheidet, das andere, was wichtiger und schwer, oder gar zu strittige Partheyen auf das Rathaus zum höhern Gericht anderer Richter, oder zur Straff u. *Poen* an den Rath selbst kommt. . . . Darneben an der Rathstub sind die bestellten *Doctores, Juristen, Advocaten, Syndici*, bey welchen als des Rechts Gelehrten alle hohe Fäll und fürnehmste Sachen überschlagen, und doch ohne deren eigenen Gewalt darinn zu schaffen oder zu gebieten, wo es vonnöthen, sonderl. in Haupt- und *Malefiz*-Sachen ihr Urthl, *Sentenz* und Rathschluß beygezogen wird." Grünewaldt, *Ratisbonae oder Summarische Beschreibung der Uralten Nahmhafften Stadt Regenspurg Auf- und Abnehmung, und wie man sie heut nach siehet; deren führnehmsten Geist- und weltlichen Zierden, darum sie sowol heut als ein Kayl. Gefreyte*

*ReichsStadt, als vor Alters ein Bayl. Königl. und Fürstl. Residenz und Haupt-Stadt, ansehnl. u. beruhmt ist* (ms., 1615), pp. 355–356. StAR, MS Ratisb. IAe 2 Nr. 9. Johann Holdpöck, *Schultheiß 1582/ 1583*, is the first Regensburg municipal judge for whom I have been able to find evidence of university degrees in law; it is, however, probable that his predecessor Michael Hiltner (Schultheißengericht Beisitzer and Äußerer Rat 1561, Schultheiß 1562–1563) also had such training. *Regensburger Ratswahlbücher*: (1558–1575), StAR, M.S. Ratisb. IAc 3; (1576–1599), StAR, M.S. Ratisb. IAc 4.

Cf. Christoff Scheurl's description of the similar procedures in Nuremberg, translated in Gerald Strauss, *Nuremberg in the Sixteenth Century* (New York, 1966), pp. 58–67.

2. Georg Troescher, "Weltgerichtsbilder in Rathäusern und Gerichtsstätten," *Wallraf-Richartz Jahrbuch* 11 (1939), pp. 156, 193 no. 86, and fig. 114, mistakenly states that the council meeting took place in the "Blauer Saal" and that this part of the Regensburg Rathaus was destroyed in the nineteenth century. The identification is repeated by Craig S. Harbison, *The Last Judgment in Sixteenth-Century Northern Europe: A Study of the Relation between Art and the Reformation* (New York, 1976), pp. 54, 177, and fig. 16. In fact, the "Blauer Saal" remains intact and the council met not there but in the larger room that is called now, in the aftermath of the Perpetual Diet, the "Kurfürstenkollegium." That room, which was clearly renovated sometime in the last decades of the sixteenth century, also survives and is, despite its alterations, still identifiable with the room in Hans Mielich's miniature. Cf. figure 38 below, and Walter Boll, *Reichstagsmuseum* [Sammlungen der Stadt Regensburg 9 (Regensburg, 1973)], pp. 23–25; Felix Mader, *Die Kunstdenkmäler von Bayern*, vol. 22: *Stadt Regensburg* (Munich, 1933), part 3, p. 100.

3. Cf. Troescher, "Weltgerichtsbilder," p. 193 no. 87.

4. Meder 161, Panofsky 272, Bartsch 52.

5. HStAM, R L Regensburg 546.

6. Troescher, "Weltgerichtsbilder," p. 193 no. 87, incorrectly identified it as a Last Judgment scene; close examination of the miniature proves that the panel is identical with the panel by Isaac Schwendtner which hangs today in the Rathaus. Cf. Boll, *Reichstagsmuseum*, p. 24; Mader, *Kunstdenkmäler*, vol. 22, part 3, p. 100; Andreas Kraus and Wolfgang Pfeiffer, eds., *Regensburg. Geschichte in Bilddokumenten* (Munich, 1979), no. 267; Karl Bauer, *Regensburg. Aus Kunst-, Kultur- und Sittengeschichte* (3rd ed., Regensburg, 1980), pp. 146–147.

7. On the Lorenzetti frescoes, see Nicolai Rubinstein, "Political Ideas in Sienese Art: The Frescoes of Ambrogio Lorenzetti and Taddeo di Bartolo in the Palazzo Pubblico," *Journal of the Warburg and Courtauld Institutes* 21 (1958), pp. 179–207; Ernst H. Kantorowicz, *The King's Two Bodies: A Study in Medieval Political Theology* (Princeton, 1957), pp. 107–113; and Randolph Starn, "The Republican Regime of the 'Room of Peace' in Siena, 1338–1340," *Representations* 18 (1987), pp. 1–32; on Lorenzetti's possible use of the iconic form of the Last Judgment in his design for the frescoes, see Samuel Y. Edgerton, *Pictures and Punishment: Art and Criminal Prosecution during the Florentine Renaissance* (Ithaca, 1985), pp. 34–40.

Isaac Schwendtner's public career began with his election to Regensburg's Äußerer Rat in 1581. To his service in the outer council was added the duties of a juror on the *Schultheißengericht* in 1583; from 1591 he served on both the outer council and as an assessor in the city's *Bauamt*. *Regensburger Ratswahlbuch* (1576–1599); StAR, M.S. Ratisb. IAc 4.

8. Writing toward the end of the sixteenth century, the Italian Gian Paolo Lomazzo discussed the scenes from the Old Testament and the classical authors which were appropriate for the halls in which clerical councils met and then noted that the other halls "in quelli dei principi e signori secolari si possono accomodare d'altra maniera." The scenes he mentioned in this latter connection were all from Greek and Roman authors. Only in his discussion of courtrooms did Solomon appear together with the ancient orators and heroes. No mention of the Last Judgment was made, but several lines were spent describing how Justitia was to be depicted. See book 6, chapter 23, "Quali pitture si richieggono ne i templi chiari e concistori, e ne' luoghi privilegiati e di dignità," *Trattato dell'arte della pittura, scoltura et archittetura* (1584) in Gian Paolo Lomazzo, *Scritti sulle arti*, ed. Roberto Paolo Ciardi, vol. 2 (Florence, 1974), pp. 295–297.

On one of the few Last Judgment depictions to be found in an Italian town hall, see Staale Sinding-Larsen, *Christ in the Council Hall: Studies in the Religious Iconography of the Venetian Republic* [Institutum Romanum Norvegiae, Acta ad Archaeologiam et Artium Historiam Pertinentia 5 (Rome, 1974)], pp. 80–83. For an interpretation of Italian allegorical depictions of Justice and Good Government as images utilizing the "icon" of the Last Judgment, an icon conceived in accordance with the everyday sights familiar to the medieval town-dweller, see Edgerton, *Pictures and Punishment*, pp. 21–40.

9. On the variety of judgment images to be found in northern council chambers from the medieval period into the seventeenth century, see Ursula Grieger Lederle, *Gerechtigkeits-darstellungen in deutschen und niederländischen Rathäusern* (Heidelberg Ph.D. dissertation; Philippsburg, 1937). Lederle, who organized the depictions she considered according to subject matter, devoted her first section to the Last Judgment images because they were the most popular and most widespread of the Justice images. Ibid., pp. 14, 26. See also Hans Fehr, *Das Recht im Bilde* (Munich and Leipzig, 1923), pp. 40–44, 49–51.

10. Ulrich Tengler's *Layen spiegel* was printed in Augsburg in 1509 and in Straßburg in 1510 and 1511; his *Der neü Layenspiegel* appeared in Augsburg in 1511 and 1512, Straßburg in 1513, 1514, 1515, 1518, and 1527; the *Laienspiegel* appeared in Straßburg in 1530, 1532, 1536, 1538, 1544, 1550, 1560. In all, eight printers/printshops were involved, although piracy and inheritance also played their rôle in the *Laienspiegel*'s history. I have been able to examine the following editions: Augsburg: Hans Otmar, 1509, 1511, and 1512; Straßburg: M. Hupfuff, 1510, 1511, 1514, and 1518 (pirated editions); Straßburg: Johann Knobloch, 1527; Straßburg: Johann Knobloch der Jüngere, 1530 and 1532; Straßburg: Johann Albrecht, 1538; and Straßburg: Knoblochs druckery, 1544. These editions will be cited hereafter by location and date.

For the printing history and general background, see Wolfgang Schmitz, ed. *Der Teufelsprozess vor dem Weltgericht nach Ulrich Tengglers "Neuer Layenspiegel" von 1511 (Ausgabe von 1512)* (Cologne, 1980), 13–83; Roderich Stintzing, *Geschichte der populären Literatur des römisch-kanonischen Rechts in Deutschland am Ende des fünfzehnten und im Anfang des sechszehnten Jahrhunderts* (Leipzig, 1867), pp. 411–447; *Short-Title Catalogue of Books Printed in the German-speaking Countries and German Books Printed in Other Countries from 1455 to 1600 Now in the British Museum* (London, 1962), pp. 851–852; Miriam Chrisman, *Bibliography of Straßburg Imprints, 1480–1599* (New Haven, 1982), p. 45.

11. ". . . an meer enden ain löblicher gebrauch ist, das man gewonlich in den radtstuben, und bey gerichtzsteten, da über das blüt und ander sachen geurtailt, ayd geschworn, und ander gerichtlich, peinlich und burgerlich sachen gehandelt, die figurn des jnngsten [sic] gerichts thüt fürbilden." Tengler, *Der neü Layenspiegel* (Augsburg: Hans Othmar for I. Rynnman, 1511), fol. CLXV. This edition was listed in the sixteenth-century register of the library of the Regensburg Rat (see below, chapter three, notes 20, 21): *Index*, fol. 91'; *Catalogus*, fol. 81. Cf. *Laienspiegel*: (Augsburg, 1509), fol. Cvi'; (Straßburg, 1511), fol. XIII'; (Augsburg, 1512), fol. XIX', CLXXXVI; (Straßburg, 1514), fol. XVI, CL; (Straßburg, 1518), fol. XVI, CL. The passage was omitted from the following editions, although a similar injunction remains in an earlier section: (Straßburg, 1527), fol. XVII; (Straßburg, 1530), fol. XVII; (Straßburg, 1532), fol. XVII; (Straßburg, 1538), fol. XIV'; (Straßburg, 1544), fol. XIV'.

12. Gustav Portig, *Das Weltgericht in der bildenden Kunst* [Zeitfragen des christlichen Volkslebens 10, part 5] (Heilbronn, 1885).

13. Lederle, *Gerechtigkeitsdarstellungen*.

14. Troescher, "Weltgerichtsbilder," pp. 139–214. To Troescher's list should be added the mid-fifteenth-century depiction of the council meeting of Count Eberhard the Mild of Württemberg; available now only in sixteenth-century copies, it showed the count and his councillors seated in a chamber in which a small Last Judgment panel hung. One of the copies, from the Württembergisches Landesmuseum in Stuttgart, Inv. Nr. 2735, is reproduced without comment on the judgment image in *Martin Luther und die Reformation in Deutschland* (exhib. cat., Germanisches Nationalmuseum, Nuremberg, 1983), no. 167.

15. Gisela Spiekerkötter, *Die Darstellung des Weltgerichtes von 1500–1800 in Deutschland* (Dusseldorf, 1939).

16. Ibid., p. 22.

17. Ibid., pp. 18–19. This she concludes by counting uses of the *deesis*, the image of Mary and John the Baptist as intercessors before Christ, as well as appearances of the instruments of passion, etc. Because of the relatively small number of images whose initial location and confessional identity is known, such conclusions are inconclusive. I will show in the course of this chapter why I think this approach was doomed to fail.

18. Harbison, *Last Judgment*.

19. Ibid., p. 60.

20. This despite his insistence that "Sixteenth Century iconography must almost always be seen in the exact context in which it was created." Ibid., p. 262.

21. Paradoxically, Harbison's choice of Last Judgment depictions as his exclusive focus, his sweeping periodization and attempt to encompass all of Northern Europe and all of Protestant-

ism, prevented him from discovering the impact of religious change on the use of the image. He explained the absence of a transformation by an appeal to the extreme individuality of each artist's symbolism: "General statements or symbolic traditions are no longer valid or even applicable." The evidence produced by Harbison to show that the Protestants continued to commission Last Judgment images for their council chambers is marred by inaccurate dating in the case of Regensburg (which became officially Lutheran in 1542, not in 1533 as Harbison supposed) and by his failure to distinguish between isolated depictions and those included as part of a series of exemplary images. Ibid., pp. 177–178, 262. My own analysis is concerned only with the transformation wrought by Lutheranism. Cf. ibid., pp. 92–101, where Harbison does recognize the uniqueness of the Lutheran position with regard to the Last Judgment and its impact on versions of the Cranach school *Allegory of Law and Grace*, as well as the conclusion he reached in an earlier article: "the idea of the *Last Judgment*, however, seems to have been an almost total casualty of the time in Protestant circles. . . . A theme that had been a keystone of earlier Christian dogma found little interest at this time when the Man on the cross seemed a more potent Redeemer than the Almighty on judgment day." "Introduction to the Exhibition," in *Symbols in Transformation: Iconographic Themes at the Time of the Reformation: An Exhibition of Prints in Memory of Erwin Panofsky*, ed. Hedy Backlin-Laudman (exhib. cat., Princeton University Art Museum, Princeton, 1969), p. 26.

22. "Ich Swere . . . allain got unnd das Recht vor augen habenn als ich das am Jungstentag gen dem Allmechtigenn got veranntwortenn will. . . ." This and the other oaths sworn in the late-medieval city closed with the appeal: "hilff mir Gott unnd alle Heilligenn." Hausgenossen Eid, quoted from the *Kaiserliche Regimentsordnungen* written for the city of Regensburg in 1500 and 1514. HStAM, R L Regensburg 376, fol. 4'; R L Regensburg 381, fol. 10'.

For a list of the Last Judgments we know existed in Rathäuser, see Troescher, "Weltgerichts-bilder," pp. 157–205. It is interesting to note that in Nuremberg, famous among art historians for the histories taken from the pages of Valerius Maximus, Plutarch, and Aulus Gellius which decorated the walls of its Rathaus at least by the last quarter of the fourteenth century, a Last Judgment panel hung in the council chamber itself in the late-medieval period. Two detailed drawings of that chamber from the first quarter of the seventeenth century reveal its absence by that time. Cf. Ernst Mummenhoff, *Das Rathaus in Nürnberg* (Nuremberg, 1891), pp. 58, 315 no. 158; Matthias Mende, ed., *Das alte Nürnberger Rathaus; Baugeschichte und Ausstattung des großen Saales und der Ratsstube*, vol. 1 (Nuremberg, 1979), pp. 188–190 nos. 150–151 and figs. 65–66; and Lederle, *Gerichtigkeitsdarstellungen*, p. 17.

23. Illustrated in Fehr, *Recht im Bilde*, pp. 44–45 and fig. 28; Harbison, *Last Judgment*, p. 53 and fig. 15.

24. "Animaduertite quid faciatis alios iudicaturi non enim hominis sed Dei exercetis iudicium." Quoted in Fehr, *Recht im Bilde*, p. 44. Interestingly, this is not an exact transcription of either Jerome's Vulgate translation, "videte ait quod faciatis. Non enim hominis exercetis iudicium sed domini," or of the (later) published Latin translation of the Septuagint. The Vulgate, however, was clearly its source, since the two verses were tied together by the phrase "Quodcunque iudicaue[ri]tis in vos redundabit," which, while an exact transcription of Jerome's translation at II Chronicles 19:6, also served as a paraphrase of the first clause of Matthew 7:2 (quoted below, note 25). I have consulted the Complutensian Polyglott: *Secunda pars Veteris testamenti*, fol. rriii'–rriiii; *Novum testamentum*, fol. Av'.

25. "Quodcunque iudicaue[ri]tis in vos redundabit qua enim mensura mensi fueritis re-metetur vobis." Matthew 7:2. Quoted in Fehr, *Recht im Bilde*, p. 44. Here, the artist took the first five words from the Vulgate translation of II Chronicles 19:6: "quodcunque iudicaueritis in vos redundabit," and the remainder of his text from the Vulgate translation of Matthew 7:2: "In quo enim iudicio iudicaveritis iudicabimini. Et in qua mensura mensi fueritis remetietur vobis." Complutensian Polyglott, *Novum testamentum*, fol. Av'.

26. Harbison, *Last Judgment*, p. 60.

27. Ibid., pp. 59, 63.

28. Samuel Y. Edgerton, "Icons of Justice," *Past and Present* 89 (1980), pp. 23–38. (The substance of the article is repeated in the first chapter of his *Pictures and Punishment*, pp. 21–58.)

29. Ibid., pp. 14–15. A more sophisticated argument about the use of words/images from temporal law in theological discussion and the use of words/images with theological implications in legal discussion has been given by Gerald Strauss, *Law, Resistance, and the State: The Opposition to Roman Law in Reformation Germany* (Princeton, 1986), pp. 194–196.

30. See above, note 8.

31. Konrad Burdach, *Der Dichter des Ackermann aus Böhmen und seine Zeit* [Vom Mittelalter zur Reformation. Forschungen zur Geschichte der Deutschen Bildung 3 (Berlin, 1932)], pp. 462–464; Friedrich Wilhelm Strothmann, *Die Gerichtsverhandlung als literarisches Motiv in der deutschen Literatur des ausgehenden Mittelalters* [Deutsche Arbeiten der Universität Köln 2 (Jena, 1930)]; Schmitz, *Teufelsprozess*, pp. 57–59, 62–68; Ernst Wilken, *Geschichte der geistlichen Spiele in Deutschland* (Göttingen, 1872), pp. 111, 153–158; also, particularly on the use of these themes in *Piers Plowman* (a theme also treated by Burdach), see Jeffrey Burton Russell, *Lucifer: The Devil in the Middle Ages* (Ithaca, 1984), pp. 85–87, 237–240.

32. Burdach, *Dichter des Ackermann*, p. 460.

33. Ibid., pp. 238–240; Strothmann, *Gerichtsverhandlung*, pp. 45–53.

34. An embroidered Regensburg rationale, or liturgical vestment, from the early thirteenth century complemented the depiction of Christ in the mandorla of the Last Judgment which decorated the garment's rear central panel by representations of the four daughters of God with the quotation from Psalm 85 in Latin: "MISERICORDIA ET VERITAS OBVIAVERVNT SIBI" and "JVSTITIA ET PAX OSCVLATAE SVNT" on the garment's shoulders. Reproduced in Felix Mader, *Die Kunstdenkmaler von Bayern*, vol. 22: *Regensburg* (Munich, 1933), part 1, pl. XVI and pp. 136–138. Cf. the enamel triptych from Stabio in which the souls rose on either wing at the angels' trumpeted summons, but the final judgment in the central panel was represented by a Justitia who held a balance, while Veritas and Iudicium stood above her on either side and Misericordia and Pietas (rather than Pax) held level the pans of the balance. The central panel was surmounted by a Christ Pantocrator in the clouds above; discussed and illustrated by Kantorowicz, *King's Two Bodies*, p. 112 n. 73 and fig. 19. Also, the French tapestry from the end of the fifteenth century, now in the Louvre, in which Misericordia and Justitia shared in the Last Judgment—the former, holding the lily associated with Christ's right side in more traditional depictions, escorted souls to heaven; the latter, holding the sword usually seen at his left, drove souls to hell; discussed and reproduced in Emile Mâle, *L'art religieux de la fin du moyen âge en France. Etude sur l'iconographie du moyen âge et sur ses sources d'inspiration* (2nd ed., Paris, 1922), p. 459 and fig. 254.

35. See above, note 10. Of the editions I have been able to examine, those of Augsburg 1509–1512 and Straßburg 1510–1518 included the "Teufelsprozess." *Laienspiegel*: (Augsburg, 1509), fols. Piii–Rvi; (Straßburg, 1511), fols. LXII'–LXXII; (Augsburg, 1512), fols. CXXXVIII–CLI; (Straßburg, 1514), fols. CXIII–CXXIII'; (Straßburg, 1518), fols. CXIII–CXXIII'. In addition the Augsburg 1511 and 1512 and Straßburg 1514 and 1518 editions reinforced the interpenetration of the "sacred" and "secular" spheres by the introduction of a verse dialogue along similar lines as the conclusion to the third section of Tengler's opus: "So werden zü beschluß des dritten tails, bey der figur und vorbildung des jungsten gerichts etlich mainung durch teütsch verß oder sprüchweiß eingefürt, wie es den verdampten, so schnell, grausam mit erschrocklichen angsten unversehenlich und ewiger peen." Quoted from the Augsburg edition of 1511, fol. CLXIV. Cf. (Augsburg, 1512), fols. CLXXXVI–CXCVIII'; (Straßburg, 1514), fols. CXLIX'–CLXIII'; (Straßburg, 1518), fols. CXLIX'–CLXIII.

Strauss, *Law, Resistance*, p. 195, mentions Tengler's work in conjunction with the depiction of the Last Judgment in German council chambers but does not examine the "Teufelsprozess" with which Tengler closed his second section.

36. Schmitz, *Teufelsprozess*, p. 71, citing Albertus Magnus, *Summa de laudibus christiferae virginis*, questio 23, 5. Cf. the similar woodcut in Bartolus de Saxoferrato, *Ein nützlicher gerichtes handel vor got dem almechtigen unserm herren durch die gloriwirdigisten Jungkfrawen Marien fursprecherin des menschlichen geschlechts an einem unvormaledeyten Sathanan anwalt der hellischen schalckeit am andern teil geübet* (Leipzig: Martin Landsberg, 1490s ?); reprinted in Albert Schramm, *Bilderschmuck der Frühdrucke* (Leipzig, 1920–1943), vol. 13, no. 134.

37. Here, as throughout, the woodcuts in the Augsburg 1511 edition are the same as those in the Augsburg edition of 1509, upon which the woodcuts of the (pirated) Straßburg editions were based. I have here chosen to use photographs of the edition of 1511 because the woodcuts in this edition were in better condition in the copies available to me. Cf. *Laienspiegel*: (Augsburg, 1509), fol. Pvii'; (Straßburg, 1510), fol. LXIV'; (Augsburg, 1511), fol. CLXIX'; (Straßburg, 1511), fol. LXIIII'; (Augsburg, 1512), fol. CXLII; (Straßburg, 1514), fol. CXV'; (Straßburg, 1518), fol. CXV'.

38. The woodcuts to the three editions of Jacobus de Theramo—Augsburg: Günther Zainer, 1472; Straßburg: Heinrich Knoblochtzer, 1477; and Magdeburg: Moritz Brandis, 1492—are published by Schramm, *Bilderschmuck*, vol. 2, nos. 235–267; vol. 12, nos. 412–450; vol. 19, nos. 11–44. On Jacobus, see Schmitz, *Teufelsprozess*, p. 79 n. 24. For the edition of Bartolus' work, see above, note 36.

39. Burdach, *Dichter des Ackermann*, pp. 475–476, discussing the manuscript *Bartoli legum doctoris processus contemplativus* attributed by Stintzing, *Geschichte der populären Literatur*, pp. 267–268, to Bartolus of Saxoferrato himself. Attribution denied by Burdach and others.

40.

> Ain proceß, durch ainen hochgeleerten zü underricht seinen jungern im latain geformiert, ist im besten zu mer verstentnuß des hyeuor an getzaigten tails, doch nit gleich nach dem lateinischen büchstaben, Sunder mit etlicher zülegung geteütschet, zü beschluß ditz tails ein gefürt. Doch sol es nyemant dafür versteen oder glauben, das diser krieg zwischen den Teüfeln hellischer poßhait, und der hochgelobten junckfraw Marie, von des menschlichen geschlechts wegen vor dem allmechtigen got also beschehen. Sunder das sich ain schlechter ainfaltiger lay dest baß erkunden. So yemants in seinem ab wesen umb bekörung personlicher dienstperkait, oder in ander weg vor ainem richter beklagt und zü kurtzem außtrag fürgehaischen wurden, wie man den selben entschuldigen und verantwurten mög.

Tengler, *Der neü Layenspiegel* (Augsburg, 1512), fol. CXXXVIII'. Cf. *Laienspiegel* (Augsburg, 1509), fol. Piii'; (Straßburg, 1511), fol. LXII'; (Straßburg, 1514), fol. CXIII; (Straßburg, 1518), fol. CXIII.

On the various texts of the "Teufelsprozess" as handbooks to legal practice, see also Strothmann, *Gerichtsverhandlung*, p. 42, and Stintzing, *Geschichte der populären Literatur*, pp. 259–279, 411–447.

41. Harbison, *Last Judgment*, pp. 53, 58–59; cf. my discussions of the panel by Derick Baegert and the anonymous Graz panel below.

42. "So nun bey den ordnungen so hyeuor in peinlicher rechtuertigung angetzaigt sein, etlich aigenschafft des jungsten gerichts, mögen als prefiguriert und bedeüt, auff das dann die schlecten layen deß ee zü der gerechtigkait geraitzt So werden zü beschluß des dritten tails, bey der figur und vorbildung des jungsten gerichts etlich mainung durch teütsch verß oder sprüchweiß eingefürt, wie es den verdampten, so schnell, grausam mit erschrocklichen angsten unversehenlich und ewiger peen." Quoted from the Augsburg edition of 1511, fol. CLXIV. Cf. *Laienspiegel*: (Augsburg, 1512), fol. CLXXXVI; (Straßburg, 1514), fol. CXLIX'; (Straßburg, 1518), fol. CXLIX'.

43. For the growing personalization of the Last Judgment in the late-medieval period, see Philippe Ariès, *Images of Man and Death*, trans. J. Lloyd (Cambridge, Mass., 1985), p. 147, and esp. Helmut Appel, *Anfechtung und Trost im Spätmittelalter und bei Luther* [Schriften des Vereins für Reformationsgeschichte (Leipzig, 1938)].

44. ". . . videte ait quod faciatis. Non enim hominis exercetis iudicium sed domini: et quodcumque iudicaueritis in vos redundabit. Sit timor domini vobiscum & cum diligentia cuncta facite. Non est enim apud dominum deum nostrum iniquitas nec personarum acceptio: nec cupido munerum." II Chronicles 19:6–7. Complutensian Polyglott: *Secunda pars Veteris testamenti*, fol. rriii'–rriiii.

45. "Unnd urtailenn nach meiner gewissen und hochsten verstenntnuß dem Armen als dem Reichen dem Gasst als dem Burger das rechtlichist nach meinem pessten versteen unnd darinnen nit ansehen weder lieb noch laid gunst forcht myet oder gab fruntschafft veintschafft noch ainicherlay ander sachen dann allain got unnd das Recht vor augen habenn als ich das am Jungstentag gen dem Allmechtigenn got veranntwortenn will alles trewlich on geverde." Hausgenossen Eid, quoted from the *Kaiserliche Regimentsordnungen* written for the city of Regensburg in 1500 and 1514. HStAM, R L Regensburg 376 (1500), fol. 4'; R L Regensburg 381 (1514), fol. 10'. The *Ordnung* of 1514 also specified (fol. 10) that a copy of the oath he had taken as well as of his duties be given anyone who held public office. Compare the reason given by Tengler for depicting the Last Judgment in every courtroom and council chamber: "das ain yeder, es sein Richter, urtailer, Radtgeben, zeügen, oder ander gerichtz person, allain die gerechtigkait so am jungsten tag gebraucht und erscheinen wirt, vor augen haben und betrachten sol, wie er am jungsten tag volkommen rechnung und antwurt geben müß, umb all und yed haimlich unnd offenlich handlungen und versaumnuß biß auff den minsten Quadranten bey der peen ewiger verdambnuß." *Der neü Layenspiegel* (Augsburg: Hans Othmar for I. Rynnman, 1511), fol. CLXV. Cf. *Laienspiegel*: (Augsburg, 1512), fol. CLXXXVI; (Straßburg, 1514), fol. CXLIX'; and (Straßburg, 1518), fol. CXLIX'.

46. Harbison, *Last Judgment*, p. 58.

47. ". . . ist das aller grössest torheit, das er spricht: Das brod bedeute odder sey ein gleichnis seines leibs fur uns gegeben, Und der becher odder wein sey ein gleichnis seines bluts fur uns vergossen." Martin Luther, "Vom Abendmahl Christi. Bekenntnis" (1528), *WA* 26:391. On the development of Luther's doctrine of the Mass, see Reinhold Seeberg, *Lehrbuch der Dogmen-*

*geschichte*, vol. 4 (4th ed., Darmstadt, 1933), pp. 397–405; Hermann Sasse, *This Is My Body: Luther's Contention for the Real Presence in the Sacrament of the Altar* (Adelaide, Australia, 1977), pp. 62–91.

48. "Dis abendmal ist ihenem ynn keinen weg zu vergleichen mit deutung und gleichnis, Darumb, so ym newen testament alles völliger sein sol denn ym alten, auch die gleichnis, so hette billich Christus uns bey ihenem abendmal lassen bleiben, odder wird nicht war sein, das schlecht brod und wein ynn unserm abendmal sey, Denn es mus warlich ihenes abendmal Mosi gar weit ubertreffen, Christus hette sonst ihenes nicht auffgehaben." Luther, "Vom Abendmahl," *WA* 26:395–396.

49. Ibid., 391; "ein Gottes opffer und gotte geopffert ist," ibid., 493. In addition to the "Vom Abendmahl" of 1528, see also Luther's *Daß diese Wort Christi 'Das ist mein Leib' noch fest stehen wider die Schwarmgeister* (1527), *WA* 23:64–283. On the Lutheran Mass as a "sacrifice of thanksgiving" rather than a "sacrifice of atonement," see Jaroslav Pelikan, " 'Once for All the Sacrifice of Himself' (Heb. 9:26)," *Luther the Expositor: Introduction to the Reformer's Exegetical Writings* [*Luther's Works*, Companion Volume (St. Louis, 1959)], pp. 237–254; Sasse, *This Is My Body*, pp. 67–68.

50. "Duplicia sunt signia: philosophica et theologicia. Signum philosophicum est nota absentis rei, signum theologicum est nota praesentis rei." Martin Luther (1540), *WA Tischrede* 4:5106; quoted by Sasse, *This Is My Body*, pp. 90–91. Cf. the reconstruction of the fourth session of the Marburger Colloquy among Luther, Zwingli, and Oecolampadius in ibid., pp. 211–212. For the medieval background of the relation between *signum* and *res*, see Hennig Brinkmann, *Mittelalterliche Hermeneutik* (Tübingen, 1980).

51. "Es ist ein unterscheid unter seiner gegenwertickeit und deinem greiffen. . . . Christus menscheit zur rechten Gotts ist und nu auch ynn allen und uber allen dingen ist nach art Göttlicher rechten hand, so wirstu yhn nicht so fressen noch sauffen als den kol und suppen auff deinem tissch, Er wölle denn. Er ist nu auch unbegreifflich worden, und wirst yhn nicht ertappen, ob er gleich ynn deinem brod its, Es sey denn, das er sich dir anbinde und bescheide dich zu eim sonderlichen tissch durch sein wort und deute dir selbs das brod durch sein wort, da du yhn essen solt, Welchs er denn thut ym abendmal." Martin Luther, *Daß diese Wort Christi*, *WA* 23:151. Cf. Sasse, *This Is My Body*, pp. 124–128.

52. Martin Luther, *WA* 31, 1:415; cf. Margaret Stirm, *Die Bilderfrage in der Reformation* [Quellen und Forschungen zur Reformationsgeschichte 45 (Gütersloh, 1977)], p. 87. For a discussion of the place of the Last Supper in the altarpieces produced by the Cranach school (including the altarpiece produced by Michael Ostendorfer for the reopening of the Regensburg Neupfarrkirche after the Interim had ended), see Craig Christensen, *Art and the Reformation in Germany* (Athens, Ohio, 1979), pp. 136–154.

53. Martin Luther, "Predigt aus dem dritten Kapitel Johannes" (7 September 1538), *WA* 47:99.

54. Lennart Pinomaa, *Der Zorn Gottes in der Theologie Luthers. Ein Beitrag zur Frage nach der Einheit des Gottesbildes bei Luther* (Helsinki, 1938), pp. 122–123.

55. I am thinking here of Erich Auerbach's figural interpretation of Dante's *Divina Commedia*: "But earthly existence remains always manifest, for it is always the basis of God's judgment and hence of the eternal condition of the soul; and this condition is everywhere not only a matter of being assigned to a specific subdivision of the penitent or blessed but is a conscious presentment of the soul's previous life on earth and of the specific place it duly occupies in the design of God's order. For it is precisely the absolute realization of a particular earthly personality in the place definitively assigned to it, which constitutes the Divine Judgment." *Mimesis. The Representation of Reality in Western Literature*, trans. W. R. Trask (Princeton, 1953), pp. 174–202; here, pp. 192–193.

56. Munich, Bayerische Staatsbibliothek. Clm. 13031. Albert Boeckler, *Die Regensburg-Prüfeninger Buchmalerei des XII. und XIII. Jahrhunderts* (Munich, 1924), pp. 15–16, 88–89, and fig. 5.

57. "Scriptoris miseri dignare, deus, misereri. Noli culparum pondus pensare mearum. Parva licet bona sint, superexalta malis sint, nox luci cedat, vite mors." Ibid. Cf. Martin Luther's anger at a similar story in which the chalice donated by Kaiser Heinrich to the honor of St. Lawrence was tossed by the saint into the balance at the judgment of Heinrich's soul, outweighing all the evil committed by the emperor: "Ich halt, es sei vil mer der schwarz teuffel gewest, dan sant lorencz." Martin Luther, "Ein mercklicher Sermon Von der gepurt Marie, der mutter gottes wie sy, und die heiligen sollen geehrt werdn von einem iczlichen christen menschen" ([Regensburg: Pauls Kohl], 1522), fols. Aiii–Aiii'. Schottenloher 16. StBM, Res. 4° Th. U. 103. XXVI, 29 (= *WA* 10, 3:312–331, which does not, however, mention the Regensburg edition. Cf. *WA* 10, 3:CLII–CLIV).

58. For a good illustration of Matthew 25, see the woodcut by Jörg Breu the Younger of the death of the penitent man and the Last Judgment with the works of mercy. Passavant III, 380, 30.

59. "Then shall the King say unto them on his right hand, Come, ye blessed of my Father, inherit the kingdom prepared for you from the foundation of the world." Matthew 25:34.

60. Cf. Harbison's discussion of the doctrine of good works and Last Judgment depictions, *Last Judgment*, pp. 106–110.

61. Discussed in Volker Liedke, "Regensburger Bildschnitzer und Schnitzaltäre der Spätgotik," *Ars Bavarica* 8 (1980), pp. 14–17.

62. Cf. *Laienspiegel*: (Augsburg, 1509), fol. Cviii; (Straßburg, 1510), fol. Av'; (Augsburg, 1511), fol. Ciii; (Straßburg, 1511), fol. Av'; (Augsburg, 1512), fol. +ii; (Augsburg, 1514), fol. Ai; (Straßburg, 1518), fol. Ai; (Straßburg, 1527), fol. Cvii'. On Tengler's work, see above, note 10.

63. A still useful summary of the empowering philosophy of Dionysius the Areopagite (pseudo-Dionysius), the anonymous Syrian (c. 500) whose writings were made available to the medieval West in a translation by John Scotus, is given by Erwin Panofsky in the introduction to his *Abbot Suger on the Abbey Church of St.-Denis and Its Art Treasures* (Princeton, 1946), pp. 17–26.

64. Mâle, "L'art religieux traduit des sentiments nouveaux le pathetique," in *L'art religieux de la fin du moyen âge*, pp. 85–144; Erwin Panofsky, " 'Imago Pietatis'. Ein Beitrag zur Typengeschichte des 'Schmerzensmanns' und der 'Maria Mediatrix,' " in *Festschrift für Max J. Friedländer zum 60. Geburtstage* (Leipzig, 1927), pp. 261–308; Gert von der Osten, *Der Schmerzensmann. Typengeschichte eines deutschen Andachtsbildwerkes von 1300 bis 1600* [Forschungen zur deutschen Kunstgeschichte 7 (Berlin, 1935)]; Sixten Ringbom, "Devotional Images and Imaginative Devotions: Notes on the Place of Art in Late Medieval Private Piety," *Gazette des beaux-arts*, ser. 6, 73 (1969), pp. 159–170; Craig Harbison, "Visions and Meditations in Early Flemish Painting," *Simiolus. Netherlands Quarterly for the History of Art* 15 (1985), pp. 87–118; James H. Marrow, "Symbol and Meaning in Northern European Art of the Late Middle Ages and the Early Renaissance," *Simiolus. Netherlands Quarterly for the History of Art* 16 (1986), pp. 150–169; Robert W. Scribner, "Popular Piety and Modes of Visual Perception in Late-Medieval and Reformation Germany," *Journal of Religious History* 16 (forthcoming, 1990).

65. Reproduced in Troescher, "Weltgerichtsbilder," p. 198 no. 106 and fig. 128; Harbison, *Last Judgment*, p. 53 and fig. 14.

66. Harbison, ibid., barely mentions this panel that constitutes the best case for the analogy of gesture and seating he wants to prove. He makes no mention at all of the angel and devil in the temporal courtroom. Cf. Lederle, *Gerichtigkeitsdarstellungen*, pp. 61–62.

67. "Dergleichenn soll Schulthaiß dem so sweren soll furhalltenn was geverlichs unnd Swers auf ainem aide lige unnd ainen vermanen wie er ain Ayd thun bedencken und veranntworten muesse an dem Jungstenn tag Auch ermeldenn wo ainer befunden wurde der ain falschen aid Swuer das Im darumb ain Stat zu ewigenn Zeiten verboten. . . ." *Regensburger kaiserliche Regimentsordnungen*, HStAM, R L Regensburg 376 (1500), fols. 6'–7; R L Regensburg 381 (1514), fol. 13'. He should also see to it that oaths were taken according to the proper "book" form and—because of the seriousness of an oath—try to prevent the swearing of unnecessary oaths in his courtroom. Cf. *Schultheisen und dessen Gerichts-Ordnung de Anno 1514* (parchment ms., 1514), StAR, MS Ratisb. IAf no. 10, fols. 9'–10.

68. The same woodcut also introduced the second part of the *Laienspiegel*. Cf. (Augsburg, 1509), fols. Jii, Mii; (Straßburg, 1510), fol. LXXX'; (Augsburg, 1511), fol. XCIX; (Straßburg, 1511), fols. XXXVI', XLIX'; (Augsburg, 1512), fols. LXXXII, CVIII; (Straßburg, 1514), fols. LXVIII, LXXXVIII'; (Straßburg, 1518), fols. LXVIII, LXXXVIII'; (Straßburg, 1527), fols. LXXII', XCIII'; (Straßburg, 1530), fols. LXXII', XCIII'; (Straßburg, 1532), fols. LXXII', XCIII'; (Straßburg, 1538), fols. LXI, LXXVIII'; and (Straßburg, 1544), fols. LXI, LXXVIII'.

69. The printer is again Günther Zainer. Woodcut published in Schramm, *Bilderschmuck*, vol. 2, no. 719.

70. The painting today in the Johanneum is actually a seventeenth-century copy of a lost fifteenth-century original. Troescher, "Weltgerichtsbilder," p. 172 nos. 36–37 and fig. 126. Cf. Harbison, *Last Judgment*, pp. 58–59 and fig. 23, and Lederle, *Gerichtigkeitsdarstellungen*, p. 63. The latter sees the panel as primarily a portrait of the judges and claims that "the youth, who stands outside the barrier and probably should represent the public, pays close attention to the process of the swearing in." She calls the Last Judgment scene a panel hanging in the background, a characterization even more problematic than Harbison's suggestion that it is a fresco on the wall.

71. Cf. *Laienspiegel*: (Augsburg, 1509), fols. Cvi, Dvi; (Straßburg, 1510), fol. XIII; (Augsburg, 1511), fol. XXII'; (Straßburg, 1511), fols. XIII, XVII'; (Augsburg, 1512), fols. XIX, XXVIII'; (Straßburg, 1514), fols. XV, XXIII'; (Straßburg, 1518), fol. XV'.

72. "Alda ain ernstliche bildung des jungstenn gerichts voraugen steen." Tengler, *Layen Spiegel* (Augsburg: Hans Otmar, 1509), fol. Cvi'. Cf. *Laienspiegel*: (Straßburg, 1511), fol. XIII; (Augsburg, 1512), fol. XIX'; (Straßburg, 1514), fol. XVI; (Straßburg, 1518), fol. XVI; (Straßburg, 1527), fol. XVII; (Straßburg, 1530), fol. XVII; (Straßburg, 1532), fol. XVII; (Straßburg, 1538), fol. XIV'; (Straßburg, 1544), fol. XIV'.

73. For quotation, see note 42 above.

74. See above, note 45. Emphasis mine.

75. The standard phrase in wills, here quoted from the last testament of Niklas Schweller, 1517. HStAM, Regensburger Testamente.

On the seriousness of oaths, see above, note 67, and the effort by the authors of the *Reformacion der Kayserlichen Stat Nuremberg* (Nuremberg: Hieronymus Holtzel, 1503), fol. 23', to see that any oath taken by an attorney had its impact on the appropriate soul: "Und sollichen ayde zuschwern durch ein anwalt, ist nit gnug ein gemeyner gewalt, ime von seiner parthey gegeben, mit dem zusatz und bevelch, das er einem yegklichen ayde in deß gwaltgebe sele schwern mug, sunder gepürt sich mit nemlichen außgedruckten worten, solichen ayde der geverdt in des gwaltgebers sele zuschwern in den gewalt zusetzen. Wo aber das also nit beschicht, wirdet der anwalt den zuschwern in die sele des gewaltgebers nit zugelassen Wol möcht er den on bevelch schwern in sein selbs sele. Und wo gleich ein anwalt in die sele des gewaltgebers schwert, So ist dannoch solichen ayde der geverde zuvermeyden in sein sele auch zuschwern schuldig, wo das von der parthey begert, oder ime von den urteylern aufgelegt wirdt." See also the discussion in Strauss, *Law, Resistance*, pp. 194–196.

76. For a vehement defense of the value of the visual and verbal image against the Scholastics' logical and questioning words, see Martin Luther's defense of painted and dramatic depictions of Christ's harrowing of hell: "Die Dritte Predigt, auff den Ostertag" (1533), *WA* 37:62–72.

77. "In den vrteyl darinnen ir vrteyle werdet jr geurteylt. Matthei am. vii." *Brandenburgische halczgerichts ordnung* (Nuremberg: J. Gutknecht, 1516), fol. 1'. Harbison, *Last Judgment*, pp. 58, 275 no. 49, and fig. 18.

78. The Last Judgment woodcuts that introduced Johann von Schwartzenberg's Bamberger *Ordnung*, in the single Bamberg edition printed by Johann Pfeyl in 1507 or in the first Mainz edition of 1508, are, in fact, the probable source for Schön's choice of inscriptions. I have examined the 1508 and 1538 editions of the Bamberger *Ordnung*. The woodcut from the rare Bamberg edition is reprinted by Hugh Davies, ed., *Catalogue of a Collection of Early German Books in the Library of C. Fairfax Murray* (London, 1962), vol. 2, pp. 748–749.

Eight editions of the *Carolina* were published in Mainz between 1537 and c. 1557; all contain the Last Judgment depiction: J. Kohler and Willy Scheel, *Die peinliche Gerichtsordnung Kaiser Karls V. Constitutio criminalis Carolina* [Die Carolina und ihre Vorgängerinnen. Text, Erläuterung, Geschichte 1 (Halle, 1900)], pp. xxv–xxxii. None of the editions printed in Lutheran cities before the middle of the century include such depictions. However, several of the Frankfurt editions that I have examined (David Zephel, 1558; Johann Rasch zum Bock, 1559; David Zephel, Johann Rasch, and Sigmund Feyerabend, 1562; Johann Lechler in Verlegung Sigmund Feyerabend und Simon Hüter, 1563; Sigmund Feyerabend and Simon Hüter, 1565) again included a woodcut of the Last Judgment, apparently a copy of an earlier one, since the image was reversed.

*Chapter 2*  God among the Councillors: The Iconography of Justice
             after the Reformation

1. A useful although by no means complete starting point for the search for such images in Luther's writings is Hans Preuß, *Martin Luther der Kunstler* (Gütersloh, 1931), pp. 28–43.

2. Martin Luther, "Das XVI. Capitel S. Johannis gepredigt u. ausgelegt" (printed 1539), *WA* 46:8.

3. Martin Luther, "Predigt über Matth. 18,9ff." (1537), *WA* 47:275–276.

4. I have omitted data for the beginning of the period because of the scarcity of wills—only three for the years 1490–1500, five for the years 1501–1510. See chapter four, table 2. In addition, the wills drawn up in these decades were generally written by imperial rather than local notaries; the language used by imperial notaries was extremely lean—these wills lack the spiritually oriented prefatory remarks to be found in those drawn up by municipal notaries and clerks. For more information on the Regensburg wills now housed in the Bayerisches Hauptstaatsarchiv, Munich, see below, chapter four.

5. On this gesture and on the rôle of Mary as intercessor before Christ in general, see the

comments of Erwin Panofsky, " 'Imago Pietatis'. Ein Beitrag zur Typengeschichte des 'Schmer-zensmanns' und der 'Maria Mediatrix,' " in *Festschrift für Max J. Friedländer zum 60. Geburtstage* (Leipzig, 1927), pp. 283–294. For Luther's comments on paintings depicting this and the next scene, see *WA* 47:257.

6. The woodcut of Mary pleading for human souls before a God armed with arrows was specifically linked by the *Heilspiegel* or *Spiegel menschlicher behaltnis* to Bernard's statement of her gentleness (as opposed to Christ's anger): "Marie ist eyn mittleryn czwischen gott und des menschen Spricht Bernhardus." *Heilspiegel* (Augsburg: Günther Zainer, 1470s), fol. 203'; *Spiegel des menschlicher behaltnis* (Augsburg: Anton Sorg, 1476), fol. 83'. Cf. the Maria Misericordia woodcuts in the same works, fols. 209' and 85'. All are illustrated in Schramm, *Bilderschmuck*, vol. 2, nos. 493, 497; vol. 4, nos. 144, 148. On Bernard's statement, see Luther's comment, cited below, note 8.

7. "Und das edle kind, die Mutter Maria, schlecht an Christus stat gesetzt und Christum zum Richter ertichtet und den elenden gewissen einen Tyrannen furgebildet, das alle zuversicht und trost von Christo genomen und auff Maria gewendet ist." Martin Luther, "Warnung an seine lieben Deutschen" (1531), *WA* 30, 3:312. Cf. Martin Luther, "Vermahnung an die Geistlichen versammelt auf dem Reichstag zu Augsburg" (1530), *WA* 30, 2:299.

8. Martin Luther, "Predigt aus dem dritten Kapitel Johannis" (7 September 1538), *WA* 47:99–100. Cf. figures 5 and 6.

9. The popularity of the Confraternity of the Rosary, founded in 1475 at Cologne, is attested by the many prints and altarpieces dedicated to the devotion. Cf. Erhard Schön, *Brotherhood of the Heavenly Rosary*, woodcut for *Speculum passionis* (Nuremberg, 1519), fol. 78, in *Illustrated Bartsch* 1301.018 (b); Erhard Schön, *The Great Rosary*, woodcut, c. 1515 in ibid., 1301.133 S1; and Albrecht Dürer, *The Feast of the Rose Gardens*, panel, Prague.

10. The "Marien Gebet" printed in Leipzig by Martin Landsberg (1490s?) combined the Maria Misericordia with the Coronation of the Virgin, the whole surrounded by saints and a rosary; still, the text printed beneath the woodcut utilized the same quotation from Genesis. Reprinted in Schramm, *Bilderschmuck*, vol. 13, no. 132. Cf. Mary's position as defense attorney in the "Teufelsprozess" Ulrich Tengler appended to the second part of his *Laienspiegel*.

11. Cf. "Ich kondte ihnen nicht anruffen, jha seinen namen nicht wohl nennen horen," Luther, "Predigt über Matth. 18,9ff.," *WA* 47:275, and "Jesus Du hoch wirdiger hailiger nam, du bist allen andächttigen hertzen süß zühoren und liebblich zu nennen," Johannes Geiler von Kaisersberg, *Das buch Granatapfel* (Augsburg: H. Otmar and I. Diemar, 1510), fol. A2ᵃ.

12. "Nun du anhebender mensch du fründ gotes, wann so du hast gebeycht dein sünde und hast allen deinen fleyß gethon unnd fürohyn thün wilt, als zü der beichte gehört, so bist du in den genaden gottes Wann allso spricht Sannt Augustein Es ist kayn hailsamer ertzney der sünd dann beicht unnd büß Wann sy macht aus dem feind gottes ainen fründ gottes, unnd auß dem kind der bößen feind, ain kind gottes. . . . Sannt Bernhardt spricht O du selige büß O du güte hoffnung der reüwigen menschen über ir sünde . . . . O wie gar bald hastu uß dem zornigen richter gemacht ainen gütigen vater." Johannes Geiler von Kaisersberg, *Granatapfel*, fol. A4ⁱ⁻ʲ. Cf. Luther's reference to penance in note 3 above.

13. Erik H. Erikson, *Young Man Luther: A Study in Psychoanalysis and History* (London, 1958), pp. 145–164. On Luther's rejection of late-medieval Marianism, see the discussion "Marialia, Stellaria, Rosaria, Coronaria und ganz eitel Diabolaria und Satanaria" in Martin Luther, "War-nung an seine lieben Deutschen" (1531), *WA* 30, 3:312, and his 1523 letter to the Regensburg Cammerer and Rat protesting the pilgrimage "zur Schönen Maria": *WA Briefe* 5:141–142.

14. " 'Wer do gleubet an mich, der darff das Jungste gerichte nicht furchten.' Den das Gerichte ist auffgehoben, es gehet ihnen so wenig an, als es die Engel angehet." Martin Luther, "Predigt aus dem dritten Kapitel Johannis" (7 September 1538), *WA* 47:102. On attrition in Luther's thought, see Helmut Appel, *Anfechtung und Trost im Spätmittelalter und bei Luther*, [Schriften des Vereins für Reformationsgeschichte (Leipzig, 1938)].

15. On his doctrine of the two realms, see W. D. J. Cargill Thompson, *The Political Thought of Martin Luther*, ed. Philip Broadhead (Brighton, Sussex, 1984), pp. 36–61; Hermann Jordan, *Luthers Staatsauffassung. Ein Beitrag zu der Frage des Verhältnisses von Religion und Politik* (Darm-stadt, 1968); Quentin Skinner, *Foundations of Modern Political Thought*, vol. 2: *The Age of the Reformation* (Cambridge, 1978), pp. 8–19; and the articles in Gunther Wolf, ed., *Luther und die Obrigkeit* [Wege der Forschung 85 (Darmstadt, 1972)].

16. For a discussion of Luther's absolute separation of human and divine love, see Anders Nygren, *Agape and Eros*, trans. Philip S. Watson (London, 1954), pp. 722–725.

17. "Nun secht ir das der Christus nichts anders thüt, den das er uns den vatter sueß mach und durch sich bring zum vatter, unnd dahyn geet eß alles was Christus thut, das wir zu dem vater ein feine liepliche zuversicht gewinnen, dan wenn wir den vater forchten so ists geschehen, sonder sollen ein feine kindliche lieb zu im tragen, Nu sagt er hie der vatter hab die welt so lieb gehabt, also auch das er sein liebs kindt für sie geben hat und setzt uns ein mittel wie wir zum vater sollen kummen, welchs Christus ist." Martin Luther, "Ein sermon zu wittemberg gepredigt von D. M. L. In was mittel allein: die seligkeyt zuerlangen sey" (Regensburg: Paul Kohl, 1522), fol. Bii. StBM, Reserve 4° Th. U. 104 (VII, 23). Cf. *WA* 10,3:CIX–CXII, 160–169, here 161, which, however, omits the Regensburg edition. Josef Benzing, *Lutherbibliographie. Verzeichnis der gedruckten Schriften Martin Luthers dis zu dessen Tod* (Baden-Baden, 1965), p. 160 no. 1366, appears to connect the Regensburg edition with the edition of 1522 listed in *WA* 10, 3:CIX no. A, as being from Nuremberg.

18. Romans 8:15. Cf. Augustine's many references to God's spiritual adoption of his mortal "children": letter to Macedonius (= Epistola LIIII in *Opera omnia*, ed. Desiderius Erasmus [Basel: Johann Froben, 1528], vol. 2, p. 158 = Epistola CLIII in *Patrologia*, vol. 33, cols. 658–659); letter to Honoratus (= Epistola CXX in *Opera*, vol. 2, p. 375 = Epistola CXL in *Patrologia*, vol. 33, cols. 541–542); *De consensu evangelistarum* II, iii (= *Opera*, vol. 4, p. 281 = *Patrologia*, vol. 34, cols. 1073–1074); *De sermone domini in monte* I (= *Opera*, vol. 4, p. 807 = *Patrologia*, vol. 34, col. 1268); *Contra Faustum Manichaeum* III, iii (= *Opera*, vol. 6, p. 151 = *Patrologia*, vol. 42, col. 215); *Contra secundum Manichaeum* I, v (= *Opera* vol. 6, p. 369 = *Patrologia*, vol. 42, col. 581).

19. Not in Schottenloher, but see the catalogue *Reformation in Nürnberg—Umbruch und Bewahrung* [Germanisches Nationalmuseum (Nuremberg, 1979)], pp. 129–130, no. 132. Cf. the unmediated relationship between the Christian and God the Father depicted on the verso of the 1551 medallion for Hans Rosenberger, the Nuremberg-born Dresden Bürger and *Plattner* for Elector August of Saxony: an angel helped a lame man to stand while another man prayed to a paternal God who looked down on him from the clouds. The accompanying inscription—GIB GOT. BIT GOT. DANCK GOT—stressed the immediacy of the relationship. Habich, no. 1457 and pl. CLIX, 1; for the same medallion in a smaller version, see no. 1458 and pl. CLIX, 2.

20. "Ein schons tractetlein von dem Götlichen und romischen Ablas" (J. Schmidt, Speyer, 1525); for a discussion of the woodcut, see below, chapter three, pp. 100–101.

21. Cf. John 6:32–35, 48–51.

22. "Uber das (spricht S. Paulus) ist er nicht allein ein vater, sondern 'der rechte vater uber aller, was vater heist ynn hymel und erden.' . . . alles, was auff erden 'vater' heysset, ist nur ein scheyn odder schadwe und ein gemalt bylde gegen disem vater." Martin Luther, "Predigt aus dem dritten Kapitel Pauli an den Epheser" (1525), *WA* 17, 1:430.

23. "Deus non ist menschlich bild, ut Daniel malet: Ein schon, alt man, hat schne weis har, bard, rotae ac. et strale giengen ac. non habet nec barbem, har ac. et tamen sic pingit deum verum in imagine viri antiqui. Sic mus man unserm herr Gott ein bild malen propter pueros et nos, si etiam docti." Martin Luther, "Predigt am Sonnabend vor Ostern" (20 April 1538), *WA* 46:308.

24. Hans Feldbusch, "Dreifaltigkeit," *Reallexikon zur deutschen Kunstgeschichte*, ed. Otto Schmidt, Ernst Gall, and L. H. Heydenreich, vol. 4 (Stuttgart, 1958), cols. 421–441; A. Legner, "Das Christusbild der gotischen Kunst," *Lexikon der christlichen Ikonographie*, ed. Engelbert Kirschbaum et al., vol. 1 (Rome, 1968), cols. 414–425; Wolfgang Braunfels, "Dreifaltigkeit," ibid., vol. 1, cols. 525–537, "Gott, Gottvater," ibid., vol. 2 (Rome, 1970), cols. 165–170, and *Die heilige Dreifaltigkeit* (Düsseldorf, 1954); Gertrud Schiller, *Ikonographie der christlichen Kunst* (Gütersloh, 1968), vol. 2, pp. 133–136, 233–240; Wolfgang Schöne, "Die Bildgeschichte der christlichen Gottesgestalten in der abendländischen Kunst," *Das Gottesbild im Abendland*, ed. Günter Howe (Witten and Berlin, 1959), pp. 34–35; and esp. Adolf Krücke, "Der Protestantismus und die bildliche Darstellung Gottes," *Zeitschrift für Kunstwissenschaft* 13 (1959), pp. 59–90.

25. Emile Mâle, *L'art religieux de la fin du moyen âge en France. Etude sur l'iconographie du moyen âge et sur ses sources d'inspiration* (2nd ed., Paris, 1922), pp. 140–144.

26. M. Burbach, "Worship and Custody of Eucharist," *New Catholic Encyclopedia* (New York, 1967), vol. 5, pp. 615–617; W. J. O'Shea, "Corpus Christi," ibid., vol. 4, pp. 345–347.

27. Panofsky, "'Imago Pietatis,'" pp. 261–308.

28. Georg Troescher, "Die 'Pitié-de-Nostre-Signeur' oder 'Notgottes,'" *Wallraf-Richartz Jahrbuch* 9 (1936), pp. 148–168. Dagobert Frey, "Ikonographische Bemerkungen zur Passionsmystik des späten Mittelalters," *Neue Beiträge zur Archäologie und Kunstgeschichte Schwabens; Julius Baum zum 70. Geburtstag am 9. April 1952 gewidmet* (Stuttgart, 1952), pp. 107–123, provides a good

survey of the mystic background to the image. On the pathetique, see the still intriguing discussion by Mâle, *L'art religieux*, pp. 84–144; on the humanization of the first person of the Trinity, see esp. pp. 140–144.

29. "Und Jhesus rieff lautt und sprach, vater ich befelh meynen geyst ynn deyne hend, und als er das gesaget, gab er den geyst auff." Luke 23:46; in translation by Luther (1522, 1546), *WA Bibel* 6:318–319. For a catalogue of the various types of *Notgottes*, see Tadeusz Dobrzeniecki, "U Zródeł Przedstawień: 'Tron Łaski' i 'Pietas Domini,'" *Rocznik. Museum Narodowego w Warszawie* 15 (1971), pp. 221–312.

30. Compare the Trinitarian image by the Master of the Berliner Passion, in which God the Father and the Holy Spirit, depicted as a winged man, support the suffering Christ before and under a literal *Himmelszelt* whose sides were held out as shelter for the triune godhead by two angels.

31. Troescher, "Die 'Pitié-de-Nostre-Signeur.'" Carolyn Bynum has noted a blurring of previously sharp sexual stereotypes associated with "a growing sense . . . of God's accessibility" in the devotional writings of the thirteenth and fourteenth centuries. *Jesus as Mother: Studies in the Spirituality of the High Middle Ages* (Berkeley, 1982), pp. 153–154, 158.

32. On the complicated rôle of art in shaping religious devotions, visions, and visualizations, see Panofsky, " 'Imago Pietatis,' " and Craig Harbison, "Visions and Meditations in Early Flemish Painting," *Simiolus. Netherlands Quarterly for the History of Art* 15 (1985), pp. 87–118.

33. Mâle, *L'art religieux*, p. 143; Frey, "Ikonographische Bemerkungen," pp. 109–111. For a more recent and controversial discussion of the sensual aspects of this image of Christ's humanity, see Leo Steinberg, *The Sexuality of Christ in Renaissance Art and in Modern Oblivion* [vol. 25 (1983) of *October*], esp. pp. 106–108 and excursus 39.

34. Otto Brunner, "Das 'ganze Haus' und die alteuropäische 'Ökonomik,'" *Neue Wege der Sozialgeschichte. Vorträge und Aufsätze* (Göttingen, 1956), p. 44, referring to Jost Trier, "Vater. Versuch einer Etymologie," *Zeitschrift der Savigny-Stiftung für Rechtsgeschichte: germanistische Abteilung* 65 (1947), pp. 259–260. For an interpretation that tries, however briefly, to bring some account of the impact of Luther on the emotional content of the "family," see Dieter Schwab, "Familie," in Otto Brunner, Werner Conze, Reinhart Koselleck, eds., *Geschichtliche Grundbegriffe* (Stuttgart, 1975), vol. 2, pp. 262–263.

35. Martin Luther, "Consolatio Lutheri ad consulem Lucam Khranach de filio suo in Italia mortuo " (1 December 1537), *WA Tischreden* 4:505–507, here 507 [no. 4787]. Cf. Luke 11:13.

36. Dürer's woodcut was the source of many of the stone funerary reliefs executed by the South German master Loy Hering and of the later woodcut of Johannes Crato praying before the *Notgottes*, as well as of works in less familiar media such as the panel stamp that appeared on an Augsburg (?) leather bookbinding c. 1600 and two papier-mâché reliefs by Albert von Soest, who also executed papier-mâché portraits of Martin Luther, Erasmus, Philipp Melanchthon, and Matthias Flacius Illyricus. Peter Reindl, *Loy Hering. Zur Rezeption der Renaissance in Süddeutschland* (Ph.D. dissertation, Basel, 1977), catalogue nos. A13, A95a, A103a, A121, A127, A131; *Dürer through Other Eyes: His Graphic Work Mirrored in Copies and Forgeries of Three Centuries* (exhib. cat., Williamstown, Mass., 1975), pp. 42–43 and fig. 24; Hanna Dornik-Eger, *Albrecht Dürer und die Graphik der Reformationszeit* [Schriften der Bibliothek des Österreichischen Museums für angewandte Kunst 2 (Vienna, 1969)], p. 63 no. 81; W. Behncke, *Albrecht von Soest, ein Kunsthandwerker des XVI. Jahrhunderts in Lüneburg* [Studien zur deutschen Kunstgeschichte 28 (Straßburg, 1901)], pp. 59–60 and fig. 22.

37. "O Herr Gott Vatter für die augen deiner Maiestat, uber dz werck deiner unaussprechlichen gütte, Sihe an deinen süssen Son der mit gantzem heiligen leib aussgespannet ist, beschaw alle theil an ime, von der scheitel des haubts, biß auff die versen der füs so würdet kein schmertz erfünden, wie sein schmertz war, Siehe auch lieber Vatter, sein herlich haubt, mit was elender kron es beschwert, mit was dornen es vorsert. nim war das Göttlich angesicht wie ist es mit lebendigem blüt vertunckelt, O der zart Leichnam wie hart und schmertzlich ist er gegeisselt, die heilig nackende brust, wie ist sie zerknitscht, Die bluttende seiten wie gentzlich wurde sie durchstochen. . . . [the catalogue continues]." "Ein gebet aus Heiliger Göttlicher geschrifft gezogen, allen Gottliebenden Christen in disen geferlichen und letzten zeitten zu Gott schreiendt, sehr nutzlich, von ainem Christlichen Predicanten zu Wienn in Osterreich gemacht." (Regensburg: Hans Kohl, 1555), fols. C–Cii. StBM, Reserve 8° Asc. 2023.

38. Panofsky, " 'Imago Pietatis,' " p. 286.

39. "Als ich im kloster in der kappen steckete, do wahr ich Christo so feind, das, wen ich sein

gemelde oder Bildniss sahe, wie ehr am Creutz hienge etc. so erschrack ich darfur und schluge die augen nidder und hette lieber den Teuffel gesehen." Martin Luther, "Predigt über Matth. 18,21f." (1537), *WA* 47:310.

40. Nevertheless, as Johann Agricola's comment on the German proverb "God's five wounds shame you" demonstrates, even committed Lutherans were capable of reintroducing ambivalence when confronted with the Peasants' War and the threat it presented to their teachings. Agricola insisted on the wounds of Christ as a joy and comfort to the believer, but also on their function as reproaches and on Christ as the damning judge to anarchists and blasphemers. "Das dich Gotts fünffwunden schennden. Ich erschricke darvor, das ichs nennen und schreyben soll, noch ist der flüch unnd schwür gemain, ynn Schweytz und Schwaben, unter den Landts knechten und kriegs gorgeln, Christus wirdt mit den Fünffwunden an dem Jüngsten tage das gericht sitzen, darumb sehen dyse Gottes lesterer zü, er wirdt ynen die Fünffwunden zaigen, zü irem ewigen verdamniß, Inn den wunden ist frewde unnd trost, wie S. Bernhard sagt, Der kelch den du getruncken hast, macht das ich dir von hertzen holdt bin, Jesu. . . ." Johann Agricola, *Das ander teyl gemainer Tewscher Sprichwörter, mit ihrer außlegung, hat fünff halb hundert newer wörtter* (Nuremberg: Johann Stüchs, 1530), fol. 114'.

41. ". . . als unglaubige und herte kinder, haben wir dich in eitelkeit unsers hertzen geraitzt, heiliger vatter wir haben gesundigt im himel und in dich, und sein nicht wirdig das wir deine kinder genent werden." "Ein gebet aus Heiliger Göttlicher geschrifft gezogen," fols. Avi–Avi'.

42. "Du getrewer Vatter gedenck an die Menscheit deines Sons und Erbarm dich uber unser schwacheit, an welche dein Son soviel muhe und arbeit gelegt hat. Gedenck der straff Gott des menschen, und Erbarmdich deren, für die ers unschuldig gelitten hat, sihe an die Peen des Erlösers, und vergis der unschuldt des erlösten." Ibid., fol. Cii.

43. "Es kan der heilige Geist solche lib nit genugsam durch den mund der propheten und apostel Aussprechen, wir konnen solche lieb in dieser verderbten Na[tur?] mit unseren verstand nit erreichen, wir konnen es mit unseren Zungen nit Aussprechen. . . ." Bartholomeus Rosinus, "Karfreitagspredigt auf Jesaias 53" (1577); sermon notes given in Theodoric and Bartholomeus Rosinus and Samuel Gallus, *Passion gepredigt 1577* (paper ms. 1577), fols. 118–128', here fol. 118. StBR, Rat. civ. 563.

44. "Erstlich, erkhenne und bekhenne Ich fur Gott, das Ich, wie andere Menschen, mit meinen angebornen und von mir selbst darzue gethanen Sünden, nicht schlecht allein der Zeitlichen Tode und alles unglückh, sonder auch den ewigen Tode sambt ewigem verderben, tausantmal wol, mit gemelten und allen meinen Sünden verdienet hab, sonderlich do Er mich als ein gerechter Gott und Richter, welchem Gottloses wesen gar nicht gefellt, in meiner angebornen blindheit, Bäbstischen Abgötteri, unglauben und andern meinen begangenen Sünden, verstockhter weis, Zu meinem ewigen verdamnus hette mögen und sollen stöckhen lassen, Das Er sich aber als ein Barmherziger Vatter, mein lieber Gott unnd Herr, on all mein denckhen, würckhen, werckhe und verdienst, uber mich armen Menschen und grossen Sünder erbarmet . . . . der Allmechtige Himmelische Vatter, aus herzlicher lieb, seinen allerliebsten Son Jesum Christum fur mich lassen Mensch werden, leiden und sterben, und mich also durch sein eiliche Gerechtigkeit und genuegthueung, von meinen Sünden, vom Teufel, Helle und Tod, darzue auch von aller anklag deß Gesezs erläset, mit seinem himmelischen Vatter versühnet, und Zum kind unnd Erben deß ewigen lebens gemacht hat." Will of Wolfgang Waldner, Lutheran preacher in Regensburg's Neupfarrkirche (1582); HStAM, Regensburger Testamente.

45. "Nemlich und Zum Ersten, Schaff unnd will Ich, wann Ich meine tag, hie In disem Jamer taill uff erden geendet hab, und mein Eellende sel von meinem leib geschaiden ist, die Ich dann got Irem Schöpffer der himlkinigin marie, Und meinem heiligen engl, In Ewige seligkait Zubelaitten befolhen haben wil, das alsdann mein leichnem, gein Sanndt Haimeran uff den freithoff getragen, und undter den stain dasselbs, da mein lieber seliger begraben ligtt, Zuererden bestättigt, und mit begengkhnus und allen sachen, Zw meiner sell haill, wie sich geburt, nach Rat, und gut bedungkhen, hernach benannter meiner Tesstamentari und geschefftiger gehallten und ausgericht werde." Burial clause (following lengthy introduction) from last will of Niklas Schweller, Regensburg Bürger; written by Cunz Vischer, the Stadtschreiber's *Substitut* in 1517. HStAM, Regensburger Testamente, Fasc. 84. Despite the assertion that the will was written "nach [Schwellers] angeben und aus [seinem] Mundt," the burial clause, the lengthy introduction, and the assertion itself are all formulaic, typical of Regensburg wills from the early decades of the sixteenth century. For more details concerning these formulas and the impact of the Reformation on them, see chapter four.

46. The Nördlingen sermon shows the impact of the Lutheran Reformation on what had become the traditional donation of three annual Masses to the honor of God, the Trinity, Mother Mary, and all the heavenly hosts for the city's salvation from treachery in the fifteenth century. After the end of the Interim in 1552, God was begged for his "vatterlichen schirm" and "das er seinenn Gottlichen billichen Zorn gegen unns ablegen unnd unns nachmalen mitt gnaden vatterlich bewarn, schutzen unnd schirmen woll." Hans-Christoph Rublack, *Eine bürgerliche Reformation: Nördlingen* [Quellen und Forschungen zur Reformationsgeschichte 51 (Gütersloh, 1982)], p. 15.

47. Martin Luther, "Ein Sermon, von Christlicher gerechtigkeit, oder vergebung der sünden, gepredigt zu Marpurg in Hessen. 1528" with preface by Nicolaus Gallus (Regensburg: Hans Kohl, 1554). StBM, 4° Hom. 1192. Schottenloher 113. Cf. Luther, WA 29:562–582. On the publishing history of this sermon, which was first printed in Wittenberg in 1530, see ibid., pp. 562–563.

48. Ibid., fols. Aiii, Aiii', Bii' = WA 29:562–582.

49. Cf. the discussions in Carl Christensen, *Art and the Reformation in Germany* (Athens, Ohio, 1979), pp. 124–130 and figs. 2–4; Craig S. Harbison, *The Last Judgment in Sixteenth-Century Northern Europe: A Study of the Relation between Art and the Reformation* (New York, 1976), pp. 92–102, 255–256. Interestingly, Harbison characterizes the later version of the "Allegory of the Law and the Gospel" by Cranach as "a reversion to an almost pre-Lutheran form" because of the artist's elimination of the Last Judgment as a symbol of the law. Ibid., p. 256.

On the altarpiece painted by Michael Ostendorfer for the Neupfarrkirche in Regensburg (1553–1555), the Last Judgment on the rear panel, visible to the communicants during their perambulation to receive the Sacrament, was seen always in relation to the story of Christ's descent to earth and sacrifice for the sake of the redemption of sinners from the Last Judgment. The depiction itself varied from that of the medieval period in its image of the triune godhead, in the banner of the Resurrection held by Christ, and in its strictly horizontal discrimination between the saved and the damned who sank without any condemnation from Christ himself. On the communicants' perambulation, see Nicolaus Gallus, "Kirchenordnung der neuen pfarre zu Regenspurg" (ms. 1567?), StAR, Eccl. I 22, 45f. 227–277. Reprinted in Emil Sehling, ed., *Die evangelischen Kirchenordnungen des XVI. Jahrhunderts*, vol. 13, 3: *Altbayern* (Tübingen, 1966), p. 462.

For the Last Judgment, like the Rosary, as a specifically Catholic image, see the quotation from the eighteenth century in Martin Scharfe, *Evangelische Andachtsbilder* (Stuttgart, 1968), p. 52.

50. In Lutheran churches the Last Judgment continued to appear in series depicting the history of the world and/or Christ's life and rôle as savior. Most usually, it appeared on the back panels of altarpieces such as Michael Ostendorfer's for the Regensburg Neupfarrkirche (1552), discussed above, note 49. In addition, elements of the traditional image of the Last Judgment were utilized by Protestant propagandists who continued the medieval tradition of depicting cardinals and popes in the jaws of hell. In this latter case, however, the leaders of the Catholic church appeared in hell not as mortal sinners condemned for their earthly works, but as the Antichrist or as devils, as they were imaged by Luther himself.

51. Cf. above, notes 6 and 8.

52. Friedrich Wilhelm Strothmann, *Die Gerichtsverhandlung als literarisches Motiv in der deutschen Literatur des ausgehenden Mittelalters* [Deutsche Arbeiten der Universität Köln 2 (Jena, 1930)], pp. 42–44.

53. Andreas Musculus, *Gründliche Anzeygung, was die Theologen des Churfürstentums der Mark Brandenburg von der christlichen evangelischen Lehre halten* (1552), translated in Gerald Strauss, *Law, Resistance, and the State: The Opposition to Roman Law in Reformation Germany* (Princeton, 1986), p. 194. For a summary of the theological controversy that was the context for Musculus' tract, see pp. 194–195 and n. 5.

54. For further examples of the penetration of legal language into Lutheran theological discussion, see ibid., pp. 201–202. Although the sophistication of Strauss' discussion of the interpenetration of law and theology far surpasses Harbison's, Strauss sees the Last Judgment image in the late-medieval courtroom as an expression "of that mutually beneficial close association in which church and state coexisted for so long in the Christian era. The Reformation caused no disruption in this symbiosis." His discussion of the rôle of the Last Judgment in this "symbiosis" is based on late-medieval rather than Lutheran documents (principally on the 1514 edition of Ulrich Tengler's *Laienspiegel*; I discuss the transformations the Reformation wrought in that text below)—with the result that his characterization of the relationship between temporal law and the Last Judgment as undisrupted by the Reformation transforms the Protestant concept of justification into a works-related judgment. Ibid., pp. 195–196.

55.

> Quisquis Senator Curiam officii caussa
> ingredis, ante ostium privatos affectus
> abjicito, iram, vim, odium, amicitiam,
> adulationem, Reip. personam et curam
> suscipito, nam ut aliis aequus aut
> iniquus fueris, ita quoque, Dei judicium
> exspectabis & sustinebis.

This is the "Tafl, mit ainem geezten stain und Lateinischer vergulder schrifft" listed in the inventory made at the end of the sixteenth century as being in the *Ratsstube* itself; HStAM, R L Regensburg 546.

56. Cf. Regensburg Hausgenossen Eid quoted above, chapter one, note 45.

57.

> Ein jeder Rathherr der do gaht,
> Von seines ampts wegen in Rath,
> Soll sein on alle boß affect,
> Dardurch sein hertze wirdt bewegt,
> Als feindtschafft Zorn und heuchlerley,
> Neid gunst gewaldt und tyranney,
> Und sein durchaus ein gleich person,
> Dem armen und dem reichem man,
> Auch sorgen für die gantz gemain,
> Derselben nutz betrachten rain,
> Dann wie er richten wirdt auf erdn,
> So wirdt in Gott auch richten werdn,
> Am jungsten tag nach seinem rath,
> Den er ewig beschlossen hat.
> MDLIIII

"Tafl mit ainer gulden schrifft, Reimbweis gestelt" from the inventory cited above, note 55. The plaque now hangs in the Reichsstädtisches Kollegium of the Regensburg Rathaus. It is illustrated in Karl Bauer, *Regensburg, Aus Kunst-, Kultur- und Sittengeschichte* (3rd ed., Regensburg, 1980), p. 151 and fig. 70.

58. For Luther and his followers, works were not necessarily an accurate predictor of the final disposition of the human soul. On the different place of works in the theologies of Luther and Calvin: "We grasp the actual depth of the difference between Lutheran and Calvinist, i.e., between Germany and Western Europe, if we consider the great importance of the concept of predestination and the question of certainty of election for Calvin's system of thought. In comparison with the days of his youth, the elder Luther was comparatively uninterested in the concept of predestination. The Calvinist emphasis on predestination resulted in a new evaluation of works. Luther and Calvin had equally rejected works as causing justification—for Luther they were the sign and fruit of faith; for Calvin, above all the sign of election." Hermann Heimpel, "Luthers weltgeschichtliche Bedeutung," *Der Mensch in seiner Gegenwart* (Göttingen, 1954), p. 154.

59. Lennart Pinomaa, *Der Zorn Gottes in der Theologie Luthers* (Helsinki, 1938), p. 135.

60. "Und hilft mir Gott, dass ich zu Doctor Martinus Luther kumm, so will ich ihn mit Fleiss kunterfetten und in Kupfer stechen, zu einer langen Gedächtnuss des christlichen Mannes, der mir aus grossen Aengsten geholfen hat." Letter reprinted in Ernst Heidrich, *Albrecht Dürers schriftlicher Nachlass* (Berlin, 1910), pp. 180–181. Cf. the famous diary entry Dürer made 17 May 1521, when news of Luther's supposed arrest and murder reached him in the Netherlands: "Und lebt er noch oder haben sie in gemördert, das ich nit weiß, so hat er das gelitten umb der christlichen wahrheit willen und umb das er gestrafft hat das unchristliche pabstumb, das do strebt wieder Christus freÿ lassung mit seiner grossen beschwerung der menschlichen gesecz." Ibid., p. 170.

61. "In dem vrteyl darinnen jr vrteyle werdet jr geurteylt. Matthei am.vij."

"Der herr thut die Barmherczigkeyt vnd das vrteyl / Allen den die erleyden das vnrecht. Psalmo. c.j.ij."

62. Mack Walker has drawn to my attention the fact that the coins spilt by Caritas can be read as landing in one of the pans of the balance held by Justitia—a still more direct indication of the rôle Caritas was construed to play in the judgment issued, and one befitting the Misericordia

who, as one of God's four daughters, argued against her sister Justitia in favor of a merciful judgment of humankind. On the four daughters of God, see chapter one, notes 32 and 34.

For the flaming heart in association with Caritas in theological writings, see Nygren, *Agape and Eros*, pp. 431, 445–446; for the development of the allegorical figure in general, see R. Freyhan, "The Evolution of the Caritas Figure in the Thirteenth and Fourteenth Centuries," *Journal of the Warburg and Courtauld Institutes* 11 (1948), pp. 68–86, esp. 73–80. It might here be noted that the iconography discussed by Freyhan in terms of Italy suggests that the almost nude woman holding flaming heart and cornucopia and accompanied by two boys in the small engraving executed in the second decade of the sixteenth century by Albrecht Altdorfer (B. 32; Winzinger, 114) after a niello by Peregrino da Casena (Pass. 654) would better be identified as Caritas than, as is traditionally the case, as Venus. Cf. Andrea Pisano's Caritas for the door of the Florentine Baptistery; Freyhan, "Evolution of the Caritas Figure," pl. 15d.

In the year in which he executed the *Sancta Justicia*, Dürer was also commissioned by the Nuremberg Rat to plan the frescoes for the Rathaussaal. Here again the outcome was not a single grand Last Judgment, but a series of judgment depictions from classical and biblical sources. Cf. Ursula Greiger Lederle, *Gerechtigkeitsdarstellung in deutschen und niederländischen Rathäusern* (Philippsburg, 1937).

Dürer's *Sancta Justicia* woodcut, created for the *Nürnberger Reformation*, was repeated on the reverse of the last page of the Apocalypse in the 1530 Vulgate, *Biblia sacra utriusque Testamenti: iuxta veterem translationem: qua hucusque Latina utitur Ecclesia* printed at Nuremberg by Fridericus Peypus in 1530: fol. Ddv'. I found it in a copy from the library of the Regensburg Discalced Carmelites, now in the Special Collections Room of the Library of the Andover-Harvard Divinity School: Safe f307 Lat. 1530.

63. Cf. *Zancken und zu gerich gen*, in the edition of Sebastian Brant, *Das Narren schyff* (Basel: Johann Bergmann von Olpe, 1494) for which Dürer also designed woodcuts (other editions with the same or related woodcuts—Reutlingen: Michael Greyff, 1494; Nuremberg: Peter Wagner, 1494; Straßburg: Johann Grüninger, 1494ff.); *Dye figure der gerechticheit*, from *Der doernen krantz van Collen* (Cologne: Johannes Koelhoff, 1490); and *Horatius* (Straßburg: Johann Grüninger, 1498); with Jacobello del Fiore's *Justice with Sts. Michael and Gabriel*, painted for the Doges' Palace in Venice in 1421. The similarity between the woodcut for the *Horatius* and the image painted by Jacobello is particularly strong. The German woodcuts are illustrated in Schramm, *Bilderschmuck*, vol. 8, no. 320; vol. 9, no. 558; vol. 18, no. 486; vol. 20, nos. 208, 448. Jacobello del Fiore's panels, now in the Accademia in Venice, are illustrated in Raimond Van Marle, *The Development of the Italian Schools of Painting* (The Hague, 1926), vol. 7, figs. 231–232, and Frederick Hartt, *History of Italian Renaissance Art* (3rd ed., New York, 1987), fig. 391.

64. See chapter one, note 34, and note 62 above. Dürer had executed several earlier designs in which allegorical figures were winged; see his Prudentia woodcut of 1494, in which the winged and crowned Virtue held a staff on which the dove of the Holy Spirit sat, the hand of God extending down from the clouds; before her stood the crowd of fools to whom she preached. Sebastian Brant, *Das Narren schyff* (Basel: Johann Bergmann von Olpe, 1494); reproduced in *Illustrated Bartsch*, 1001.513v. Also, Dürer's better known images, *Nemesis* (1500–1503) and *Melancolia* (1514).

65. On the conflict between this broad customary definition of justice and written law, see Günther Franz, *Der deutsche Bauernkrieg* (Munich, 1933); Strauss, *Law, Resistance*, pp. 6–16, 98–99, 196–198.

66. On Luther's attitude toward the late-medieval shift to Roman law, see Strauss, *Law, Resistance*, esp. pp. 191–224.

67. Martin Luther on charity (bread for the poor) and the duties of the prince: *WA Tischreden* 4:329–330, no. 4472. Cf. Hans Sachs' praise for the Nuremberg Rat that "speisset [die Bürger] aus durch den wintter kalte;" in "Der lieblich draum," quoted in full by Hartmut Kugler, "Die Stadt im Wald. Zur Stadtbeschreibung bei Hans Sachs," in *Studien zur frühbürgerlichen Literatur im 16. Jahrhundert*, ed. Thomas Cramer and Erika Kartschoke [Beiträge zur Älteren Deutschen Literaturgeschichte 3 (Bern, 1978)], pp. 85–87. On the Regensburg Rat's responsibility for grain for the poor and in times of general need, see Franciscus Hieremia Grünewaldt, *Ratisbonae oder Summarische Beschreibung der Uralten Nahmhafften Stadt Regenspurg Auf- und Abnehmung, und wie man sie heut nach siehet; deren führnehmsten Geist- und weltlichen Zierden, darum sie sowol heut als ein Kayl. Gefreyte ReichsStadt, als vor Alters ein Bayl. Königl. und Fürstl. Residenz und Haupt-Stadt, ansehnl. u. beruhmt ist* (ms., 1615), StAR, M.S. Ratisb. IAe2 Nr. 9, p. 356, as well as the earlier provisions documented in StBM, Cgm. 308, fols. 64–66'(11394); *Das sogenannte schwarze oder pergamentene*

*Buch d. ao. 1526* (1526) [= StAR, Pol. I Nr. 1], fols. 54, 66', 74 (1534); 69–70 (1501); and in the fragmentary municipal account book for 1505, HStAM, Gemeiners Nachlaß 26. Even after the Thirty Years' War, the responsibilities of the Regensburg *Hannsgrafenamt* included daily weighing of the bread produced by the city's bakers to assure that each roll and loaf weighed its full measure. Walter Fürnrohr, *Das Patriziat der Freien Reichsstadt Regensburg zur Zeit des Immerwährenden Reichstags. Eine sozialgeschichtliche Studie über das Bürgertum der Barockzeit* [*Verhandlungen des historischen Vereins von Oberpfalz und Regensburg* 92 (1951)], p. 165.

68. See above, fig. 17 and notes 4, 44. The omission of the Last Judgment and the substitution of the neutral appeal to the Gospel for the traditional appeal to the saints in the oath form adopted as a part of the *Carolina* during the Regensburg Reichstag of 1532 may well have been a concession to the Protestants present. Cf. the discussion of the transformed meaning attached to oaths in Protestant England in Keith Thomas, *Religion and the Decline of Magic* (New York, 1971), pp. 67–68.

69. Sebald Beham, title page woodcut to Justinus Gobler, *Der Gerichtlich Proceß, Auß geschribenen Rechten, und nach gemeynem im Heyligen Reich Teutscher Nation gebrauch unnd ubung, in zwey theyl verfaßt* (Frankfurt, 1534). For other cases of the exemplification of justice in historical scenes, see the title page woodcut to the 1562 edition of the same work published at Frankfurt by Christian Egenolff's heirs and the title page woodcut to the *Statuten Buch, Gesacz, Ordnungen und Gebräuch, Kaiserlicher, Algemainer, und etlicher Besonderer Land und Stett Rechten*, published by the same press in 1556.

70. Both the "Teufelsprozess" and the similar verse dialogue that had closed the third section in the earlier editions are missing from the Straßburg editions of 1527, 1530, 1532, 1538, 1544, and 1550; I have not seen the editions of 1536 and 1560.

71. Particularly interesting here are the Straßburg editions of 1527, 1530, and 1532, where the scene was replaced in its first appearance with a woodcut that had previously served only to introduce sections on courtroom practices involving Jews—apparently a quickly made decision—and in its second with the depiction of a capital trial, also already present as an illustration of other sections in previous editions. The injunction to display the Last Judgment before the eyes of those with business in the council chamber, which was imbedded in the section "Ordnung und Sizt im Rath und Rechten," remained, despite the elimination of the woodcut itself. *Laienspiegel* (Straßburg, 1527), fols. XVI', XXIIII; (Straßburg, 1530), fols. XVI', XXIIII, LI; (Straßburg, 1532), fols. XVI', XXIIII, LI.

72. Fol. I', all editions. Cf. figs. 10 and 16 above.

The replacement of images was, of course, an uneven process. The Straßburg edition of 1527, cited above, retained the image of Christ with the balance scales despite its omission of the "Teufelsprozess" and its replacement of the image of the Last Judgment in the council chamber. The Straßburg editions of 1538, printed by Johann Albrecht; of 1544, printed in "Knoblochs druckery"; and of 1550, printed by W. Rihel and G. Messerschmidt, are even more confusing. Although they substituted an image of God/Christ in the clouds above a magistrate for the image of Christ with the balance scales and omitted the "Teufelsprozess" and the verse treatment of the same subject at the end of the third section, they restored one of the depictions of the Last Judgment in the council chamber (fol. XIV', all editions), and reintroduced a reference to Mary in the author's closing remarks as well as a woodcut showing the author looking up to God/Christ and Mary in the heavens (fols. CXXII', CXXIII, all editions). It must, however, also be observed that not only did the "Teufelsprozess" and the verses at the end of the third section disappear, but in general where sections of the text referring to the Last Judgment could conveniently be removed, these textual references too were eliminated.

73. On one of the images that frequently replaced the Last Judgment in the Protestant council chamber (most notably in Albrecht Dürer's designs for the Nuremberg Rathaus), see David Cast, *The Calumny of Apelles: A Study in the Humanist Tradition* (New Haven, 1981), esp. pp. 89–120. Cast, who mentions the Last Judgment image only in passing, acknowledges its religous content but regards it only as a "model," reminding the judges of the seriousness of "the judgment taking place *in reality* below." Ibid., p. 107, emphasis mine.

74. Georg Troescher, "Weltgerichtsbilder in Rathäusern und Gerichtsstätten," *Wallraf-Richartz Jahrbuch* 11 (1939), p. 165, no. 21; Lederle, *Gerechtigkeitsdarstellungen*, p. 70. The series is not mentioned by Harbison. Despite the inscription's use of the genitive plural, I take it to be an echo of Wisdom of Solomon 1:1: "Diligite iustitiam, qui iudicatis terram," rather than a labeling of the judge as judge of "many lands."

75. Cf. Harbison, *Last Judgment*, pp. 127–129; Gisela Spiekerkötter, *Die Darstellung des Welt-*

*gerichtes von 1500–1800 in Deutschland* (Düsseldorf, 1939), p.64; Lederle, *Gerechtigkeitsdarstel-lungen*, pp. 22–23.

76. Troescher, "Weltgerichtsbilder," p. 165 no. 20. Cf. Harbison, *Last Judgment*, p. 301 no. 252. The stained-glass window in the Emden town hall, mentioned by Harbison as an example of the continued demand for Last Judgment images in secular locations, even by Calvinists who otherwise "hindered the production of totally religious works," is also one of a series: eight extant, forty-eight at the time of creation! Cf. Harbison, *Last Judgment*, p. 178; Spiekerkötter, *Darstellung des Weltgerichtes*, pp. 60, 88; Lederle, *Gerechtigkeitsdarstellungen*, p. 19.

There is no evidence to support the thesis proposed over the years and most recently restated by Mende that a Last Judgment image dominated the west wall of the large reception hall of the Nuremberg Rathaus as a result of the redecorating of the hall according to Albrecht Dürer's designs in 1521/1522. It is presumably for this reason that Troescher lists only the late-medieval panel from the Ratsstube itself under Nuremberg in his catalogue. If such a depiction was there in the sixteenth century, it was replaced by the allegorical depictions of Fama and Victoria in the repainting of 1613. After that time the only Last Judgment in either the reception hall or the Ratsstube was the small (in the context of the room) fresco that appeared on the west end of the south wall, behind the Vischer screen that separated the *Halsgericht* area from the body of the hall. Cf. Matthias Mende, ed., *Das alte Nürnberger Rathaus; Baugeschichte und Ausstattung des großen Saales und der Ratsstube*, vol. 1 (Nuremberg, 1979), pp. 296–297 no. 349, 330, 317–318 nos. 373–375; figs. 144 and 165; and pl. 10; Ernst Mummenhoff, *Das Rathaus in Nürnberg* (Nuremberg, 1891), pp. 97, 323 no. 272; Troescher, "Weltgerichtsbilder," p. 191 no. 79; and chapter one, note 22 above.

77. ". . . sie sind unsers Herrgots Stockmeister, richter und hencker." Martin Luther, "Predigten über das 2. Buch Mose" (29 October 1525?), *WA* 16: 488.

78. Martin Luther, "Ein Sermon, von Christlicher gerechtigkeit," fol. Aiii'. StBM, 4° Hom. 1192. Schottenloher 113. Cf. Luther, *WA* 29:565.

79. The Schmalkaldic War, for example, was interpreted by the Nördlingen Ratsherren as being the result of "Gottlichen billichen Zornn," its conclusion the result of God's *Gnade* and "vatterlichen schirm." Hans-Christoph Rublack, *Eine bürgerliche Reformation: Nördlingen* [Quellen und Forschungen zur Reformationsgeschichte 51 (Gütersloh, 1982)], p. 15.

80. Preuß, *Martin Luther*, pp. 28–43.

81. Martin Luther, "Predigt aus dem dritten Kapitel Johannis" (7 September 1538), *WA* 47:98. Woodcut reproduced in Max Geisberg, *Die Buchillustration in der ersten Hälfte des XVI. Jahrhunderts*, vol. 1 (Munich, 1930), pl. 66.

82. The woodcut was accompanied by the inscription

Ich rich die sünd mit sterbend not
In deren yetz iung and alt stat.

*Tractat contra pestem* (Straßburg: Bartholomäus Kistler, 1500). Illustrated in Schramm, *Bilder-schmuck*, vol. 20, nos. 2062, 2064.

83. Albrecht Dürer, *Sts. John, Peter, Paul, and Mark.* Munich, Alte Pinakothek. Translated inscription given in Carl C. Christensen, *Art and the Reformation in Germany* (Athens, Ohio, 1979), pp. 183–185. Quoted is II Timothy 3:1–4.

84. Strauss, *Law, Resistance*, pp. 43–58; quotations from pp. 44, 57. Regardless of the extent to which Hans Sachs and the members of the Nuremberg Rat may have considered Luther's pessimistic assessment of human moral action as the core of his theology, Luther's own perspective was quite different. For him, in contrast to the Catholic theologian, the problem of human depravity was not essentially concerned with works on earth or the need to punish earthly misdeeds; it was instead a problem of the utter impossibility of *earning* divine love, however pious and acceptable earthly actions might be. In this conception the essential human depravity could be controlled by no human magistracy; it was an element not of humankind's temporal existence but of its relationship to its god. "One must," Luther had said, "wol und eigentlich wissen zuunterscheiden die zwei Regiment . . ." Luther, "Ein sermon, von christlicher gerechtig-keit," fol. Aiii. For more detailed description of the two regimes referred to by Luther, see note 48 above, and Justus Menius, *An die hochgeborne Furstin / Fraw Sibilla Hertzogin zu Sachsen / Oeconomia Christiana / das ist / von Christlicher Haushaltung*, introduction by Martin Luther (Wittenberg: Hans Lufft, 1529), fols. Biii–Biii'.

85. "Nach dem vil treffenlicher Geschichten und Exempel, Bede der hailigen Göttlichn schrifft, unnd annderer glaubwirdigen Historien unnd Chronickn, lauter inn sich halten, unnd

anzaigen, Mit was grawsamen unnd erschrockenlichem zorn Gott der Almechtig die verachtung seyner Vätterlichen heymsuchung, unnd zuvorab die Abgotterey, unnd, wider seyn hailigs Wort, von Menschen erfunden und angerichten Gotsdienst, Je unnd alwegen gestrafft hat, Also, das offtmalns grosse weite Lannd, unnd mechtige Stette, durch Krieg, Feur, unnd andere mehr derogleichen Plagen, Zu grund verheeret worden." Regensburg Rat, "Vermahnung und Gebot, etliche fürnehme ärgerliche Laster betreffend" (September 1543); reprinted in Johann Friedrich Kayser, ed., *Sammlung derer von einem Wohledlen Hoch- und Wohlweisen Herrn Stadt Cammerer und Rath der des Heil. Röm. Reichs Freyen Stadt Regenspurg an Ihre untergebene Burgerschafft von Zeit zu Zeit im Druck erlassenen Decreten* (Regensburg, 1754), No. XIII, p. 29.

86. Rublack, *Bürgerliche Reformation*, p. 53.

87. Hans-Christoph Rublack, "Grundwerte in der Reichsstadt im Spätmittelalter und in der frühen Neuzeit," in *Literatur in der Stadt. Bedingungen und Beispiele städtischer Literatur des 15. bis 17. Jahrhunderts*, ed. Horst Brunner [Göppinger Arbeiten zur Germanistik 343 (Göppingen, 1982)], pp. 24–27. In a justly famous essay, Bernd Moeller explained the success of the Zwinglian/Bucerian Reformation in terms of its successful continuation and expansion of the medieval sense of the free imperial city as a "sacred community." *Reichsstadt und Reformation* [Schriften des Vereins für Reformationsgeschichte 180 (Gütersloh, 1962)]. On the difference between the place of ethics in the thought of Luther and Zwingli, cf. Reinhold Seeberg, *Lehrbuch der Dogmengeschichte*, vol. 4, part 1: *Die Entstehung des protestantischen Lehrbegriffs* (4th ed., Leipzig, 1933), pp. 442–444.

88. Rublack, "Grundwerte," p. 30.

89. Lucas Cranach the Younger, *Unterschied zwischen der waren Religion Christi, und falschen Abgöttischen lehr des Antichrists in den fürnemsten stücken*, woodcut, c. 1545; G. 654–655; H. 18; Berlin. Cf. R. W. Scribner, *For the Sake of Simple Folk: Popular Propaganda for the German Reformation* (Cambridge, 1981), pp. 201–205.

90. On this pious psychology, see the now classic study of Quattrocento Italian paintings in their social context by Michael Baxandall, *Painting and Experience in Fifteenth-Century Italy: A Primer in the Social History of Pictorial Style* (Oxford, 1972), pp. 40–56.

91. Lucas Cranach the Younger, *Taufe Christi mit Friedrich dem Weise und Martin Luther*, woodcut, c. 1548, Vienna. On this woodcut and the rôle of baptism in Protestant thought, see Scribner, *For the Sake of Simple Folk*, pp. 226–227. For an earlier Italian example in which the Italian patricians seem already observers *within* the scene, see the fresco of the Baptism of Christ painted in 1416 for the Oratorio of San Giovanni in Urbino by Lorenzo and Jacopo Salimbeni; reproduced in Pietro Zampetti, *Paintings from the Marches, Gentile to Raphael* (London, 1971), pl. 22.

92. On this woodcut and a similar one set in front of Nuremberg, see Scribner, *For the Sake of Simple Folk*, pp. 224–226. Cf. the fifteenth-century altarpiece showing the events of St. James' life set before the marketplace of Rothenburg ob der Tauber, which was executed for the St.-Jakobs-Kirche in Rothenburg in 1466. A small panel attributed to the school of Altdorfer and now in the Museen der Stadt Regensburg set the stoning of St. Stephen on the square before the Regensburg cathedral.

93. I here follow the account of the sequential cooperation on the project by Melchior Bocksberger and his nephew or cousin Johann Bocksberger der Jüngere given by Max Goering, "Die Malerfamilie Bocksberger," *Münchner Jahrbuch der bildenden Kunst* N .F. 7 (1930), pp. 229–239, 253–257. Goering dates Johann Bocksberger's work on the project to 1564, the same year he designed the woodcuts executed by Jost Amman for the *Neuwe Biblishce Figuren, desz Alten und Neuwen Testaments* (Frankfurt: Sigmund Feyerabend, 1564). Ibid., pp. 231, 244, 253–255.

94. A scene described by Goering as simply "a gathering of old men in oriental costume," with the further comment that "the scene is difficult to explain iconographically." Ibid., p. 255 and fig. 51.

95. Among the scenes frescoed by the Bocksbergers on the adjacent outer wall of the city's large reception hall—in which the Reichstag would later often meet—were other judgment scenes from ancient history: the judgment of Trajan and the punishment of the traiterous schoolmaster. In design both scenes were clearly based on Hans Schäufelein's woodcuts of the same subjects for Johann von Schwartzenberg, *Das Büchle Memorial, das ist ain angedänckung der Tugent* (published as second part of *Der Teütsch Cicero*; Augsburg: Heinrich Steiner, 1535), fols. cxiii, cxvii'. A complete iconographic reading of this very complex wall, which included scenes from the life of Moses as well as scenes from antiquity and myth (the fall of Ganymede) is outside the scope of this book. As we have already seen (note 69 above), the mixing of scenes of biblical

judgment with scenes of judgment from antiquity also occurred on woodcut title pages and inside council chambers after the Last Judgment lost its exclusive or dominant position.

96. *Der Stat Nurnberg Verneute Reformation 1564* (Nuremberg, Valentin Geißler, 1564). The MS Master, active in Nuremberg 1545–1580, is not mentioned by Bartsch. Ulrich Thieme and Felix Becker, *Allgemeines Lexikon der bildenden Künstler von der Antike bis zur Gegenwart*, vol. 78 (Leipzig, 1950), p. 436.

Cf. the binding panel used on a copy of Luther, *Schrifften* (Wittenberg, 1551): the allegorical figures are the same, their features and costumes coarser; two cities or a city on two hills occupy the background. The arms of the electorate and duchy of Saxony incorporated in the twin columns that frame the scene suggest a Saxon origin for the panel. Presumably it was based on the MS Master's woodcut, although the reverse explanation could also be true; both could also go back to an unknown original. The binding panel is sketched by Cyril J. H. Davenport, *Cameo Book-Stamps Figured and Described* (London, 1911), p. 183, who was, however, unfamiliar with the MS Master's woodcut.

In 1625 Andrea Betzel combined a literal repetition of the MS Master's woodcut for the Nuremberg *Reformation* of 1564 with a literal repetition of the frame the Nuremberg master had designed for the title page of the same work: a triumphal arch above which two putti held the imperial shield surmounted by the imperial crown; to the left stood the emperor with law book and lance on a pedestal labeled IMP: CUSTOS LEGUM; to the right Moses with tablets inscribed LEX DONUM DEI. The resulting woodcut, of very poor quality, served as the title page for *Der Stadt Magdeburgk Reformirter Wilkühr und Statuta* (Magdeburg, 1625). Illustrated in the facsimile of the *Wilkühr* (Osnabrück, 1979).

The allegorical depiction of the Nuremberg *Reformation* soon found a response in an edition of the *Carolina* published in Frankfurt. Johann Wolff's (?) 1565 edition replaced the Last Judgment woodcut with a Justitia image titled "Mundanae Iustitiae Effigies" and the first verse from the Sapientia Solomonis (Wisdom of Solomon): "Diligite Iustitiam, qui iudicatis terram." StBM, Handschriftenabteilung, Reserve 4° Crim. 42/2, fol. 8.

97. Thus Grünewaldt in his chronicle referred to the wise and industrious "Oeconomic" of the city where, he wrote, "the open purse is never completely emptied onto the ground." *Ratisbonae* (1615), p. 358; StAR, M.S. Ratisb. IAe2 Nr. 9.

98. Carl Theodor Gemeiner, *Reichsstadt Regensburgische Chronik*, ed. Heinz Angermeier (Munich, 1971), vol. 4, p. 490 n. 906.

99. *Regensburger kaiserliche Regimentsordnung* (1514), fols. 1, 47–49; HStAM, R L Regensburg 381.

100. The ordinance of 1523 is quoted by Gemeiner, *Chronik*, pp. 490–492. In Nördlingen the painting of Christ as Man of Sorrows placed above the *Almosenkasten* in 1522 reminded the Bürger that donations to the *Almosenkasten* fed the poor (= fed the suffering Christ himself) and were acts of mercy in accordance with Matthew 25 and the teaching of the medieval church. Städtisches Museum, Nördlingen.

101. On Concordia as a normative value in late-medieval / early modern German cities, see Hans-Christoph Rublack, "Political and Social Norms in Urban Communities in the Holy Roman Empire," in *Religion, Politics, and Social Protest: Three Studies on Early Modern Germany*, ed. Kaspar von Greyerz (London, 1984), pp. 26–28, 44–45. On Concordia as a "daughter" of Justitia, see Ernst H. Kantorowicz, *The King's Two Bodies: A Study in Medieval Political Theology* (Princeton, 1957), pp. 112–113, citing Bartolus and Baldus.

102. In this he was presumably imitated by his Regensburg disciple, but the size and poor condition of the sketch for the Rathaus frescoes makes any buildings in the background indecipherable. The artist of the binding panel discussed in note 96 above, interpreted the cuff of Justitia's long-sleeved gown as a bracelet; Andreas Betzel reinterpreted the cuff/bracelet as a glove. For an early sixteenth-century account of the rôle of *respublica* or the commonweal, see book II of Jacob Wimpheling's *Germania* (1501), discussed briefly in Rublack, "Political and Social Norms," pp. 44–45.

103. Cf. the Virtues carved by Albert von Soest to frame the doors of the council chamber in Lüneburg, 1568–1584, especially Justitia, who was crowned by God himself. W. Behncke, *Albert von Soest, ein Kunsthandwerker des XVI. Jahrhunderts in Lüneburg* [Studien zur deutschen Kunstgeschichte 28 (Straßburg, 1901)], pp. 16–36, esp. p. 26.

104. The source of Schwendtner's iconography was Jost Amman's woodcut for Georg Lauterbeck, *Regentenbuch* (Frankfurt: Peter Schmid in Verlegung Sigmund Feyerabends und Georgen Fischers, 1579), p. 59, illustrated in Hanna Dornik-Eger, *Albrecht Dürer und die Graphik der Reformationszeit* [Schriften der Bibliothek des Österreichischen Museums für angewandte Kunst

2 (Vienna, 1969)], pl. 60 and p. 59. For introducing me to the Amman print, I am grateful to Wolfgang Pfeifer, director of the Regensburg Stadtmuseum, who will publish a lengthier examination of the connection between Schwendtner's panel and Amman's woodcut. The copies of the *Regentenbuch* owned by the Regensburg Ratsbibliothek in the sixteenth century were of earlier editions (*Catalogus* 101, Hist. 53 = StBR, 2° Jur. 9662, printed at Leipzig in 1557, bound in Regensburg 1558 or later, was a gift of the author himself to the Cammerer and Rat of Regensburg; *Catalogus* 81, Jur. 34 = StBR, 2° Jur. 968 [?], was printed at Leipzig in 1567), without the Amman print; no doubt other editions existed within the city, possibly Schwendtner himself owned one. A Frankfurt edition of 1600, too late to be the source of Schwendtner's iconography, but with the Amman woodcut and bound in Regensburg, is in the collection of the Bayerische Staatsbibliothek, Munich (2° Pol. g. 43). In the absence of Dr. Pfeifer's analysis we can only hypothesize, but the fact that Jost Amman executed woodcuts after designs by Johann Bocksberger the Younger for Feyerabend's Frankfurt printshop—*Neuwe Biblische Figuren, desz Alten und Neuwen Testaments* (1564), illustrations to an edition of Livy (1568 with text, 1571 without), and *Ein Neuw Thierbuch* (1569)—during the period in which he was designing the Regensburg Rathaus façade raises the possibility that Bocksberger himself constituted the link between the two allegories of Good Government.

Schwendtner's panel varied from its predecessor only in its substitution of the older anthropomorphized Gottvater for the tetragramm supplied by the Zwinglian Amman (the strict Calvinist/Zwinglian interpretation of the commandment against graven images of God had begun influencing printers in Lutheran cities by the end of the sixteenth century) and its depiction of Regensburg's towers in the background.

My own position on the transformation of political *Bildsprache* by Lutheranism is to be contrasted with that expressed by Dornik-Eger in her analysis of the Amman woodcut, *Albrecht Dürer*, p. 59: "An eccentric mixture of allegorical figures and Christian symbolism, in which the image of God has been replaced by a tetragramm in strict accordance with Zwingli's and Calvin's prohibition. In its composition and details as well as in its conception of space, it must be considered as a direct descendent of Italian Mannerism; its immediate connection is to the works of the School of Fontainebleu. It breaks away completely from the stylistic tradition of German prints from the first half of the sixteenth century, as well as from the iconography of the German Reformation." Cf., however, the *Allegory of Royalty* engraved by Jean Duvet, the French "Master of the Unicorn" active as an engraver 1520–1555. Reproduced in *Illustrated Bartsch*, vol. 13, 1, no. 43 (514).

105. Hesiod, *Erg.* 197ff. told of Nemesis and Aidos leaving the earth to live with the gods. Ovid, *Metamorphoses* I, 149–162, was apparently the first to refer to the goddess as Astraea (he called her Iustitia in *Fasti* I, 249, as did Vergil, *Georgics* II, 437f); in his retelling, her abandonment of earth is followed by the battle of the Titans. Anchises' prophecy from *Aeneid* VI was transformed into praise of Charles V by Ariosto in the fifteenth canto of the *Orlando furioso*. Cf. Dante, *De monarchia* I, 11. Frances A. Yates, *Astraea: The Imperial Theme in the Sixteenth Century* (London, 1975), pp. 22–23, 29–33, 53. Baldus, citing Huguccio, also knew of the goddess Astraea as a personification of justice; Kantorowicz, *King's Two Bodies*, p. 101 n. 41.

Visually, the use of the chain to link the allegorical figures may be connected to the rope in Lorenzetti's Sienese fresco (see above, chapter one, note 7), a rope that has been linked by Starn to a passage from the opening of *Il tesoretto* (1263) by Ser Brunetto Latini, a thirteenth-century notary and politician active in (and exiled from) the Italian city republic of Florence; compare the inscription on Schwendtner's panel with the following passage from Latini:

> Ma tutti per commune
> Tirassero una fune
> Di Pace e di ben fare
> Che già non puo scampare
> Terra rotta di parte

> But all in common
> should pull together on a rope
> of Peace and Welfare
> because there is no surviving
> for a land divided by faction
> —ll. 175–180

Quoted and translated in Randolph Starn, "The Republican Regime of the 'Room of Peace' in Siena, 1338–1340," *Representations* 18 (1987), p. 12. For a complete edition and translation, see

Brunetto Latini, *Il Tesoretto*, ed. and trans. by Julia Bolton Holloway [Garland Library of Medieval Literature 2 (New York, 1981)]. Whether or not the chain of the Jost Amman woodcut and Schwendtner's panel are to be connected with the rope in Lorenzetti's fresco, the chain functioned as a reversal of the heavy links by which an enthroned Justitia with flaming sword, scales, and nimbused crown controlled the Vices at her feet in the frontispiece for an engraved series on the seven deadly sins executed by Jean Mignon c. 1547. Henri Zerner, *Ecole de Fontainebleau. Gravures* (Paris, 1969), fig. 85.

    106.

> CERNE,AGE,QVAMPIVSESTNEXVS,QVAMFIRM[VS],ETINQVE:
> VITASINE HOC NEXVCEV LANIENA FORET.
> DIVA TENENS ENSEM,LANCES,ASTRAEA,CVIQ[VE].
> REDDERE PROFACTI CONDITIONE IVBET.
> STORGEANIMOSIVNGIT,PRVDENTIAFACTAGVBERNAT,
> PAX MARTEMSVBIGIT,PACIS ALVMNA CERES.
> PVBLICARESNEXVHOCSOLIDAEST:Q[VI]SIABSITABVRBE
> VRBISQVIDMONSTRIEST,DICMIHI,VITA—CHAOS.

Isaac Schwendtner, *Das gute Regiment* (1592). Museen der Stadt Regensburg, Altes Rathaus.

    107. For his municipal career, see chapter one, note 7.

*Chapter 3*  Widow, Wife, Daughter: The Iconography of Resistance to the Emperor

    1. For fifteenth-century examples of the combination of political and religious "languages" to describe the relation between cities and the emperor, particularly in cases where the relation had become tense, see Heinrich Schmidt's excellent Ph.D. dissertation, *Die deutschen Städtechroniken als Spiegel des bürgerlichen Selbstverständnisses im Spätmittelalter* [Schriftenreihe der historischen Kommission bei der Bayerischen Akademie der Wissenschaften 3 (Göttingen, 1958)], pp. 64–82.
    2. The theological justification for the new militancy was expressed most succinctly by Martin Luther in the sentence that serves as epigraph to this chapter. "Denn ein Friede muß völlig verbannt und abgelehnt werden, der auf Kosten des Evangeliums erkauft wird und es hindert und verletzt." Martin Luther, "Bedenken" (August 1531?), quoted by Hermann Jordan, *Luthers Staatsauffassung. Ein Beitrag zu der Frage des Verhältnisses von Religion und Politik* (Darmstadt, 1968), p. 167 n. 279.
    3. "Habn vorgemelte herrn Camerer und Rathe, Wie sie von Ambts wegen, zu forderst Gott dem almechtigen, auch der Rö. Kay. und Kö. Ma. unsern allergnedigsten herrn, ihnen selbst, und irer gemaynen gehorsamen burgerschafft, auch andern fridsamen menschen schuldig, nit umbgeen mögen solchem unrathe fürzukomen. . . ." "Das öffentliche Einreden denen Predigern auf der Canzel und in Religions Sachen sich gebührend aufzuführen betreffend" (1534), reprinted in Johann Friedrich Kayser, ed., *Sammlung derer von einem Wohledlen Hoch- und Wohlweisen Herrn Stadt Cammerer und Rath der des Heil. Röm. Reichs Freyen Stadt Regenspurg an Ihre untergebene Burgerschafft von Zeit zu Zeit im Druck erlassenen Decreten* (Regensburg, 1754), p. 10. Cf. the language of the earlier decree, "Die Freyheiten für diejenige, welche sich hier wollen häußlich niederlassen, betreffend" (1523): "Wir wollen uns auch in solchem allem, gegen ainem yeden, auch in gemainer unser Stat Regirung, ordnung, statuten und polliceyen, dermassen halten unnd beweysen, daran zuvor die Rom. Kayserl. Majestät etc. Unser allergnedigster her, alle stend des heyl. Reichs, und meniglich genedigs und guts gefallen haben sollen." Ibid., p. 2.
    4. Quoted in Carl Theodor Gemeiner, *Geschichte der Kirchenreformation in Regensburg aus den damals verhandelten Originalacten beschrieben* (Regensburg, 1792), p. 146. Cf. Leonhart Widmann, *Chronik von Regensburg* (ms., 1511–1543, 1552–1555), ed. E. V. Oefele [Die Chroniken der deutschen Städte 15 (Leipzig, 1878)], p. 197.
    5. Ibid., p. 179 and n. 132. Based on a military census now lost, Gemeiner found a loss of eight hundred men between the beginning of the religious controversy and 1548. For more discussion of the problem of calculating population size for sixteenth-century Regensburg, see chapter four, notes 13–16.
    6. Ibid., pp. 193, 196, 198; Leonhard Theobald, *Die Reformationsgeschichte der Reichsstadt Regensburg* [Einzelarbeiten aus der Kirchengeschichte Bayerns 19 (Munich, 1936; Nuremberg, 1951)], vol. 2, pp. 114–120, for a day-by-day account of the troop movements around the city.

7. *Reichsstadt Regensburgische Chronik*, 4 vols. (Regensburg, 1800–1824; 2nd ed., ed. Heinz Angermeier, Munich, 1971), and *Kirchenreformation*, pp. 189–268.

8. Theobald, *Reformationsgeschichte*, vol. 2, pp. 84–184.

9. The material for the earlier phases (up to 1525) of Regensburg's history was saved by Carl Theodor Gemeiner's interest in that period—an interest that resulted in his preservation of those documents from the omnivorous paper mill and in his production of the magnificent *Regensburgische Chronik*. During the search for books and manuscripts which followed the secularization of the Bavarian cloisters in the nineteenth century, the documents preserved by Gemeiner were confiscated and removed to Munich, where they are now housed in the Bayerisches Hauptstaatsarchiv under the rubric "Gemeiners Nachlaß." Cf. the history of the transfer of valuable books and manuscripts from the municipal and clerical libraries in Regensburg to the Hofbibliothek (now Bayerische Staatsbibliothek) in Munich outlined in Christine Elisabeth Ineichen-Eder, *Mittelalterliche Bibliothekskataloge Deutschlands und der Schweiz*, vol. 4, part 1: *Bistümer Passau und Regensburg* (Munich, 1977), p. 475.

10. Widmann, *Chronik*. Although he moved to Regensburg initially to obtain better medical care for his ailing wife, the imperial mercenary Schmidt soon accepted a position as Stadthauptmann; his entry for 1552 includes a brief account of his participation in the city delegation that pled (successfully) before the emperor for permission to reopen the city's Lutheran churches. Heinrich Schmidt, *Chronik* (ms., begun 1583), fols. 4, 6', 7, 7'; AHVR, M.S. Ratisb. 357.

11. Schottenloher 96, 97.

12. Schottenloher 98. On this Dutch educator and playwright in the tradition of Terence and Plautus, see Daniel Jacoby, "Georg M. Macropedius," *Allgemeine Deutsche Biographie* (Berlin, 1884), vol. 20, cols. 19–28; Thomas Best, *Macropedius* (New York, 1972); Macropedius, *Two Comedies: Rebelles (The Rebels), Bassarus*, ed. and trans. Yehudi Lindeman (Nieuwkoop, 1983), pp. 11–19.

13. Schottenloher 99.

14. Ibid. 100.

15. Ibid. 95, 97–100. Although Schottenloher catalogues only four editions—102 (Hans Kohl, 1552), 148 and 149 (Heinrich Geißler, 1559), and 305 (Hans Burger, 1574)—of Nicolaus Gallus' summa or catechism, Hans Kohl printed one in 1547 while his press was located in the Minoritenkirche in Regensburg, and the date 1546 on the title page woodcut of the city's shield suggests that another even earlier edition may have been printed. Nicolaus Gallus, *Ein Kurtze Ordenliche suma der rechten Waren Lehre unsers heiligen Christlichen glaubens / Welche lere ein yeder Christlicher haußvatter nit allain für sich selb zuwissen sonder auch seine Kinder und Ehalden zuleren oder leren zulassen schuldig ist. Sampt einem kurtzen außzug einer Gotseligen Haußhaltung* (Regensburg: Parfueser Closter, Hans Kohl, 1547). StBR, 8° Rat. civ. 675.

The 2nd (3rd?) edition of Nocolaus Gallus' catechism (Schottenloher 102) was one of only two items printed by Hans Kohl in 1552, the year of the Interim's end in Regensburg. The second was a conciliar ordinance pertaining to the pestilence (Schottenloher 101).

16. Ineichen-Eder, *Mittelalterliche Bibliothekskataloge*, p. 471.

17. Ibid., pp. 471–472.

18. Ibid., p. 472.

19. Grünewaldt, *Ratisbonae* (1615), fols. 164–165. The duplication of entries in the two catalogues discussed below (assumed by Ineichen-Eger to cover the books in two different collections) is additional proof of the identity of the two libraries.

20. AHVR, AA R 44; referred to hereafter as *Index*. The presence on the list of a book published in 1574 provides the *terminus post quem* for its compilation, Ehinger's *Catalogus* of 1638 (see below, note 21) the *terminus ante quem*. The attribution to Jonas Paulus Wolf is suggested by Ineichen-Eder, *Mittelalterliche Bibliothekskataloge*, p. 473, following Christian Heinrich Kleinstauber, "Geschichte d. ehemaligen Stadtwagegebäudes und d. k. Kreisbibliothek in Regensburg," *Conversationsblatt*, supplement to *Regensburger Tagblatt* (1875), Nr. 70.

21. StBR, Rat. civ. 430; referred to hereafter as *Catalogus*.

22. Grünewaldt particularly praised the careful preservation of the books in the Stadtbibliothek; he said even the old Catholic books there were more gently handled than those in the city's Catholic institutions. Grünewaldt, *Ratisbonae* (1615), fols. 164–165.

23. Thus the edition of the business correspondence of Nuremberg's Koberger printing house contains nothing about binding the works printed on their presses. Oscar Hase, *Die Koberger: Eine Darstellung des buchhändlerischen Geschäftsbetriebs in der Zeit des Übergangs vom Mittelalter zur Neuzeit* (Leipzig, 1885).

24. ". . . grosse schöne pergamenene puecher," *Regensburger kaiserliche Regimentsordnung*, HStAM, R L Regensburg 376 (1500), fol. 35'; R L Regensburg 381 (1514), fol. 43'. *Ratswahlbücher*: StAR, M.S. Ratisb. IAc 1 (1500–1539); M.S. Ratisb. IAc 2 (1540–1557); M.S. Ratisb. IAc 3 (1558–1575); M.S. Ratisb. IAc 4 (1576–1599).

25. See, however, the isolated references to bindings and Protestantism in the catalogues produced for recent Luther exhibitions, particularly *Kunst der Reformationszeit* (exhib. cat., Staatliche Museen zu Berlin [East], Berlin, 1983), pp. 344–355, 403–417. Also: Hanna Dornik-Eger, *Albrecht Dürer und die Graphik der Reformationszeit* [Schriften der Bibliothek des Österreichischen Museums für angewandte Kunst 2 (Vienna, 1969)], pp. 61–65; Doris Fouquet-Plümacher, "Deutsche Renaissance-Einbände mit Rollen- und Plattenstempeln" (brief exhib. brochure, Universitätsbibliothek der Freien Universität Berlin, 1983); Kristin E. S. Zapalac, "Eiserne Männer, eiserne Jungfrauen: Luther, Lukretia und das Kennzeichnen der Stadt Regensburg auf Einbänden, 1542–1575" (brief exhib. cat., Staatliche Bibliothek, Regensburg, 1983); and the pages on the influence of Protestantism in Ilse Schunke, *Die Einbände der Palatina in der Vatikanischen Bibliothek* (Vatican City, 1962), vol. 1. See also E. Ph. Goldschmidt, *Gothic and Renaissance Bookbindings Exemplified and Illustrated from the Author's Collection* (London, 1928), pp. 62–68, still useful despite his assertion (p. 63) that the mid-sixteenth-century German panels "are far from offering the same interest as the earlier Netherlandish and French panels, either from the artistic or from the iconographic point of view."

26. "So wöllet, lieben herrn und freunde, dis gedechtnis meiner ewigen liebe gegen euch und dise keiserliche stat nicht alleine freuntlich und gerne annemen, sondern auch um euer selen seligkeit willen bedencken, was dis für ein zeichen seie, das der engel zu Regenspurg zween schlüssel im schild füret.

"Denn weil in der schrift durch die lieben engel prediger und durch schlüssel das evangelion, welches allen gleubigen den himmel aufschleust, bedeutet werden, was kund ich diser alten herrlichen stad des reichs besseres geben denn wünschen, das lebendige gottesengel mit der predigt des gesetzs und evangelii als schlüsseln das himelreich allen sündern und büßern aufschließen?" From the forward dedicated to the Regensburg city councillors: Johannes Drach, "Der 117. Psalm ausgelegt" (Regensburg: Hans Kohl, 1541). Schottenloher 77, p. 195.

27. Theobald, *Reformationsgeschichte*, vol. 2, p. 114.

28. Ibid.

29. Discussed above, chapter two, notes 62–64.

30. On the Ratsbibliothek as the provenance of this copy, see *Index*, fol. 91', Juristica 7. It was not, however, bound for the city as its binding is dark leather rather than the light pigskin usual on the city's books; at some point after it was acquired by Regensburg, the city's arms were stamped on the binding using a tool dating from the end of the sixteenth century but in use into the eighteenth century. For Nuremberg as guide, esp. in matters of religion, see Theobald, *Reformationsgeschichte*, vol. 2, pp. 15–16.

Griffins, a symbol of empire and imperial majesty, and the imperial eagle had together crowned Hans Mielich's miniature for the Regensburg *Freiheitsbuch* of 1536 (fig. 1); the source for Mielich's choice of the symbol was that encyclopedia of imperial iconography, the *Triumphal Arch of Maximilian* by Albrecht Dürer, Hans Springinklee, Wolf Traut, and Mielich's teacher Albrecht Altdorfer (1515) [Bartsch 137; Meder 251; Panofsky 358], from which he took not only the two griffins, but also the imperial crown that topped both works. The fabled beasts, however, could also refer to imperial power in a negative sense: griffins were commonly associated with Alexander the Great, who, in his griffin-accompanied attempt at flight, symbolized Superbia for the Middle Ages. Cf. O. Holl, "Alexander der Grosse," in *Lexikon der christlichen Ikonographie*, ed. Engelbert Kirschbaum (Rome, 1968), vol. 1, cols. 94–96. According to Johann Georg Humel, procurator in Regensburg, a "gemeines Teutsches Verßlein" about Hoffart (= Superbia or Pride) began "Wer fliegen will, der flieg also, Weder zunider": *Thesaurus centum electissimorum proverbiorum* (Regensburg: Christoff Fischer, 1636), no. 13. StBR, Rat. civ. 637. Although the verse continued with a reference to the fall of Icarus in Humel's version, the flight of Alexander would have been the more familiar medieval exemplum. Humel's commentary on pride included the reference to the loss of their hegemonies by the Jews and the Romans which was also to be found in Martin Luther's sermon on the two realms: "Ein Sermon, von Christlicher gerechtigkeit, oder vergebung der sünden, gepredigt zu Marpurg in Hessen. 1528" (Regensburg: Hans Kohl, 1554), fol. Aiii. It is perhaps in this negative sense that we are to understand the ex libris personification of empire who clutched the Regensburg arms in his claws at the end of the Schmalkaldic War; he, too, appears to have had his formal origin in Dürer's griffins on Maximilian's triumphal arch. Cf., however, note 63 below, for a griffin who held the shield bearing the single-keyed arms of the Catholic city of Worms in the editions of Sebastian Münster's *Cosmographiae* published at Basel beginning in 1550.

31. On the city seal attached to a document of 1211 the enthroned saint held book and key. Erich Keyser and Heinz Stoob, eds., *Deutsches Städtebuch: Handbuch städtischer Geschichte*, vol. 5: *Bayern* (Stuttgart, 1974), p. 586; Karl Bauer, *Regensburg* (Regensburg, 1980), p. 9. The so-called great seal of 1248 shows him with the same accoutrements but surrounded by architecture representative of cathedral or city. Original in HStAM. The admission tokens sold for the tournament held in Regensburg in 1487 were stamped with the keys of the city, as were the city's coins, its weights, the insignia required to be worn by beggars permitted in the city, and the tokens "paid" Ratsherren for their attendance at council meetings. HStAM, R L Regensburg 583, fol. 2; Georg Gottlieb Plato-Wild, *Regensburgisches Münz-Kabinet oder Verzaichniß der d. H.R.R. freien Stadt Regensburg Kurrent und Schau-Münzen* (Regensburg, 1779); Egon Beckenbauer, *Die Münzen der Reichsstadt Regensburg* [Bayerische Munzkataloge 5 (Grünewald, 1978)]; R L Regensburg 381, fols. 5, 27, 47.

32. Two of the other panels of the altarpiece—*Purgatory* and *Works of Mercy*—are reproduced in *Martin Luther und die Reformation in Deutschland* (exhib. cat., Germanisches Nationalmuseum, Nuremberg, 1983), fig. 41 a–b.

33. On the early history of Regensburg bookbinding, see the occasional references to payments for the binding of municipal registers, etc., in the fragments of municipal accounts preserved by Gemeiner for 1501 and 1512: HStAM, Gemeiners Nachlaß 25 and 29. Also see Paul Adam, "Buchbindekunst im alten Regensburg," *Archiv für Buchbinderei* 19 (1919/1920), pp. 49–57, 62–70; 20 (1920), pp. 1–5, 13–17, 25–30, 37–38, 41; Schottenloher, pp. 10–11, 27–28, 97–98.

34. Until the construction of the mill, Regensburg had bought paper produced in Venice and Ravensburg for municipal use: HStAM, Gemeiners Nachlaß 29. For the watermarks on the paper produced in the city's mill in the course of the sixteenth century, see Gerhard Piccard, *Wasserzeichen: Schlüssel* (Stuttgart, 1979), pp. 10–11, and figs. 201–556, 701–733; on the mill itself, see *Bauamtschronik*, fol. 21, and Schottenloher 78, and p. 29.

35. See below, fig. 48 and note 78.

36. For the city ordinances, see Schottenloher 22, 28, 39, 40, 51, 59, 60, 62–65, 71, 72, 74, 76, 79–81. The decrees issued by the bishopric are Schottenloher 34 and 50; the editions of *Indictionis concilii* are Schottenloher 69 and 70. The keys of St. Peter were also, of course, the symbol of the pope as St. Peter's successor, and appropriate to the Regensburg see because of its patron.

37. E.g., those volumes of the *Ratswahlbücher* which were bound before 1542: StAR, M.S. Ratisb. IAc 1 (1500–1539) and M.S. Ratisb. IAc 2 (1540–1557).

38. Schottenloher 83. The "regimen against pestilence" (1532), edited by Kaspar Kolb and by him dedicated to the Regensburg Rat, which saw to its distribution door to door within the city, although not commissioned by the Rat can be seen as a partial exception to this rule. In it the announcement on the title page that the work was dedicated to the council was accompanied by the city arms, followed by the announcement of imperial privilege. Schottenloher 54 publishes the dedicatory foreword. For the distribution by the city, see Widmann, *Chronik*, p. 126.

39. Schottenloher 43 and 47.

40. Schottenloher 48.

41. Among the most striking of his works are Bede's *Abacus atque veterum latinorum per digitos manusque numerandi consuetudo* (edited by Johann Aventinus) and Paul Ricius' *Statera prudentum*, both printed in 1530 with woodcuts attributed to Michael Ostendorfer. The woodcuts in the two works, Schottenloher 52 and 53, are discussed by Alfred Hagelstange, "Ein Schriftchen über Zeichensprache von 1532, mit Holzschnitten von Michael Ostendorfer," in *Studien aus Kunst und Geschichte, Friedrich Schneider zum 70. Geburtstage gewidmet* (Freiburg i. Br., 1906), p. 275. The *Abacus*, actually the first chapter of the Venerable Bede's *De temporum ratione* with glosses, was frequently published as a separate work, both in manuscripts (e.g., in a ninth-century ms. from Regensburg: StBM, Handschriftenabteilung, Clm. 14725) and printed books (e.g., *Patrologia*, vol. 90 [Paris, 1850], cols. 685–698). Charles W. Jones, *Bedae Pseudepigrapha: Scientific Writings Falsely Attributed to Bede* (Ithaca, 1939), pp. 22–23, 53–54.

42. See Schottenloher 52, 53, 56.

43. See note 38 above.

44. Schottenloher 83, 84.

45. P. Schmidt, *Die Illustration der Luther Bibel 1522 bis 1700* (Basel, 1962), pp. 93–112. The

September Testament and its followers in Basel (1523) and Wittenberg (1534) are discussed in Robert W. Scribner, *For the Sake of Simple Folk: Popular Propaganda for the German Reformation* (Cambridge, 1981), pp. 169–174.

46. For an illustration of the title page woodcut of this German edition of the bull *Exsurge, domine,* see *Reformation in Nürnberg—Umbruch und Bewahrung* (exhib. cat., Germanisches Nationalmuseum, Nuremberg, 1979), no. 108.

47. "On Aplas von Rom kan man wol selig werden" (Augsburg: Melchior Ramminger, 1520), illustrated in *Martin Luther und die Reformation in Deutschland,* no. 200.

48. "Ein schons tractetlein von dem Götlichen und romischen Ablas" (Speyer: J. Schmidt, 1525). Discussed and illustrated in Scribner, *For the Sake of Simple Folk,* pp. 116–117.

49. Hans Sachs, *Ein wunderliche Weyssagung von dem Babstum. wie es yhm an das endt der welt gehen sol* (Nuremberg: Hans Guldenmund, 1527). The title page claimed that the illustrations were taken from frescoes in the Nuremberg Carthusian monastery, but when threatened with confiscation of the work by the Nuremberg Rat Guldenmund produced the Bolognese work as proof that the work was not of recent invention. The preface was by Andreas Osiander. *Illustrated Bartsch,* vol. 13, part 2, pp. 136–150.

50. Ibid., no. 1301.048 (i).

51. Philipp Melanchthon's "Der Bapstesel zu Rom" first appeared in 1523 together with Luther's "Das Munchkalb zu freyberg," the joint production titled "Deuttung der czwo grewlichen Figuren Bapstesels zu Rom und Munchkalb zu freyberg." For its fifteenth-century predecessor, see Dieter Koepplin and Tilman Falk, *Lukas Cranach, Gemälde, Zeichnungen, Druckgraphik* (Basel, 1974), vol. 1, pp. 361–363, 370–371.

52. The image is discussed in Scribner, *For the Sake of Simple Folk,* pp. 131–133.

53. This count includes one French and one English translation and editions both with and without Luther's "Monchkalb" text; see *WA* 11:357–365. One Wittenberg edition goes to the extreme of referring in the title to the Castel Sant'Angelo as the pope's "synagogue"; *WA* 11:363, α.

54. Letter reprinted by Gemeiner, *Kirchenreformation,* pp. 18–19.

55. Born in the last decade of the fifteenth century in Lichtenfels, Johann Hiltner was son of the *Kastner* and *Forstmeister* to the bishop of Bamberg. After having studied at the University of Wittenberg (magister artium 1510) and in France (doctor jura 1517), Hiltner himself became councillor to the Bamberg bishop. In 1523 he was called to Regensburg by Thoma Fuchs, the city's imperial Hauptmann whose brothers Jacob and Andreas, cathedral canons at Bamberg, had become Protestants. Hiltner seems to have married only after his arrival in Regensburg; at any rate, his first wife was Felicitas, daughter of Hans Schwebl, a member of the Innerer Rat in Regensburg. Although not himself born in the city, it was not only in this marriage that Hiltner typified the intermarried politically active families of Regensburg; Hans Huemer, one of his stepsons by his third wife, Barbara (d. 1568), was a member of the city's Äußerer Rat. He was also mentioned as an intimate in the will of Karl Gartner, a member of the Innerer Rat. And the preface to Aventinus' *Annal Bavarica* referred to that historian's friendship with Hiltner. On 15 October 1542, Hiltner was the second (after the Cammerer Andreas Wolff) to receive Communion in both kinds at the first official celebration of the Lutheran Communion in Regensburg. He died twenty-five years later, in 1567. Günter Schlichting, "Dr. Johann Hiltner, der Reformator der Reichsstadt Regensburg," *Verhandlungen des Historischen Vereins für Oberpfalz und Regensburg* 120 (1980), pp. 455–456; Gartner and Huemer wills, Regensburger Testamente, HStAM; Theobald, *Reformationsgeschichte,* p. 128.

56. Gemeiner, *Kirchenreformation,* pp. 34–35.

57. Ibid., pp. 42–43; *WA Briefe* 5:490.

58. Theobald, *Reformationsgeschichte,* vol. 1, pp. 229, 251.

59. Ibid., p. 240.

60. Ibid., p. 243.

61. Physicians: D. Pauls Flettacher (whose son Haubolt entered the Äußerer Rat in 1559, the Innerer Rat in 1561), D. Nicolaus Salzinger. Members of the Äußerer Rat: Hans Steuerer der Ältere (Innerer Rat, 1546), Wilhelm Radecker, Hans Klemperl, Georg Paumkircher, Hans ("Jung"?) Stuchs (Innerer Rat, 1543), Paulus Kohl (printer), Hans Heusinger (Innerer Rat, 1564), Georg Perger, Wolf Schweller.
My source is an early eighteenth-century copy of the petition by Johann Georg Gölgel, *Regenspurgische Kirchen-Historia* (ms., 1707), StaBM, Cgm. 2012, fols. 27–28'. Cf. Theobald, *Reformationsgeschichte,* pp. 249–250, and Gemeiner, *Kirchenreformation,* pp. 120–122. Gemeiner

claims thirty-two signers but lists only thirty-one; Theobald lists thirty-three. Neither Gemeiner nor Theobald quote the petition. The names given by Gemeiner and Gölgel are the same except for minor differences in spelling; Theobald appears to have added two to his list through misreading. My source for the public careers of these men is the Regensburger *Ratswahlbücher*: (1540–1557), StAR, M.S. Ratisb. IAc 2; (1558–1575), StAR, M.S. Ratisb. IAc 3.

62. *Schultheißengericht Beisitzer*: Jeronimus Seittentaler (Innerer Rat, 1547), Michael Fuchsprunner (a cabinetmaker, he had been *Wachtgericht Beisitzer* 1532–1541, had been accused of Anabaptism in 1539 but recanted, and in 1542 was elected to the Schulteißengericht), Michael Marr ("Mayr"; Äußerer Rat, 1543), Wolfgang Pfaffenreutter, Georg Enckofer, and Michael Mullner. *Hannsgrafenamt Beisitzer*: Hans Eysen. *Procurator*: Hans Kranberger. *Ungeltschreiber*: Erhard Niddermayer, Cristoff Egker (1545). *Bauamtschreiber* (name not given in any of the three sources). *Bauamt*: Hans Lang (1553). *Donauwacht Ausschuß*: Wilhelm Wieland (1548). For sources, see preceding note.

63. The arms of Worms itself were a single key on a shield; see Master HSD, *Civitas Wormaciensis*, woodcut c. 1550 in which a griffin held the city's shield above a profile view of Worms itself. Printed as a four-sheet foldout for Sebastian Münster, *Cosmographiae universalis Lib. VI.* (Basel: Henrich Petrus, 1550), inserted between pp. 652 and 653. Repeated in later editions: (Basel: Henrich Petrus, 1552), between pp. 480 and 481; (Basel: Henrich Petrus, 1554), between pp. 480 and 481; and, in German edition: *Cosmographey oder beschreibung aller länder, herrschafften* (Basel: Henrich Petrus, 1564), as paginated insert, pp. dxciii–dcxcv.

64. Martin Luther, "Von den Schlüsseln" (1530), WA 30, 2:468.

65. The iconography of the woodcut is analyzed by Scribner, *For the Sake of Simple Folk*, pp. 80–81. The date 1538 (in contrast to c. 1545 assigned by Geisberg/Strauss; G.922) is taken from an entry in Antonius Lauterbach's daybook; cf. O. Clemen, "Abbildung des Papstums 1545," in WA 54:346–347.

66. E.g., the woodcut *ADORATVR PAPA DEVS TERRENVS* published in 1545, in which the verse

> Bapst hat dem reich Christi gethon
> Wie man hie handelt seine Cron.
> Machts ir zweifeltig: spricht der geist
> Schenckt getrost ein: Gott ists ders heist.

was signed by Martin Luther and accompanied by a depiction of three farmers, one of whom defecated into an inverted papal tiara balanced above a papal shield on which the keys had been transformed into thieves' lock picks. WA 54:351–352, 365–366; pl. 11.

67. Martin Luther, "Ein Christlicher sermon, Von gewalt Sand Peters" (Regensburg: Pauls Kohl, 1522). Schottenloher 13. Quoted from WA 10, 3:215, which does not, however, list the Regensburg edition; ibid., cxxvii–cxxviii.

"Das Ampt der schlüsseln dadurch Wir Wider auffgericht und angenommen Werden so Wir gefallen sind" is the title above a woodcut of an open confessional labeled *BEICHT* in the catechism by Regensburg's Lutheran pastor, Nikolaus Gallus, *Ein Kurtze Ordenliche suma der rechten Waren Lehre unsers heiligen Christlichen glaubens* (Regensburg: Hans Kohl, 1547), fol. 27'. StBR, 8° Rat. civ. 675. On the omission of this edition from Schottenloher's catalogue, see above, note 15.

68. Heinrich Lilienfein, *Lukas Cranach und seine Zeit* (Bielefeld, 1944), pl. 127; Carl C. Christensen, *Art and the Reformation in Germany* (Athens, Ohio, 1979), fig. 9 and pp. 139–141. Cf. Michael Ostendorfer's altarpiece for the Neupfarrkirche (1553/1555), in which the call to confession and the confession itself occupied more than a third of the central panel. Reproduced in *Martin Luther und die Reformation*, fig. 539 and pp. 400–402.

69. Augsburg: Johann Miller, 1513. Harbison, *Last Judgment*, p. 151 and fig. 75, and idem, "Reformation Iconography: Problems and Attitudes," *Tribute to Wolfgang Stechow*, ed. Walter L. Strauss (*Print Review* 5 [1976]), p. 80 and fig. 2.

70. See above, chapter two, note 12.

71. Martin Luther, "Disputatio de potestate concilii" (10 October 1536?), WA 39, 1:193. Cf. Luther, "Disputatio contra privatam missam" (29 January 1536), WA 39, 1:146; and, again, the earlier "Von den Schlüsseln" (1530), WA 30, 2:465–507.

72. Text given above, note 26. I am grateful to Dr. Günter Schlichting of Regensburg for alerting me to Johannes Drach's interpretation. On Drach himself, see Schottenloher, pp. 18–19.

73. Schottenloher, pp. 18–19, 98–99.

74. Schottenloher 83.

75. "... hat er Christus unser lieber herr den gewalt der schlüssel, das ist, die macht leüt von sunden zu entpinden, und inen die sunde in seinem namen zuvergeben, seiner gemain hie auff erden gelassen und bevolhen, als da er spricht Joan. am xx." "Ein Vermanung Und unterricht deren, so die Absolution irer sünden, und das Hochwirdig Sacrament Zur sterckung ires glaubens empfahen wöllen, wie alle Sambstag nach der vesper zu Regenspurg ab der Cantzel offenlich verlesen wirdt" (Regensburg: Hans Kohl, c. 1544), fol. Av'. Schottenloher 89. StBM, 8° Polem. 1310, 3. A woodcut of the Regensburg arms appeared on the title page. Cf. among other references to the "Amt der Schlüsseln": "Warhafftiger Bericht"; "Vermahnung vor der beicht" (ms. 1542), StAR, Eccl. I 10, ad 142f.; "Christliche Vermanungen, Wie die vor der Beicht, Communion und Predig, zu Regenspurg inn der newen Pfarr, der Gemeine offentlich fürgelesen werden" (Regensburg: Heinrich Geißler, 1567), Schottenloher 265. All reprinted in Emil Sehling, ed., *Die evangelischen Kirchenordnungen des XVI. Jahrhunderts*, vol. 13, 3: *Altbayern* (Tübingen, 1966), pp. 389–402, here p. 398.

76. At least three chalices were created for the Lutheran Neupfarrkirche in the course of the sixteenth century; each bore the city's arms: a hexagonally footed chalice from 1542, with crossed keys, Regensburg silvermark, and master's sign; a chalice from 1545, with crossed keys; and a hexagonal chalice from 1597, with enameled keys and angel's head, Regensburg silvermark, and master's sign. The church's sixteenth-century pyx, a round silver box with small ball feet meant to hold the consecrated Host, bore the crossed keys and date 1542 in enamel and the Regensburg silvermark. Felix Mader, *Die Kunstdenkmäler von Bayern*, vol. 22: *Stadt Regensburg* (Munich, 1933), part 2, pp. 206–207.

77. See *Ratswahlbücher*: StAR, M.S. Ratisb. IAc 1 (1500–1539) and M.S. Ratisb. IAc 2 (1540–1557).

78.

*Concordantiae maiores sacrae bibliae* (Basel 1531).
binding: 2° beveled wooden boards with clasps; white pigskin.
large square Regensburg arms / CONCORDANTIAE / MDXXXXIII / antique medallion roll.

*Index*, fol. 8 (Theologia 9). StBR, 2° Script. 337. It was overlooked by Adam, "Buchbindekunst," *Archiv für Buchbinderei* 20 (1920), p. 26, who found no *Stadtwappen* before that appearing on the *Ratswahlbuch* for 1558–1574 (StAR, IAc 3); however, cf. ibid. 19 (1919/1920), p. 50.

There is virtually no information on bookbinders active in Regensburg during the sixteenth century. Schottenloher found city accounts revealing that Martin Haider, a servant in the tax office, was paid in 1501 to bind the *Kaiserliche Regimentsordnung* written for the city in 1500; that from 1506–1512, Johann Holnstain was paid by the city as a binder of municipal registers; and that Hans Wagner was paid to bind some municipal registers in 1522. Schottenloher, p. 11. In addition to the entries given by Schottenloher, I have been able to locate a few more references to Regensburg bookbinders in documents preserved in the Bayerisches Hauptstaatsarchiv in Munich. The municipal registers mentioned above were generally bound in simple leather covers, but Martin Haider bound the *Regimentsordnung* in boards (as was specified by the *Regimentsordnung* itself); on Haider and Holnstain: HStAM, Gemeiners Nachlaß 25, "Ausgeben ze ainitzen daß Jahre 1501," fols. 2, 4', 9'; Gemeiners Nachlaß 29, "Ainitz ausgeben" (1512), fols. 3', 8, 14'. On 27 January 1525, a city scribe took a deposition from "Steffan puchpinter" concerning a sermon preached by Paul Schmidl, the pastor of St. Cassian's, on 27 January 1525; HStAM, Gemeiners Nachlaß 40. More relevant to the decades with which we are concerned, the bookbinder and Anabaptist Gabriel Weinberger underwent interrogation and was exiled from the city in 1539; Schottenloher, pp. 27–28. The cleric (?) Conrad Demerl, who in 1542 willed his 231 books to the Regensburg Rat in order that they not be divided up (a practice not uncommon among those who left the monasteries in this period), also willed a metal-bound cask containing weapons to the bookbinder Valentin Wibenperger; HStAM, Regensburger Testamente. Documents filed two decades later by the Nuremberg Rat on behalf of a book dealer in that city against a Regensburg bookbinder named Michel Wibenperger (Schottenloher 88 and p. 159 n. 3) suggest that at least two generations of Wibenpergers were active as bookbinders in Regensburg in the relevant period. Unfortunately, I have been able to locate no bindings signed with the initials GW, VW, or MW among Regensburg-owned books.

79. Martin Luther, *WA Tischreden* I, 326–327; translated in Cynthia Grant Schoenberger, "Luther and the Justifiability of Resistance to Legitimate Authority," *Journal of the History of Ideas* 40 (1979), p. 17.

80. On the connection between binding stamps and woodcuts, see Bernard McTigue, "English Bookbinding and the Continental Woodblock Tradition," *Printing History* 3 (1981), pp. 20–29. In Regensburg the wooden boards of the early sixteenth-century bindings were frequently leather-wrapped only at the spine, the leather extending over only one-quarter or one-half of the wooden cover. Large folio volumes were, however, generally fully leather-bound even in the first decades of the century.

81. "Item In ainem peitel etlich alt haidnisch pfening / Item In einem peitelein etlich alt haidnisch pfening guet und pöß." The inventory made at Altdorfer's death by Hans Linck, Wolfgang Schweller, and Georg Haider, and the will Altdorfer made on his deathbed are in the Stadtmuseum, Regensburg. They are reprinted in Walter Boll, "Albrecht Altdorfers Nachlass," *Münchner Jahrbuch der bildenden Kunst* N.F. 13 (1938/1939), pp. 91–102, here, p. 101. For binding, see above, note 78.

82. Cf. the same roll-stamp without visible IH, located in the possession of Caspar Angler, bookbinder to Herzog Albrecht of Prussia in Königsberg, by Konrad Haebler and Ilse Schunke, *Rollen- und Plattenstempel des XVI. Jahrhunderts* (Leipzig, 1928), vol. 1, p. 14. Roll-stamps (e.g., the Virtues roll discussed below) bearing the initials IH have been identified by the same scholars with the Augsburger bookbinder Jacob Hall. Ibid., vol. 1, p. 185. The separation of the initials I—H on the tool would, according to Haebler, "Der Rollstempel und seine Initialen," *Nordick Tidskrift för Bok- och Bibliotekväsen* 11 (1924), pp. 24–52, indicate that they refer to the binder who owned the stamp, rather than to the craftsman who created it. Nevertheless, locating the binder by the tools he used is a hazardous enterprise at best, since tools changed hands by sale and inheritance and were copied.

83. The volumes are today in the Staatliche Bibliothek, Regensburg:

Herodotus, *Libri novem* (Basel 1540).
binding: 2° beveled wooden boards with clasps; brown leather, blind.
Virtues roll signed I H 1546 / flower stamps / H N / 1546 / Reformers roll signed I H 1539 / garland roll. Cf. *Index*, fol. 85 (Art. 2), StBR, 2 Class. 32.

Martin Luther's letter, dated Monday after St. Catherine's day (27 November), 1542, is in the collection of the Museen der Stadt, Regensburg; reprinted in *WA Briefe* 10:208–209.

84. See preceding note. The significance of the lack of municipal watermark and choice of leather is lessened by the lack of data on the sale of paper from the city-owned mill to individuals in Regensburg, and the lack of information on books bound for and owned by the city's Bürger.

85. Two common features help to identify the books bound for the Regensburg Ratsbibliothek: the iron leaf-shaped boss affixed to the back of each binding, possibly to attach a chain since the title of *Index* referred to "alle bücher, so in eines erbarn Camerer und Rhats Liberei alhie zu Regenspurg an Ketten, gelegt sind"; and the distinctive double depressions cut (for ease in using clasps?) in the long side of the beveled wooden boards next to the clasps. Unfortunately, little work has been done on beveling styles, which appear to be regional. See the comment by E. Ph. Goldschmidt, *Gothic and Renaissance Bookbindings Exemplified and Illustrated from the Author's Collection* (London, 1928), vol. 1, pp. 295–296, and the similar beveling described and illustrated by Fritz Juntke-Halle, "Georg Rumler, ein Hallischer Buchbinder aus der zweiten Hälfte des 16. Jahrhunderts," in *Beiträge zum Rollen- und Platteneinband im 16. Jahrhundert. Konrad Haebler zum 80. Geburtstage am 29. Oktober 1937 gewidmet*, ed. Ilse Schunke (Leipzig, 1937), p. 205 and pl. X.

Adam, "Buchbindekunst," *Archiv für Buchbinderei* 20 (1920), p. 1 and fig. 1a–b, presents another case that suggests Augsburg or Saxony-Regensburg connections. The Regensburg roll used on the binding of the *Schreiner-Handwerksordnung* of 1565 appears to be an adaptation (complete with Saxon arms only thinly disguised) of the narrow Saxon arms/antique medallion roll used by Jakob Kraus, an Augsburg bookbinder called to work for the court in Saxony.

86. Cf. McTigue, "English Bookbinding."

87. These medallion and binding portraits are strikingly dissimilar to the images of the fifteenth-century reformer in woodcuts illustrating the account of Hus' martyrdom in Ulrich von Reichenthal, *Conciliumbuch* (Augsburg: Anton Sorg, 1483), fols. 33' and 34'. Reproduced in Schramm, *Bilderschmuck*, vol. 4, nos. 1072–1073.

88. At least one senior member of the Innerer Rat, however, was presumably still Catholic in the period of the Schmalkaldic War and Interim: Wolfgang Steuerer, characterized by Gemeiner, *Kirchenreformation*, p. 157n, as the leader of the Catholic opposition within the council, was a member of the Innerer Rat from 1519 until his death in 1552. See *Ratswahlbücher*: (1500–1539), StAR, M.S. Ratisb. IAc 1; (1540–1557), StAR, M.S. Ratisb. IAc 2.

89. E.g., another stamp by the same IH Master dated one year earlier (1538), depicting five reformers (including the reluctant but frequently claimed "Protestant" Erasmus) in medallions labeled "MARTINVS LVTHERVS—H FRIDERI.DVX.SAXO—D.ERASMVS ROTERDAMVS—PHILIPPVS MELANTHON 15–38—IOAN.FRIDERI.DVX.SAXO." This stamp was used on a volume purchased and possibly bound in Augsburg in 1558. It entered the Ratsbibliothek sometime after 1638. StBR, 2° Class. 14.

90. An amazing portrait of Johann Friedrich as rebel armed as he was when captured at Mühlberg, painted by Titian or members of Titian's workshop c. 1548 in Augsburg, has been published by Wolfgang Braunfels, "Ein Tizian nach Cranach," *Festschrift für Herbert von Einem zum 16. Februar 1965*, ed. Gert von der Osten (Berlin, 1965), p. 46 and pl. 2, who suggests that the painting was intended as the shaming portrait of a criminal, similar to those painted on the walls of the Bargello in Florence. In contrast to this portrait stands a series of woodcuts by the Saxon HM Master which celebrated the duke as a Protestant martyr after his death in 1554. One showed the reception of the duke by his wife and sons on his return from captivity. The fact that, despite his adventures, he was allowed to die peacefully at home was interpreted by the author of the verses accompanying the woodcut as a "clear sign from heaven"—an interpretation echoed in the woodcut by the rays that streamed down on Johann Friedrich from the hand of an angel sent by a God whose hand was raised in benediction. Strauss, *Woodcut, 1550–1600*, vol. 3, p. 1244. A second woodcut showed the important events in the duke's life as a series of vignettes, beginning with his father's instructions to him as a child and ending with the transportation of his soul to heaven to await the Last Judgment. Ibid., pp. 1245–1248.

91. Martin Luther, "Wermanunge zum Gebet, Wider den Türcken" (Wittenberg: Nickel Schirlentz, 1541), WA 51:586.

92. Georg Swarzenski, *Die Regensburger Buchmalerei des X. und XI. Jahrhunderts. Studien zur Geschichte der deutschen Malerei des frühen Mittelalters* (2nd ed., Stuttgart, 1969), pp. 32–33, 97–98 and figs. 1, 31; Adolf Katzenellenbogen, *Allegories of the Virtues and Vices in Medieval Art from Early Christian Times to the Thirteenth Century* (London, 1939), p. 35 and fig. 36.

93. Discussed in Swarzenski, *Regensburger Buchmalerei*; Katzenellenbogen, *Allegories*, pp. 36–37 and fig. 38; and Stephan Beissel, *Vaticanische Miniaturen* (Freiburg i. Br., 1893), pp. 35–36 and pl. XVIII. The *Gospel Book* may well have been commissioned by Heinrich II for the Benedictine abbey at Monte Cassino; for the evidence for such a commission and donation, and the interpretation of the illumination in the light of this evidence, see Herbert Bloch, *Monte Cassino in the Middle Ages* (Cambridge, Mass., 1986), vol. 1, pp. 19–30.

94. Katzenellenbogen, *Allegories*, p. 36. I have relied for my explication de texte on the descriptions given by Swarzenski and Katzenellenbogen. My interpretation, however, differs substantially from that of the latter scholar in its understanding of the causal connections depicted. See also the analysis by Ernst H. Kantorowicz, *The King's Two Bodies: A Study in Medieval Political Theology* (Princeton, 1957), pp. 113–115, who rightly insists (pp. 114–115) that "the picture's language is theological, and not jurisprudential."

95. Heinrich II, crowned king by Archbishop Willigis in Mainz and emperor by Pope Benedict VIII in Rome, was canonized by the church a century after his death. He "viewed his role as king, and as emperor as well, in a theocratic light." Jonathan W. Zophy, ed., *The Holy Roman Empire: A Dictionary Handbook* (Westport, Conn., 1980), p. 198. According to Percy Schramm, the dedicatory miniature to be found in another manuscript copied for Heinrich II by a monk of the Regensburg school, depicting Christ himself crowning the king while two angels handed him the sword and holy lance awarded him in the Mainz ceremony, demonstrated that "Willigis had acted in the place of Christ, the true *coronator* of the *rex Dei gratia*, and the insignia with which Heinrich had received his *corrobatio* as such a king were granted—as is made clear by the image—by heaven." Percy Ernst Schramm, *Herrschaftszeichen und Staatssymbolik. Beiträge zu ihrer Geschichte vom dritten bis zum sechzehnten Jahrhundert* [Schriften der Monumenta Germaniae historica 13 (Stuttgart, 1955)], vol. 2, p. 508. For further discussion, see idem, *Kaiser, Könige und Päpste. Gesammelte Aufsätze zur Geschichte des Mittelalters* (Stuttgart, 1968–1971), vol. 3, pp. 116–121, 178–180; vol. 4, pp. 80–83.

96. StBM, Clm. 13002, fol. 4. The pen drawings are discussed in Albert Boeckler, *Die Regensburg-Prüfeninger Buchmalerei des XII. und XIII. Jahrhunderts* (Munich, 1924), pp. 24–26 and figs. 15–16. Cf. Katzenellenbogen, *Allegories*, p. 57 and figs. 54–55.

97. "Deus superbis resistit." James 4:6. "Excelsus dominus humilia respicit." Psalms 137:6. Boeckler, *Die Regensburg-Prüfeninger Buchmalerei*, pp. 24–26.

98. Hans Sachs and Erhard Schön, *Schandenport: Die zwelff grausamen Tyrannen des alten*

*Testaments, mit irem wüterischen leben und erschröcklichem undergang zu trost allen ellenden Christen, so unter dem schweren Joch des blutdurstigen Türcken und andern Tyrannen verstricket sind, etc.* (Nuremberg, 1531; Nuremberg: Hans Guldenmund, 1545). *Illustrated Bartsch* 1301.119.

99. "Zu trost allen ellenden Christen, so unter dem schweren Joch des blütgyrigen Türken, und anderer Gotlosen Tyrannen, zwancknuß beschwert sind. . . . welches doch auß verhentnuß Gottes zu straff irer sündt und manigfeltiger ubertrettung, auß väterlicher heymsuchung geschehen ist. . . . das sie von eygener Oberkeyt gedrucket, oder von frembden Heydnischen Tyrannen uberzogen, begweltigt, beraubt, ermördt, zinßbar gemacht, gefangen, hingefart, von Gottes gesetz zü abgötterey gedrungen wurden. Alßdenn erkennet das volck Gottes sein ubertrettung, keret sich zu Got, schrey umb hilff, so erbarmet sich Got desselben seines volcks gnedigkliche, rrettet (sic) sie auß der Tyrannen hendt. . . . Wie auch Got alle mal den hochmüt der Tyrannen, sambt irem anhang, durch sein gwaltigen Arm, mit irem schendlichen unehrlichen tödten, so wunderbarlich zeiget, das sich solche unehrliche tödte mit irem schendtlichen leben wol vergleichet." Hans Sachs, *Schandenport,* fol. 1.

100. Desiderius Erasmus, *Ein nutzliche underwisung eines Christenlichen fürsten wol zü regieren* (Zurich: Christoph Froschouer, 1521), fols. XVI–XX'. The other German edition is *Die unterweysung aines frummen Fürsten an den herrn Karln den fünfften,* trans. G. Spalatinus (Augsburg: S. Grimm and M. Wirsung, 1521); cited in *Short-Title Catalogue of Books Printed in the German-Speaking Countries and German Books Printed in Other Countries from 1455 to 1600 Now in the British Museum* (London, 1962), p. 282.

101. On the long history of Luther's move toward advocating resistance to imperial efforts to reinstitute the sacramentary practices of the Catholic church in the empire, see most recently Mark U. Edwards, Jr., *Luther's Last Battles: Politics and Polemics, 1531–1546* (Ithaca, 1983), pp. 20–37. Weighing the rhetorical force of Luther's argument against the reformer's own disclaimers, Edwards concludes (p. 36) that, "as a practical matter, all of [Luther's] polemics on the issue of resistance *encouraged* Protestants to resist a Catholic attack, even if led by the emperor."

102.

> Fünff und achtzig Priester ermort
> Saul, unschuldig an einem ort
> Ir weyber und sewgende kinder
> Ermört ir Esel und ir Rinder.

Sachs, *Schandenport,* fol. 3; Martin Luther, *WA Tischreden* I, 326–327 (see above, note 79). A similar connection was apparently intended by the two engravings depicting the *Punishment of Tyranny* in Hendrick Goltzius' series *The Allegories of Faith;* Bartsch 73–74. Perceived mistreatment was, of course, also regarded as a crime against Christianity during the medieval period; writing in the mid-fifteenth century, the Augsburger Burkard Zink called Karl IV a "durchächter der christenhait" for his imposition of a *Judensteuer* on Augsburg: Schmidt, *Deutsche Städtechroniken,* p. 70.

103. Martin Luther to Johann Ludicke, pastor of Kottbus (8 February 1539), *WA Briefe* 8:367. The story of David and Saul could, of course, be reiterated to make an entirely different point; cf. the earlier (1531) *Gutachten* written for Margrave Georg von Brandenburg-Ansbach by theologians gathered in Ansbach, in which a paragraph was devoted to the example of Saul in order to conclude with David's assertion that "wollt er sein schwert nie wider den konig Saul furn. . . . sagt er doch allweg: Das sei fern von mir, das ich hand anleg an den gesalbten des herrn, dann wer solt das unschuldigclich thun mogen?" The complete opinion is reprinted in Heinz Scheible, ed., *Das Widerstandsrecht als Problem der deutschen Protestanten 1523–1546* [Texte zur Kirchen- und Theologiegeschichte 10 (Gütersloh, 1969)], pp. 83–88, here p. 88.

104.

> Sein warer freünde Lucius
> Halff yhm zu nacht auß der gfengknus
> Verließ weyb kindt hab ehr und güt
> Und mit seym freündt in aremüt
> Verließ sein liebes vatterlandt

Hans Sachs and Erhard Schön, *Die Neun getrewesten Römer, mit yhren wunder getrewen thaten* (Nuremberg: Niclas Meldeman, [1531]). "Und wo ein Fürst odder Herr das Evangelion nicht wil leyden, Da gehe man ynn ein ander Fürstenthum, da es gepredigt wird, wie Christus spricht [Matthew 10:23]: 'Verfolgen sie euch ynn einer stad, so fliehet ynn die andere'." Martin Luther, "Ob kriegsleutte auch ynn seligem stande seyn künden" (Wittenberg, 1526), *WA* 19:634.

Individual stories and songs of ancient heroes and tyrants were also popular; there were at least two editions published at Nuremberg c. 1521 of Ludwig Binder's "Diß lied sagt von Nero dem Küng." Emil Weller, *Annalen der politischen National-Literatur der Deutschen im XVI. und XVII. Jahrhundert* (Freiberg i. Br., 1862–1864), vol. 2, no. 38.

105. For a sixteenth-century example of the traditional nine heroes, see the woodcut executed by Hans Burgkmair the Elder in 1519; B. 68. Nevertheless, in 1528 in the instructions for parish visitations for which Martin Luther himself wrote the preface, Philipp Melanchthon paired Julius Caesar with the notorious Nero and labeled both "tyrann." *Unterricht der Visitatoren an die Pfarhern ym Kurfurstenthum zu Sachssen*, preface by Martin Luther (Wittenberg: Nickel Schirlentz, 1528), fol. Diii.

Hans Baron's *Crisis of the Early Italian Renaissance* (Princeton, 1966) remains, despite possible chronological flaws, a most compelling account of a similar perspectival shift in Quattrocento Florence. In that case, the tyrant was the lord of Milan, Giangaleazzo Visconti. Cf. Niccolai Rubenstein, "Political Ideas in Sienese Art: The Frescoes of Ambrogio Lorenzetti and Taddeo di Bartolo in the Palazzo Pubblico," *Journal of the Warburg and Courtauld Institutes* 21 (1958), pp. 179–207.

106. Sachs' description somewhat misleadingly says simply "Brutus"; according to Valerius Maximus (IIII, 7, 6), Servius Terentius accompanied not the more famous Marcus Iunius Brutus, the leader of the conspiracy against Julius Caesar (as Sachs at least implies), but his relative and fellow conspirator Decius Iunius Brutus Albinus when he fled Rome in 43 B.C. Terentius identified himself as Brutus to save his friend's life when caught by pursuers but was recognized and released. "Ser. Terentius," *Paulys Real-Encyclopädie der classischen Altertumswissenschaft* (Stuttgart), ser. 2, vol. 9, col. 598; Münzer, "D. Iunius Brutus Albinus," *Paulys Real-Encyclopädie*, suppl. vol. 5, cols. 369–385.

107. Hans Sachs and Erhard Schön, *Die Neun getrewesten heydnischen Frawen, mit yhren wunder getrewen thaten* (Nuremberg: Niclas Meldeman, [1531]).

108. Livy, *Ab urbe condita* I, 57–59; Ovid, *Fasti* II, 721–852. German translations of Livy's history were popular throughout the sixteenth century; they were printed at Mainz (1505, 1514, 1530, 1551, 1557), Straßburg (1507, 1562, 1574, 1581, 1590, 1596), and Frankfurt (1568). In addition, Ludwig Binder's song "Dieß lied sagt von Lucretia, wie sie umb ir ere kam, unnd sich selbst ertödtet," published at Straßburg c. 1520, was reprinted in Nuremberg c. 1530 and 1560. Weller, *Annalen*, vol. 2, no. 23.

109. In Livy's account Brutus actually carried Lucretia's body to the forum in Collatina, the better to rouse his colleagues for a march on Rome.

110. Lucretia's appearance among the nine heroines (three from pagan antiquity, three from the Old Testament, and three from Christian antiquity) was not without precedent; Jacob Burckhardt cites a German fifteenth-century cycle that included her: "Die Sammler," *Beiträge zur Kunstgeschichte von Italien* (Basel, 1898), p. 415.

111. *Gesta romanorum* 135; Augustine, *De civitate Dei* 1: 19. Hans Galinsky, *Der Lucretia-Stoff in der Weltliteratur* [Sprach und Kultur der Germanisch-romanischen Völker, Section B: Germanistische series 3 (Breslau, 1932)].

112. See, for instance, the translation of Boccaccio's work into German by Hainrich Steinhöwel, *Des Giovanni Boccaccio Buch: von den berühmten Frawen*, printed at Augsburg (Anton Sorg, 1479), Straßburg (Johann Prüss, 1488), and Augsburg (H. Stayner, 1541).

113. *De mulieribus claris* (Ulm: Johann Zainer, 1473), fol. 49; the same illustrations without text in *Kurczsinn von etlichen Frauen* (s.l., s.d.); Augsburg edition translated by Heinrich Steinhöwel, *von den berühmten Frawen*, fol. 69'. Illustrated in Schramm, *Bilderschmuck*, vol. 4, no. 440; vol. 5, no. 57. On Martin Luther's knowledge of Boccaccio's work, see "Deinde recitavit historiam von frawen liste aus eynem buche, cuius titulus est: Die Florentzisch frawen. . . ." (January 1537), *WA Tischreden* 3:374, no. 3521.

114. E.g., Hans Burgkmair, *Drei güt haidin Lucrecia. Veturia. Virginia*, from a series of nine good Christian, Jewish, and pagan women (Augsburg: Jost de Negker, 1519); B. 69.

115. Later Pope Leo X. Wolfgang Stechow, "Lucretia Statua," *Essays in Honor of Georg Swarzenski* (Chicago, 1951), p. 118 and fig. 2. Stechow's short article is a useful survey of the early sixteenth-century history of the Lucretia image, particularly in Italy. He does not, however, provide much help in understanding the grounds for the acknowledged popularity of its northern versions, which he dismisses as "various degrees of imitation of the Italian monologues, . . . without adding anything of importance to either interpretation or form" (p. 124). Borrowings across the Alps were not, of course, unidirectional; works by Dürer and Lucas van

Leyden influenced two of the most "influential" of Marcantonio Raimondi's engravings after Raphael—his Dido of 1510, and his Lucretia of 1511/1512. Ibid., pp. 327, 328.

116. F. Winkler, *Die Zeichnnugen Albrecht Dürers* (Berlin, 1936), 436; now in the Albertina, Vienna.

117. Barthel Beham, *Lucretia with Column*, Bartsch 14, and *Lucretia in Niche with Column*, Bartsch 15; Hans Sebald Beham, *Lucretia with Column*, Bartsch 79. All three images are undated, although Passavant attributes another, columnless, *Lucretia* dated 1520 to Barthel Beham, Passavant IV, 283, 199; and Pauli attributes a *Lucretia before Her Bed* (1530) and a *Lucretia with Tree* (1519) to Hans Sebald Beham, see Gustav Pauli, *Hans Sebald Beham, ein kritisches Verzeichniss* (Straßburg, 1901), nos. 82, 912; Bartsch 78. Cf. Hans Baldung Grien, *Lucretia with Fruit Garlands* (1519), Passavant 73. See also the reverse of the medallion with the portrait of Hans Pflaum (1536), on which Lucretia sat under a tree as she stabbed herself. The inscription: RICHT.NICHT.ON. SCHVLT.ANN.M.D.XXXVI. Georg Habich, no. 1303 and pl. CXLV, 8. *Die deutschen Schaumünzen des XVI. Jahrhunderts*, vol. 1, part 2 (Munich, 1931).

At least one of the books in the Regensburg Ratsbibliothek cited Lucretia, Pyramis, Thisbe, and Dido, as exempla of Fortitudo; Jacobus Faber Stapulensis (= Jacques Le Fèvre d'Etaples), *Artificialis introductio in Decem Ethicorum Libros Aristotelis* (s.l., s.d.), fol. XIX' [= *Index*, fol. 84, Math. 18]; StBR, Philos. 3272. The virtue of fortitude seems to have been most susceptible to personification in the guise of historical or mythological figures. In Italy the thirteenth-century sculptor Nicolo Pisani, whose marble pulpit for the cathedral at Pisa depicted the Nativity in the stylistic language of pagan funerary sculpture, introduced Hercules into the medieval church as a representation of Fortitudo. While it would be wrong to claim that Mantegna turned St. Sebastian into a mere personification of Fortitudo, his depiction of the arrow-pierced patron of plague victims against a column certainly stressed the saint's fortitude at the same time that it recalled the column of Christ's flagellation. Cf. Mantegna's use of the column in two of his three surviving *St. Sebastian*s: panel (1459?), Vienna, Kunsthistorisches Museum; canvas (c. 1470), Paris, Louvre. The column as a symbol of Fortitudo had its origin in the name of one of the columns erected by Solomon before the temple, and in Samson's feat of strength. W. Messerer, "Säule," *Lexikon der christlichen Ikonographie*, ed. Engelbert Kirschbaum (Rome, 1968–1972), vol. 4, cols. 54–56. The *Sebastian*s by Albrecht Altdorfer and Hans Burgkmair were among the very few German depictions of the saint to show him with a column instead of the more usual tree: B. 23, B. 25. See also *Die Sterck* from Burgkmair's series of the seven cardinal Virtues, the Basel impression of which included "antique" medallions in its architectural frame: B. 52-III.

118. Max Friedländer and Jakob Rosenberg, *Die Gemälde von Lucas Cranach* (Berlin, 1932), list thirty-one *Lucretia*s (three presumably by Cranach the Younger), as well as fifteen paintings of the exemplar of Sanctimonia more popular in the medieval period—Judith (including one history picture). This count includes a diptych of Judith and Lucretia dating from after 1537; several of the other panels may be halves of such pairs. The dated Judith panels are from 1530 (1) and 1531 (2). *Judith*s dated on stylistic grounds: 1526–37 (8), after 1537 (4). Cranach's interest in the Lucretia image had deeper roots: the Küpferstichkabinett in Dahlem, Berlin, has a *Lucretia* drawing by Cranach dated 1509, and a painted *Lucretia* by Hans Döring dated 1514 may be based on an earlier (lost) Cranach. Ibid., p. 66 no. 198c. Dated Cranach *Lucretia*s: 1525 (1), 1528 (2), 1530 (1), 1532–1539 (7). The remainder are dated on stylistic grounds: c. 1525 (2), 1526–1537 (14), after 1537 (5). Cf. the Netherlandish *Lucretia*s described in Dietrich Schubert, "Halbfigurige Lucretia-Tafeln der 1. Hälfte des 16. Jahrhunderts in den Niederländen," *Jahrbuch des Kunsthistorischen Institutes der Universität Graz* 6 (1971), pp. 99–110. I will address the tension between the political use of the virtuous matron and the salacious tone of most of the Cranach panels—which apparently were intended for bedrooms rather than council chambers—in a future work.

History paintings and prints detailing the entire story of Lucretia did not, of course, completely die out. See the title page woodcut to the edition of Erasmus' *De duplici Copia verborum ac rerum* printed at Basel in 1519; StBR, 4° Lat. rec. 197; the panels by Jörg Breu der Ältere (for the Herzog of Bavaria, 1528, now in the Alte Pinakothek, Munich) and Hans Baldung Grien (fragment dated 1530, now in Museum Narodzowe, Poznan), as well as the 1515 woodcut by Hans Burgkmair (Passavant 118); and the drawings and woodcut by Baldung Grien (Gert von der Osten, *Hans Baldung Grien. Gemälde und Dokumente* [Berlin, 1983], pp. 203–205 and figs. 71, 71a). Also the later history woodcut by Jost Amman illustrating Livy I:58 for Philipp Lonicer, *Icones Livianae: Praecipuas romanorum historias magno artificio ad vivum expressas oculis repraesentantes, succinctis Versibus illustratae* (1572). *Illustrated Bartsch*, vol. 20, no. 3.16. Hans Schäufelein's woodcuts of Judith and Lucretia for Johann von Schwartzenberg, *Das Büchle Memorial, das ist ein angedänckung der Tugent* [= fols. XCVI–CXLVII' of *Der Teütsch Cicero* (Augsburg: Heinrich Steiner, 1534)], fols. CIX' and CXV', occupy a place between the isolated figure with attribute and the history paintings. The work was reprinted in the following year with the same woodcuts, but with spelling and pagination slightly altered; all further citations are to the edition of 1535.

119. Werner Schade, "Das unbekannte Selbstbildnis Cranachs," *Dezennium 2. Zwanzig Jahre VEB Verlag der Kunst* (Dresden, 1972), p. 374. Schade's hypothesis has been repeated without elaboration by other scholars: Dieter Koepplin and T. Falk, *Lucas Cranach. Gemälde, Zeichnungen, Druckgraphik* (exhib. cat., Basel, 1974–1976), vol. 1, p. 417; *Kunst der Reformationszeit*, pp. 303–304. Interestingly, Schade himself does not mention his hypothesis in his own later work, *Die Malerfamilie Cranach* (Dresden, 1974). Cf. Herbert Zschelletzschky, *Die "Drei Gottlosen Maler" von Nürnberg: Sebald Beham, Barthel Beham und Georg Pencz* (Leipzig, 1975), pp. 123–130.

120. Karl Hartfelder, *Philipp Melanchthon als Praeceptor Germaniae* [Monumenta Germaniae Paedagogica 7 (Berlin, 1889)], pp. 561, 595 no. 280. Hartfelder omits the reprint of Melanchthon's edition of the *Fasti* published at Basel in 1551. StBR, 2° Classic. 52. An edition of the *Fasti* also appeared in the Ratsbibliothek *Catalogus* of 1638, fol. 125 (Poet. 96).

In 1528, in his instructions to parish visitors in electoral Saxony, Melanchthon had listed Ovid's *Metamorphoses* (but not the *Fasti*) together with Vergil, and Cicero's *De officiis* and letters as appropriate reading for school children who were "practiced" in grammar. *Unterricht der Visitatorn*, preface by Luther, fol. Miii. On Melanchthon's rôle in the popularization of another classical "history" that assumed allegorical dimensions in Northern council chambers, see David Cast, *The Calumny of Apelles: A Study in the Humanist Tradition* (New Haven, 1981), pp. 94–96. For the availability of translations of Livy, see note 108 above. Another source of the story available to the Germans was the *Cronica von allen Kaisern und Künigen* (Augsburg, 1476). It is described briefly by Galinsky, *Der Lucretia-Stoff*, pp. 70–72.

121. *Ein schön spil von der geschicht der Edlen Römerin Lucretiae, unnd wie der Tyrannisch küng Tarquinius Superbus von Rhom vertriben, und sunderlich von der standthafftigkeit Iunii Bruti, des Ersten Consuls zü Rhom* was reprinted in Straßburg in 1550. The play and its history are printed in Heinrich Bullinger and Hans Sachs, *Lucretia-Dramen*, ed. Horst Hartmann (Leipzig, 1973). For an analysis that sets the play more firmly in its literary context, see Galinsky, *Lucretia-Stoff*, pp. 70, 76–79.

122. It was first staged in 1527. *Lucretia-Dramen*, and Galinsky, *Lucretia-Stoff*, pp. 70–75. Cf. Hans Sachs' poem "Die keusch Römerin Lucrecia erstach sich selber, ir er zw retten" (1548), reprinted in *Hans Sachs*, ed. A. von Keller and E. Goetze, vol. 22 [Bibliothek des Litterarischen Vereins in Stuttgart 201 (Tübingen, 1894)], pp. 448–449.

123. *Lucretia-Dramen*, p. 30.

124. I here occupy a middle ground between Galinsky, who insists that in Sachs' play "the marriage-moralizing content steps into the background in contrast to the political," and Hartmann, who can find no political content before Bullinger.

Another German version of the Lucretia story deserves mention here: the *Cronica von allen Kaisern und Künigen* (published at Augsburg in 1476) was a prose account, flatter in tone and emphasis than either of the two later dramas, and with a description of a leaderless mass uprising against the Tarquins which would have surely been unacceptable in the empire after the Peasants' War. Cf. Galinsky, *Lucretia-Stoff*, pp. 70–71.

125. *Luretia-Dramen*, pp. 16–23.

126. "Spiritus Sanctus laudat mulieres. Exempla sunt Iudith, Esther, Sara, et apud gentes laudantur Lucrecia, Artemisia." *WA Tischreden* 1:3. Cf. ibid., 4:4783. Although the passage occurred in a defense of marriage as an institution, it is interesting to note that of the women in Luther's list, one—Artemisia of Halikarnassos—was a political leader in her own right, and two others—Judith and Esther—took more active rôles in the preservation of their communities than did Lucretia.

127. Lucretia served Luther as a contrast to the false claims to chastity and innocence of Portiphar's wife and her charges against Joseph in Genesis 39:13–18: "Sic ipsa est pudica, casta et sanctissima Lucretia. . . ." *In Primum Librum Mose Enarrationes* (1543/1544) WA 44:366. And: ". . . aut si casu, aut temeritate potius Ioseph accidisset, ut solus ipse domi se contineret, et animo stuprandi venisset in cubiculum, etiam per vim inferre stuprum repugnanti et frustra luctanti potuisset: Sicut Lucretiam violatam esse historia Romana testatur: nihil patietur, nec rea est mortis." Ibid., 368. Also: "An non indignum est tantam dominam hac ignominia adfici, quae in hoc toto regno castissima Lucretia et exemplum pudicitiae fui aliis matronis. . . . Postremo

nequaquam aufugisset si vim inferre cogitasset, clamorem vero facile compescuisset, sicut Tarquinius ad Lucretiam inquit: Ferrum in manu est, moriere si emiseris vocem." Ibid., 370.

128.
> LVCRETIA.DI.FROM.SCHON.VND.ZART . . VON.
> SEXTO.DES.KONIGS.SON.ZU.ROM.BEZWUNGEN.WART.
> VNKEYSCH.MIT.IM.ZV.LEBEN.
> DARVM.SI.SICH.IN.DOT.DET.GEBEN.

Michael Ostendorfer, *Lucretia* panel of 1530. Museen der Stadt Regensburg. In addition, Arnulf Wynen, *Michael Ostendorfer (um 1492–1559). Ein Regensburger Maler der Reformationszeit* (Ph.D. dissertation, Freiburg i. Br., 1961), nos. 7–9, 176a, lists three *Judith* panels by Ostendorfer—one of them possibly to be linked with the *Lucretia* panel as a diptych—and another *Judith* panel by an anonymous Donau-school master.

129. Schwartzenberg, *Memorial . . . der Tugent* (Augsburg: Heinrich Steiner, 1534). On Schwartzenberg (1463–1528), whose Lutheran beliefs forced him to give up his Bamberg position in 1522, see *Allgemeine deutsche Biographie* (1891), vol. 33, pp. 305–306. Just when Schwartzenberg composed the verses of the *Memorial* is not clear. The page devoted to the Last Judgment hints at heterodoxy in the printed inscription in the middle of Hans Schäufelein's woodcut:

> Stet auff ir todten zu gericht
> Kein werk bleibt ungeurteilt nit

but the verses composed by Schwartzenberg himself avoided the causal relation, representing only the cry of those whose earthly treasures and pleasures had left them in eternal pain while those they had despised were acknowledged as God's children; fol. CXV'.

130.
> Der sibent küng zü Rom regiert,
> Sein sun mit frümbkeit ungeziert.
> Lucretia trüg neid und haß,
> Umb lob das man ir geben was.
> Drümb er mit ir auß laster rang,
> Und sy mit not zum eebruch zwang.
>
> Das öffnet sy mit grossem schmertz,
> Und stach ain messer durch ir hertz.
> Wolt lieber leiden todes pein,
> Dann eebruchs ein exempel sein.
> Bey frümen haiden ir das zam
> Und Sextus hies deß Täters nam.
>
> Umb dise lästerlichen sünd,
> Dy hy von Sexto ist verkünt.
> Sen alle küng auß Rom verjagt,
> Als uns die selb Histori sagt.
> Darümb ward darnach alweg fast,
> Zü Rom der Küngklich nam gehaßt.
> Das noch biß heüt zu diser frist,
>
> Kein Küng zü Rom regirn ist.
> Dergleich man mer geschehen findt,
> Genötzwängt frümme weib und kind.
> Auch dringt man manchen mit der tat,
> Den sein zü schanden geben statt.
> Sölchs hatt zerstört vil Regiment,
> Das seyt gewarnet alle ständt.

*Memorial der Tugent*, fol. CXIII.

131. On the iconography of Judith as given in the *Biblia pauperum* and *Speculum humanae salvationis* and incorporated by Donatello into his famous sculpture of the Old Testament heroine, see Edgar Wind, "Donatello's Judith: A Symbol of 'Santimonia,'" *Journal of the Warburg Institute* 1 (1937–1938), pp. 62–63. Cf. the engravings of FORCE trampling HOLOFERNE and ATRENPANCE (= Temperantia) trampling TARQUIN in the *Heures* printed by the French bookbinder and printer Simon Vostre in 1498ff. and the popular medieval image of Mary triumphing over the devil, linked to the stories of Judith and Jael by the *Spiegel menschlicher*

*Behaltnis* (Augsburg: Anton Sorg, 1476), fols. 67'–68'. The Vostre *heures* appear to have been widely distributed in Europe; the library of the Nuremberg Sebaldskirche owned an earlier 1491 edition. W. von Seidlitz, "Die gedruckten illustrierten Gebetbücher des XV. und XVI. Jahrhunderts," *Jahrbuch der königlich preussischen Kunstsammlungen* 5 (1884), p. 132. The 1498 Vostre illustrations are reproduced in Emile Mâle, *L'art religieux de la fin du moyen âge en France. Etude sur l'iconographie du moyen âge et sur ses sources d'inspiration* (Paris, 1922), p. 336 and figs. 186–188. This latter connection was repeated with the appearance of Judith in a rondelle set into the wall of Mary's bedroom in a woodcut *Annunciation* by Albrecht Dürer (c. 1503); B. 83. For a German example in which the story was clearly a political as well as religio-moral fable, see Hans-Christoph Rublack, *Eine bürgerliche Reformation: Nördlingen* [Quellen und Forschungen zur Reformationsgeschichte 51 (Gütersloh, 1982)], pp. 11–15.

132. Cf. "Und sy mit not zum eerbruch zwang" (1534; fol. CXV') and "Und sy mit not zum eebruch zwang" (1535; fol. CXIII').

133. Cassius Dio, *Roman History* II, 15 = Zonaras' *Epitome* 7,11. Both given in Cassius Dio, *Roman History*, trans. Earnest Cary (London, 1914), vol. 1, p. 85.

134. Ibid., p. 89.

135. Cf. Zschelletzschky, *Die "drei gottlosen Maler"*, pp. 123–130, where, because of the author's focus on the Nuremberg "rebels," the images of Lucretia and Judith are seen as entirely "analoge Darstellung[en] einer 'in tyrannos' gerichteten patriotischen Tat." In Italy the story of Judith appears to have been more popular than that of Lucretia; in the North, despite the biblical authority for the story of Judith as well as her continuous appearance in illustrated Bibles and her popularity in the first decades of the sixteenth century in images similar to those of Lucretia, the latter heroine superceded Judith in the paintings of the Wittenberg school. Cf. the Judith history scenes of the Bibles printed at Augsburg in 1477 by Anton Sorg and at Nuremberg from 1476 to 1478 by Johann Sensenschmidt (Schramm, *Bilderschmuck*, vol. 4, no. 304; vol. 18, no. 257), the undated *Judith* by Albrecht Altdorfer (B. 1), the 1523 and 1525 *Judiths* of Barthel Beham and his undated Venetian/Cranach school *Judith*: (B. 2–4), and Hans Sebald Beham's three *Judiths* (two undated, one from 1547: B. 10–12). In none of these German depictions of Judith is there any sign of an attempt to transform the figure into a personification of Fortitudo or Sanctimonia through the addition of attribute or inscription. Cf., however, the Hans Sachs' *Meisterlied*, published at Nuremberg c. 1550 by Friderich Gutknecht, "Ein schön meister Lied, Von der Gottsförchtigen Frawen Judit, wie sie Holofernes das haupt abschlug," and the undated medallion signed by Lorenz Rosenbaum (active at Schaffhausen and Augsburg, 1535–1565) with Judith on the obverse (inscription: DER HERR.HAT NIT VERLAS:DIE.DIE IM VERTRVV.IV.XIII) and Jael, the Old Testament heroine who drove a stake through Sissera's head, on the reverse (inscription: ALSO MVSSEN VMKMEN HERR ALL DEINE FEIND.IVDIC:V DER HERR NA VMB° D.SISSERA). Weller, *Annalen*, vol. 2, no. 136; Habich, no. 1534, pl. CLXV, 8, 8a.

Martin Luther himself doubted the historicity of the Judith story, reading it instead as a metaphorical "Poema und Gedicht" in which Judith represented the whole Jewish people. *WA Tischreden* 1:193–194, 208, 210, 337–338; 3:137–139; "Vorrhede auffs buch Judith," *Apocrypha. Das sind Bücher: so nicht der heiligen Schrifft gleich gehalten: vnd doch nützlich vnd gut zu lesen sind.* (Wittenberg: Hans Lufft, 1534), fol. II.

136. Martin Luther, *WA Tischreden* 1:326–327; translated in Schoenberger, "Luther and the Justifiability of Resistance," p. 17. Cf. the language of Luther's later, more public statement on resistance: "19. Denn wer Reuber und Mörder verteidiget, und für sie krieget (er sey wer er wölle) Der mus die fahr seines Kriegs, zu sampt ewiger verdamnis gewertig sein. 20. Und hilfft die Könige noch Fürsten, auch der Keiser nichts, das sie rhümen, sie sind Schutzherrn der Kirchen, Denn sie sind schuldig zu wissen, was da sey die Kirche, Und was dieser Weerwolff sey." "Siebentzig Schlußreden, Von den dreien Göttlichen Hierarchiis" (1539), *WA* 39,2:51.

The necessity to defend wife and children had already appeared in Philipp Melanchthon's 1528 instruction to parish visitors (with preface by Martin Luther)—not as a justification for resisting the emperor, but as a justification for waging war against the Turks. Melanchthon had attacked those who argued that one should not resist the attacks of the Turks on the grounds that vengeance was forbidden to Christians: "Denn die Türcken gar keine erbarkeit wissen noch achten, Die gewaltigen nemen den andern gut, weib und kind, nach yhrem mutwillen. . . . Wenn schon der Christiche glaube nichts were, so ists dennoch not, das wir streiten widder die Türcken, umb unser weib und kind willen, Denn wir lieber tod sein wollen, ehe wir solche schande und unzucht an den unsern sehen und leiden wollen." *Unterricht der Visitatorn*, fols. Jiii–Jiii'.

137. Whether it was the emperor or his entourage, or the emperor as a member of the papal entourage, whom Luther wished to hold responsible is less than clear; cf. ". . . so wollen dennoch wir, als die treuen Untertanen, nicht glauben, daß S.K.M. tue, sondern dencken, das es ander Tyrannen unter dem Namen K. M. tun." Martin Luther to Gregory Brück, chancellor emeritus of Electoral Saxony (5 August 1530), *WA Briefe* 5:532. And "Caesar non sit nec possit persona illa esse, quae hoc bellum moveret aut movere posset, sed papa et episcopi, qui Caesare velut milite uti volunt pro suis horrendis tyrannidibus et diabolicis flagitiis defendis contra agnitam veritatem." Martin Luther to Johann Ludicke, preacher in Kottbus (8 February 1539), *WA Briefe* 8:367.

138. Martin Luther, Justus Jonas, Martin Bucer, and Philipp Melanchthon, "*Gutachten* for Johann Friedrich of Saxony and Landgrave Philip of Hesse" (13–14 November 1538). Printed in Heinz Scheible, ed., *Das Widerstandsrecht als Problem der deutschen Protestanten, 1523–1546* [Texte zur Kirchen- und Theologiegeschichte 10 (Gütersloh, 1969)], p. 93. Translation in Schoenberger, "Luther and the Justifiability of Resistance," p. 16. Justus Jonas, it should be remembered, would accept a call to Regensburg in 1552.

Michael McCormick has informed me that the phrase "open or notorious force" encapsulates a concept of Roman law. The same concept was used during the sixteenth century in pamphlets such as that by the Lutheran Johannes Brenz to justify the war against the Turks: "Every civil authority owes it to God to maintain law and order, to protect the land and the people from wrongful violence and murder, as St. Paul teaches in Romans 13. Now, the Turk is attacking Germany even though he has no right or provocation to do so; his assault is like that of a murderer. Just as the government is obligated to punish thieves and murders, or to take preventative action as soon as the aggressive intentions of such persons became known, so the government is obligated to resist the Turk, an undisguised brigand and murderer." Johannes Brenz, "Wie sich Prediger und Leien halten sollen, so der Türck das Deudsche Land uberfallen würde" (Wittenberg: Georg Rhaw, 1537), translated in John W. Bohnstedt, *The Infidel Scourge of God: The Turkish Menace as Seen by German Pamphleteers of the Reformation Era* [Transactions of the American Philosophical Society 58, part 9 (Philadelphia, 1968)], p. 47. It is noteworthy that Brenz used the vocabulary of civil law and the New Testament but did not appeal to the paternal language with which we are primarily concerned.

139. His argument was that there was no marriage between Jacob and Leah since neither had given willing consent; he was deceived and she compelled by her father's threats as Lucretia had been by the threats of Sextus. *In Primum Librum Mose Enarrationes* (1542), *WA* 43:637–638.

140. According to some scholars, the use of the natural law theory in the 1538 recommendation suggests that Melanchthon rather than Luther was its primary author. Edwards, *Luther's Last Battles*, pp. 30–31, 218 n. 25.

141. On the problem of resistance and the political thought of Martin Luther and his lieutenants, see Quentin Skinner, *The Foundations of Modern Political Thought*, vol. 2: *The Age of the Reformation* (Cambridge, 1978), pp. 3–19, 195–209; W. D. J. Cargill Thompson, *The Political Thought of Martin Luther*, ed. Philip Broadhead (Brighton, Sussex, 1984); Gunther Wolf, ed. *Luther und die Obrigkeit* (Darmstadt, 1972); Jordan, *Luthers Staatsauffassung*; and Hermann Kunst, *Evangelischer Glaube und Politische Verantwortung. Martin Luther als politischer Berater seiner Landesherrn und seine Teilnahme an den Fragen des öffentlichen Lebens* (Stuttgart, 1976), pp. 225–261, esp. pp. 239–261.

A very interesting case is the 1547 treatise *Von der Notwehr Unterricht* written by Justus Menius with revisions by Philipp Melanchthon. One of the few analyses of the text is Luther D. Peterson, "Melanchthon on Resisting the Emperor: The *Von der Notwehr Unterrichte* of 1547," in *Regnum, Religio et Ratio: Essays Presented to Robert M. Kingdon* [Sixteenth-Century Essays and Studies 8 (Kirksville, Mo., 1987)], pp. 133–144. Although Peterson translates "Notwehr" as "self-defense," the exempla given are of the defense of wives, children, subjects, and household members against unjust authority, rather than the individual's defense of him- or herself. It would appear that even in this case it was responsibilities rather than rights which were at stake and that the responsibilities adhering to the office of the inferior magistrates were conceived in terms of the responsibilities of the father to his wife and children rather than the reverse. After all, in an earlier work Justus Menius himself had insisted not that the household was the kingdom writ small, but that Politia had its origin in Oeconomia, its fountainhead: "aus der Oeconomia odder haushaltung, mus die Politia odder landregirung, als aus einem brunnequel, entspringen und herkommen. . . ." *An die hochgeborne Furstin, Fraw Sibilla Hertzogin zu Sachsen, Oeconomia Christiana, das ist, von Christlicher Haushaltung* (Wittenberg: Hans Lufft, 1529), fol. Biiii. Thus the hypothetical right of the subject Uriah to defend his wife against King David was not a right but a responsibility and not a "remarkable exception." Peterson, "Melanchthon," pp. 141–143. Nor does this treatise—as Peterson asserts—contradict Skinner's statement that Melanchthon had insisted "that 'it is never permissible' for private individuals 'to engage in acts of sedition' on their own behalf against any legally constituted authority." It did not grant the right to resist "on their own behalf" but insisted instead on the responsibility of the father to defend wife and child against aggression. Ibid., pp. 143–144. Our perspective turns Peterson's thesis—that "William Tell, the wife of the Thessalonian tyrant, and the husbands of Rhodes are examples of just resistance because they held offices in the household order that obligated them to protecting others"—on its head. Ibid., p. 144. It was not the father whose rôle is imagined as an office on the model of the magistrate, but the magistrate whose office was conceptualized on the model of the father.

Luther himself had recommended and used the term "pater" of Charles V in the early 1530s; this very restricted use is discussed in the following chapter. Once it had become clear to the Protestants that no religious compromise was possible and that the emperor would not reverse his attempts to force a return to the Catholic church on his Protestant "children," Charles V was no longer their "father." This "depaternization" explains how it was possible for the Lutherans and Luther himself eventually to sanction resistance—a possibility overlooked by Paul Münch, "Die 'Obrigkeit im Vaterstand'—Zu Definition und Kritik des 'Landesvaters' während der frühen Neuzeit," *Daphnis* 11 (1982), pp. 28–29.

Many of the songs written and published to raise Protestant morale during the Schmalkaldic War even denied Charles V the dignity of his title and formal address: "Ach Karl großmechtiger Man / Wie hast ain Spiel gefangen an / On not in Teutschen landen." Opening lines to "Ain Lied für die landsknecht gemacht. Inn disen Kriegßleüffen, nützlich zusingen" (1546, and three later editions). Weller, *Annalen*, vol. 1, no. 197; see also vol. 1, nos. 196 and 199. Other songs referred to him as a minion of the pope = Antichrist; vol. 1, nos. 194 and 200.

Apparently even after the end of the Interim, during the period when the Regensburg Rat frequently referred to its relationship with its subjects in paternal terms, the term was used of the relationship between emperor and subjects only infrequently. I have found no use of the image in the formal appeals to the emperor by the Rat. Schneidt's 600-page collection of documents relating to the *Kurfürstentag* held in Regensburg in 1575 for the purpose of electing a successor to the dying Maximilian II reveals the use of such paternal language in only one exchange. On 11 October the emperor himself referred to his paternal concern for the empire in his opening address. He had, he said, acted: "zu des geliebten Vatterlands ehr, nuz und wohlstandt Immer dienlich gewesen, mit allem getreüen vätterlichen eifer gesuchett und gefürdert." On the next day the elector of Saxony responded on behalf of the electors in similar language: "Dieweil die freye Wahl gelassen, hab man Kays. Mai. vor solche vätterliche Sorgfältigkeit zu danken, und zu bitten sich der Administration gleichwol nicht zu entschlagen, das *Interregnum* sey gefährlich, und müsse vieler unruhigen Ungehorsam nothwendig gesteüret, auch der genachbarten *Practiquen* begegnet werden, derowegen zu Erhaltung Friedens der beste Weg, daß ein Röm. König erwehlet werde." Joseph Maria Schneidt, ed., *Vollständige Geschichte der römischen Königs-Wahl Rudolphs II, aus meistens annoch ungedruckten Urkunden als ein Beytrag zur Geschichte der Churfürsten-Tage und Römischen Königs-Wahlen* (Würzburg, 1792), pp. 429, 431, 492, 494.

142. Charles Seymour, *Michelangelo's David: A Search for Identity* (New York, 1974), pp. 142–145. For a more complete discussion of the context of the herald's statement (a meeting called to determine the best location for Michelangelo's *David*, which was, according to the herald *not* a symbol of death), see Saul Levine, "'Tal Cosa': Michelangelo's *David*—Its Form, Site, and Political Symbolism" (Ph.D. dissertation: Columbia University, 1969), pp. 135–170, esp. 146–147. Levine includes a new transcription by Enzo Settesoldi, archivist of the Archivio dell'Opera del Duomo, Florence, of the minutes of the meeting as an appendix to his dissertation, pp. 287–291.

143. Cf. the image of militant self-help, the Old Testament heroine Jael, who saved her city by driving a spike into the ear of the sleeping tyrant Sisera. Less popular than Lucretia or even Judith, she nevertheless also appeared on bindings; e.g., the panel that showed her gruesome solution with the inscription SIC PEREANT OMNES INIMICI TVI DOMINE IVDICVM. Germanisches Nationalmuseum, Nuremberg, Einbände Sammlung B. 228.

144. Hermann Heimpel, "Luthers weltgeschichtliche Bedeutung," *Der Mensch in seiner Gegenwart* (Göttingen, 1954), p. 155.

It was not necessarily clear in the Protestants' writings precisely who was to exert authority in this case. "Ein New Lied von der Weltlichen Oberkeit," published in 1546 and again at Augsburg in 1547 opened simply with the (perhaps now, for Protestants) comforting reminder that "Kein gwalt uff dieser Erd bleibt fest." Weller, *Annalen*, vol. 1, no. 201. Cf.: "Et cum Saul etiam vellet filium Ionathani occidere, restitit ei et populus per vim. Et cum rex Ioiakim vellet Ieremiam occidere, restiterunt principes, Ahikam et alii. Nam Principes Germaniae plus iuris habent contra Caesarem, quam illic populus contra Saul, vel Ahikam contra Joiakim, ut qui communi consilio gubernent imperium cum Caesare, et Caesar non sit monarcha nec posset deiectis Electoribus mutare formam imperii, nec esse ferendum, si tentaret." Martin Luther to Johann Ludicke, preacher in Kottbus (8 February 1539), *WA Briefe* 8:367.

It was, of course, not always necessary or even useful to be explicit; as Mark Edwards has pointed out, the ultimate outcome of Luther's polemics on resistance, however cautiously couched, was to encourage Protestants to resist a Catholic attack, even if the emperor himself were one of its leaders. *Luther's Last Battles*, pp. 20–37.

145. The mirror appeared as the attribute of all three allegorical figures on the woodcut title pages of the sixteenth century. E.g., Venus with mirror: Arnobius Afrus, *Commentarius in Psalmos*, ed. Desiderius Erasmus (Basel, 1522) = *Index*, fol. 11' (Theologica 9). StBR, 2° Patr. 429. Prudentia with mirror: Laurentius Valla, *Romani dialecticarum disputationum* (Cologne: Johannes Gymnicus, 1530) = *Index*, fol. 82 (Medica 8). StBR, Lat. rec. 408.

146. Katzenellenbogen, *Allegories*, pp. 45 n. 2, 56, 62 n. 2. The frequent depiction of John the Baptist holding or wearing a disk with the *Agnus dei* as a reference to Christ (ibid., p. 77 n. 5) suggests that the dove disk held by Prudentia referred to the Holy Spirit, i.e., to divine Wisdom.

147. "Candor est enim lucis eterne & speculum sine macula dei magestatis: & imago bonitatis illius." Sapientia Solomonis 7:26. Complutensian Polyglott: *Tertia pars Veteris testamenti*, fol. Aiii'. Cited in Gustav Friedrich Hartlaub, *Zauber des Spiegels* (Munich, 1951), p. 161.

148. The dove of the Holy Spirit sat on Prudentia's staff. The origin of Prudentia's wisdom was further identified in the woodcut by the hand of God which extended from the clouds in approbation of her teaching. Despite this, the crowd of fools paid her no heed. Sebastian Brant, *Das Narren schyff* (Basel: Johann Bergmann von Olpe, 1494); reproduced in *Illustrated Bartsch* 1001.513v.

149. See above, "Prolegomena," note 6, and Pierre Courcelle, *Connais-toi toi même de Socrate à saint Bernard* (Paris, 1974), pp. 129–163.

150. Heinrich Schwarz, "The Mirror in Art," *Art Quarterly* 15 (1952), p. 109. James H. Marrow, "Symbol and Meaning in Northern European Art of the Late Middle Ages and the Early Renaissance," *Simiolus. Netherlands Quarterly for the History of Art* 16 (1986), pp. 150–169.

151. ". . . nach meiner gewissen unnd höchsten verstenntnnuß, . . . das rechtlichist nach meinem pessten versteen." Schulthaissen and Hausgenossen oaths (same language in both), *Regensburger kaiserliche Regimentsordnung* (1500), fol. 4': HStAM, R L Regensburg 376; (1514), fols. 10–10': HStAM, R L Regensburg 381. Particularly interesting from the point of view of Strauss' work on the resistance to the imposition of Roman law in Germany is the fact that the oaths did not include vows to adhere to written law, but only to judge according to the juror's/judge's "best understanding of the right."

152. The members of the Innerer Rat took oaths "ainem yeden zu seinem rechten unnd sachen furderlich on verzug zu helfenn unnd das getrewest und pessts thun Raten Richten und verhelffen"; *Regensburger kaiserliche Regimentsordnungen*: (1500), fol. 3., HStAM, R L Regensburg 376; (1514), fol. 4, HStAM, R L Regensburg 381.

153. Goldschmidt, *Gothic and Renaissance Bookbinding*. The basic difference is one of style. Wittenberg school bindings gave the central panel of the binding face to a large panel stamp; Lucretia and Justitia were frequently paired on the recto and verso of the bindings. In Regensburg such large panel stamps were not used on the bindings because the central panel was filled by a stamp bearing the city's arms.

154. Kantorowicz, *King's Two Bodies*, pp. 107–113.

155. See, e.g., Tobias Stimmer's design for a stained-glass window c. 1562/1563, in which a crowned Justitia, holding sword and scales raised triumphantly, looked down on the emperor, pope, Turk, and pagan she had trampled underfoot. *Die Renaissance im deutschen Südwesten* (exh. cat., Badisches Landesmuseum, Karlsruhe, 1986), vol. 1, p. 337. Such images of justice struck directly at imperialist images such as the illumination of Heinrich II from the *Gospel Book of Heinrich II* or the language of Friedrich II's *Liber augustalis*: "The Caesar, therefore, must be at once the Father and Son of Justice, her lord and her minister: Father and lord in creating Justice and

protecting what has been created; and in like fashion he shall be, in her veneration, the Son of Justice and, in ministering her plenty, her minister." Text and translation in Kantorowicz, *King's Two Bodies*, p. 99.

156. See above, chapter two, note 62.

157. See, for example, the two Minne tapestries produced in Regensburg c. 1390–1420, now in the Stadtmuseum; reproduced in Leonie von Wilkens, *Bildteppiche* (Museum der Stadt Regensburg, 1980); Georg Pencz' woodcut of Venus as heavenly planet after an Italian model: Pauli 908 (attributed to Hans Sebald Beham); and Lucas Cranach's many versions of Venus and Cupid. On *"Minne*-piety," see Anders Nygren, *Agape and Eros*, trans. Philip S. Watson (London 1954), pp. 659–664.

158. Kantorowicz, *King's Two Bodies*, pp. 468–471.

159. Wolf Traut, *Plea for the Lost Souls* (c. 1510) and *Holy Sacraments* (c. 1510); reproduced in Geisberg/Strauss, *The German Single-Leaf Woodcut, 1500–1550*, vol. 4, pp. 1368, 1369. The gesture of the wounding was itself familiar from the Passion scenes that included the depiction of Longinus piercing Christ's side with his lance. Cf. Peter Strieder, "Folk Art Sources of Cranach's Woodcut of the Sacred Heart," *Tribute to Wolfgang Stechow*, ed. Walter L. Strauss [*Print Review* 5 (1976)], pp. 160–166.

160. A similar point is made by Caroline Walker Bynum, "The Body of Christ in the Later Middle Ages: A Reply to Leo Steinberg," *Renaissance Quarterly* 39 (1986), pp. 399–439. Cf. the complex of images associating the nursing breast and Christ's lance-pierced side, milk and blood, explored by Bynum in *Jesus as Mother: Studies in the Spirituality of the High Middle Ages* (Berkeley, 1982), pp. 110–169.

161. Isolated images of the Mater Dolorosa whose heart was pierced by a single sword were even more common in the early decades of the sixteenth century. Cf. Hans Sebald Beham's *Mater Dolorosa* medallion, c. 1522; Hans Burgkmair's large *Mater Dolorosa* surrounded by the seven sorrows of the Virgin (1524); and Hans Schäufelein's *Mater Dolorosa with St. Joseph*, c. 1539; reproduced in Geisberg/Strauss, *German Single-Leaf Woodcut, 1500–1550*, vol. 1, p. 197; vol. 2, p. 420–421; vol. 3, p. 997.

162. In contrast to the title of the Latin version, "Querulosa Christi consolatio: ad dolorosam virginis Marie compassionem," the German title, "Von den klagbaren leyden und mitleyden christi: und seiner wirdigen muter Marie," emphasized not the dialogic answer of Christ to his mother's co-suffering, but the equality of the two passions.

163. Translated from the German version of the woodcut: "O Müter mildt, was quelst dein hercz. . . . Welcher mit andacht peycht und rewigem herczen anschawet die waffen der barmherczigkeyt Christi."

164. Luke 2:34–35. Quoted in James H. Marrow, "Symbol and Meaning in Northern European Art of the Late Middle Ages and the Early Renaissance," *Simiolus. Netherlands Quarterly for the History of Art* 16 (1986), pp. 150–169, here p. 153. This article provides a good introduction to the rôle of Northern art of the late-medieval period in "structuring experience."

165. According to Adolf Spamer, *Das kleine Andachtsbild vom XIV. bis zum XX. Jahrhundert* (Munich, 1930), pp. 11, 307–308 and pl. IV, the source of the image was an allegory falsely attributed to St. Bernard. See also the interesting late medieval "folk art" images of the heart of Jesus illustrated in Strieder, "Folk Art Sources," pp. 160–166.

166. G.1410. On Traut's activity in Dürer's workshop, cf. Thieme-Becker, vol. 33, p. 351, and Geisberg/Strauss, *German Single-Leaf Woodcuts*, vol. 4, p. viii.

167. Considered exemplary of Augustine's own attempt to comprehend the Trinity and of his own acknowledgment (*De trinitate* XV), of the extent to which human incapacities set limits on any such attempt, the story of Augustine and the child, listed in the *Acta sanctorum* under "Aliqua incerta," was attributed by Ambrosius Staibano, *Templo Augustiniano*, chap. 8, to "plures medii aevi scriptores." *Acta sanctorum*, ed. J. Bollandus et al., August VI (Antwerp, 1743), pp. 357–358, no. 707. However apocryphal, the scene was a popular one in the lives of the saint produced by artists from the fifteenth century on; cf. Jeanne and Pierre Courcelle, *Iconographie de saint Augustin*, vol. 2: *Les cycles du XVᵉ siècle* (Paris, 1969), pls. LX, C, CV; vol. 3: *Les cycles du XVIᵉ et du XVIIᵉ siècle* (Paris, 1972), pls. X, XIII, XXII, XXVI, XXVII, XXX, LXXII, XCIII, CXXIX, CL; vol. 4: *Les cycles du XVIIIᵉ siècle. L'Allemagne* (Paris, 1980), pls. XXXV (panel painted by Rubens in 1637, now in Prague), LXXII. In two of these (vol. 3, pls. X, XIII; vol. 4, pl. LXXII), the connection between the scene and the Trinity was made explicit by the appearance of the *Gnadenstuhl* in the clouds above the saint and child.

168. *Enarratio in Psalmum XXXVII*, in *Opera omnia*, ed. Desiderius Erasmus, vol. 8 (Basel: Jo-

hann Froben, 1529), p. 213 = *Patrologia*, vol. 36, col. 398. Augustine's quotation from the Song of Songs (2:5 and 5:8) is a Latin translation of the Septaugint. It agrees with the interlinear translation given in the so-called Complutensian Polyglott: *Vetus testamentum multiplici lingua nunc primo impressum* (Alcalá de Henares: Arnaldus Guillelmus de Brocario, 1517), vol. 3, fols. pv and pvii.

Other examples of the same image can be found in *Enarratio in Psalmum CXIX*, ibid., vol. 8, p. 973 = *Patrologia*, vol. 37, col. 1600, and *Enarratio in Psalmum CXLIII*, ibid., vol. 8, p. 1142 = *Patrologia*, vol. 37, col. 1865.

169. Augustine, *Confessiones* IX, ii; in Erasmus ed. (1528) vol. 1, p. 107. The images chosen were drawn from the Psalms; cf. Augustine's exegesis of Psalm 140:10, with its reference to Psalm 120:4, "Sharp arrows of the mighty, with coals of juniper": *Enarratio in Psalmum CXXXIX*, ibid., vol. 8, p. 1108 = *Patrologia*, vol. 37, col. 1811.

On the love of God and the flaming heart in general, see R. Freyhan, "The Evolution of the Caritas Figure in the Thirteenth and Fourteenth Centuries," *Journal of the Warburg and Courtauld Institutes* 11 (1948), pp. 73–80; the same symbolism, together with the arrow, is discussed by Nygren, *Agape and Eros*, pp. 431–434, 441–446, 658–662, and esp. the illumination from a manuscript of Heinrich Suso's autobiography, *Seuses Leben*, facing p. 616 (discussed pp. 613–615). Cf. Altdorfer's *Venus/Caritas* (Bartsch 32) after the niello by Peregrino da Casena (Passavant 654), discussed above, chapter two, note 62.

Similar imagery appeared in the vernacular. One fifteenth-century German hymn called Jesus the "götlicher minne flamme." August Heinrich Hoffmann von Fallersleben, *Geschichte des deutschen Kirchenliedes bis auf Luthers Zeit* (3rd ed., Hannover, 1861), p. 99 no. 27. On Jesus as the "word" sprung out of God's heart: ibid., p. 101 no. 29; Waldtraut Ingeborg Sauer-Geppert, *Sprache und Frömmigkeit im deutschen Kirchenlied* (Kassel, 1984), p. 130.

Cf. the rejection of Venus' powers in *De civitate dei* XXI, 6–8.

170. Filippo Lippi's praedella to the Barbadori altar expanded the simple slit of the more usual image: three arrows pierced Augustine's heart as he contemplated the image of the Trinity. Florence, Uffizi, no. 8351.

171. E.g., the *Augustine* of the Zwolle IAM Master, active in Zwolle, Gouda, and Delft in the last decades of the fifteenth century. Reproduced in F. W. H. Hollstein, *Dutch and Flemish Etchings, Engravings, and Woodcuts c. 1450–1700* (Amsterdam, n.d.), vol. 12, p. 269.

An engraving of Augustine holding a flaming heart through which the Christ child, held by Mary, pushed an arrow was executed by Schelte a Bolswert at Paris in 1624 as a part of a series commissioned by Georges Maigret, prior of the Augustinian Hermits at Malines, who also wrote the legends for each engraving. The engraving seems to have served as the model for the panel of the same subject painted by Murillo in 1678 for the Sevillian friars of the same order (now in the Museo in Seville). Courcelle, *Iconographie*, vol. 3, pp. 45, 137–138, and pls. XLVII, CXLIX.

The irony of Augustine's adoption of the Venus imagery to describe the love of God did not escape later artists who used it also to describe his misspent youth. In his fresco cycle for the Augustinerkirche in Mainz the eighteenth-century artist Johann Baptista Enderle depicted two scenes that incorporated Venus' archer-son Cupid: Augustine's mother Monica knelt before St. Ambrose with her son who was held on a lead by the archer Cupid; Augustine's dissipated youth was symbolized by a devil, prostitutes, and Cupid with his bow and arrow. E. Sauser, "Augustinus von Hippo," *Lexikon der christlichen Ikonographie*, ed. Engelbert Kirschbaum (Rome, 1973), vol. 5, col. 287. In an engraved scene designed by Johann Anwander, a painter active in Swabia and Franconia (at the Bamberger Residenz), and executed by the brothers Josef-Sebastian and Johann-Baptist Klauber in 1758, a putto drew his bow at the winged and enflamed heart that descended from Christ's breast to Augustine's. Since God the Father was present in the Hebrew letters enclosed in a triangle above the scene, the heart's wings seem to have been intended to transform it into the presence of the third person of the Trinity, the Holy Spirit. Courcelle, *Iconographie*, vol. 4, p. 82 and pl. LXXIV.

172. See references to works by Rubens, Günther, and Murillo in Sauser, "Augustinus von Hippo," col. 284; illustrations in Courcelle, *Iconographie*, vols. 3 and 4.

173. See the discussion of Titian's *Heavenly and Earthly Love* (1511–1517), another image of two types of love, in Erwin Panofsky, *Studies in Iconology* (New York, 1967), pp. 150–169. Two engravings from the end of the sixteenth century by Hendrik Goltzius repeated the iconography of the IH Master—Cupid held his arrow to Venus' heart—and combined arrow-pierced hearts traditional to Venus with the flaming hearts symbolic of the love of God. Bartsch 160b, Bartsch 160e. Cf. Kantorowicz, *King's Two Bodies*, pp. 242, for a thirteenth-century transformation of the theological Caritas into a political virtue: *amor patriae*.

174. See above, Prolegomena, note 166.

175. It is here worth noting that Dürer himself had proposed tondi scenes of the "power of women" (David and Bathsheba, Sampson and Delilah, Aristotle and Phyllis) between the arched windows on one wall of the reception hall in the Nuremberg Rathaus; in the frescoed decorations painted by Hans Sebald Beham and Georg Penz according to Dürer's designs more conventional judgment scenes took their place. Dürer's ink drawing for the "power of women" tondi is in the Morgan Library in New York; Winkler 921; Hans Kauffmann, "Albrecht Dürer 'Die Vier Apostel'. Vortrag gehalten den 18. April 1972 im Kunsthistorischen Institut der Rijksuniversiteit" (Utrecht, 1973), pp. 15–16. Kauffmann's comment that the original scenes would not have been inappropriate to a room in which his *Adam and Eve* of 1507 also hung can scarcely be called an explanation of their meaning or significance in the context. At least one of the judgment scenes which replaced the depictions of "the power of women" in the Nuremberg Rathaus—the judgment of Trajan— also appeared on one wall of the Regensburg Rathaus as frescoed by the Bocksbergers.

176. Perhaps indicative of the disappearance of a context in which the appearance of Lucretia had assumed a political significance is the extent to which her story instead became the locus for the display of an artist's dramatic skill. The Lucretia images of the later sixteenth century, particularly in Baroque Italy, differed radically from their Northern and Italian predecessors, stressing not the self-sacrifice of the woman for the sake of her honor and that of her husband, but rather the swirling violence of the rape itself. Cf. the dramatic contrapposto of Titian's three panels of c. 1570/1571, which showed not the pious suicide but the violent rapist lunging with his drawn sword. The panels are reproduced in Rodolfo Pallucchini, *Tiziano* (Florence, 1969), vol. 1, pp. 325–326 and figs. 527–529, pls. 58–59.

*Chapter 4  Gottvater, Stadtväter, Hausväter*: Paternal Imagery in the
        Dialogue between Bürger and Rat

1. Hans-Christoph Rublack, "Grundwerte in der Reichsstadt im Spätmittelalter und in der frühen Neuzeit," in *Literatur in der Stadt. Bedingungen und Beispiele städtischer Literatur des 15. bis 17. Jahrhunderts*, ed. Horst Brunner [Göppinger Arbeiten zur Germanistik 343 (Göppingen, 1982)], p. 24.

2. See, e.g., the case of Ulm cited by Eberhard Naujoks, *Obrigkeitsgedanke, Zunftverfassung und Reformation: Studien zur Verfassungsgeschichte von Ulm, Esslingen und Schwäbisch Gmünd* [Veröffentlichungen der Kommission für geschichtliche Landeskunde in Baden-Württemberg, series B, 3 (Stuttgart, 1958)], p. 15. Cf., however, the cyclical model suggested for a later period by Mack Walker, *German Home Towns* (Ithaca, 1971), p. 69, which appears to fit the events occurring in Regensburg at the end of the fifteenth century, at least so far as they have been researched. Whichever model is applied, the possibility for tension between those in the political center of the town and those outside it encouraged the development of a language or of competing languages for the discussion, legitimation, and negotiation of political relationships.

3. Naujoks dates the beginning of a language of "ruler" and "subject" in the free imperial city of Ulm to the late fifteenth century and finds that the council began replacing the informal "Du" with the formal (noble) "Ihr" in official letters after 1500. *Obrigkeitsgedanke*, pp. 15, 29; cited by Bernd Moeller, *Reichsstadt und Reformation* [Schriften des Vereins für Reformationsgeschichte 180 (Gütersloh, 1962)], trans. into English from expanded French version (1966) by H. C. E. Midelfort and M. U. Edwards, Jr., as "Imperial Cities and the Reformation" in *Imperial Cities and the Reformation: Three Essays* (Philadelphia, 1972), p. 52.

4. Max Weber, *Wirtschaft und Gesellschaft: Grundriss der verstehenden Soziologie* (4th ed., Tübingen, 1956), pp. 28, 122–123. Translation is from David Sabean, *Power in the Blood: Popular Culture and Village Discourse in Early Modern Germany* (Cambridge, 1984), p. 24.

5. "Und solch eusserlich und leiblich regiment hat Gott eingesatzt, verordnet, und, als sonst andere seine Götliche ordenung, zu halten und ehren gepotten, yn dem wort, da er saget, Du solt deinen vater und deine muter ehren." Justus Menius, *An die hochgeborne Furstin, Fraw Sibilla Hertzogin zu Sachsen, Oeconomia Christiana, das ist, von Christlicher Haushaltung*, introduction by Martin Luther (Wittenberg: Hans Lufft, 1529), fols. Biii–Biii'.

6. Weber, *Wirtschaft und Gesellschaft*, p. 122. Translated as *Economy and Society: An Outline of Interpretive Sociology*, by Guenther Roth et al. (Berkeley, 1978); here, p. 213. Cf. Robert Scribner's more recent reordering of many of the same elements under the heading "Sozialkontrolle":

"Sozialkontrolle und die Möglichkeit einer städtischen Reformation," in *Stadt und Kirche im 16. Jahrhundert*, ed. Bernd Moeller [Schriften des Vereins für Reformationsgeschichte 190 (Gütersloh, 1978)], pp. 58–59; and Quentin Skinner's brief but pointed discussion of the coercive power of language: *The Foundations of Modern Political Thought* (Cambridge, 1978), vol. 1, pp. xii–xiii.

7. Weber, *Wirtschaft und Gesellschaft*, p. 122; translated in Roth et al., *Economy and Society*, p. 212.

8. Kayser, *Dekretensammlung*.

9. Schottenloher.

10. On the use of medieval German citizens' wills as a source for social history, see Ahasver von Brandt, "Mittelalterliche Bürgertestament. Neuerschlossene Quellen zur Geschichte der materiellen und geistigen Kultur," *Sitzungsberichte der Heidelberger Akademie der Wissenschaften. Philosophisch-historische Klasse* (1973).

11. The wills are arranged alphabetically in bundles and filed under the simple rubric "Regensburger Testamente." Karl Primbs gave a list of the individuals named either as testators or witnesses in his "Uebersicht von Testamenten aus dem Archive der ehemaligen Reichsstadt Regensburg," *Archivalische Zeitschrift* N.F. 4 (1894), pp. 257–293. Unfortunately, some of the wills he lists appear to have vanished in the intervening years; the inventory numbers he gives no longer apply.

12. Because my initial interests lay in the testamentary bequests of the individuals, my count is based on the number of testators rather than the number of wills; spouses making the joint wills that became increasingly frequent toward the end of the sixteenth century are counted as separate individuals. In the charts and graphs that follow, "wills" refers therefore to the dispositions of individual testators even when only one document rather than two is involved. My resources, unfortunately, did not allow me to correlate and eliminate the duplication of the multiple wills that occasionally occurred, usually when a widow or widower remarried; the number of testators after mid-century, when joint testaments were most common, is therefore slightly inflated.

13. E.g., J. Jastrow, *Bevölkerungszahl der deutschen Städte zu Ende des Mittelalters und zu Beginn der Neuzeit* (1886), n. 8; Ivo Striedinger, *Der Kampf um Regensburg, 1486–1492* [*Verhandlungen des historischen Vereins von Oberpfalz und Regensburg* 44 (1890)], p. 47 n. 1, gives an estimate of between 12,000 and 15,000; Leonhard Theobald, *Die Reformationsgeschichte der Reichsstadt Regensburg* [Einzelarbeiten aus der Kirchengeschichte Bayerns 19, vol. 1 (Munich, 1936)], p. 8, estimates "perhaps as large as Frankfurt, which had almost 10,000 toward the end of the fifteenth century."

14. In addition, of course, the prohibition of such Protestant sacraments during the Interim skewed the Lutheran records for that period. Matthias Simon, "Beiträge zum Verhältnis der Konfessionen in der Reichsstadt Regensburg, Eine notwendige Entgegnung," *Zeitschrift für bayerische Kirchengeschichte* 34 (1964), pp. 1–33. As stressed by the subtitle, Simon's goal was to disprove the assertions concerning the growth of Lutheranism among the people of Regensburg made by Jürgen Sydow, "Die Konfessionen in Regensburg zwischen Reformation und Westfälischem Frieden," *Zeitschrift für bayerische Landesgeschichte* 23 (1960), pp. 473–491.

Death registers, which would be most useful for our purposes, were not kept by the city before 1650; Regensburg Lutherans began keeping a burial register in 1588; the Catholic parish priests in the city did not begin keeping such registers until the seventeenth century, generally not until after the Thirty Years' War. Guido Hable and Raimund Sterl, *Geschichte Regensburgs. Eine Übersicht nach Sachgebieten* [Studien und Quellen zur Geschichte Regensburgs 1 (Regensburg, 1970)], pp. 37–38 (these authors do not even hazard a population estimate for the period with which we are concerned).

15. On the death rate for a sixteenth-century German city, see R. Po-Chia Hsia, "Civic Wills as Sources for the Study of Piety in Muenster, 1530–1618," *The Sixteenth Century Journal* 14 (1983), pp. 325–326.

16. In fact, Simon's estimate is probably too high since he has calculated based on an annual birth rate of 34 per 1,000; between 35 and 45 births per 1,000 inhabitants is a more accurate figure for preindustrial Europe. See Rudolf Endres, "Zur Einwohnerzahl und Bevölkerungsstruktur Nürnbergs im 15./16. Jahrhundert," *Mitteilungen des Vereins für Geschichte der Stadt Nürnberg* 57 (1970), pp. 249–250; and Christopher Friedrichs, *Urban Society in an Age of War: Nördlingen, 1580–1720* (Princeton, 1979), p. 38, citing E. A. Wrigley, *Population in History* (New York, 1969), p. 62, and Pierre Guillaume and Jean-Pierre Poussou, *Démographie historique* (Paris, 1970), pp. 168–171. A population estimate based on 40 births per 1,000 = c. 10,000 population, would give a total of only 4,400 adult deaths in Regensburg for the eighty-year period.

If we hold the population estimate constant, the representativeness of the extant wills must vary by decade. Those wills that survive for the decade 1521–1530 would represent only 7 percent of the Regensburger who died in that decade; by the century's end the figure rises to 43 percent. In actuality, the famines and plagues of the century caused great fluctuations in population, but the calculation of more accurate percentages of representativeness is beyond the scope of our sources. On the sixteenth-century epidemics and their tolls, see Endres, "Zur Einwohnerzahl," p. 250.

17. It was apparently a condition of "retirement" into such an institution that the bed linens of the retiree be bequeathed to the hospital on his or her death. On the frequency of such "prebends" in the empire, see Michel Mollat, *The Poor in the Middle Ages*, trans. A. Goldhammer (New Haven, 1986), pp. 270–271.

The survival of occasional wills by apprentices among the testaments from sixteenth-century Regensburg is unusual; according to von Brandt, "Mittelalterliche Bürgertestament," p. 12, "the equally large number of apprentices seem never to make their appearance among the medieval testators."

18. Ludwig Lindner, *Das bürgerliche Recht der Reichsstadt Regensburg* (Ph.D. dissertation, Erlangen; Regensburg, 1908), pp. 29, 64–65.

19. "Es sollen auch die Testament unnd Geschefft der letzten willen allweg nach ordnung unnd den Rechten gemeß mit den solemmpnitetn darzu gehorig aufgericht unnd mit sonnderm vleiß beschribenn werden. Es sollenn auch nw furohin alle testament der letzstenn willen Erstlich vor ainem Erbern Rate eröffennt verlesenn und den Partheyenn auff Ir begere derselbenn Copi unnd abschrifft gegebenn werdenn Unnd So alßdann die tail dieselbenn Testament unnd geschefft Rechtvertigen woltenn Sollenn haubtman Camrer unnd Rate bey Inen vleis furwenden sy In der guete unteinannder zuvertragenn Wo sy aber dieselbenn In der guete nicht verainen mochten Alßdann zu Rechtvertigung derselben fur das Schulthaissengericht als fester Instantz gewisen werden." HStAM, R L Regensburg 381, fols. 8–8'.

20. Cf. the case for Münster, described by R. Po-chia Hsia, *Society and Religion in Münster, 1535–1618* (New Haven, 1984), pp. 177–198; and "Civic Wills," pp. 321–349. Hsia argues that "a sample check of wills prepared by a number of notaries shows that the notarial formulations which give the wills a certain uniformity do not distort the religious sentiments of the testators" (p. 179). This despite the fact that "the majority of wills contain no clues concerning the confessional loyalty of the testators. . . . Most wills have religious formulae which are ambiguous to interpret: they invoke the Holy Trinity and Christ but make no mention of the Virgin and the saints, although in many cases the testators specifically characterize themselves as Catholics" (p. 185). As the following analysis reveals, the situation for Regensburg is similar.

21. Quoted above, chapter two, note 45.

22. Schweller was an unusually pious Catholic on his deathbed; he ordered that his house be sold and one-half of the profit realized from the sale be used "Zw meiner sell haill." Nevertheless, even here he himself did not specify what arrangements were to be made but instead dictated that the decision should be made "durch meine geschefftiger." The dedication of half his immovable goods—the other half, together with all his movable goods, was bequeathed to his wife—to the salvation of his soul at the discretion of his executors was unusual. Medieval law in the city had decreed that, in the absence of a will and of descendants, only one-ninth of a man's property be expended for the good of his soul; two-thirds of his property was to fall to his wife, the remaining two-ninths to his next of kin (the property of a deceased wife was divided similarly, but the language of the law considered the masculine case only). Lindner, *Bürgerliches Recht*, pp. 28–29.

23. Rublack, "Grundwerte," p. 40.

24. Ibid.

25. Cf. Sabean, *Power in the Blood*, pp. 27–30, who argues (pp. 29–30): "What is common in community is not shared values or common understanding so much as the fact that members of a community are engaged in the same argument, the same *raisonnement*, the same *Rede*, the same discourse, in which alternative strategies, misunderstandings, conflicting goals and values are threshed out. . . . What makes community is the discourse." And, most recently, Lyndal Roper, "'The common man', 'the common good', 'common women': Gender and Meaning in the German Reformation Commune," *Social History* 12 (1987), pp. 1–22. I would modify Sabean's point to argue that if they do not necessarily share values or a common understanding, a shared language or languages, shared images, and a shared discourse may disguise that lack of agreement from the speakers themselves.

26. "Wir wollen uns auch in solchem allem, gegen ainem yeden, auch in gemainer unser Stat Regirung, ordnung, statuten und polliceyen, dermassen halten unnd beweysen, daran zuvor die Rom. Kayserl. Majestät etc. Unser allergnedigster her, alle sten des heyl. Reichs, und meniglich genedigs und guts gefallen haben sollen." "Die Freyheiten für diejenige, welche sich hier wollen häußlich niederlassen, betreffend" (1523), Kayser, *Dekretensammlung*, no. I, pp. 1–2; here, p. 2.

27. On 19 August 1485, for instance, when Regensburg was in the midst of an economic crisis and guildsmen had taken over the city's gates, an open meeting held in the city's Dominican church led to the creation of a citizens' committee whose suggestions were presented to the council on 20 August 1485; two days later the council presented its written response. Out of this exchange came a reformed "constitution," signed and sealed by Cammerer, inner and outer council, and eleven representatives of the community on 23 August. Striedinger, *Der Kampf um Regensburg*, pp. 51–52.

On the other hand, in 1492, after the emperor had forced his son-in-law to return Regensburg from Bavarian to imperial control, "the members of the town council, for the first time in years again in the position to act independently, could think of nothing better to do than to hear from the long oppressed community." This time the representatives elected from the city's eight administrative quarters were reluctant to accept any responsibility, saying only that they expected the council itself would fulfill its appointed rôle and protect the city from damage and danger. Ibid., pp. 196–197.

During the related unrest of the second decade of the sixteenth century, the community was called together so frequently in quarter meetings that they finally elected ten men from each quarter as an *Ausschuß*; these met daily with the Rat itself, and the Rat appears to have feared to undertake anything without their consideration. The debate and unrest continued, according to a contemporary chronicler, until it at last seemed counterproductive even to the most rebellious; his account provides us yet another definition of government: "und kundten nit finden, das also recht thet, wo kain regiment weer, und sach sy für gut an, das dy herren solten wider regiren und ein ausschus bey inen etc. da huben sy an, bevalhen, man soll wider straffen wie vor dy ungehorsamen, gaben wider den gewalt einem ratht. . . ." Leonhard Widmann, *Chronik von Regensburg*, ed. E. V. Oefele [Die Chroniken der deutschen Städte 15 (Leipzig, 1878)], p. 17.

28. ". . . der sol und mag sich deß für einen erbern Camerer und Rate, als die hohern öbrigkeyt alhie, wie sich gepürt, berüeffen. Wo aber disem eines erbern Camerern unnd Rates notwendigem fürnemen, yemandt ungehorsam unnd entgegen erscheinen wirdet, der sol darumb ernstlicher straff gewartend sein, Davor wisse sich menigklich zuverhüeten." "Die Verweisung an nachgeordnete gerichtliche Behörden betreffend" (18 October 1531), reprinted in Kayser, *Dekretensammlung*, no. II, p. 4. The adjective "hohern" in this case referred to the Rat's position as the highest in a series of municipal courts.

29. Hans-Christoph Rublack, "Political and Social Norms in Urban Communities in the Holy Roman Empire," in *Religion, Politics, and Social Protest: Three Studies on Early Modern Germany*, ed. Kaspar von Greyerz (London, 1984), pp. 24–60.

30. Heinrich Bornkamm, "Die Frage der Obrigkeit im Reformationszeitalter," *Das Jahrhundert der Reformation. Gestalten und Kräfte* (2nd ed., Göttingen, 1961), pp. 291–315; Erich Maschke, " 'Obrigkeit' im spätmittelalterlichen Speyer und in anderen Städten," *Archiv für Reformationsgeschichte* 57 (1966), p. 7; Rainer Postel, "Obrigkeitsdenken und Reformation in Hamburg," *Archiv für Reformationsgeschichte* 70 (1979), p. 170.

31. Cf. the very different situation in Hamburg, where, according to Postel, the Rat willingly legitimated its authority to outsiders in more communitarian terms and the emperor "was apparently named as overlord only when it was opportune or unavoidable—demonstrating an interest in independence which was well content to leave political connections unexpressed." Postel, "Obrigkeitsdenken und Reformation," pp. 182, 196. Cf. Maschke, "Obrigkeit," pp. 8–9, 14.

32. ". . . und kayserlicher Maiestat des heiligen Reichs darnach gemainer Stat frumben zu furdernn," *Kaiserliche Regimentsordnung* 1514 (HStAM, R L Regensburg 381), fol. 4. The oath in the *Regimentsordnung* of 1500 substitutes the word "königlicher" for "kayserlicher." HStAM, R L Regensburg 376, fol. 3. On the further problem of swearing to "obey" ("gehorsam sein") the emperor in a free city, see Maschke, "Obrigkeit," pp. 16–17.

33. Maschke, "Obrigkeit," pp. 9, 19–22; Postel, "Obrigkeitsdenken und Reformation," pp. 171–172.

34. Widmann, *Chronik von Regensburg*, pp. 15–26; esp. p. 17.

35. On Nuremberg, see Gerald Strauss, *Nuremberg in the Sixteenth Century* (New York, 1966), pp. 61–62, 78–81, 85.

36. Ibid.

37. "Wann man den Eussern Rate erfordern soll

"Item wann man von der Stewr reden will

"Item wenn man ewig gellt oder Zins verkaufen will

"Item wenn gemaine Stat abgesagt veindt uberkame

"Item wenn man Raisen thun musste

"Item wenn von koniglicher [kaiserlicher] Maiestat unnd des heiligen Reichs wegenn ettwas Zugebenn oder groß zuthun begert wurde unnd sunst albegenn wann mercklich geschefft furfallenn darzue ainen Innern Rate notturfftig ansehenn wirdet den Grossenn Rate darzue zuerfordern

"Item Haubtman Camrer unnd Inner Rate mogen auch In allenn anndern sachenn Soofft sy wollenn unnd fur guet ansehenn ainen Eussern Rate wol erfordernn."

HStAM, R L Regensburg 376 (1500), fols. 20'–21; R L Regensburg 381 (1514), fol. 9'. Bracketed word indicates change from text of 1500 to text of 1514.

38. HStAM, R L Regensburg 376 (1500), fol. 20'.

39. The Ausschuß was elected annually by the Gemeinde in *Wachtgedinge* or quarter meetings during February or March; the five men elected from each quarter were empowered by the Bürger resident in that quarter to act on their behalf ("denselbigenn ganntz volmechtigen gewallt gebenn Inn sachen darumb sy von haubtman Camrer Innerm unnd Ausserm Rate erfordert an Irer als ainer ganntzen Erbern gemain stat zu hanndeln unnd zu besliessenn"); after presentation to the Rat by the master for that quarter, their names were inscribed in the annual register. HStAM, R L Regensburg 381 (1514), fol. 33'.

The separation of governing committee and community was, of course, a process with much older origins. Originally the Äußerer Rat itself had functioned as just such an Ausschuß of the Gemeinde; nevertheless, by the end of the fourteenth century it had already ceased to fulfill that function (hence the demand of the guildsmen in 1485 for a new Ausschuß). On the constitutional developments of the medieval period, see the dissertation by Berta Ritscher, *Die Entwicklung der Regensburger Ratsverfassung in der gesellschaftlichen und wirtschaftlichen Struktur der Zeit von 1245– 1429* [*Verhandlungen des historischen Vereins für Oberpfalz und Regensburg* 114 (1974), pp. 7–126; 115 (1975), pp. 7–63; 116 (1976), pp. 7–110, esp. 114 (1974), pp. 123–126].

40. "Doch alle Jar an Sand Steffans tag In den Weyhnacht feyrtagenn sol man ain gemain auf das Rathaus samentlich berueffenn unnd In Irem beywesen dise ordnung verlesenn / Aber sonnst soll man ain ganntze gemain zu erfordern nicht bemuhen." HStAM, R L Regensburg 381 (1514), fol. 33'.

41. Quoted from "Der Vormünder Pflicht betreffend" [1537], Kayser, *Dekretensammlung*, no. IX, pp. 20.

42. "Dieweil nuhn ein erberer Camrer und rathe diser Stat, Regenspurg, als der hochgenanten Römischen Kayserlichen und Königlichen Maiestat gehorsame underthone." "Verbot den Verkauf einer Französischen Schrifft wieder Kayserliche Majestät betreffend" (1535), Kayser, *Dekretensammlung*, no. VII, p. 16.

43. "Als Unnserm Ainigem naturlichen rechten Herrn, und Höchsten khayserlichen Obrigkhait, getrew, gewhar, gewärttig Zusein, Alles zuthuen, was wir alle, und jede Insonnderhait E: Khayß: Mayt: und derselben nachkommen, Als getrewe, gehorsame Undterthanen, Irem naturlichen rechten Herrn Zuthuen schuldig sindt." Oath taken by Regensburg Rat and Bürger to Emperor Rudolph II, 1576. Text given in Johann Linda, *Warhaffte beschreibung deß Acts, so Auff Ableyben deß Aller Durchleuchtigisten, Großmechtigisten Fürsten und Herrn Herrn Maximiliani, Deß Anndern Römischen Khaysers etc. Hochlöblichster und seeligster gedächtnus, mit Irer Mayt. Leich und derselben Clag, besinckhnus, und anndern Ceremonien Alhie zu Regenspurg gehalten worden* (ms., 1576), Archiv des Historischen Vereins für Oberpfalz und Regensburg, R. MS 105, fols. 10–10'. Linda added to the text the comment that the Rat had seen and approved the form of the oath in advance.

44. Cf. the following cases of men who gave up or were removed from their "offices," all translated as "Amt" in Martin Luther's German Bible (1523, 1545): "Und es begab sich, da er Priesters ampt ["cum sacerdoto" in Vulgate] pfleget fur Gott, zur zeit seiner ordnung." Luke 1:8. "Und es begab sich, da die zeit seines Ampts ["officii" in Vulgate] auswar, gieng er heim in sein haus." Luke 1:23. "Der haushalter sprach bey sich selbs, Was sol ich thun? mein Herr nimpt das

ampt ["villicatio" in Vulgate] von mir, graben mag ich nicht, so scheme ich mich zu betteln. Ich weis wol was ich thun wil, wenn ich nu von dem ampt ["villicatio" in Vulgate] gesetzt werde, das sie mich inn ire Heuser nemen." Luke 16:3–4.

In Regensburg, where only the bare register recorded the careers of the individual councillors, we must usually guess at the reasons for the disappearance of a name from the annual list. The best guess is usually "death," but it is, as the sources remind us, only a guess and surprises are possible: at least one council member was removed from the Innerer Rat before his death for adultery. Walter Fürnrohr, *Das Patriziat der Freien Reichsstadt Regensburg zur Zeit des Immerwährenden Reichstags. Eine sozialgeschichtliche Studie über das Bürgertum der Barockzeit* [*Verhandlungen des historischen Vereins von Oberpfalz und Regensburg* 92 (1951)], p. 274. The emperor, of course, also referred to his "office," in the sense of his responsibilities as emperor, but avoided any language that would suggest that the electors had the right to revoke his election. During the *Kurfürstentag* of 1575, Maximilian II referred to his "imperial office," but prefaced mention of his having been "raised to it by the unanimous vote of the electors" with insistence on "divine investiture": "Irem obliegenden Kaiserlichen Ambtt von der zeit an sie vermittelst Göttlicher verleihung und des heiligen Reichs Churfürsten einheliger Wahl darzu erhoben." Joseph Maria Schneidt, ed., *Vollständige Geschichte der römischen Königs-Wahl Rudolphs II, aus meistens annoch ungedruckten Urkunden als ein Beytrag zur Geschichte der Churfürsten-Tage und Römischen Königs-Wahlen* (Würzburg, 1792), p. 429.

45. Cf. the Nördlingen *Ratsordnung* from 1480 in which the phrase "wer zü gewalt erwelt wirt" occurs in the context of a preamble defining God as the source of Obrigkeit and omitting all mention of the community. Hans-Christoph Rublack, *Eine bürgerliche Reformation: Nördlingen* [Quellen und Forschungen zur Reformationsgeschichte 51 (Gütersloh, 1982)], pp. 40–41. Especially interesting here is the one situation in which the Nördlingen Rat did broaden its language to include an appeal to the community as a source of legitimation: the Peasants' War. Ibid., pp. 44–51.

46. "Camerer und Rathe, Wie sie von Ambts wegen, zu forderst Gott dem almechtigen, auch der Rö. Kay. und Kö. Ma. unsern allergnedigsten herrn, ihnen selbst, und irer gemaynen gehorsamen burgerschafft, auch andern frid·amen menschen schuldig. . . ." "Das öffentliche Einreden denen Predigern auf der Canzel und in Religions Sachen sich gebührend aufzuführen betreffend" (1534), Kayser, *Dekretensammlung*, no. V, p. 10.

Hans-Christoph Rublack has recently traced the development of the concept of Obrigkeit or "magistracy" in the decrees issued by the Nördlingen council in the century between 1450–1550. According to his investigation, the theoretical legitimation of the magistracy as an authority instituted from above was first joined to the older statement of the practical necessity of the Nördlingen Bürger's obedience to the Rat in an ordinance of 1480. "After 1500 the formula 'der Rat als Obrigkeit' appears: the council perceives itself then as an institution, as the secular 'upper hand.'" Rublack, *Bürgerliche Reformation*, p. 42.

47. "From God the council received very valuable legitimation of its activities; obedience was now expected because required by God—not, as one might expect implicitly, on the basis of any transfer of authority by the community. The individual Ratsherr bore final responsibility not only toward the community, but also *for* the community, at the Last Judgment." Rublack, "Grundwerte," p. 25.

48. The usual German phrase was "beschirmen und hand haben."

49. Edward F. Campbell, ed., *Ruth* [The Anchor Bible 7 (Garden City, N.Y., 1975)], p. 123, citing not only ancient and modern Arabic custom but also the presence of the same motif in the metaphorical marriage of Yahweh and Israel at Ezekiel 16:8.

50. Jacob Grimm, *Deutsche Rechtsaltümer* (4th ed., Leipzig, 1899), vol. 1, pp. 219–221, includes examples from medieval England, France, and Germany, as well as from classical sources; cf. J. Seibert, "Schutzmantelschaft," in *Der Lexikon der christlichen Ikonographie*, ed. Engelbert Kirschbaum, vol. 4 (Rome, 1971), cols. 128–129, 133.

51. The image gained great popularity with the Cistercian order after Caesarius of Heisterbach reported that a Cistercian monk, disappointed to see none of his fellows in heaven in a vision he had of that place, was comforted by the Virgin, who opened her cloak to reveal her dear Cistercians sheltering there. Cited in Seibert, "Schutzmantelschaft," col. 129.

52. E.g., the Maria Misericordias in the woodcuts for Ulrich Tengler's *Laienspiegel* (figs. 5 and 6) and in the center panel of the Regensburger *Armseelenaltar* (fig. 20).

53. On Jesus in the rôle more often given to Mary, see the work of Carolyn Walker Bynum,

"The Body of Christ in the Later Middle Ages: A Reply to Leo Steinberg," *Renaissance Quarterly* 39 (1986), pp. 399–439, and *Jesus as Mother: Studies in the Spirituality of the High Middle Ages* (Berkeley, 1982).

54.

> In meinem götliche[m] schirm will ich sy haben.
> die meine[m] name[n] ihu[s] in irer begird welle[n] trage[n].
> Die ewig Weyßhait

Inscription from anonymous woodcut for Heinrich Suso, *buch genant der Seusse* (Augsburg: Anton Sorg, 1482), fol. LXXXVIIII; reprinted in Schramm, *Bilderschmuck*, vol. 4, no. 776.

55. E.g., "das ewer keiserlichen maiestet ampt ist . . . fromme, rechte prediger schützen und handhaben." Philipp Melanchthon, "Apologia zur Augsburgischen Confession," in *Corpus doctrinae christianae* (Leipzig, 1560), p. 184; quoted in Jacob and Wilhelm Grimm, *Deutsches Wörterbuch*, vol. 4, part 2 (Leipzig, 1877), col. 396. On the two phrases "hand haben" and "beschirmen" used together in the Regensburg wills before the Reformation of the city, see ibid., vol. 4, part 2, cols. 393–396, and vol. 1 (Leipzig, 1854), col. 1569.

56. Hartmut Kugler, "Die Stadt im Wald. Zur Stadtbeschreibung bei Hans Sachs," in *Studien zur frühbürgerlichen Literatur im 16. Jahrhundert*, ed. Thomas Cramer and Erika Kartschoke [Beiträge zur Älteren Deutschen Literaturgeschichte 3 (Bern, 1978)], pp. 83–103.

57.

> Ich plickt gen dem gartten hinwarz,
> darin ein edler vogel het geheket,
> gros als ein adlar, war kol schwarz.
> sein linke seitten, die war im bedeket
> mit liechten rosen, rot und weis
> gedailt mit fleis.
> mit seim gefider macht er einen werbel,
> und sein Junge hielt er in hut,
> der wol gemut.
> er speisset sie aus durch den wintter kalte.

Hans Sachs, "der lieblich draum" (1527), ll. 11–19. Both *Meisterlieder* are given in full by Kugler, "Stadt im Wald," pp. 85–89, from whom I have taken these excerpts.

58.

> der vogel deut die reichstat nürnberk.
> In Irem wapen sie ein adlar füret,
> die linke seitten rot und weis,
> das ir vom römischen reich ist herkumen.
>
> . . .
>
> sein Junge all Burger bedeut,
> reich und arme in der stat hin und wider,
> kauffherren und die handswerkleut.
> darum der vogel schwinget sein gefider,
> bedeut, das dreu auffmerken hat
> ein erber rat
> auff Ire untterthon und thut wartten,
> und halten sie in dreuem schuz;

Hans Sachs, "auffschluss des draums" (1527), ll. 1–4, 11–18. Cf. Kugler's own comments on the same subject, "Stadt im Wald," pp. 99–100.

59. ". . . in umbra alarum tuarum protege me." Psalms 17:8. Complutensian Polyglott: *Tertia pars Veteris testamenti*, fol. av. "Sicut aves volantes sic proteget dominus exercituum hierusalem." Isaiah 31:5. Complutensian Polyglott: *Quarta pars Veteris testamenti*, fol. dvi.

60. "Be schirm mich under dem schatten deiner vettich:" Psalm 16:9 in first printed German Bible (Straßburg: Johann Mentel, c. 1466); reprinted as *Die Erste Deutsche Bibel*, ed. W. Kurrelmeyer [Bibliothek des Litterarischen Vereins in Stuttgart 234 (Tübingen, 1904), 238 (1905), 243 (1907), 246 (1907), 249 (1908), 251 (1909), 258 (1912), 259 (1913), 266 (1915)], vol. 7, p. 260, ll. 26–27. This translation was published at least fourteen times by printers in Augsburg, Straßburg, and Nuremberg between c. 1466 and 1518; ibid., vol. 1, pp. ix–xix.

Cf. Psalm 17:8, "beschirme mich unter dem schatten deiner flügel," in the editions of Martin Luther's Psalter translation (1524/1545); *WA Bibel* 10,1:144–145.

"Als die fliegenden vogel, also beschirmt der herre der here iherusalem." Isaiah 31:5 in *Erste Deutsche Bibel*, vol. 8, p. 433, ll. 44–46.

"Und der HERR Zebaoth wird Jerusalem beschirmen (wie die vögel thun mit flügeln)." Isaiah 31:5 in Luther (1528/1545), *WA Bibel* 11,1:100–101.

The word "beschirmen" was also common in works by writers such as Johannes Geiler von Keisersberg. See the nine citations to Geiler's *das buch der sünden des munds* (Straßburg, 1518), in Grimm, *Deutsches Wörterbuch*, vol. 1, col. 1569.

61. Cf.: "Und der herre widergeb dir umb dein werck: das du entphachest vollen lon von dem herrn got israhel zü dem du bist komen: und under des vettich du bist entphlohen. . . . Ich bins ruth dein diern Breit deinen mantel auf dein diern: wann du bist nachwendig." Ruth 2:12, 3:9; translated in *Erste Deutsche Bibel* (c. 1466), vol. 4, p. 430, ll. 22–25; p. 433, ll. 25–27. And: "Reddat tibi dominus pro opere tuo: & plenam mercedem recipias a domino deo israel ad quem venisti: & sub cuius confugisti alas. . . . Ego sum ruth ancilla tua. Expande pallium tuum super famulam tuam: quia propinquus es." Ruth 2:12, 3:9; translated by Jerome, Complutensian Polyglott: *Secunda pars Veteris testamenti*, fols. iv', ivi. And: "Der HERR vergellte dyr deyne that, und musse deyn lohn volkomen seyn bey dem HERRN dem Gott Israel, zu wilchem du komen bist, das du unter seynen flugeln zuversicht hettist. . . . Ich bin Ruth deyne magd, breyte deynen flugel uber deyne magd, Denn du bist der Nachman ["Erbe" in 1545]." Ruth 2:12, 3:9; translated by Luther (1524/1545), *WA Bibel* 9,1:174–175, 178–179. Cf. Alexander Cruden, *A Complete Concordance to the Holy Scriptures of the Old and New Testaments* (Philadelphia, 1879), p. 686; and esp. Campbell, ibid., pp. 100, 123.

62. "Wie eyn Adeler auffweckt seyn nest, und uber seynen iungen schwebt, er breyttet seyne fittich aus, und nam yhn und trug yhn auff seynen flugeln." Deuteronomy 32:11 = 5. Moses 32:11 = 5. Moses 32:11 in Luther (1523/1545), *WA Bibel* 8:662–663.

Cf. in addition to the passages cited above, Psalms 36:7, 57:1, 61:4, 63:7, 91:4; Isaiah 8:8; Ezekiel 17:1–24; also the threatening wings of God in Isaiah 18:1; Jeremiah 48:40, 49:22. On the motif of the magnificent bird in Canaanite and biblical literature, see Mitchell Dahood, ed., *Psalms* I [The Anchor Bible 16 (Garden City, N.Y., 1966)], pp. 107–108.

63. "JErusalem, Jerusalem, die du tödtest die Propheten, und steinigest die zu dir gesand sind, Wie offt habe ich deine Kinder versamlen wöllen, wie eine Henne versamlet ire Küchlin, unter ire flügel, Und ir habt nicht gewolt?" Matthew 23:37 in Martin Luther's translation (1522/1546); *WA Bibel* 6:104–105; cf. Luke 13:34, in *WA Bibel* 6:278–279. Also: *Erste Deutsche Bibel* (c. 1466), vol. 1, pp. 90, 273.

64. "So sol man nun fur Christo und Gott, dem himmelisschen vater, nicht fliehen, sondern er wil, wir sollen uns zu im halten wie die kuchlein undter der Hennen flugel sich versamlen, und wie Kinder zu den Eldtern sich halten, also sollen wir auch eine kindliche zuflucht haben zu Christo und dem himmelisschen vater." Luther, "Predigt aus dem dritten Kapitel Johannes" (7 September 1538), *WA* 47:99. Cf. "id ago sub alis tuis nimis cum ingenti periculo; nisi quia sub alis tuis tibi subdita est anima mea, et infirmitas mea tibi nota est. Parvulus sum, sed vivit semper Pater meus, et idoneus est tutor meus. . . ." Augustine, *Confesssiones* X, iv.

65. "Wir hernachbenandte bitten Eüer Erbar Weißheit ganz unterthaniglich, alß unsere Vatter und Obrigkeit, die unß Von Gott Verordnet und furgesezet ist dises unser Christliches bitten und herzliches begehren gnädiglich Zuvernehmen, dieweil der Vatter aller barmherzigkeit Gott der Allmächtige in diesen lezten fährlichen Zeiten uns sein heylig Evangelion auß grosser Lieb und barmherzigkeit geben und predigen läst. . . ." Johann Georg Gölgel, *Regenspurgische Kirchen Historia* (ms., 1707), fol. 27. StBM, Cgm. 2012.

66. "Ein heilsamer fürst (als kunstlich Plutarchus dar von sagt) ist ettlicher maß ein läbendig byldung gottes, deer da ist der aller best, und da mit ouch der aller gwaltigest, Dem gütheit das gybt, das er allenn welly nütz sin, der gwalt gibt im, das er sölichs so er wil, ouch vermag." Desiderius Erasmus, *Ein nutzliche underwisung eines Christenlichen fürsten wol zü regieren* (Zurich: Christoph Froschauer, 1521), fol. XII'.

67. Quoted by Rublack, "Political and Social Norms," p. 47.

68. See, e.g., "Verschiedene Laster, Sünden und nächtlichen Unfug betreffend" (1562), Kayser, *Dekretensammlung*, no. XVIII, pp. 45–47.

69. ". . . vor alters aber hat man die landesherrn veter und die underthanen lude oder kinder genennt. . . ." Cited from Grimm, *Deutsches Wörterbuch*, vol. 12, part 1 (Leipzig, 1956), col. 19. On Mathesius himself, see *Allgemeine Deutsche Biographie* (1884), vol. 20, pp. 586–589.

70. "Honor thy father and mother, that thy days may be long upon the land which the Lord

thy God giveth thee" (Exodus 20:12; cf. Deuteronomy 5:16), was considered the Fourth Commandment by Augustine, who based his numbering on the text given in Deuteronomy; Jerome, following rabbinic tradition, based his numbering on the Exodus text and called it the Fifth Commandment. In the sixteenth century the issue of "graven images" and the rôle of art in liturgy and piety was involved in the question of the numbering and division of the Commandments; Hans von Campenhausen, "Die Bilderfrage in der Reformation," *Zeitschrift für Kirchengeschichte* 68 (1957), p. 109; Margarete Stirm, *Die Bilderfrage in der Reformation* [Quellen und Forschungen zur Reformationsgeschichte 45 (Gütersloh, 1977)], pp. 21–22, 46. In the twentieth century, Jews, Eastern Orthodox, and all Protestants except Lutherans follow Jerome, while Catholics and Lutherans follow Augustine as they both did in the sixteenth century. For the sake of convenience, I adopt the Augustinian numbering in the discussion that follows.

71. "Dû solt êren vater unde muoter, die dich an die werlt brâhten. . . . dû solt dînen geistlîchen vater êren; daz sint die priester, wan die hât got selbe gewirdiget unde geêret über alle menschen." Berthold von Regensburg, "Von den zehen Geboten unsers Herren," printed in Franz Pfeiffer, ed., *Berthold von Regensburg. Vollständige Ausgabe seiner Predigten*, vol. 1 (Vienna, 1862), pp. 275–276. In the late-medieval period, the application of the paternal appositive to "spiritual fathers" ranged from the lawyer's formulaic appeal to "our most holy father and lord, Lord Innocent the eighth, Pope by divine providence" to the diarist's entry: ". . . bemiet sich der hochwürdig, durchleuchtig, hochgeporn fürst und herr Johans, administrator hie zu Regenspurg, pfalzgraff bey Rhen, hirtzog in Bahren etc., wie er dan alß ein treuer pfarherr thet, in allen auffrürn, wen sy am allerunsinnigisten waren auff den plezen, das er ob 12 maln under sy rith, so vetterlich patt, ermanet mit früntlichen reden. . . ." Appeal of 14 May 1485, given in Striedinger, *Der Kampf um Regensburg*, p. 156. Diary entry from Leonhard Widmann, *Chronik von Regensburg*, sixteenth-century manuscript diary edited by E. V. Oefele [Die Chroniken der deutschen Städte 15 (Leipzig, 1878)], p. 19.

72. "Ir sult ouch êren iuwer geistlîche muoter, daz ist diu heilige kristenheit, daz dû dînen ebenkristen êrest, daz er dîn genôze ist, daz wir kristenliute alle einander gebrüeder sîn in gote, als wir alle tage dâ sprechen in dem pater noster." Berthold von Regensburg, "Zehen Geboten," p. 276.

73. Berthold von Regensburg, "Von Gotes Minne," printed in Pfeiffer, ed., *Berthold von Regensburg*, pp. 165–173.

74. "Als verre ein muoter ir lieben kindes vergezzen wil als wênic wil unser got vergezzen und er wil unser halt verre minre vergezzen dan ein muoter ir kindes vergezzen muoz." Ibid., p. 166. This sexual stereotyping is similar to that discovered by Carolyn Bynum in twelfth-century Cistercian writings. *Jesus as Mother*, pp. 148–149, 154, 167.

75. ". . . non habet nec barbem, har ac. et tamen sic pingit deum verum in imagine viri antiqui. Sic mus man unserm herr Gott ein bild malen propter pueros et nos, si etiam docti." Martin Luther, "Predigt am Sonnabend vor Ostern" (20 April 1538), WA 46:308.

76. Thomas Aquinas, *Selected Political Writings*, ed. A. P. D'Entreves (Oxford, 1954), p. 9; cited in Michael Walzer, *The Revolution of the Saints* (New York, 1974), p. 184n. After noting that Aquinas had "held that the virtue of *pietas*, often hardly distinguishable from *caritas*, was the power animating devotion and reverence to both parents and *patria*," Kantorowicz nevertheless adds: "Usually, however, Aquinas means 'Heaven' or 'Paradise' when talking about *patria*." Ernst H. Kantorowicz, *The King's Two Bodies: A Study in Medieval Political Theology* (Princeton, 1957), p. 243 n. 154.

77.

> wer nit seynem obersten ist underthon
> Geistlich weltlich, und inn thut widerston
> Gott strafft die sünd mit dem dot
> Als das vicesimo Levitici stot.

Last four lines under rubric "Das vierd gebott" in Johannes Geiler von Kaisersberg, *Dis büchlin wiset wie sich ein yeglicher Cristen mensch schicken soll zu einer gantzen volkomnen und gemeiner beych* (Basel: Niclaus Lamparter, c. 1518), fol. 9'; reprinted in *Die Aeltesten Schriften Geilers von Kaysersberg*, ed. L. Dacheux (Breisgau, 1882), p. 148. Cf. Jean Gerson, *Opusculum tripartitum de preceptis decalogi, de confessione et de arte moriendi*, translated into German by Johannes Geiler von Keisersberg as *Der dreieckecht Spiegel* (Straßburg: Matthias Schürer, [1510]), VIII. capitel; reprinted in Johannes Geffcken, *Der Bildercatechismus des funfzehnten Jahrhunderts und die catechetischen Hauptstücke in dieser Zeit bis auf Luther* (Leipzig, 1855), cols. 40–41.

78. For medieval examples in Latin, see Paul Münch, "Die 'Obrigkeit im Vaterstand'—zu Definition und Kritik des 'Landesvaters' während der frühen Neuzeit," *Daphnis* 11 (1982), pp. 22–26.

79. "Ein frommer fürst sol ein sölich gmüt und hertz haben gegen sinem volck, als da hat ein güter Hußvatter gegen sinem hußgsind." Erasmus, *Ein nutzliche underwisung*, fol. XX'.

80. In addition to the edition just quoted, see *Die unterweysung aines frummen Fürsten an den herrn Karln den fünfften*, trans. G. Spalatinus (Augsburg: S. Grimm and M. Wirsung, 1521); cited in *Short-Title Catalogue of Books Printed in the German-Speaking Countries and German Books Printed in Other Countries from 1455 to 1600 Now in the British Museum* (London, 1962), p. 282.

81. "Wie auch von alters her die Römer und andere sprachen herrn und frawen ym haus Patres et matres familias, das ist haus veter und haus mutter, genennet haben. Also yhre landsfursten und oberherrn haben sie Patres patriae, das ist veter des gantzen lands geheissen, uns die wir Christen sein wöllen, zu grossen schanden, das wir sie nicht also heissen oder zum wenigsten dafur halten und ehren." Martin Luther, *Deudsch Catechismus* (1529), WA 30,1:152.

In tracing the development in the German city of a language of political paternity with Lutheran roots I am aware of blurring the line separating Luther's writings on municipal government from those on princely government. Luther's ignorance or ignoring of municipal government, particularly in its communal or participatory aspect, has been stressed by Hans-Christoph Rublack, "Martin Luther und die städtische soziale Erfahrung," in *Martin Luther: Probleme seiner Zeit*, ed. Volker Press and Dieter Stievermann [Spätmittelalter und Frühe Neuzeit. Tübinger Beiträge zur Geschichtsforschung 16 (Stuttgart, 1986)], pp. 88–123; esp. pp. 92–99.

82. Luther's lieutenant Melanchthon also included the magistracy in his consideration of the Fourth Commandment: *Unterricht der Visitatorn an die Pfarhern ym Kurfurstenthum zu Sachssen*, preface by Martin Luther (Wittenberg: Nickel Schirlentz, 1528), fols. Civ'–E'.

83. "Wylliger gehorsam und undertenikeit, allerley gewalt umb gottes wolgefallen willen, als der Apostel S. Petrus sagt, an als widderbellen, clagen und murmulen." Martin Luther, "Die zehen gepot gottes. mit einer kurtzen außlegung irer erfullung und ubertretung" (printed in Wittenberg, Nuremberg, Basel, and Augsburg in 1518[?]; Leipzig and other Augsburg editions, 1519–1522), WA 1:250–256; here, 254; cf. the definition of violation of the Fourth Commandment at 1:252–253: "Wer briester standt unehret, nach redet und beleidigt. Wer seine hern und uberkeyt nicht ehret, trewe und gehorsam ist, sie sein gut oder bosze."

84. The epigraph with which we began this chapter. Martin Luther, "Predigt über das 2. Buch Mose" (29 October 1525?), WA 16:486.

85. "Denn der Fürsten und Herrn Obirkeit ist nicht eine liepliche Obirkeit, sondern erschreckliche, Denn sie sind unsers Herrgotts Stockmeister, richter und hencker, mit den er die bösen buben strafft, aber Vater und Mutter sind nicht also erschrecklich, sondern gantz freüntlich." Ibid., 16:488.

86. *WA Briefe* 5:313; quoted by Eike Wolgast, *Die Wittenberger Theologie und die Politik der evangelischen Stände. Studien zu Luthers Gutachten in politischen Fragen* [Quellen und Forschungen zur Reformationsgeschichte 47 (Gütersloh, 1977)], p. 174. *WA Tischrede* 2:645 no. 2768.

87. See above, note 81.

88. Münch, "Die Obrigkeit," pp. 26–27.

89. Seneca, "De clementia," I, xiv. Translation taken from Seneca, *Moral Essays*, trans. John W. Basore (London, 1928), vol. 1, pp. 398–399.

90. Seneca, *De clementia*, ed. and commentary by Jean Calvin (Paris: Louis Blaubloem, 1532; reprinted Geneva: P. Santandreanus, 1576 and 1597). On the publishing history of Seneca's essay, see bibliography in Jean Calvin, *Calvin's Commentary on Seneca's De Clementia*, ed. and trans. by Ford Lewis Battles and André Malan Hugo (Leiden, 1969), pp. 398–399.

91. "Nütz und güt bedunckt mich, zü hören, mit was titel Julius Pollux, dem Keyser Comodo (des kintheit er underricht hat) bezeichnet und entworffen hab ein Künig und ein Tyrannen, Dann so er ein künig glich bald den götten nach hat gesetzt, als einen der inen der nächst und glichest wer, hat er also gesprochen, Ein Künig solt du loben mit sölichen namen, Vatter, dugenthafft, senfft, milt, gütig, fürsichtig, billich, fründlich, großmütig. . . ." Erasmus, *Ein nutzliche underwisung*, fol. XXI'. The passage continues at some length.

92. "Wo die underthon [von iren obern lieb gehabt auch die obern durch die underthon] mit der gehorsam in Eren gehalten, das frid und ainigkait dest bestendiger und yedes in seinem ordenlichen wesen beleiben." The lines appeared as part of the "Layenspiegels einfürung," a section apparently introduced in the Augsburg 1511 edition of the *Neü Layenspiegel*. Cf. (Augs-

burg, 1512), fol. I; (Straßburg, 1527), fol. I; (Straßburg, 1530), fol. I; (Straßburg, 1532), fol. I; (Straßburg, 1538), fol. II; and (Straßburg, 1544), fol. II, which contain the bracketed material, with (Straßburg, 1514), fols. I–I' and (Straßburg, 1518), fols. I–I', from which it was omitted.

In 1528 Martin Luther had used a similar phrase in praise of Herzog Johann of Saxony; he had acted "out of Christian love (since it isn't required of temporal authority)" in ordering that ecclesiastical visitors conduct a visitation of the parishes in his lands. Preface to Melanchthon, *Unterricht der Visitatorn*, fol. Aiv.

93. "Daher gewachsen ist ein solche liebe und trew seiner unterthanen zu yhm, das sie yhn Gotte vergleicht haben, umb solcher veterlicher freundlicher wolthat willen. . . . Die Römer haben wol Augustum, Ciceronem, und andere, Patrem Patriae genennet, Ein vater, welcher als ein vater bey seinen kindern thut, bey und mit yhnen gehandelt habe, aber so hoch haben sie keinen gesetzt aus freyer eygener wilkür, Denn Augustus und Domitianus woltens haben bey einer straffe, das man yhn wie, Göttern, opffern muste, und war ein lauter gezwang." Johann Agricola, *Dreyhundert Gemeyner Sprichwörter, der wir Deudschen uns gebrauchen, und doch nicht wissen woher sie komen* (Leipzig: Michael Blum, 1530), fol. 45'. The proverb explicated was: "Wenn Gott ein land segnet, so gibt er yhm ein klugen Fürsten, der friede helt, Widderümb wenn Gott ein land straffet und plagen wil, so gibt er yhm ein Tyrannen und wütrich, der es alles one radt mit der faust wil ausrichten." Ibid., fol. 45. Like Luther, Agricola used praise in an attempt to shape the emperor's actions. After praising Maximilian's protection of the empire and foundation of the Schwäbish League, Agricola mentioned the wars the emperor had fought "aber dieses hat er verhütet, das, widder Franckreich, noch Venedigen, oder der Bapst ein pferd hetten an einen zaun ynn Deudschen landen anbinden dürffen," adding that "wiewol dis alles fur Gott nicht viel gilt," it had nevertheless garnered the emperor much praise. Ibid., fol. 46'.

94. It would be some time before a Lutheran would again speak of the emperor in paternal terms. At the *Kurfürstentag* held in Regensburg in 1575 at the insistence of the dying Maximilian II to elect his son Rudolph as his successor, both Maximilian and the elector of Saxony referred to the emperor's "true paternal concern" ("getreüen vätterlichen sorgveltigkeit") for his empire. Cf. "Kayserl. *Proposition* auf den Churfürstentag zu Regensburg 1575" and "Geheimes *Protocollum*, welches 1575. auf dem Churfürstlichen Collegialtage zu Regensburg bey damalig vorgewesener Königswahl Rudolphi II. gehalten worden," in *Vollständige Geschichte der römischen Königs-Wahl Rudolphs II, aus meistens annoch ungedruckten Urkunden als ein Beytrag zur Geschichte der Churfürsten-Tage und Römischen Königs-Wahlen*, ed. Joseph Maria Schneidt (Würzburg, 1792), pp. 429, 431, 492, 494.

95. See above, chapter three, notes 136 and 138.

96. Münch, "Obrigkeit im Vaterstand."

97. Cf. Erik Erikson, *Young Man Luther* (New York, 1958). Interestingly enough, John Wycliff, the pre-Luther English Protestant, also connected the Fourth Commandment to honor the father and mother to the heavenly as well as the earthly father. In this he was joined by Herolt, the author of *der Sele Trost*, and Rus. The extension of the commandment to the priests as fathers was widespread, the extension to worldly magistrates and to mother church somewhat less so. John Wycliff, "The Poor Caitiff" or "Pauper rusticus," quoted in Geffcken, *Bildercatechismus*, col. 215; cf. cols. 182–183, 198, 204, 210; and pp. 69, 70–71, 72.

A similar point about the impact of theological conceptions on the conceptualization of political relationships in the medieval period has been made by Kantorowicz, *King's Two Bodies*. His discussion of *patria* is here particularly relevant: "There was nevertheless one domain in which the idiom *patria* retained, as it were, its full original meaning and its former emotional values, if only by transference and in a transcendentalized form: in the language of the Church. The Christian, according to the teaching of the early Church and the Fathers, had become the citizen of a city in another world. His true *patria* was the Kingdom of Heaven, the celestial city of Jerusalem. . . . From the outset, therefore, one should at least consider the possibility whether— before the full impact of legal and humanistic doctrines became effective—the new territorial concept of *patria* did not perhaps develop as a re-secularized offshoot of the Christian tradition and whether the new patriotism did not thrive also on ethical values transferred back from the *patria* in heaven to the polities on earth." Ibid., pp. 234–235; cf. Kantorowicz' conclusion in the affirmative, pp. 267–268.

98. For the signers, see above, chapter three, notes 61 and 62.

99. In the German phrase, the Rat was considered or begged to act out of its presumed "vätterliche liebe" for its subject. Interestingly enough, the older invocation of God as "Schopfer" still appeared, although the invocation of the saints was replaced by a reference to the

Trinity. The testator was presumably a devout Catholic; at any rate, she included a bequest to a *Domherr*, a member of the cathedral chapter. HStAM, Regensburg Testamente.

100. The sole exception was Jacobus Bronn, *tabellionus publicus*, who wrote only one extant will opened before the Rat. The will was written in Latin for a Scotsman residing in the city. HStAM, Regensburger Testamente.

101. "So bfyll ich mein arma Sundige sell, dürch Cristüm meinen Erloser und seligmacher meinem dreüem Lieben gott und vatter voll aller gnaden und parmherzigkheydtt, In seine gwaldige handt amen bfyl Im auch meine verlasne khinder alß einem Reichrn vatter der sy khan erhallten vor allem ubll amen." Will of Elisabeth, widow of Hans Cammerer (1) and Karl Gartner (2) (9 March 1554); HStAM, Regensburger Testamente.

102. To each of them, she left a "keepsake," expressing the hope that they would oversee the pious nurturing of her orphans: "solche khleina leth und gdenckzaichen wollen meine günstige herrn ayden und schweger von mir Im pesten anemen. mein darpey gdencken. und Im um gottes willen Meine waisen Lasen bfollen sein mit Cristlicher vermanüng daß sy gozfürchtig und wol erzogen wern." Ibid.

103. "Und bin Zu Irer E.E.F.E.W. des demütigen getrostens, sy werden deßhalb meinen Universal Erben in gunstigem Vätterlichem Schutz, doch der Religion halben, Unbetrangt halten und bevohlen sein lassen." Will of Katherina, widow of Hans Haider (1586); HStAM, Regensburger Testamente.

104. "Und bitte hierauf einen Erbarn Camerer unnd Rathe alhie, als meine gönstige liebe Oberherrn unnd Vätter gehorsamblichen, das Ire Wl: Jeztgemelten meinen lieben Geschwistrigeten solche Ire *Legata* zum besten, in ein Erbar Löblich vormundambt legen, und Zum besten erhalten wöllen." Will of Michael Schuester, bath-house attendant (1581); HStAM, Regensburger Testamente. On the Vormundamt, see below, notes 119–120.

105. "Ferner und Zum Andern befihle ich mein Liebe hausfraw Margareth meinem Lieben threwen Gott und einem Erbarn Cammerer und Rath dieser Löblichen und uralten Reichs Statt Regenspurg, die wöllen sich irer mit gnaden und umb Gottes willen annemen, Ir die Zeit ires Lebens, weil sie hie kheine bluets freund hat, allen gunstigen und vätterlichen willen erweisen, solches wirdt der getrewe und Barmherzige Gott, Als ein Vatter der waisen und Richter wittwen nicht unbelohnet lassen [Psalm 68.] dessen bin ich in meinem herzen gewiß." Will of Lorenz Ludwig from Amberg, minister in St. Lazarus, Regensburg (1599); HStAM, Regensburger Testamente. Ludwig's will was also one of the few to refer to the "fatherland"—in his case, apparently his natal city, Amberg.

The magistrate's rôle as protector of women and children had been stressed—and linked to God—by Philipp Melanchthon as early as 1528 in his instructions to the parish visitors of Saxony: "Wer nu Gott also ynn der öbrickeit sehen möchte, der würde die öbrickeit hertzlichen lieb haben. . . . Wenn du wissest, das yemand dein kind von dem todte errettet hette, du würdest dem selbigen gütlichen dancken. Warumb bistu denn nicht danckbar der öbrickeit, die dich, deyne kinder, dein weib, von teglichem mord errettet? . . . Darumb, wenn du weib und kind ansihest, so soltu gedencken, dis sind Gottes gaben, die ich durch öbrickeit behalten mag, Und als lieb du deine kinder hast, also lieb soltu auch die öbrickeit habe." *Unterricht der Visitatorn*, preface by Luther, fol. Dii.

106. "Zu Executoren und volstreckern dis meines lezten willens, Bitt Ich demutiglichen und Zum höchsten, Die Edlen, Ehrnuessten, Fürsichtigen, Ersamen und Weysen Herrn Camerer und Rathe, der Statt Regenspurg sie wöllen inen obemellten Jörgen Mair, meinen liben hauswurt, dann meine lieben Söne, alß Endresen, Georgen, Thobiasen und Jeremiasen, die Gruenwaldt trewlich lassen befohlen sein So wol die *Execution* dises meines lezten Willens, wie dann mein Vertrauen Zu inen dis falß steet. Das wird der Allmechtige, der ein Vater aller Wittib und Weysen ist, inen reichlich vergellten." Will of Margaret Kradl, widow of Hans Grünewaldt, wife of Georg Meier (1588); HStAM, Regensburger Testamente. The fact that this will was written by Paulus Hartingius, an imperial notary—and wills written by imperial notaries were generally lacking in such formulations—strongly suggests that Margaret Kradl herself was reponsible for the language, especially the adapted biblical quotation.

107. Will of Wolfgang Waldner (1582); HStAM, Regensburger Testamente. The passage is quoted at length above, chapter two, note 44.

108. "Ich danckhe auch einem Erbarn Cammerer unnd Rathe alhie, als meinen lieben Herren und vättern, das Sie mich im Praedigambt und bei diser rainen Kirchen, undter Irem genedigen Schuz, uber Zwainzig Jar, unnd iezt in meinem schwachen alter mit reicher undterhaltung versorget haben, Gott wöll Inen seinen reichen seegen dafur geben. . . . Inen [my children] allen

wol bewust, was fur Vätterlicher trew und guetes, die Zeit meiner Haushaltung, Ich an Inen gethan, das Ich es offtmals lieber uber mir, dann uber Inen, hab ausgeen lassen." Ibid.

109. ". . . dieweil Ein Erbar Rathe, obgemelt meine Liebe Herrn, von der Zeit An, Ich hiehero einkhommen, mich nit Allein Zum Burger Aufgenommen, sonnder auch vor Andern Zw ainem Irem Ambt, mich dest Leichter Zuernehren, unnd Aufzuenthalten, unnd Zu Annder meiner wolfarth, gannz vätterlich befürdert, und gehalten darumben Ich mich dann gegen denselben höchster dannckhbarkhait schuldig erkhenne, Demnach ich nit unbillich bewegt widerumben mit ainem khlainen Legaten oder verehrung Zwbedennckhen." Will of Wolfgang Klopfinger, Bürger and scribe in municipal salt-tax office (1572); HStAM, Regensburger Testamente.

110. Martin Luther, "Predigt über das 2. Buch Mose" (29 October 1525?), WA 16:488.

111. See above, notes 81 and 86.

112. "Eben solche imbevustige lieb treget der Herr Christus gegen uns, die er bewiesen in dem, das er seinen Vatter den gehorsam geleistet, sich willig unsert halben in das leiden eingelassen." Bartholomeus Rosinus, "Karfreitagspredigt auf Jesaias 53" (1577); notes in Theodoric and Bartholomeus Rosinus, and Samuel Gallus, *Passion gepredigt 1577* (paper ms., 1577), fol. 123; StBR, Rat. civ. 563.

113. ". . . so müssen doch ihre Weyßheiten, als die ihr Ambt der Obrigkeit bishero lieber mit Vätterlicher sanfftmüt und gelindigkeit, dann strenger schörpff und ernstlicher Straff, gegen ihrer lieben Burgerschafft und gemaindt führen wöllen, mit betrübtem Hertzen und schmertzen erfahren, das die Vätterliche lieb und naygung nicht allein zu gebürlichem gehorsam nichts früchten noch verfangen will. . . ." "Die Policey betreffend" (1591), Kayser, *Dekretensammlung*, no. XXXIII, pp. 87–88.

114. I direct the reader's attention to Quentin Skinner's argument from the preface to *The Foundations of Modern Political Thought* (Cambridge, 1978), vol. 1, pp. xii–xiii.

115. ". . . aus der Oeconomia odder haushaltung, mus die Politia odder landregirung, als aus einem brunnequel, entspringen und herkommen." Menius, *An die hochgeborne Furstin*, fol. Biiii. Cf. Otto Brunner, "Das 'ganze Haus' und die alteuropäische 'Ökonomik,' " *Neue Wege der Sozialgeschichte. Vorträge und Aufsätze* (Göttingen, 1956), p. 44, referring to Jost Trier, "Vater. Versuch einer Etymologie," *Zeitschrift der Savigny-stiftung für Rechtsgeschichte: germanistische Abteilung* 65 (1947), pp. 259–260.

116. "Es ist aber mit dem allein noch nicht gnug, das frome kinder yhren Got, schepffer herr und vater allein furchten, sondern sollen auch erkennen, das er yhnen wil gnedig und barmhertzig sein, und sich ynn allem gegen yhnen der massen und also erzeygen, wie ein trewer, freundlicher, lieber vater gegen seinen geliebten kindern thun sol. . . ." Menins, *An die hochgeborne Furstin* fol. Jiiii'.

117. Cf. ibid., chapters XII–XIII, fols. Liiii–Mii', on the treatment of servants/apprentices and the obedience they owed masters.

118. Cf. the distinction drawn between the attitudes of servants and mercenaries to their masters and children to their fathers, in a sermon by Bernard of Clairvaux on the love of God: "Est qui confitetur domino quoniam potens est: & est qui confitetur quoniam sibi bonus est: & item qui confitetur quoniam simpliciter bonus est. Primus servus est: et timet sibi. Secundus mercenarius: et cupit sibi. Tertius filius: et defert patri." Bernard of Clairvaux, "Sermo de charitate"; quoted from *Mellifui devotique doctoris . . . opus preclarum suos complectens sermones de tempore, de sanctis & super cantica canticorum Aliosque plures eius sermones & sententias*, ed. Andrea Bocardus ([Paris]: Iehan Petit, 1508), fol. CCxcvi = Migne, vol. 182, col. 995. The "Sermo de charitate," regarded as a separate work, but generally following immediately after the "Sermo de diligendo deo" in many of the fifteenth and sixteenth century editions I have examined, is in Migne's edition a part of Bernard's "Sermo de diligendo deo." The thoughtful editor of one early edition separated the two sermons by almost 250 pages but prefaced the second with this note: "Hic sermo in eo exemplari ende est excerptus intitulatur sermo de charitate: sed verius in multis aliis exemplaribus libello de diligendo deum annectitur: ut unus sit duntaxat idemque tractatus." *Opuscula* (Brixia: Angelus et Jacobus de Britannicis fratres, 1494/1495), fol. Nii' (hand numbered 316'). Cf. Bernard of Clairvaux, *Opera* (Louvain: Jacobus de giuncti, 1530), fol. 276.

119. "Got dem almechtigen zu lobe, und gemaynem nutze zu gut." "Die Errichtung des Vormund-Amts betreffend" (1537), Kayser, *Dekretensammlung*, no. VIII, p. 17.

120. "Als dann auch keyn bestendigers und Got gefelliges Regiment ist, oder seyn kan, Dann woe soliche verstendige und wolgezogne leüte regieren und regiert werden." Ibid. The city council acknowledged its responsibility in this direction not only before its official acceptance of Lutheranism, but before Luther himself had broken away from the Catholic church. The few

pages of accounts which survive for the late-medieval city reveal payments to the women and men into whose care the Cammerer and Rat had entrusted orphans and abandoned infants on an individual basis. HStAM, Gemeiners Nachlaß 26, "Ainitz ausgebn" (1505), fols. 1, 2', 3', 4, 4', 5, 9, 9', 10', 12'. On the Vormundamt itself, see Ludwig Lindner, *Das bürgerliche Recht der Reichsstadt Regensburg* (Ph.D. dissertation; Regensburg, 1908), pp. 49–54. Cf. discussion of concilliar Caritas in chapter two, note 62, above.

121. "Darzu auch, in sonderheyt, die Eltern spüren und sehen mögen das nach irem absterben ire kinder nit verlassen, sonder durch der Oberkeyten fürsorg nit weniger bedacht, fürsehen, und erzogen werden, als ob sie, die Eltern, ungeverlichen, selbst noch lebetn, und dabey weren." Ibid., p. 18.

122. The phrase is "Vätterliche heymsuchung Gottis." "Vermahnung und Gebot, etliche fürnehme ärgerliche Laster betreffend" (1543), Kayser, *Dekretensammlung*, no. XIII, pp. 29, 30.

123. "Damit dan ein Erbar Rate alhie, als die ordenliche Oberkeyt, nit geacht werden möchte, als ob solche schendliche Sunde unnd Laster mit irem wissen und willen geschöhen, sonder das, zu irer entschuldigung vor Gott und der Welt, Ir billich mißfallen heirin gespürt werde. . . ." Ibid., p. 31.

124. "Nach dem der Almechtig gütig GOtt, Unser Himlischer Vatter, in diser letzten Zeit der Welt, sein Heiligs Göttlichs Wort, sampt den hochwirdigen Sacramenten, dardurch wir zu ime kommen, und lernen selig werden, aus der tieffen Finsternuß des Bapstums, Sonderlich aber am ersten dem Teutschland, Unserm lieben Vatterland, widerumb auffs rainest und reichlichst herfür scheinen lassen. . . ." "Religions-Sachen betreffend" (1566), Kayser, *Dekretensammlung*, no. XIX, p. 48.

125. "So vermanen sie demnach hiemit gantz trewlich und väterlich, alle ire Unterthane, Burger und verwandte, das sie sich zu solcher irer verordneten, Pfarrers, und anderer Predicanten und Kirchendiener Predigen, und der hochwirdigen Sacrament raichung, fleissig finden, dieselben auch gern und offt besuchen, anhören und empfahen. . . ." Ibid., p. 50.

126. "Die sollen als verächter Gottes und der Obrigkeiten, sampt deß Heiligen Reichs auffgerichten Abschiden, und darinn verleibten Religionsfriden, . . . mit ernst darumb gestrafft werden." Ibid., pp. 51–52.

127. In the last decades of the century the increasing incidence of joint wills in which children were neither mentioned nor their eventuality specifically excluded, in which property was not specified but only reserved to the surviving partner, and which were opened more than one year after the making of the will suggests that these wills, rather than being made late in life in contemplation of a coming death, were made shortly after a couple's marriage, possibly as a surrogate marriage contract. Although reference was made in all of these virtually identical wills to God the Father and to the Trinity, they included no apostrophe to the Rat as "Vater," "Weisheit," or "Obrigkeit"—or, indeed, in any other guise.

128. Gerald Strauss, "Protestant Dogma and City Government: The Case of Nuremberg," *Past and Present* 36 (1967), pp. 37–58.

129. "Unser Son Petro, dem soll nicht mehr den 50 Fl. für alles folgen . . . weil Er seinen Beruff und studirn verlass, von mir entlauffen, Sich Zu Zwickaw ubel gehalten unnd von dannen wider weg gelauft, seine Mutter Zu Tode dadurch gekrencket. Mir ganz unkindlich ungehorsam wonen, unnd mich In die hoechste todliche Gremug bracht, Unnd In des nie seine buß bewiß, noch verzeihung gesucht." Will of Bartholomeus Rosinus, Lutheran minister and *Superintendent* in Regensburg (1584); HStAM, Regensburger Testamente.

130. "Ein vatter kan ehe zehen kinder erneeren, denn zehen kinder einen vatter." Johann Agricola, *Das ander teyl gemainer Tewscher Sprichwörter, mit ihrer außlegung, hat fünff halb hundert newer wörtter* (Nuremberg: Johann Stüchs, 1530), fol. 33'.

131. Now in the Alte Pinakotek, Munich. For the inscription and a discussion of the painting, see Carl C. Christensen, *Art and the Reformation in Germany* (Athens, Ohio, 1979), pp. 181–206.

In contrast to others who saw in such disobedience evidence that the end of the world was at hand, Agricola proved the unfortunate antiquity of children's tendency to disregard their parents despite the sacrifices their parents had made for them; if this had not always been the case, he wrote, God would not have directed the Fourth Commandment to children alone. Agricola, *Das ander teyl gemainer Tewscher Sprichwörte*, fol. 34'.

132. Here, as in all following references to children in the wills and the analysis using them, "children" is understood to refer to biological offspring, regardless of age, and regardless of domicile. Not surprisingly, tension between parent and child appears to have increased with the child's adolescence and adulthood.

133. Cf. *Laienspiegel* (Augsburg, 1509), fols. Fiii–Fiii'; (Straßburg, 1511), fols. XXIIII–XXIIII'; (Augsburg, 1512), fols. XXXIX–XXXIX'; (Straßburg, 1514), fols. XXXII–XXXII'; (Straßburg, 1518), fols. XXXII–XXXII'; (Straßburg, 1527), fols. XXXIII'–XXXIIII; (Straßburg, 1530), fols. XXXIII'–XXXIIII; (Straßburg, 1532), fols. XXXIII'–XXXIIII; (Straßburg, 1538), fol. XXIX; and (Straßburg, 1544), fol. XXIX with *Reformacion der Kayserlichen Stat Nuremberg* (Nuremberg: Hieronymus Holtzel, 1503), fols. 55–55', and *Der Stat Nürmberg verneüte Reformation* (Nuremberg: Valentin Geißler, 1564), fols. 179'–181.

134. "Zum Neundten, Nach dem mein ehleibliche thochter, Margaretha, Conradten Schilttennpergers, webers am Regenn alhie bei Regennspurg hausfraw, Sich Inn Zeittenn ires lebenns, gegen mir, unnd meinem lieben hauswirt, Irem vatter seeligenn, nit als ein gehorsam frumbkindt, erzaigt unnd gehaltten, Sunder in Irem Junckhfreulichen Stanndt, Inn ein unzuchtig ergerlich lebenn gerathen, unnd ausser der ehe, Ein khindt erobert, volgennts sich auch one mein, und Ires vattern, meines lieben haußwirts seeligen wissen, unnd willen verheurat Unnd Inn Summa sich ye unnd allwegen, bis auf dise Stunndt dermassen mit schmachreden unnd sunsten, gegenn mir hören lassen, Das Ich guette fuegliche ursachenn gehabt, Sy mein Thochter Margaretha, Inn disem meinem Testament, unnd lezsten willen, allerdinng Zu umbgeen, unnd auszuschliessen, Damit aber diser mein lezster will, nach meinem absterben, desto weniger angefochtenn werde. . . ." Will of Margaretha, widow of Leonhart Aichenseer, Bürger (1557); HStAM, Regensburger Testamente.

135. ". . . alles unnd yedes vermein unnd vermach ich, meinem lieben Sone., Hannsen Aichenseer, Von welichem mir vil Khinndtliche lieb unnd trew widerfarn." Ibid.

136. "Und Wiewol sich unser beeder Sohn Hans Heinrich, also, wie Menigclich bewusst, verhalten, dz Wir Ihne wol und billich von Rechts wegen gar von Unser beeder Verlassung außzeschliessen fueg und Recht hetten, . . . Wiewol Wir sonst ein mehrers Dann Ihme gebüert, auf Ihne gewendet, Auch ein mehrers Unß Zethuen schuldig were, Welches Wir doch aus vätterlicher und Müetterlicher Zunaigung." Will of Heinrich and Margaretha Schmidt (1584); HStAM, Regensburger Testamente. The bitterness of the chronicle entries was reflected in the section heading: "Hernach vollgt meines Sunns Hannsen Hainrichen Schmidts Alle gepflegte Hanndlung so er gegen mir unnd seiner Muetter geuebt hatt Sambt der schullden unnd Anderm von dem 1572 Jarrs An bis äuf das 1583 Jars Alls er von weib unnd khindt An unser frauen tag in der fasten bey der nacht hinweckh gezogen Alles Ime zur gewerung wan Im gott wider Anhaimbs helffen sollt." Heinrich Schmidt, *Item In dissem Buech ist beschriben Allerlay Handlungen so mich Hainrichen Schmidt der Zeyt Stadthauptman zu Regenspurg sambt den Mainigen von Jharn zu Jharn betroffen unnd durch unns ist gehandellt worden wellchs von dem 1523 Jar Anfacht unnd ferner bis Ins 1583 Jars beschribn worden unnd gendt ist gott der Almechtig gebe sein genad ferner Ammen.?* (ms. begun 1583); AHVR, M.S. Ratisb. 357, fols. 23–38; esp. fols. 23, 25', 29', 30 ("Aus vetterlicher lieb"). I am preparing an edition of this chronicle.

137. At issue was what Schmidt described as a resurgence of the Manichean heresy ("Allte verdampte Seckht der Maniches") among the pastor Oppius, Jeronymous Pister, the sexton Vireckl, and the school rector Haubolt. The school rector was dismissed after "ain Erber Camer und Ratthe Deen pforer und khirchendiner auch den Reckhtor zum offern malls Ermant und gannz fetterlichen gewernet sich in sollchem woll Zubedenckhen." The others attempted to acquit themselves of the charges after "ain Erber Camer unnd Ratthe aus vätterlicher Sorgfelltigkhait zu Andern stenden des Heilligen Reichs und sunderlichen zu denen dy der worn Augspurgischen Confession verwant umb Ire Censur geschickht," but the Rat found itself forced "zur dem die sach bey dern unverstendigen* burgern die disen betrug nit verstanden von tag zu tag Jhe mer Aingewurtzlt Auch da sy lenger Zugesechen mit der Zeitt Ain Auflauf gepern Dörhin haben sy Ain Ertzney miessen Erdenckhen damit das faul fleisch vom leib Ausgeschnitten werdt und die ubrigen glider frisch und gesund pleibn." They therefore dismissed the pastor himself. Schmidt, *Allerlay Handlungen*; AHVR, M.S. Ratisb. 357, fols. 41–41'.

*The adjective here seems to refer to a willful blindness on the part of the Bürger rather than to hint at a lack of education or money among the pastor's followers; Schmidt later referred to the group that left the city to follow their pastor as "zum thail Alle fast wolhabent." Ibid., fol. 41'.

138. Agricola, *Das ander teyl gemainer Tewtscher Sprichwörter*, fols. 121'–122.

139. On remarriage in early modern European society, see Barbara Diefendorf, "Remarriage in Sixteenth-Century Paris," *Journal of Family History* 7 (1982), pp. 379–395; J. Dupâquier et al., eds., *Marriage and Remarriage in Populations of the Past* (London, 1981); Christopher R. Friedrichs, "Marriage, Family, and Social Structure in an Early Modern German Town," *Historical Papers*, Canadian Historical Association (1975), pp. 17–40; J. Hajnal, "European Marriage Patterns in

Perspective," in *Population in History*, ed. D. V. Glass and D. E. C. Eversley (London, 1965), pp. 101–143; Ralph A. Houlbrooke, "Death and the Broken Family," *The English Family 1450–1700* (London, 1984), pp. 202–227; John Knodel and Katherine A. Lynch, "The Decline of Remarriage: Evidence from German Village Populations in the Eighteenth and Nineteenth Centuries," *Journal of Family History* 10 (1985), pp. 34–59; Johann Peter Süssmilch, *Die Göttliche Ordnung in den Veränderungen des menschlichen Geschlechts, aus der Geburt, dem Tode und der Fortpflanzung derselben erwiesen* (Berlin, 1775).

140. For a more positive interpretation of the impact of Lutheranism on the family, see Steven Ozment, *When Fathers Ruled* (Cambridge, Mass., 1983).

141. "Sovil aber meinen Sun Niclasen belangt, Allweil ich denselben ein ehrlich handtwerckh lernen lassen, Sich aber von solchem begeben, und wider meinen Willen Zu dem Jesuitischen Schwarm, also von der rainen Lehr Göttliches worts abgefallen, geschlagen. . . ." Will of Friderich Sebaldt, Lutheran deacon and *Kirchendiener* (1588); HStAM, Regensburger Testamente.

142. "Unnd wann auch meynn *adoptirter* suen unnd erb, von der rechten waren Christlichen kirchen unnd Religion, der Augspurgischen confession abfallen solte, darvon Ine Got genediglich behüetten wolle, Alßdann soll er durch di obrigkheit, diser stat Regennspurg, umb Zwaythausennt gulden gestrafft, Unnd dieselbe suma geltß, Zuerhalttung der Kirchen bemelter Augspurgischen *Confession* angelegt werdenn." Will of Edl and Gestreng Herr Georg Weynsbrünner, Ritter von Salzburg, Pfandherr zu Eggmühl (1562); HStAM, Regensburger Testamente.

143. *Der Stat Nürmberg verneüte Reformation* (Nuremberg: Valentin Geißler, 1564), fols. 179', 181.

# Bibliography

ARCHIVAL SOURCES

### Regensburg, Stadtarchiv
[StAR]

*Hannsgrafenamtbuch*: Pol. III 57.

*Ratswahlbücher*: 1500–1539, M.S. Ratisb. IAc 1
1540–1557, M.S. Ratisb. IAc 2
1558–1575, M.S. Ratisb. IAc 3
1576–1599, M.S. Ratisb. IAc 4.

Dimpfel, Christoph Gottlieb. *Ratisbona Nova Antiqua* (1740). MS Ratisb. IAe2 Nr. 1–5.

Grünewaldt, Franciscus Hieremia. *Ratisbonae oder Summarische Beschreibung der Uralten Nahmhafften Stadt Regenspurg Auf- und Abnehmung, und wie man sie heut nach siehet; deren führnehmsten Geist- und weltlichen Zierden, darum sie sowol heut als ein Kayl. Gefreyte Reichs-Stadt, als vor Alters ein Bayl. Königl. und Fürstl. Residenz und Haupt-Stadt, ansehnl. u. beruhmt ist* (1615). MS Ratisb. IAe2 Nr. 9.

*Das sogenannte schwarze oder pergamentene Buch d. ao. 1526*. Pol. I 1.

*Schultheisen und dessen Gerichts-Ordnung de Anno 1514* (ms., 1514). MS Ratisb. IAf Nr. 10.

Partial listing of Ratsherren, last decades of 15th century (compiled at end of 18th century?). Hist. II Nr. 9.

### Regensburg, Archiv des Historischen Vereins für Oberpfalz und Regensburg
[AHVR]

*Index Generalis Secundum ordinem Pulpitorum confectus ostendens, quae scripta singulis voluminibus contineantur; Ein gemein Register Uber alle bucher, so in eines erbarn Camerer und Rhats Liberei alhie zu Regenspurg an Ketten, gelegt sind, und dieselben nach einander auf den Pulpiten ligen, etc. Wievil auch Tractetlein in einem ieden buch zusamen gebunden sind* (compiled after 1574, possibly in 1593 by Jonas Paulus Wolf; cf. Ineichen-Eder, *Mittelalterliche Bibliothekskataloge*, p. 473). AA R 44.

Linda, Johann. *Warhaffte beschreibung deß Acts, so Auff Ableyben deß Aller Durchleuchtigisten, Großmechtigisten Fürsten und Herrn Herrn Maximiliani, Deß Anndern Römischen Khaysers etc. Hochlöblichster und seeligster gedächtnus, mit Irer Mayt. Leich und derselben Clag, besinckhnus, und anndern Ceremonien Alhie zu Regenspurg gehalten worden. Item Wie sich Camerer und Rathe gegen dem Auch Aller Durchleuchtigisten Großmechtigisten und unüberwindlichisten Dazumal Angehenden Römischen Khayser Rudolpho dem Anndern, dieses nhamens Unserm Alle genedigisten Herrn, Biß auff Irer Khayß: Mayt Abreysen, mit der Huldigung, Clag, Glückhwuntschung und Schanckhung, erzaigt und verhallten. Anno 1576* (early 18th-century copy made by Christoph Georg Gumpelzhaimer of ms. dated 1576). Ms. Ratisb. 105.

Schmidt, Heinrich. *Item In dissem Buech ist beschriben Allerlay Handlungen so mich Hainrichen Schmidt der Zeyt Stadthauptman zu Regenspurg sambt den Mainigen von Jharn zu Jharn betroffen unnd durch unns ist gehandellt worden wellchs von dem 1523 Jar Anfacht unnd ferner bis Ins 1583 Jars beschribn worden unnd gendt ist gott der Almechtig gebe sein genad ferner Ammen.?* (begun 1583). Ms. Ratisb. 357 [an edition and commentary on this chronicle is in preparation].

Zerzog, Adolf von. *Geschriebene Regensburger Chronik samt Urkundensammlung* (description of death and funeral of Kaiser Maximilian II; 1835). Ms. Ratisb. 105.

### Regensburg, Staatliche Bibliothek
#### [StBR]

Ehinger, Elia. *Catalogus Bibliothecae Amplissimae Reipub. Ratisbonensis* (Johann Rhelino, amanuensis, 1638). Rat. civ. 430.

Rosinus, Theodoric and Bartholomeus, and Samuel Gallus. *Passion gepredigt 1577* (paper ms., 1577). Rat. civ. 563.

Sneckner, Erhart. "Rechnung Register Erhart Sneckner Paumaister ym LXXVI jar und yn das LXXVII jar." (1475/1476). Rat. civ. 152.

### Munich, Bayerische Staatsbibliothek
### Handschriftenabteilung
#### [StBM]

Gölgel, Johann Georg. *Lebens-Beschreibung aller Herren Räthen und Consulanten Welche in des H: Röm. ReichsFreyen Stadt Regensburg Von der Zeit der eingeführten Evangelischen Religion an, biß auf gegenwärtige Zeit gewesen* (1706). Cgm. 2014.

Gölgel, Johann Georg. *Regenspurgische Kirchen-Historia oder Kurzer Bericht von der durch Gottes Gnade in des Häyligen Römischen Reichs freyen Stadt Regenspurg eingeführten Evangelischen Religion* (1707). Cgm. 2012.

### Munich, Bayerisches Hauptstaatsarchiv
#### [HStAM]

Material relating to discussions of 1485/1486. R L Regensburg 596.

*Regensburger kaiserliche Regimentsordnung* (1500). R L Regensburg 376 [contemporaneous paper copy with officeholders' names: R L Regensburg 380].

*Regensburger kaiserliche Regimentsordnung* (1514). R L Regensburg 381.

Regensburg Rathaus inventory (end of 16th century). R L Regensburg 546.

Regensburg wills (15th–18th centuries, arranged alphabetically). Regensburger Testamente. fasc. 1–102.

Gemeiners Nachlaß. (41 cartons of miscellaneous material in rough chronological order).

Material concerning relations with Bavaria. Kurbayern Äußeres Archiv.

## PUBLISHED PRIMARY SOURCES

Academia Complutensi, ed. *Novum testamentum grece et latine in academia complutensi noviter impressum.* Alcalá de Henares: Arnaldus Guillelmus de Brocario, 1514.

Academia Complutensi, ed. *Vetus testamentum multiplici lingua nunc primo impressum. Et imprimis Pentateuchus Hebraico Greco atque Chaldaico idiomate. Ad iuncta unicuique sua latina interpretatione.* Alcalá de Henares: Arnaldus Guillelmus de Brocario, 1517.

Academia Complutensi, ed. *Vocabularium hebraicum atque chaldaicum totius veteris testamenti cum aliis tractatibus prout infra in prefatione continetur in academia complutensi noviter impressum.* Alcalá de Henares: Arnaldus Guillelmus de Brocario, 1515.

Agricola, Johann. *Das ander teyl gemainer Tewscher Sprichwörter, mit ihrer außlegung, hat fünff halb hundert newer wörtter.* Nürnberg: Johann Stüchs, 1530.

Agricola, Johann. *Dreyhundert Gemeyner Sprichwörter, der wir Deudschen uns gebrauchen, und doch nicht wissen woher sie komen.* Leipzig: Michael Blum, 1530.

Angermann, Jacob. *Carmen heroicum, de dignitate et praestantia politici Magistratus. Amplissimis prudentissimis, generis nobilitate, doctrina et authoritate, omnique virtutum splendore praestantissimis viris, Dominis Coss. Consularibus, reliquisque celeberrimae Imperialis Reipub: Ratisbonensis Senatoribus, Dominis atqu; Mecoenatibus suis summa fide perpetuaq; observantia colendis.* Marburg: Paulus Egenolphus, 1598. StBR, 8º Rat. civ. 655.

Augustinus, Aurelius. *Opera omnia,* ed. Desiderius Erasmus. Basel: Johann Froben, 1528 [volumes 1–7 dated 1528; volumes 8–10, and table of contents and index bound at front of first volume dated 1529].

Augustinus, Aurelius. *Opera omnia,* ed. J.-P. Migne. *Patrologiae cursus completus. Series latina prior.* Volumes 32–47. Paris.

Augustinus, Aurelius. *Opuscula plurima.* Straßburg: Martin Flach, 1491.

Boccaccio. *De mulieribus claris,* translated into German as *Des Giovanni Boccaccio Buch: von den berühmten Frawen* by Hainrich Steinhöwel. Ulm: Johann Zainer, 1473. reprinted by Karl Drescher [Bibliothek des litterarischen Vereins in Stuttgart 205]. Tübingen, 1895.

Bodenstein von Karlstadt, Andreas. *Von abtuhung der Bylder, Und das keyn Betdler unther den Christen seyn soll.* Wittenberg: Nikell Schytlentz, 1522.

Boll, Walter. "Albrecht Altdorfers Nachlaß," *Münchner Jahrbuch der bildenden Kunst* N.F. 13 (1938/1939), pp. 91–102.

Bonaventure. *Lignum vitae.* In *Seraphici doctoris S. Bonaventurae decem opuscula ad theologiam mysticam stectantia.* Quaracchi, 1965.

Breitenbach, Edgar. *Speculum humanae salvationis, eine typengeschichtliche Untersuchung.* Strasbourg, 1930.

Bullinger, Heinrich. *Ein schön spil von der geschicht der Edlen Römerin Lucretia unnd wie der Tyrannisch küng Tarquinius Superbus von Rhom vertriben und sunderlich von der standhafftigkeit Iunii Bruti des Ersten Consuls zü Rhom uff Sontag den andern tag Mertzens im 1533 jar zü Basel gehallten.* Basel: Thomas Wolff, 1533. Reprinted in Heinrich Bullinger and Hans Sachs, *Lucretia- Dramen.* ed. Horst Hartmann. Leipzig, 1973. pp. 39–97.

*Christliche Vermanung Wie die vor der Beicht Communion und Predig zu Regenspurg inn der newen Pfarr, der Gemeine offentlich fürgelesen werden.* Regensburg: Heinrich Geißler, 1567. Schottenloher 265. StBR, Rat. civ. 162ª.

Clarius Brizianus, Isidorus, ed. *Vulgata aeditio veteris ac novi testamenti, quorum alterum ad Hebraicam, alterum ad Graecam emendatum est diligentissimè.* Venice: Peter Schoeffer of Germany, 1542.

*Concilium tridentinum, diariorum, actarum, epistolorum, tractatum nova collectio,* ed. Societas Goerresiana. Freiburg, 1901–.

Donauer, Christoph. *Epigrammatum selectorum, res varias, suo quodam modo, explicantium, fasciculus. Cum religionis, justiciae, pacis, ad S.P.Q. Ratisponensem, prosopopoeia.* Nuremberg: officina typographica Gerlachiana, 1592. StBR, Rat. civ. 501.

Drach, Johannes. "Der 117. Psalm ausgelegt." Regensburg: Hans Kohl, 1541. Schottenloher 77.

Durandus de Saint-Pourçain, Guillelmus. *Lectura prima super Sentencias.* In *La controverse sur le péché originel au début du XIV^e siècle. Textes inédits,* ed. Raymond Martin, O.P. [Spicilegium sacrum lovaniense études et documents 10 (Louvain, 1930)].

*Ein Vermanung Unnd unterricht deren so die Absolution irer sünden und das Hochwirdig Sacrament zur sterckungs ires glaubens empfahen wollen wie die alle Sambstag nach der Vesper zu Regenspurg ab der Canzel offenlich verlesen wirdt.* Regensburg: Hans Kohl, c. 1544. Schottenloher 89. StBR, 8° Polem. 1310, 3.

Erasmus, Desiderius. *Ein nutzliche underwisung eines Christenlichen fürsten wol zü regieren.* Zurich: Christoph Froschauer, 1521.

Erasmus, Desiderius. *Hyperaspistae liber secundus adversus librum Martini Lutheri, cui titulum fecit Seruum arbitrium.* Basel: Johann Froben, 1527.

Erasmus, Desiderius. *Novum instrumentum omne, diligenter recognitum & emendatum, non solum ad graecum veritatem, verumetiam ad multorum utriusque linguae codicum, eorumque veterum simul & emendatorum fidem, postremo ad probatissimorum autorum citationem, emendationem & interpretationem, praecipue, Origenis, Chrysostomi, Cyrilli, Vulgarii, Hieronymi, Cypriani, Ambrosii, Augustini, una cum Annotationibus, quae lectorem doceant, quid qua ratione mutatum sit. Quisquis igitur amas veram Theologiam, lege, cognosce, ac deinde iudica. Neque statim offendere, si quid mutatum offenderis, sed expende, num in melius mutatum sit.* Basel: Johann Froben, February 1516.

Erasmus, Desiderius. *Novum Testamentum omne, multo quam antehac diligentius recognitum, emendatum ac translatum, non solum ad Graecum veritatem, verumetiam ad multorum utriusque linguae codicum, eorumque veterum simul & emendatorum fidem, postremo ad probatissimorum autorum citationem, emendationem & interpretationem, praecipue Origenis, Athanasii Nazianzeni, Chrysostomi, Cyrilli, Theophylacti, Hieronymi, Cypriani, Ambrosii, Hilarii, Augustini, una cum Annotationibus recognitis, ac magna accessione locupletatis, quae lectorem doceant, quid qua ratione mutatum sit. Quisquis igitur amas veram Theologiam, lege, cognosce, ac deinde iudica. Neque statim offendere, si quid mutatum offenderis, sed expende, num in melius mutatum sit. Nam morbus est non iudicium, damnare quod non inspexeris. SALVO VBIQVE ET ILLABEFACTO ECCLESIAE IVDICIO.* Basel: Johann Froben, 1519.

*Die erste deutsche Bibel,* ed. W. Kurrelmeyer [Bibliothek des Litterarischen Vereins in Stuttgart 234, 238, 243, 246, 249, 251, 258, 259, 266]. Tübingen, 1904–1915.

*Etliche Sprüch aus Heiliger Göttlicher Schrifft in disen schweren spaltungen unnser Christlichen Religion den Gottseligen Gewissen zu unterricht und trost das sie bey der erkanten reinen warheit des H. Evangelii bestendig bleiben Und zur warnung der andern das sie wider Gottes zorn und straff die Buß nit zu lang auffziehen Trewer guter meinung zusamen gebracht.* Regensburg: Heinrich Geißler, 1560. Schottenloher 169. StBR, Rat. civ. 669/I.

Faber Stapulensis, Jacob. *Martyrii beati Pauli apostoli a lino papa graece scripti orientalibus ecclesiis traditi et subinde in latinum conversi.* Paris, 1512; 2nd edition, Paris, 1515.

Gallus, Nicolaus (Lutheran minister in Regensburg). *Ein Kurtze Ordenliche suma der rechten Waren Lehre unsers heiligen Christlichen glaubens / Welche lere ein yeder Christlicher haußvatter nit allain für sich selb zuwissen sonder auch seine Kinder und Ehalden zuleren oder leren zulassen schuldig ist. Sampt einem kurtzen außzug einer Gotseligen Haußhaltung.* Regensburger Parfueser Closter: Hans Kohl, 1547. Not in Schottenloher. StBR, 8° Rat. civ. 675.

Gallus, Nicolaus. "Kirchenordnung der neuen pfarre zu Regenspurg" (ms., 1567?). StAR, Eccl. I 22, 45f. 227–277. Reprinted in Sehling, *Die evangelischen Kirchenerdnungen,* vol. 13, part 3, p. 462.

Gallus, Nicolaus. *Widerholung Und Bestetigung. Der waren nötigen Christlichen Antwort Nicolai Galli auff des Münchs Thumb Predigers erholete beharliche unter Christen unerhörte grewliche*

*Rabsacische Gottslestering wider alle Kirchen der Christlichen Augspurgischen Confession.* Regensburg: Heinrich Geißler, 1562. Schottenloher 191. StBR, 8º Rat. civ. 617.

Geiler von Kaisersberg, Johannes. *Das buch Granatapfel.* Augsburg: H. Otmar and I. Diemar, 1510.

Heidrich, Ernst, ed. *Albrecht Dürers schriftlicher Nachlass.* Berlin 1910.

Humel, Johann Georg. *Thesaurus centum electissimorum proverbiorum.* Regensburg: Christoff Fischer, 1636. StBR, Rat. civ. 637.

Kayser, Johann Friedrich, ed. *Sammlung derer von einem Wohledlen Hoch- und Wohlweisen Herrn Stadt Cammerer und Rath der des Heil. Röm. Reichs Freyen Stadt Regenspurg an Ihre untergebene Burgerschafft von Zeit zu Zeit im Druck erlassenen Decreten.* Regensburg, 1754.

Kohler, J., and Willy Scheel. *Die peinliche Gerichtsordnung Kaiser Karls V. Constitutio criminalis Carolina* [Die Carolina und ihre Vorgängerinnen. Text, Erläuterung, Geschichte 1]. Halle, 1900.

Lomazzo, Gian Paolo. "Trattato dell'arte, della pittura, scoltura et archittetura." In *Scritti sulle arti*, ed. R. P. Ciardi. Florence, 1974.

Luther, Martin. *D. Martin Luthers Werke: Kritische Gesamtausgabe.* Section 1: *Werke.* 63 volumes. Weimar, 1883–1987.

Luther, Martin. *D. Martin Luthers Werke: Kritische Gesamtausgabe.* Section 2: *Tischreden.* 6 volumes. Weimar, 1912–1921.

Luther, Martin. *D. Martin Luthers Werke: Kritische Gesamtausgabe.* Section 3: *Die deutsche Bibel.* 13 volumes. Weimar, 1906–1961.

Luther, Martin. *D. Martin Luthers Werke: Kritische Gesamtausgabe.* Section 4: *Briefwechsel.* 18 volumes. Weimar, 1930–1985.

Luther, Martin. "Ein Christlicher sermon, Von gewalt Sand Peters." Regensburg: Pauls Kohl, 1522. Schottenloher 13. = *WA* 10, 3:208–216.

Luther, Martin. "Ein mercklicher Sermon Von der gepurt Marie, der mutter gottes wie sy, und die heiligen sollen geehrt werdn von einem iczlichen christen menschen." Regensburg: Pauls Kohl, 1522. Schottenloher 16. StBM, Res. 4º Th. U. 103. XXVI, 29. = *WA* 10, 3:312–331.

Luther, Martin. "Ein Sermon, von Christlicher gerechtigkeit, oder vergebung der sünden, gepredigt zu Marpurg in Hessen. 1528," with preface by Nicolaus Gallus. Regensburg: Hans Kohl, 1554. StaBM, 4º Hom. 1192. Schottenloher 113. Cf. *WA* 29:562–582.

Luther, Martin, Justus Jonas, Martin Bucer, Philip Melancthon. *Gutachten* for Johann Friedrich of Saxony and Landgrave Philip of Hesse (13–14 November 1538). Printed in Heinz Scheible, ed. *Das Widerstandsrecht als Problem der deutschen Protestanten, 1523–1546* [Texte zur Kirchen- und Theologiegeschichte 10]. Gütersloh, 1969. P. 93.

Melanchthon, Philipp. *Commentarius in Genesis*, in *Opera omnia*, ed. Caspar Peucer. Wittenberg: Johannes Crato, 1562.

Melanchthon, Philipp. *In obscuriora aliquot capita Geneseos annotationes.* Hagenoa: Johann Secerius, 1523.

Melanchthon, Philipp. *Unterricht der Visitatorn an die Pfarhern ym Kurfurstenthum zu Sachssen.* Preface by Martin Luther. Wittenberg: Nickel Schirlentz, 1528.

Menius, Justus. *An die hochgeborne Furstin / Fraw Sibilla Hertzogin zu Sachsen / Oeconomia Christiana / das ist / von Christlicher Haushaltung.* Introduction by Martin Luther (Wittenberg: Hans Lufft, 1529).

Migne, J.-P. ed. *Patrologiae cursus completus omnium ss. patrum, doctorum scriptorumque ecclesiasticorum sive latinorum, sive graecorum. Series latina.* 221 volumes. Paris, 1844–1864.

Münster, Sebastian. *Dictionarium Chaldaicum, non tam ad Chaldaicos interpretes quam Rabbinorum intelligenda commentaria necessarium ex baal Aruch & Chal. bibliis atque Hebraeorum peruschim congestum.* Basel: Johann Froben, 1527.

Münster, Sebastian. *Hebraica Biblia Latina planeque nova*. Basel: Michael Isingrinius and Henricus Petrus, 1534.

Osius, Hieronymus (rector and professor in Regensburg's Gymnasium Poeticum). *Scriptum Continens ceu oeconomia quandam lectionum, et exercitiorum, quae publice ac pricatim adolescentiae literariae in Gymnasio Ratisponensi Proponuntur*. Regensburg: Heinrich Geisler, 1567. Schottenloher 267. StBR, Rat. civ. 523.

Ostofrancus, Christopher (= Christopher Hoffman, Benedictine in St. Emmeram). *De Ratisbona metropoli boioariae et subita ibidem iudaeorum proscriptione*. Augsburg: Silvanus Otmar for Johann Wagner of Regensburg, 1519. StBR, Rat. civ. 70.

Pagninus, Sanctes. *Biblia. Habes in hoc libro prudens lector utriusque instrumenti novam translationem aeditam*. Lyon: Antonius du Ry, 1528 [1527].

Pagninus, Sanctes. *Thesauri Hebraicae linguae*. Antwerp: Christophor Plantin, 1572.

Pagninus, Sanctes. *Thesaurus linguae sanctae, sive lexicon Hebraicum*. Augmented by Johann Mercer, Antonius Cevallerius, B. Cornelius Bertram. Lyons: Bartholomaeus Vincentius, 1575.

Pürstinger, Berthold, Bishop of Chiemsee. *Tewtsche Theologey*. Munich: Hans Schopfer, 1528.

Reuchlin, Johannes. *De rudimentis hebraicis libri III*. Pforzheim: Tho. Anselm, 1506; photographic reprint, Hildesheim, 1974.

Sachs, Hans. "Ein Lobgedicht auf Regensburg von Hans Sachs," ed. Jos. Rud. Schuegraf. Regensburg, 1845. StBR, Rat. civ. 544.

Sachs, Hans. *Tragedia. Von der Lucretia auß der beschreybung Livii, hat 1. Actus und 10. Person*. Dated 1527. Nuremberg: Christoff Heußler, 1561. Reprinted in Heinrich Bullinger and Hans Sachs, *Lucretia-Dramen*. Ed. Horst Hartmann. Leipzig, 1973. Pp. 99–110.

Sachs, Hans, and Erhard Schön. "Die Neun getrewesten heydnischen Frawen, mit yhren wunder getrewen thaten." Nuremberg: Niclas Meldeman, [1531].

Sachs, Hans, and Erhard Schön. "Die Neun getrewesten Römer, mit yhren wunder getrewen thaten." Nuremberg: Niclas Meldeman, [1531].

Sachs, Hans, and Erhard Schön. "Schandenport: Die zwelff grausamen Tyrannen des alten Testaments, mit irem wüterischen leben und erschröcklichem undergang zu trost allen ellenden Christen, so unter dem schweren Joch des blutdurstigen Türcken und andern Tyrannen verstricket sind, etc." Nuremberg, 1531; Nuremberg: Hans Guldenmund, 1545.

Scheible, Heinz, ed. *Das Widerstandsrecht als Problem der deutschen Protestanten, 1523–1546* [Texte zur Kirchen- und Theologiegeschichte 10]. Gütersloh, 1969.

Schneidt, Joseph Maria, ed. *Vollständige Geschichte der römischen Königs-Wahl Rudolphs II, aus meistens annoch ungedruckten Urkunden als ein Beytrag zur Geschichte der Churfürsten-Tage und Römischen Königs-Wahlen*. Würzburg, 1792.

Sehling, Emil, ed. *Die evangelischen Kirchenordnungen des XVI. Jahrhunderts*. Volume 13, part 3: *Altbayern*. Tübingen, 1966. Pp. 389–402.

Tengler, Ulrich. *Layen spiegel*. Augsburg: Hans Otmar, 1509 (and later editions).

*Theologia deutsch = Eyn geystlich edles Buchleynn. von rechter underscheyd und vorstand. was der alt und new mensche sey. Was Adams und was gottis kind sey. und wie Adam ynn uns sterben unnd Christus ersteen soll.*, ed. Martin Luther. Wittenberg: Johann Grünenberg, 1516.

*Theologia deutsch = Theologia. deutsch.*, ed. Martin Luther. Straßburg: Johann Knobloch, 1519.

Valla, Lorenzo. *In Latinam Novi testamenti interpretationem ex collatione Graecorum exemplarium Adnotationes apprime utiles*, ed. Desiderius Erasmus. Paris: Iehan Petit, 1505.

Waldner, Wolfgang. *Abfertigung und gründliche Widerlegung des ungegründten Gegenberichts M. Josue Opitii so er von der Erbsünde seiner enturlaubung und etlichen Special hendlen wider eines Erbarn Camerer und Raths der Stadt Regenspurg warhafften Bericht am ende des 1578. Jars hat meuchelisch in Druck außgehen lassen.* Regensburg: Johann Burger, 1580. Schottenloher 325. StBR, Rat. civ. 646.

Widmann, Leonhard. *Chronik von Regensburg,* ed. E. V. Oefele [Die Chroniken der deutschen Städte 15]. Leipzig, 1878.

## SECONDARY SOURCES

Adam, Paul. "Buchbindekunst im alten Regensburg," *Archiv für Buchbinderei* 19 (1919/1920), pp. 49–57, 62–70; 20 (1920), pp. 1–5, 13–17, 25–30, 37–38, 41.

Allen, Mowbray. *T. S. Eliot's Impersonal Theory of Poetry.* Lewisburg, 1974.

Ambronn, Karl-Otto. *Landsassen und Landsassengüter des Fürstentums der Oberen Pfalz im Sechszehnten Jahrhundert* [Historischer Atlas von Bayern; Teil Altbayern, series 2, no. 3]. Munich, 1982.

Appel, Helmut. *Anfechtung und Trost im Spätmittelalter und bei Luther* [Schriften des Vereins für Reformationsgeschichte]. Leipzig, 1938.

Bartsch, Adam von. *The Illustrated Bartsch.* ed. Walter L. Strauss. Multiple volumes. New York, 1978–.

Bauer, Karl. *Regensburg. Aus Kunst-, Kultur- und Sittengeschichte.* 3rd edition, Regensburg, 1980.

Bauerreiss, Romuald. *Pié Jesu—Das Schmerzensmann-Bild und sein Einfluss auf die mittelalterliche Frömmigkeit.* 1931.

Baumann, Urs. *Erbsünde? Ihr Traditionelles Verständnis in der Krise heutiger Theologie* [Ökumenische Forschungen, ed. Hans Kung and Joseph Ratzinger, II. Soteriologische Abteilung 2]. Freiburg, 1970.

Beckenbauer, Egon. *Die Münzen der Reichsstadt Regensburg* [Bayerische Munzkataloge 5]. Grünewald, 1978.

Berkner, Lutz K. "Recent Research on the History of the Family in Western Europe," *Journal of Marriage and the Family* 35 (1973), pp. 395–405.

Boeckler, Albert. *Die Regensburg-Prüfeninger Buchmalerei des XII. und XIII. Jahrhunderts.* Munich, 1924.

Boll, Walter. "Albrecht Altdorfers Nachlass," *Münchner Jahrbuch der bildenden Kunst* N.F. 13 (1938/1939), pp. 91–102.

Boll, Walter. *Reichstagsmuseum.* [Sammlungen der Stadt Regensburg 9]. Regensburg, 1973.

Bornkamm, Günther. "Das Vaterbild im Neuen Testament," in *Das Vaterbild in Mythos und Geschichte,* ed. Hubertus Tellenbach. Stuttgart, 1976. Pp. 136–154.

Bornkamm, Heinrich. "Die Frage der Obrigkeit im Reformationszeitalter," *Das Jahrhundert der Reformation. Gestalten und Kräfte.* 2nd edition, Göttingen, 1966. Pp. 291–315.

Bosl, Karl. *Die Sozialstruktur der mittelalterlichen Residenz- und Fernhandelsstadt Regensburg. Die Entwicklung ihres Bürgertums vom 9–14. Jahrhundert* [Bayerische Akademie der Wissenschaften, Philosophisch-historische Klasse Abhandlungen, N.F. 63]. Munich, 1966.

Brady, Thomas A. *Ruling Class, Regime, and Reformation in Strasbourg, 1520–1555.* Leiden, 1978.

von Brandt, Ahasver. "Mittelalterliche Bürgertestament. Neuerschlossene Quellen zur Geschichte der materiellen und geistigen Kultur," *Sitzungsberichte der Heidelberger Akademie der Wissenschaften. Philosophisch-historische Klasse* (1973), 3. Abhandlung.

Braunfels, Wolfgang. "Anton Wonsams Kölnprospekt von 1531 in der Geschichte des Sehens," *Wallraf-Richartz Jahrbuch* 22 (1960), pp. 115–136.

Braunfels, Wolfgang, "Ein Tizian nach Cranach." In *Festschrift für Herbert von Einem zum 16. Februar 1965*, ed. Gert von der Osten. Berlin, 1965. Pp. 44–48.

Braunfels, Wolfgang. *Die heilige Dreifaltigkeit*. Düsseldorf, 1954.

Breitenbach, Edgar. *Speculum humanae salvationis, eine typengeschichtliche Untersuchung*. Straßburg, 1930.

Brown, Peter. *Augustine of Hippo*. 2nd edition, New York, 1986.

Brunner, Otto. "Das 'ganze Haus' und die alteuropäische 'Ökonomik." In *Neue Wege der Verfassungs- und Sozialgeschichte*. Göttingen, 1968. Pp. 103–127.

Buchholz, Friedrich. *Protestantismus und Kunst im sechszehnten Jahrhundert*. Leipzig, 1928.

Buhl, Hans. "Geschichte des Hauses Obere Bachgasse 16 in Regensburg," *Verhandlungen des Historischen Vereins für Oberpfalz und Regensburg* 109 (1969), pp. 63–78.

Bundy, Murray Wright. *The Theory of Imagination in Classical and Mediaeval Thought* [University of Illinois Studies in Language and Literature 12]. Urbana, 1927.

Burckhardt, Jacob. "Die Sammler," *Beiträge zur Kunstgeschichte von Italien*. Basel, 1898.

Burdach, Konrad. *Der Dichter des Ackermann aus Böhmen und seine Zeit* [Vom Mittelalter zur Reformation. Forschungen zur Geschichte der Deutschen Bildung 3]. 3 volumes. Berlin, 1926–1932.

Bynum, Caroline Walker. "The Body of Christ in the Later Middle Ages: A Reply to Leo Steinberg," *Renaissance Quarterly* 39 (1986), pp. 399–439.

Bynum, Carolyn Walker. *Jesus as Mother: Studies in the Spirituality of the High Middle Ages*. Berkeley, 1982.

von Campenhausen, Hans. "Die Bilderfrage der Reformation," *Zeitschrift für Kirchengeschichte* 68 (1957), pp. 96–128.

Cargill Thompson, W. D. J., *The Political Thought of Martin Luther*, ed. Philip Broadhead. Brighton, Sussex 1984.

Chadwick, Henry. *Augustine*. Oxford, 1986.

Chrisman, Miriam. *Bibliography of Straßburg Imprints, 1480–1599*. New Haven, 1982.

Christensen, Carl C. *Art and the Reformation in Germany*. Athens, Ohio, 1979.

Christensen, Carl C. "The Reformation and the Decline of German Art," *Central European History* 6 (1973), pp. 207–232.

Christensen, Carl C. "The Significance of the Epitaph Monument in Early Lutheran Ecclesiastical Art (c. 1540–1600): Some Social and Iconographical Considerations." In *The Social History of the Reformation*, ed. L. P. Buck and J. W. Zophy. Columbus, Ohio, 1972. Pp. 297–314.

Courcelle, Pierre. *Les Confessions de saint Augustin dans la tradition littéraire. Antécédents et postérite*. Paris, 1963.

Courcelle, Pierre. *Connais-toi toi même de Socrate à saint Bernard*. Paris, 1974.

Darlow, T. H., and H. F. Moule. *Historical Catalogue of the Printed Editions of Holy Scripture in the Library of the British and Foreign Bible Society*. 3 volumes. London, 1911.

Davenport, Cyril J. H. *Cameo Book-Stamps Figured and Described*. London, 1911.

Davies, Hugh, ed. *Catalogue of a Collection of Early German Books in the Library of C. Fairfax Murray*. London, 1962.

Dehio, Georg. *Geschichte der deutschen Kunst*. 4th edition, Berlin and Leipzig, 1930–1934.

Diefendorf, Barbara. "Remarriage in Sixteenth-Century Paris," *Journal of Family History* 7 (1982), pp. 379–395.

Dinkler, Erich. *Die Anthropologie Augustines*. Stuttgart, 1934.

Dobrzeniecki, T. "A Gdansk panel of the 'Pitié-de-Nostre-Seigneur.' Notes on the Iconography," *Bulletin du Museum national de Varsovie* 10 (1969), pp. 29–54.

Dobrzeniecki, T. "U zrodeł przedstawien: 'Tron Łaski' i "Pietas Domini," *Rocznik Muzeum naradowego w Warszawie* 15 (1971), pp. 221–312.

Donaldson, Ian. *The Rapes of Lucretia: A Myth and Its Transformations*. Oxford, 1982.

Dornik-Eger, Hanna. *Albrecht Dürer und die Graphik der Reformationszeit* [Schriften der Bibliothek des Österreichischen Museums für angewandte Kunst 2]. Vienna, 1969.

Dubarle, A.-M. *Le péché originel. Perspectives theologiques*. Paris, 1983.

Ebeling, Gerhard. *Lutherstudien*. Volume 2: *Disputatio de homine*, part 2: *Die philosophische Definition des Menschen: Kommentar zu These 1–19*. Tübingen, 1982.

Edgerton, Samuel Y. "Icons of Justice," *Past and Present* 89 (1980), pp. 23–38.

Edgerton, Samuel Y. *Pictures and Punishment: Art and Criminal Prosecution during the Florentine Renaissance*. Ithaca, 1985.

Eliot, T. S. *The Sacred Wood*. 2nd edition, New York, 1960.

Endres, J. A. "Zwei 'Armenseelen'-Darstellungen," *Zeitschrift für Christliche Kunst* 27 (1914), pp. 157–160.

Endres, Rudolf. "Zur Einwohnerzahl und Bevölkerungsstruktur Nürnbergs im 15./16. Jahrhundert," *Mitteilungen des Vereins für Geschichte der Stadt Nürnberg* 57 (1970), pp. 242–271.

Erickson, Carolly. *The Medieval Vision: Essays in History and Perception*. Oxford, 1976.

Erikson, Erik H. *Young Man Luther: A Study in Psychoanalysis and History*. London, 1958.

Fehr, Hans. *Das Recht im Bilde*. Munich and Leipzig, 1923.

Fouquet-Plümacher, Doris. "Deutsche Renaissance-Einbände mit Rollen- und Plattenstempeln" [brief exhibition brochure, Universitätsbibliothek der Freien Universität Berlin]. Berlin, 1983.

Freundorfer, J. *Erbsünde und Erbtod beim Apostel Paulus* [Neutestamentische Abhandlungen 13]. Münster i. Westfalen, 1927.

Freyhan, R. "The Evolution of the Caritas Figure in the Thirteenth and Fourteenth Centuries," *Journal of the Warburg and Courtauld Institutes* 11 (1948), pp. 68–86.

Friedländer, Max, and Jakob Rosenberg. *Die Gemälde von Lucas Cranach*. Berlin, 1932.

Friedrichs, Christopher R. "Marriage, Family, and Social Structure in an Early Modern German Town," *Historical Papers*, Canadian Historical Association (1975), pp. 17–40.

Frühsorge, Gotthardt. "Die Begründung der 'väterlichen Gesellschaft' in der europäischen oeconomia christiana. Zur Rolle des Vaters in der 'Hausväterliteratur' des 16. bis 18. Jahrhunderts in Deutschland." In *Das Vaterbild im Abendland I: Rom, Frühes Christentum, Mittelalter, Neuzeit, Gegenwart*, ed. Hubertus Tellenbach. Stuttgart, 1978. Pp. 110–123.

Fürnrohr, Otto. "Das Patriziergeschlecht Schiltl in Regensburg," *Verhandlungen des historischen Vereins für Oberpfalz und Regensburg* 97 (1956), pp. 377–392.

Fürnrohr, Walter. *Das Patriziat der Freien Reichsstadt Regensburg zur Zeit des Immerwährenden Reichstags. Eine sozialgeschichtliche Studie über das Bürgertum der Barockzeit* [*Verhandlungen des historischen Vereins von Oberpfalz und Regensburg* 92 (1951), pp. 153–308]. Ph.D. dissertation.

Galinsky, Hans. *Der Lucretia-Stoff in der Weltliteratur* [Sprach und Kultur der Germanisch-romanischen Völker. Section B: Germanistische, series 3]. Breslau, 1932.

Geiger, Ludwig. *Johann Reuchlin, sein Leben und seine Werke*. Leipzig, 1871; reprinted Nieuwkoop, 1964.

Geisberg, Max. *Die Buchillustration in der ersten Hälfte des XVI. Jahrhunderts* 1]. Munich, 1930.

Geisberg, Max, and Walter L. Strauss. *The German Single-Leaf Woodcut, 1500–1550*. 4 volumes. New York, 1974.

Geisberg, Max, and Walter L. Strauss. *The German Single-Leaf Woodcut, 1550–1600.* 3 volumes. New York, 1975.

[Gemeiner, Carl Theodor]. *Geschichte der Kirchenreformation in Regensburg. aus den damals verhandelten Originalacten beschrieben.* Regensburg, 1792.

Gemeiner, Carl Theodor. *Reichsstadt Regensburgische Chronik.* 4 volumes. Regensburg, 1800–1824. 2nd edition ed. Heinz Angermeier. Munich, 1971.

Gerrish, Brian A. *Grace and Reason: A Study in the Theology of Luther.* Oxford, 1962.

Gerstenkorn, Hans Robert. *Weltlich Regiment zwischen Gottesreich und Teufelsmacht. Die staatstheoretischen Auffassungen Martin Luthers und ihre politische Bedeutung* [Schriften zur Rechtslehre und Politik 7]. Bonn, 1956.

Gilson, Etienne. *The Christian Philosophy of Saint Augustine,* trans. L. E. M. Lynch. New York, 1960.

Goering, M. "Die Malerfamilie Bocksberger," *Münchner Jahrbuch der bildenden Kunst* N.F. 7 (1930), pp. 185–280.

Goldschmidt, E. Ph. *Gothic and Renaissance Bookbindings Exemplified and Illustrated from the Author's Collection.* London, 1928.

Grimm, Jacob and Wilhelm. *Deutsches Wörterbuch.* 17 volumes. Leipzig, 1854–1971.

Gross, Julius. *Geschichte des Erbsündendogmas. Ein Beitrag zur Geschichte des Problems vom Ursprung des Übels.* 4 volumes. Munich, 1960–1972.

Gumpelzhaimer, Christoph Georg. *Regensburgs Geschichte, Sagen und Merkwürdigkeiten.* 4 volumes. Regensburg, 1830–1838.

Habich, Georg. *Die deutschen Schaumünzen des XVI. Jahrhunderts.* Munich, 1929.

Hable, Guido, and Raimund Sterl. *Geschichte Regensburgs. Eine Übersicht nach Sachgebieten* [Studien und Quellen zur Geschichte Regensburgs 1]. Regensburg 1970.

von Haebler, H. C. *Das Bild in der Evangelischen Kirche.* Berlin, 1957.

Haebler, Konrad. "Der Rollstempel und seine Initialen," *Nordick Tidskrift för Bok- och Bibliotekväsen* 11 (1924), pp. 24–52.

Haebler, Konrad, and Ilse Schunke. *Rollen- und Plattenstempel des XVI. Jahrhunderts.* 2 volumes. Leipzig, 1928.

Hajnal, J. "European Marriage Patterns in Perspective." In *Population in History,* ed. D. V. Glass and D. E. C. Eversley. London, 1965. Pp. 101–143.

Hamel, Adolf. *Der junge Luther und Augustine. Ihre Beziehungen in der Rechtfertigungslehre nach Luthers ersten Vorlesungen 1509–1518 untersucht.* Part 2: *Der Exeget des Römerbriefes 1515/16, des Galaterbriefes 1516/17 und des Hebräerbriefes 1517/18 in seinem Verhältnis zu Augustine.* Gütersloh, 1935; reprinted Hildesheim, 1980.

Harbison, Craig. "Introduction to the Exhibition." In *Symbols in Transformation: Iconographic Themes at the Time of the Reformation. An Exhibition of Prints in Memory of Erwin Panofsky,* ed. Hedy Backlin-Laudman [exhibition catalogue, Princeton University Art Museum]. Princeton, 1969.

Harbison, Craig. *The Last Judgment in Sixteenth-Century Northern Europe: A Study of the Relation between Art and the Reformation.* New York, 1976.

Harbison, Craig. "Reformation Iconography: Problems and Attitudes," *Tribute to Wolfgang Stechow,* ed. Walter L. Strauss [*Print Review* 5 (1976)], pp. 78–87.

Harbison, Craig. "Visions and Meditations in Early Flemish Painting," *Simiolus. Netherlands Quarterly for the History of Art* 15 (1985), pp. 87–118.

Hartfelder, Karl. *Philipp Melanchthon als Praeceptor Germaniae* [Monumenta Germaniae Paedagogica 7]. Berlin, 1889.

Heimpel, Hermann. "Luthers weltgeschichtliche Bedeutung," *Der Mensch in seiner Gegenwart* (Göttingen, 1954). Pp. 136–161.

Hollstein, F. W. H. *Dutch and Flemish Etchings, Engravings, and Woodcuts c. 1450–1700.* Multiple volumes. Amsterdam, 1949–.

Hollstein, F. W. H. *German Etchings, Engravings, and Woodcuts c. 1400–1700.* Multiple volumes. Amsterdam 1954–.

Hsia, R. Po-Chia. "Civic Wills as Sources for the Study of Piety in Muenster, 1530–1618," *The Sixteenth-Century Journal* 14 (1983), pp. 321–340.

Hsia, R. Po-Chia. *Society and Religion in Münster, 1535–1618.* New Haven, 1984.

Imhof, Arthur E. "Remarriage in Rural Populations and in Urban Middle and Upper Strata in Germany from the Sixteenth to the Twentieth Century." In *Marriage and Remarriage in Populations of the Past*, ed. J. Dupâquier et al. London, 1981. Pp. 335–346.

Ineichen-Eder, Christine Elisabeth. *Mittelalterliche Bibliothekskataloge Deutschlands und der Schweiz.* Volume 4, part 1: *Bistümer Passau und Regensburg.* Munich, 1977.

Jackson, B. Darrell. "The Theory of Signs in Augustine's *De Doctrina Christiana*," in *Augustine: A Collection of Critical Essays*, ed. R. A. Markus. New York, 1972. Pp. 92–147.

Jordan, Hermann. *Luthers Staatsauffassung Ein Beitrag zu der Frage des Verhältnisses von Religion und Politik.* Darmstadt, 1968.

Kantorowicz, Ernst H. *The King's Two Bodies: A Study in Medieval Political Theology.* Princeton, 1957.

Kantorowicz, Ernst H. *Laudes Regiae: A Study in Liturgical Acclamations and Medieval Ruler Worship*, with a study of the music of the laudes and musical transcriptions by Manfred F. Bukofzer. [University of California Publications in History 33]. Berkeley, 1946.

Kantzenbach, Friedrich Wilhelm. "Bild und Wort bei Luther und in der Sprache der Frömmigkeit," *Neue Zeitschrift für sustematische Theologie* 16 (1974), pp. 57–74.

Katzenellenbogen, Adolf. *Allegories of the Virtues and Vices in Medieval Art from Early Christian Times to the Thirteenth Century.* London, 1939.

Keach, William. "Cupid Disarmed or Venus Wounded? An Ovidian Source for Michelangelo and Bronzino," *Journal of the Warburg and Courtauld Institutes* 41 (1978), pp. 327–331.

Keyser, Erich, and Heinz Stoob, eds. *Deutsches Städtebuch: Handbuch städtischer Geschichte.* Volume 5: *Bayern.* Stuttgart, 1974. Pp. 572–597.

Kirschbaum, Engelbert. *Der Lexikon der christlichen Ikonographie.* 8 volumes. Rome, 1968–1976.

Kleinstauber, Christian Heinrich. "Geschichte d. ehemaligen Stadtwagegebäudes und d. k. Kreisbibliothek in Regensburg," *Conversationsblatt*, supplement to *Regensburger Tagblatt* (1875), Nr. 70.

Knodel, John, and Katherine A. Lynch. "The Decline of Remarriage: Evidence from German Village Populations in the Eighteenth and Nineteenth Centuries," *Journal of Family History* 10 (1985), pp. 34–59.

Koepplin, Dieter, and Tilman Falk. *Lukas Cranach, Gemälde, Zeichnungen, Druckgraphik.* Basel, 1974.

Kohler, J., and Willy Scheel. *Die peinliche Gerichtsordnung Kaiser Karls V. Constitutio criminalis Carolina* [Die Carolina und ihre Vorgängerinnen. Text, Erläuterung, Geschichte 1]. Halle, 1900.

Kolb, Robert. "The Advance of Dialectic in Lutheran Theology: The Role of Johannes Wigand (1523–1587)." In *Regnum, Religio et Ratio: Essays Presented to Robert M. Kingdon* [Sixteenth-Century Essays and Studies 8]. Kirksville, Missouri, 1987. Pp. 93–102.

Kraus, Andreas, and Wolfgang Pfeiffer, eds. *Regensburg. Geschichte in Bilddokumenten.* Munich, 1979.

Kretzenbacher, Leopold. *Die Seelenwaage.* Klagenfurt, 1958.

Kristeller, Paul. *Die Strassburger Bücher-Illustration im XV. und im Anfange des XVI. Jahrhunderts.* Ph.D. dissertation, Leipzig, 1888.

Kugler, Hartmut. "Die Stadt im Wald. Zur Stadtbeschreibung bei Hans Sachs." In *Studien zur frühbürgerlichen Literatur im 16. Jahrhundert*, ed. Thomas Cramer and Erika Kartschoke [Beiträge zur Älteren Deutschen Literaturgeschichte 3]. Bern, 1978. Pp. 83–103.

*Kunst der Reformationszeit* [exhibition catalogue, Staatliche Museen zu Berlin (East)]. Berlin, 1983.

Lederle, Ursula Greiger. *Gerechtigkeitsdarstellung in deutschen und niederländischen Rathäusern*. Heidelberg Ph.D. dissertation. Philippsburg, 1937.

Leeming, B. "Augustine, Ambrosiaster and the massa perditionis," *Gregorianum* 11 (1930), pp. 58–91.

Levine, Saul. " 'Tal Cosa': Michelangelo's *David*—Its Form, Site, and Political Symbolism." Ph.D. dissertation, Columbia University, 1969.

Liedke, Volker. "Regensburger Bildschnitzer und Schnitzaltäre der Spätgotik," *Ars Bavarica* 8 (1980), pp. 9–28.

Lilienfein, Heinrich. *Lukas Cranach und seine Zeit*. Bielefeld, 1944.

Lindner, Ludwig. *Das bürgerliche Recht der Reichsstadt Regensburg*. Ph.D. dissertation, Erlangen. Regensburg, 1908.

Lukken, M. *Original Sin in the Roman Liturgy: Research into the Theology of Original Sin in the Roman Sacramentaria and the Early Baptismal Liturgy*. Leiden, 1973.

Lyonnet, Stanislaus. "Le péché originel et l'exégèse de Rom. 5,12–14," *Recherches de science religieuse* 44 (1956), pp. 63–84.

McCool, Gerald A. "The Ambrosian Origin of Augustine's Theology of the Image of God in Man," *Theological Studies* 20 (1959), pp. 62–81.

McIntosh, John S. "A Study of Augustine's Versions of Genesis." Ph.D. dissertation. Chicago, 1912.

McTigue, Bernard. "English Bookbinding and the Continental Woodblock Tradition," *Printing History* 3 (1981), pp. 20–29.

Mader, Felix. *Die Kunstdenkmäler von Bayern*. Volume 22: *Stadt Regensburg*. Munich, 1933.

Mader, Johann. *Die logische struktur des personalen Denkens aus der Methode der Gotteserkenntnis bei Aurelius Augustinus*. Wien 1965.

Mâle, Emile. *L'art religieux de la fin du moyen âge en France. Etude sur l'iconographie du moyen âge et sur ses sources d'inspiration*. 2nd ed. Paris, 1922.

Markus, R. A. "St. Augustine on Signs," in *Augustine: A Collection of Critical Essays*, ed. R. A. Markus. New York, 1972. pp. 61–91.

Marrow, James H. "Symbol and Meaning in Northern European Art of the Late Middle Ages and the Early Renaissance," *Simiolus. Netherlands Quarterly for the History of Art* 16 (1986), pp. 150–169.

*Martin Luther und die Reformation in Deutschland* [exhibition catalogue, Germanisches Nationalmuseum]. Nuremberg, 1983.

Maschke, Erich. "Deutsche Städte am Ausgang des Mittelalters," *Die Stadt am Ausgang des Mittelalters*, ed. W. Rausch. Linz, 1974.

Maschke, Erich. " 'Obrigkeit' im spätmittelalterlichen Speyer und in anderen Städten," *Archiv für Reformationsgeschichte* 57 (1966), pp. 7–22.

Maschke, Erich. "Verfassung und soziale Kräfte in der deutschen Stadt des Spätmittelalters vornehmlich in Oberdeutschland," *Vierteljahrschrift für Sozial- und Wirtschaftsgeschichte* 46 (1959), pp. 289–349, 433–476.

Mayer, Cornelius. "Res per signa," *Revue des études augustinienne* 20 (1974). pp. 100–112.

Mayer-Pfannholz, A. "Die Trinität am Grabe," *Das Münster* 11 (1958), pp. 105–107.

Meinhold, Peter. *Die Genesisvorlesung Luthers und ihre Herausgeber* {Forschungen zur Kirchen- und Geistesgeschichte 8]. Stuttgart, 1936.

Mende, Matthias, ed. *Das alte Nürnberger Rathaus; Baugeschichte und Ausstattung des großen Saales und der Ratsstube.* Volume 1. Nuremberg, 1979.

Miles, Margaret. *Image as Insight: Visual Understanding in Western Christianity and Secular Culture.* Boston, 1985.

Moeller, Bernd. *Reichsstadt und Reformation* [Schriften des Vereins für Reformationsgeschichte 180]. Gütersloh, 1962.

Moeller, Bernd, ed. *Stadt und Kirche im 16. Jahrhundert* [Schriften des Vereins für Reformationsgeschichte 190]. Gütersloh, 1978.

Morré, Fritz. *Ratsverfassung und Patriziat in Regensburg bis 1400* [*Verhandlungen des historischen Vereins für Oberpfalz und Regensburg* 85 (1935)].

Mummenhoff, Ernst. *Das Rathaus in Nürnberg.* Nuremberg, 1891.

Münch, Paul. "Die 'Obrigkeit im Vaterstand'—Zu Definition und Kritik des 'Landesvaters' während der frühen Neuzeit," *Daphnis* 11 (1982), pp. 15–40.

Nash, Ronald H. *The Light of the Mind: St. Augustine's Theory of Knowledge.* Lexington, Kentucky, 1969.

Naujoks, Eberhard. *Obrigkeitsgedanke, Zunftverfassung und Reformation: Studien zur Verfassungsgeschichte von Ulm, Esslingen und Schwäbisch Gmünd* [Veröffentlichungen der Kommission für geschichtliche Landeskunde in Baden-Württemberg, series B, 3]. Stuttgart, 1958.

Naujoks, Eberhard. "Obrigkeit und Zunftverfassung in den südwestdeutschen Reichsstädten," *Zeitschrift für württembergische Landesgeschichte* 33 (1974), pp. 53–93.

Nygren, Anders. *Agape and Eros.* Trans. Philip S. Watson. London, 1954.

O'Connell, Robert J. *Art and the Christian Intelligence in St. Augustine.* Cambridge, Massachusetts, 1978.

Oldenbourg, M. Consuelo. *Die Buchholzschnitte des Hans Schäufelein, ein bibliographisches Verzeichnis ihrer Verwendungen* [Studien zur deutschen Kunstgeschichte 340]. Baden-Baden, 1964.

O'Meara, J. J. *The Young Augustine.* London, 1954.

von der Osten, Gert. *Der Schmerzensmann. Typengeschichte eines deutschen Andachtsbildwerkes von 1300 bis 1600* [Forschungen zur deutschen Kunstgeschichte 7]. Berlin, 1935.

Ozment, Steven E. *Homo spiritualis: A Comparative Study of the Anthropology of Johannes Tauler, Jean Gerson, and Martin Luther (1509–1516) in the Context of Their Theological Thought* [Studies in Medieval and Reformation Thought 6]. Leiden, 1969.

Ozment, Steven E. *Mysticism and Dissent: Religious Ideology and Social Protest in the Sixteenth Century.* New Haven, 1973.

Pagels, Elaine. *Adam, Eve, and the Serpent.* New York, 1988.

Panofsky, Erwin. "'Imago Pietatis'. Ein Beitrag zur Typengeschichte des 'Schmerzensmanns' und der 'Maria Mediatrix.'" In *Festschrift für Max J. Friedländer zum 60. Geburtstage.* Leipzig, 1927. Pp. 261–308.

Panofsky, Erwin. *Meaning in the Visual Arts.* Garden City, New York, 1953.

Panofsky, Erwin. *Studies in Iconology.* New York, 1967.

von Pauly, August Friedrich, and Georg Wissowa. *Paulys Real-Encyclopädie der classischen Altertumswissenschaft.* 34 volumes. Stuttgart, 1856–1972.

Pelikan, Jaroslav. *Luther the Expositor: Introduction to the Reformer's Exegetical Writings* [*Luther's Works*, Companion Volume]. St. Louis, 1959.

Peterson, Luther D. "Melanchthon on Resisting the Emperor: The *Von der Notwehr Unterrichte* of 1547." In *Regnum, Religio et Ratio: Essays Presented to Robert M. Kingdon* [Sixteenth-Century Essays and Studies 8]. Kirksville, Missouri, 1987. Pp. 133–144.

Piccard, Gerhard. *Wasserzeichen.* Volume 8: *Schlüssel.* Stuttgart, 1979.

Pinomaa, Lennart. *Der Zorn Gottes in der Theologie Luthers. Ein Beitrag zur Frage nach der Einheit des Gottesbildes bei Luther.* Helsinki, 1938.

Plato-Wild, Georg Gottlieb. *Regensburgisches Münz-Kabinet oder Verzaichniß der d. H.R.R. freien Stadt Regensburg Kurrent und Schau-Münzen.* Regensburg, 1779.

Platz, Philipp. *Der Römerbrief in der Gnadenlehre Augustins* [*Cassisiacum* 5 (Würzburg, 1938)].

Portalié, Eugène. *A Guide to the Thought of Saint Augustine.* Trans. R. J. Bastian. London, 1960.

Portig, Gustav. *Das Weltgericht in der bildenden Kunst* [Zeitfragen des christlichen Volkslebens. Volume 10, part 5]. Heilbronn, 1885.

Postel, Rainer. "Obrigkeitsdenken und Reformation in Hamburg," *Archiv für Reformationsgeschichte* 70 (1979), pp. 169–201.

Postel, Rainer. "Reformation und bürgerliche Mitsprache in Hamburg," *Zeitschrift des Vereins für Hamburgische Geschichte* 65 (1979).

Preuß, Hans. *Martin Luther, der Künstler.* Gütersloh, 1931.

*Reformation in Nürnberg—Umbruch und Bewahrung* [exhibition catalogue, Germanisches Nationalmuseum]. Nuremberg, 1979.

*Die Renaissance im deutschen Südwesten* [exhibition catalogue, Badisches Landesmuseum]. Karlsruhe, 1986.

Reu, M. *Luther's German Bible: An Historical Presentation Together with a Collection of Sources.* Columbus, Ohio, 1934.

Ringbom, Sixten. "Devotional Images and Imaginative Devotions: Notes on the Place of Art in Late Medieval Private Piety," *Gazette des beaux-arts*, ser. 6, 73 (1969), pp. 159–170.

Ritscher, Berta. *Die Entwicklung der Regensburger Ratsverfassung in der gesellschaftlichen und wirtschaftlichen Struktur der Zeit von 1245–1429* [*Verhandlungen des historischen Vereins für Oberpfalz und Regensburg* 114 (1974), pp. 7–126; 115 (1975), pp. 7–63; 116 (1976), pp. 7–110]. Ph.D. dissertation.

Ritter, Gerhard A. "Divine Right und Prärogative der englischen Könige 1603–1640," *Historische Zeitschrift* 196 (1963), pp. 584–625.

Rondet, Henri. *Le péchè originel dans la tradition patristique et théologique.* Paris, 1967. Translated into English by Cajetan Finegan under the title *Original Sin: The Patristic and Theological Background.* Shannon, 1972.

Roper, Lyndal. " 'The common man', 'the common good', 'common women': Gender and Meaning in the German Reformation Commune," *Social History* 12 (1987), pp. 1–22.

Rosenthal, Erwin I. J. "Sebastian Muenster's Knowledge and Use of Hebrew Exegesis." In *Essays in Honour of the Very Rev. Dr. J. H. Hertz, Chief Rabbi of the United Hebrew Congregations of the British Empire on the Occasion of His Seventieth Birthday,* ed. I. Epstein, E. Levine, and C. Roth. London, 1942. Pp. 351–369.

Rosenthal, Frank. "The Rise of Christian Hebraism in the Sixteenth Century," *Historia Judaica* 7 (1945), pp. 167–191.

Rubinstein, Nicolai. "Political Ideas in Sienese Art: The Frescoes of Ambrogio Lorenzetti and Taddeo di Bartolo in the Palazzo Pubblico," *Journal of the Warburg and Courtauld Institutes* 21 (1958), pp. 179–207.

Rublack, Hans-Christoph. *Eine bürgerliche Reformation: Nördlingen* [Quellen und Forschungen zur Reformationsgeschichte 51] Gütersloh, 1982.

Rublack, Hans-Christoph. "Grundwerte in der Reichsstadt im Spätmittelalter und in der frühen Neuzeit." In *Literatur in der Stadt. Bedingungen und Beispiele städtischer Literatur des 15. bis 17. Jahrhunderts,* ed. Horst Brunner [Göppinger Arbeiten zur Germanistik 343]. Göppingen, 1982. Pp. 9–36.

Rublack, Hans-Christoph. "Political and Social Norms in Urban Communities in the Holy

Roman Empire." In *Religion, Politics, and Social Protest: Three Studies on Early Modern Germany*, ed. Kaspar von Greyerz. London, 1984. Pp. 24–60.

Sabean, David. *Power in the Blood: Popular Culture and Village Discourse in Early Modern Germany*. Cambridge, 1984.

Sasse, Hermann. *This Is My Body: Luther's Contention for the Real Presence in the Sacrament of the Altar*. Revised edition, Adelaide, 1977.

Schade, W. *Die Malerfamilie Cranach*. Dresden, 1974.

Schindler, Alfred. "Geistliche Väter und Hausväter in der christlichen Antike." In *Das Vaterbild im Abendland I: Rom, Frühes Christentum, Mittelalter, Neuzeit, Gegenwart*, ed. Hubertus Tellenbach. Stuttgart, 1978. Pp. 70–82.

Schindler, Alfred. "Gott als Vater in Theologie und Liturgie der christlichen Antike." In *Das Vaterbild im Abendland I: Rom, Frühes Christentum, Mittelalter, Neuzeit, Gegenwart*, ed. Hubertus Tellenbach. Stuttgart, 1978. Pp. 55–69.

Schindler, Alfred. *Wort und Analogie in Augustines Trinitätslehre* [Hermeneutische Untersuchungen zur Theologie 4]. Tübingen, 1956.

Schlichting, Günter. "Dr. Johann Hiltner, der Reformator der Reichsstadt Regensburg," *Verhandlung des Historischen Vereins für Oberpfalz und Regensburg* 120 (1980), pp. 455–471.

Schmaus, Michael. *Die psychologische Trinitätslehre des Hl. Augustinus* [Münsterische Beiträge zur Theologie 11]. Münster, 1927.

Schmidt, Heinrich. *Die deutschen Städtechroniken als Spiegel des bürgerlichen Selbstverständnisses im Spätmittelalter* [Schriftenreihe der historischen Kommission bei der Bayerischen Akademie der Wissenschaften 3]. Ph.D. dissertation. Göttingen, 1958.

Schmidt, P. *Die Illustration der Luther Bibel 1522 bis 1700*. Basel, 1962.

Schmidt, Rolf. "Studien zur spätgotischen Plastik in Regensburg," *Zeitschrift für bayerische Landesgeschichte* 37 (1974), pp. 167–177.

Schmitz, Wolfgang, ed. *Der Teufelsprozess vor dem Weltgericht nach Ulrich Tenynglers "Neuer Layenspiegel" von 1511 (Ausgabe von 1512)*. Cologne, 1980.

Schoenberger, Cynthia Grant. "Luther and the Justifiability of Resistance to Legitimate Authority," *Journal of the History of Ideas* 40 (1979), pp. 3–19.

Schottenloher, Karl. *Das Regensburger Buchgewerbe im 15. und 16. Jahrhundert mit Akten und Druckverzeichnis*. Mainz, 1920.

Schramm, Albert. *Bilderschmuck der Frühdrucke*. 23 volumes. Leipzig, 1920–1943.

Schramm, Percy Ernst. *Herrschaftszeichen und Staatssymbolik. Beiträge zu ihrer Geschichte vom dritten bis zum sechzehnten Jahrhundert* [Schriften der Monumenta Germaniae historica 13]. Stuttgart, 1955.

Schubert, D. "Halbfigurige Lucretia-Tafeln der 1. Hälfte des 16. Jahrhunderts in den Niederländen," *Jahrbuch des Kunsthistorischen Institutes der Universität Graz* 6 (1971), pp. 99–110.

Schuegraf, J. R. "Lebensgeschichtliche Nachrichten über den Maler und Bürger Michael Ostendorfer," *Verhandlungen des historischen Vereins von Oberpfalz und Regensburg* 14 (1850), pp. 1–76.

Schunke, Ilse. *Die Einbände der Palatina in der Vatikanischen Bibliothek*. Vatican City, 1962.

Scribner, Robert W. *For the Sake of Simple Folk: Popular Propaganda for the German Reformation*. Cambridge, 1981.

Scribner, Robert W. "Popular Piety and Modes of Visual Perception in Late-Medieval and Reformation Germany, *Journal of Religious History* 16 (forthcoming, 1990).

Scribner, Robert W. "Sozialkontrolle und die Möglichkeit einer städtischen Reformation." In *Stadt und Kirche im 16. Jahrhundert*, ed. Bernd Moeller [Schriften des Vereins für Reformationsgeschichte 190]. Gütersloh, 1978. Pp. 57–65.

Seeberg, Erich. *Luthers Theologie*. Volume 2: *Christus, Wirklichkeit und Urbild*. Stuttgart, 1937.

Seeberg, Erich. *Studien zu Luthers Genesisvorlesung; Zugleich ein Beitrag zur Frage nach dem alten Luther* [Beiträge zur Förderung christlicher Theologie 36, 1]. Gütersloh, 1932.

Seeberg, Reinhold. *Lehrbuch der Dogmengeschichte*. Volume 4, part 1: *Die Entstehung des protestantischen Lehrbegriffs*. 4th edition, Leipzig, 1933.

Seeliger, S. "Die Trinität am Grabe," *Das Münster* 10 (1957), pp. 100–101.

Seymour, Charles. *Michelangelo's David: A Search for Identity*. Pittsburg, 1967.

*Short-Title Catalogue of Books Printed in the German-speaking Countries and German Books Printed in Other Countries from 1455 to 1600 Now in the British Museum*. London, 1962.

Simon, Matthias. "Beiträge zum Verhältnis der Konfessionen in der Reichsstadt Regensburg," *Zeitschrift für bayerische Kirchengeschichte* 33 (1964), pp. 1–33.

Sinding-Larsen, Staale. *Christ in the Council Hall: Studies in the Religious Iconography of the Venetian Republic* [Institutum Romanum Norvegiae, Acta ad Archaeologiam et Artium Historiam Pertinentia 5]. Rome, 1974.

Skinner, Quentin. *The Foundations of Modern Political Thought*. Volume 2: *The Age of the Reformation*. Cambridge, 1978.

Spamer, Adolf. *Das kleine Andachtsbild vom XIV. bis zum XX. Jahrhundert*. Munich, 1930.

Specht, Rainer. "Über Funktionen des Vaters nach Thomas von Aquino." In *Das Vaterbild im Abendland I: Rom, Frühes Christentum, Mittelalter, Neuzeit, Gegenwart*, ed. Hubertus Tellenbach. Stuttgart 1978. Pp. 95–109.

Spiekerkötter, Gisela. *Die Darstellung des Weltgerichtes von 1500–1800 in Deutschland*. Dusseldorf 1939.

Starn, Randolph. "The Republican Regime of the 'Room of Peace' in Siena, 1338–1340," *Representations* 18 (1987), pp. 1–32.

Stechow, Wolfgang. "Lucretia Statua," *Essays in Honor of Georg Swarzenski*. Chicago, 1951.

Steinberg, Leo. *The Sexuality of Christ in Renaissance Art and in Modern Oblivion* [October 25 (1983)].

Stintzing, Roderich. *Geschichte der populären Literatur des römisch-kanonischen Rechts in Deutschland am Ende des fünfzehnten und im Anfang des sechszehnten Jahrhunderts*. Leipzig, 1867.

Stirm, Margarete. *Die Bilderfrage in der Reformation* [Quellen und Forschungen zur Reformationsgeschichte 45]. Gütersloh, 1977.

Strauss, Gerald. *Law, Resistance, and the State: The Opposition to Roman Law in Reformation Germany*. Princeton, 1986.

Strauss, Gerald. *Nuremberg in the Sixteenth Century*. New York, 1966.

Strieder, Peter. "Folk Art Sources of Cranach's Woodcut of the Sacred Heart." In *Tribute to Wolfgang Stechow*, ed. Walter L. Strauss [*Print Review* 5 (1976)], pp. 160–166.

Striedinger, Ivo. *Der Kampf um Regensburg, 1486–1492* [*Verhandlungen des historischen Vereins von Oberpfalz und Regensburg* 44 (1890)].

Strothmann, Friedrich Wilhelm. *Die Gerichtsverhandlung als literarisches Motiv in der deutschen Literatur des ausgehenden Mittelalters* [Deutsche Arbeiten der Universität Köln 2]. Jena, 1930.

Swarzenski, Georg. *Die Regensburger Buchmalerei des X. und XI. Jahrhunderts. Studien zur Geschichte der deutschen Malerei des frühen Mittelalters*. 2nd edition, Stuttgart, 1969.

Sydow, Jürgen. "Die innerösterreichische Zuwanderung nach Regensburg im 16. und 17. Jahrhundert," *Blätter für Heimatkunde* 29 (1955), pp. 63–66.

Sydow, Jürgen. "Die Konfessionen in Regensburg zwischen Reformation und Westfälichem Frieden," *Zeitschrift für bayerische Landesgeschichte* 23 (1960), pp. 473–491.

Tellenbach, Hubertus, ed. *Das Vaterbild im Abendland I: Rom, Frühes Christentum, Mittelalter, Neuzeit, Gegenwart*. Stuttgart, 1978.

Tellenbach, Hubertus, ed. *Das Vaterbild in Mythos und Geschichte*, Stuttgart, 1976.

Theobald, Leonhard. *Die Reformationsgeschichte der Reichsstadt Regensburg* [Einzelarbeiten aus der Kirchengeschichte Bayerns 19]. 2 volumes. Munich, 1936, Nuremberg, 1951.

Thieme, Ulrich, and Felix Becker. *Allgemeines Lexikon der bildenden Künstler von der Antike bis zur Gegenwart*. 37 volumes. Leipzig, 1907–1950.

Thompson, W. D. J. Cargill. *The Political Thought of Martin Luther*. Brighton, Sussex, 1984.

Trier, Jost. "Vater, Versuch einer Etymologie," *Zeitschrift der Savigny-Stiftung für Rechtsgeschichte, Germanistische Abteilung* 65 (1947), pp. 232–260.

Troescher, Georg. "Die 'Pitié-de-Nostre-Signeur' oder 'Notgottes,'" *Wallraf-Richartz Jahrbuch* 9 (1936), pp. 148–168.

Troescher, Georg. "Weltgerichtsbilder in Rathäusern und Gerichtsstätten," *Wallraf-Richartz Jahrbuch* 11 (1939), pp. 139–214.

Vandervelde, G. *Original Sin: Two Major Trends in Contemporary Roman Catholic Reinterpretation*. Amsterdam, 1975.

Voigt, Georg. "Die Lucretia-Fabel und ihre literarischen Verwandten," *Berichte der k.-sächsischen Gesellschaft der Wissenschaften, philosophisch-historische Klasse* (1893), pp. 1–36.

Voss, Georg. *Das Jüngste Gericht in der bildenden Kunst des frühen Mittelalters. Eine kunstgeschichtliche Untersuchung*. Leipzig, 1884.

Walker, Mack. *German Home Towns: Community, State, and General Estate, 1648–1871*. Ithaca, 1971.

Weber, Max. *Wirtschaft und Gesellschaft. Grundriss der verstehenden Soziologie*. 4th edition, Tübingen, 1956.

Wilde, J. "The Hall of the Great Council of Florence," *Journal of the Warburg and Courtauld Institutes* 7 (1944), pp. 65–81.

Wilken, Ernst. *Geschichte der geistlichen Spiele in Deutschland*. Göttingen, 1872.

Wind, Edgar. "Donatello's Judith: A Symbol of 'Santimonia'," *Journal of the Warburg Institute* 1 (1937–1938), pp. 62–63.

Wlosok, Antonie. "Vater und Vatervorstellungen in der römischen Kultur." In *Das Vaterbild im Abendland I: Rom, Frühes Christentum, Mittelalter, Neuzeit, Gegenwart*, ed. Hubertus Tellenbach. Stuttgart, 1978. Pp. 18–54.

Wolf, Gunther, ed. *Luther und die Obrigkeit* [Wege der Forschung 85]. Darmstadt, 1972.

Wynen, Arnulf. *Michael Ostendorfer (um 1492–1559). Ein Regensburger Maler der Reformationszeit*. Ph.D. dissertation. Freiburg i. Br., 1961.

Zapalac, Kristin E. S. *Eiserne Männer, eiserne Jungfrauen: Luther, Lukretia und das Kennzeichnen der Stadt Regensburg auf Einbänden, 1542–1575* [brief exhibition catalogue, Staatliche Bibliothek, Regensburg]. Regensburg, 1983.

Zorn, Wolfgang. "Die politische und soziale Bedeutung des Reichsstadtbürgertums im Spätmittelalter," *Zeitschrift für bayerische Landesgeschichte* 24 (1961), pp. 460–480.

Zschelletzschky, Herbert. *Die "drei gottlosen Maler" von Nürnberg: Sebald Beham, Barthel Beham und Georg Pencz*. Leipzig, 1975.

# Index

*Library of Congress Cataloging-in-Publication Data*

Zapalac, Kristin Eldyss Sorensen.
   In his image and likeness: political iconography and religious
change in Regensburg, 1500–1600–by Kristin Eldyss Sorensen Zapalac.
      p.   cm.
   Includes bibliographical references.
   ISBN 0–8014–2269–8 (alk. paper)
      1. Regensburg (Germany)—Languages—Political aspects.   2. Visual
communication—Germany—Regensburg—History—16th century.
3. Reformation—Germany—Regensburg.   4. Regensburg (Germany)—
Politics and government.   5. Regensburg (Germany)—Church
history—16th century.   I. Title.
P119.32.G3Z36   1990
306.4′4′0943347—dc20                                              89–71209